Learn Python Programming
Second Edition

The no-nonsense, beginner's guide to programming, data science, and web development with Python 3.7

Fabrizio Romano

BIRMINGHAM - MUMBAI

Learn Python Programming
Second Edition

Commissioning Editor: Richa Tripathi
Acquisition Editor: Karan Sadawana
Content Development Editor: Rohit Singh
Technical Editor: Romy Dias
Copy Editor: Safis Editing
Project Coordinator: Vaidehi Sawant
Proofreader: Safis Editing
Indexer: Mariammal Chettiyar
Graphics: Jason Monteiro
Production Coordinator: Shantanu Zagade

First published: December 2015
Second edition: June 2018

Production reference: 2241018

Published by Packt Publishing Ltd.
Livery Place
35 Livery Street
Birmingham
B3 2PB, UK.

ISBN 978-1-78899-666-2

www.packtpub.com

To my dear dear friend and mentor, Torsten Alexander Lange.
Thank you for all the love and support.

`mapt.io`

Mapt is an online digital library that gives you full access to over 5,000 books and videos, as well as industry leading tools to help you plan your personal development and advance your career. For more information, please visit our website.

Why subscribe?

- Spend less time learning and more time coding with practical eBooks and Videos from over 4,000 industry professionals

- Improve your learning with Skill Plans built especially for you

- Get a free eBook or video every month

- Mapt is fully searchable

- Copy and paste, print, and bookmark content

PacktPub.com

Did you know that Packt offers eBook versions of every book published, with PDF and ePub files available? You can upgrade to the eBook version at `www.PacktPub.com` and as a print book customer, you are entitled to a discount on the eBook copy. Get in touch with us at `service@packtpub.com` for more details.

At `www.PacktPub.com`, you can also read a collection of free technical articles, sign up for a range of free newsletters, and receive exclusive discounts and offers on Packt books and eBooks.

Foreword

I first got to know Fabrizio when he became our lead developer a few years ago. It was quickly apparent that he was one of those rare people who combine rigorous technical expertise with a genuine care for the people around him and a true passion to mentor and teach. Whether it was designing a system, pairing to write code, doing code reviews, or even organizing team card games at lunch, Fab was always thinking not only about the best way to do the job, but also about how to make sure that the entire team had the skills and motivation to do their best.

You'll meet the same wise and caring guide in this book. Every chapter, every example, every explanation has been carefully thought out, driven by a desire to impart the best and most accurate understanding of the technology, and to do it with kindness. Fab takes you under his wing to teach you both Python's syntax and its best practices.

I'm also impressed with the scope of this book. Python has grown and evolved over the years, and it now spans an enormous ecosystem, being used for web development, routine data handling, and ETL, and increasingly for data science. If you are new to the Python ecosystem, it's often hard to know what to study to achieve your goals. In this book, you will find useful examples exposing you to many different uses of Python, which will help guide you as you move through the breadth that Python offers.

I hope you will enjoy learning Python and become a member of our global community. I'm proud to have been asked to write this, but above all, I'm pleased that Fab will be your guide.

Naomi Ceder

Python Software Foundation Fellow

Contributors

About the author

Fabrizio Romano was born in Italy in 1975. He holds a master's degree in computer science engineering from the University of Padova. He is also a certified scrum master, Reiki master and teacher, and a member of CNHC.

He moved to London in 2011 to work for companies such as Glasses Direct, TBG/Sprinklr, and student.com. He now works at Sohonet as a Principal Engineer/Team Lead.

He has given talks on Teaching Python and TDD at two editions of EuroPython, and at Skillsmatter and ProgSCon, in London.

I'm grateful to all those who helped me create this book. Special thanks to Dr. Naomi Ceder for writing the foreword to this edition, and to Heinrich Kruger and Julio Trigo for reviewing this volume. To my friends and family, who love me and support me every day, thank you. And to Petra Lange, for always being so lovely to me, thank you.

About the reviewers

Heinrich Kruger was born in South Africa in 1981. He obtained a bachelor's degree with honors from the University of the Witwatersrand in South Africa in 2005 and a master's degree in computer science from Utrecht University in the Netherlands in 2008.

He worked as a research assistant at Utrecht University from 2009 until 2013 and has been working as a professional software developer developer since 2014. He has been using Python for personal and projects and in his studies since 2004, and professionally since 2014.

Julio Vicente Trigo Guijarro is a computer science engineer with over a decade of experience in software development. He completed his studies at the University of Alicante, Spain, in 2007 and moved to London in 2010.

He has been using Python since 2012 and currently works as a senior software developer and team lead at Sohonet, developing real-time collaboration applications for the media industry.

He is also a certified ScrumMaster and was one of the technical reviewers of the first edition of this book.

> *I would like to thank my parents for their love, good advice, and continuous support. I would also like to thank all the friends I have met along the way, who enriched my life, for keeping up my motivation, and make me progress.*

Packt is searching for authors like you

If you're interested in becoming an author for Packt, please visit `authors.packtpub.com` and apply today. We have worked with thousands of developers and tech professionals, just like you, to help them share their insight with the global tech community. You can make a general application, apply for a specific hot topic that we are recruiting an author for, or submit your own idea.

Table of Contents

Preface

When I started writing the first edition of this book, I knew very little about what was expected. Gradually, I learned how to convert each topic into a story. I wanted to talk about Python by offering useful, simple, easy-to-grasp examples, but, at the same time, I wanted to pour my own experience into the pages, anything I've learned over the years that I thought would be valuable for the reader—something to think about, reflect upon, and hopefully assimilate. Readers may disagree and come up with a different way of doing things, but hopefully a better way.

I wanted this book to not just be about the language but about programming. The art of programming, in fact, comprises many aspects, and language is just one of them.

Another crucial aspect of programming is independence. The ability to unblock yourself when you hit a wall and don't know what to do to solve the problem you're facing. There is no book that can teach it, so I thought, instead of trying to teach that aspect, I will try and train the reader in it. Therefore, I left comments, questions, and remarks scattered throughout the whole book, hoping to inspire the reader. I hoped that they would take the time to browse the Web or the official documentation, to dig deeper, learn more, and discover the pleasure of finding things out by themselves.

Finally, I wanted to write a book that, even in its presentation, would be slightly different. So, I decided, with my editor, to write the first part in a theoretical way, presenting topics that would describe the characteristics of Python, and to have a second part made up of various real-life projects, to show the reader how much can be achieved with this language.

With all these goals in mind, I then had to face the hardest challenge: take all the content I wanted to write and make it fit in the amount of pages that were allowed. It has been tough, and sacrifices were made.

My efforts have been rewarded though: to this day, after almost 3 years, I still receive lovely messages from readers, every now and then, who thank me and tell me things like *your book has empowered me*. To me, it is the most beautiful compliment. I know that the language might change and pass, but I have managed to share some of my knowledge with the reader, and that piece of knowledge will stick with them.

And now, I have written the second edition of this book, and this time, I had a little more space. So I decided to add a chapter about IO, which was desperately needed, and I even had the opportunity to add two more chapters, one about secrets and one about concurrent execution. The latter is definitely the most challenging chapter in the whole book, and its purpose is that of stimulating the reader to reach a level where they will be able to easily digest the code in it and understand its concepts.

I have kept all the original chapters, except for the last one that was slightly redundant. They have all been refreshed and updated to the latest version of Python, which is 3.7 at the time of writing.

When I look at this book, I see a much more mature product. There are more chapters, and the content has been reorganized to better fit the narrative, but the soul of the book is still there. The main and most important point, empowering the reader, is still very much intact.

I hope that this edition will be even more successful than the previous one, and that it will help the readers become great programmers. I hope to help them develop critical thinking, great skills, and the ability to adapt over time, thanks to the solid foundation they have acquired from the book.

Who this book is for

Python is the most popular introductory teaching language in the top computer science universities in the US, so if you are new to software development, or if you have little experience and would like to start off on the right foot, then this language and this book are what you need. Its amazing design and portability will help you to become productive regardless of the environment you choose to work with.

If you have already worked with Python or any other language, this book can still be useful to you, both as a reference to Python's fundamentals, and for providing a wide range of considerations and suggestions collected over two decades of experience.

What this book covers

Chapter 1, *A Gentle Introduction to Python*, introduces you to fundamental programming concepts. It guides you through getting Python up and running on your computer and introduces you to some of its constructs.

Chapter 2, *Built-in Data Types*, introduces you to Python built-in data types. Python has a very rich set of native data types, and this chapter will give you a description and a short example for each of them.

Chapter 3, *Iterating and Making Decisions*, teaches you how to control the flow of your code by inspecting conditions, applying logic, and performing loops.

Chapter 4, *Functions, the Building Blocks of Code*, teaches you how to write functions. Functions are the keys to reusing code, to reducing debugging time, and, in general, to writing better code.

Chapter 5, *Saving Time and Memory*, introduces you to the functional aspects of Python programming. This chapter teaches you how to write comprehensions and generators, which are powerful tools that you can use to speed up your code and save memory.

Chapter 6, *OOP, Decorators, and Iterators*, teaches you the basics of object-oriented programming with Python. It shows you the key concepts and all the potentials of this paradigm. It also shows you one of the most beloved characteristics of Python: decorators. Finally, it also covers the concept of iterators.

Chapter 7, *Files and Data Persistence*, teaches you how to deal with files, streams, data interchange formats, and databases, among other things.

Chapter 8, *Testing, Profiling, and Dealing with Exceptions*, teaches you how to make your code more robust, fast, and stable using techniques such as testing and profiling. It also formally defines the concept of exceptions.

Chapter 9, *Cryptography and Tokens*, touches upon the concepts of security, hashes, encryption, and tokens, which are part of day-to-day programming at present.

Chapter 10, *Concurrent Execution*, is a challenging chapter that describes how to do many things at the same time. It provides an introduction to the theoretical aspects of this subject and then presents three nice exercises that are developed with different techniques, thereby enabling the reader to understand the differences between the paradigms presented.

Chapter 11, *Debugging and Troubleshooting*, shows you the main methods for debugging your code and some examples on how to apply them.

Chapter 12, *GUIs and Scripts*, guides you through an example from two different points of view. They are at opposite ends of the spectrum: one implementation is a script, and another one is a proper graphical user interface application.

Chapter 13, *Data Science*, introduces a few key concepts and a very special tool, the Jupyter Notebook.

Chapter 14, *Web Development*, introduces the fundamentals of web development and delivers a project using the Django web framework. The example will be based on regular expressions.

To get the most out of this book

You are encouraged to follow the examples in this book. In order to do so, you will need a computer, an internet connection, and a browser. The book is written in Python 3.7, but it should also work, for the most part, with any recent Python 3.* version. I have given guidelines on how to install Python on your operating system. The procedures to do that change all the time, so you will need to refer to the most up-to-date guide on the Web to find precise setup instructions. I have also explained how to install all the extra libraries used in the various examples and provided suggestions if the reader finds any issues during the installation of any of them. No particular editor is required to type the code; however, I suggest that those who are interested in following the examples should consider adopting a proper coding environment. I have given suggestions on this matter in the first chapter.

Download the example code files

You can download the example code files for this book from your account at www.packtpub.com. If you purchased this book elsewhere, you can visit www.packtpub.com/support and register to have the files emailed directly to you.

You can download the code files by following these steps:

1. Log in or register at www.packtpub.com.
2. Select the **SUPPORT** tab.
3. Click on **Code Downloads & Errata**.
4. Enter the name of the book in the **Search** box and follow the onscreen instructions.

Once the file is downloaded, please make sure that you unzip or extract the folder using the latest version of:

- WinRAR/7-Zip for Windows
- Zipeg/iZip/UnRarX for Mac
- 7-Zip/PeaZip for Linux

The code bundle for the book is also hosted on GitHub at `https://github.com/PacktPublishing/Learn-Python-Programming-Second-Edition`. In case there's an update to the code, it will be updated on the existing GitHub repository.

We also have other code bundles from our rich catalog of books and videos available at `https://github.com/PacktPublishing/`. Check them out!

Conventions used

There are a number of text conventions used throughout this book.

`CodeInText`: Indicates code words in text, database table names, folder names, filenames, file extensions, pathnames, dummy URLs, user input, and Twitter handles. Here is an example: "Within the `learn.pp` folder, we will create a virtual environment called `learnpp`."

A block of code is set as follows:

```
# we define a function, called local
def local():
    m = 7
    print(m)
```

When we wish to draw your attention to a particular part of a code block, the relevant lines or items are set in bold:

```
# key.points.mutable.assignment.py
x = [1, 2, 3]
def func(x):
    x[1] = 42  # this changes the caller!
    x = 'something else'  # this points x to a new string object
```

Any command-line input or output is written as follows:

```
>>> import sys
>>> print(sys.version)
```

Bold: Indicates a new term, an important word, or words that you see onscreen. For example, words in menus or dialog boxes appear in the text like this. Here is an example: "To open the console in Windows, go to the **Start** menu, choose **Run**, and type cmd."

Warnings or important notes appear like this.

Tips and tricks appear like this.

Get in touch

Feedback from our readers is always welcome.

General feedback: Email feedback@packtpub.com and mention the book title in the subject of your message. If you have questions about any aspect of this book, please email us at questions@packtpub.com.

Errata: Although we have taken every care to ensure the accuracy of our content, mistakes do happen. If you have found a mistake in this book, we would be grateful if you would report this to us. Please visit www.packtpub.com/submit-errata, selecting your book, clicking on the Errata Submission Form link, and entering the details.

Piracy: If you come across any illegal copies of our works in any form on the Internet, we would be grateful if you would provide us with the location address or website name. Please contact us at copyright@packtpub.com with a link to the material.

If you are interested in becoming an author: If there is a topic that you have expertise in and you are interested in either writing or contributing to a book, please visit authors.packtpub.com.

Reviews

Please leave a review. Once you have read and used this book, why not leave a review on the site that you purchased it from? Potential readers can then see and use your unbiased opinion to make purchase decisions, we at Packt can understand what you think about our products, and our authors can see your feedback on their book. Thank you!

For more information about Packt, please visit `packtpub.com`.

A Gentle Introduction to Python 1

"Give a man a fish and you feed him for a day. Teach a man to fish and you feed him for a lifetime."

– Chinese proverb

According to Wikipedia, **computer programming** is:

"...a process that leads from an original formulation of a computing problem to executable computer programs. Programming involves activities such as analysis, developing understanding, generating algorithms, verification of requirements of algorithms including their correctness and resources consumption, and implementation (commonly referred to as coding) of algorithms in a target programming language."

In a nutshell, coding is telling a computer to do something using a language it understands.

Computers are very powerful tools, but unfortunately, they can't think for themselves. They need to be told everything: how to perform a task, how to evaluate a condition to decide which path to follow, how to handle data that comes from a device, such as the network or a disk, and how to react when something unforeseen happens, say, something is broken or missing.

You can code in many different styles and languages. Is it hard? I would say *yes* and *no*. It's a bit like writing. Everybody can learn how to write, and you can too. But, what if you wanted to become a poet? Then writing alone is not enough. You have to acquire a whole other set of skills and this will take a longer and greater effort.

In the end, it all comes down to how far you want to go down the road. Coding is not just putting together some instructions that work. It is so much more!

Good code is short, fast, elegant, easy to read and understand, simple, easy to modify and extend, easy to scale and refactor, and easy to test. It takes time to be able to write code that has all these qualities at the same time, but the good news is that you're taking the first step towards it at this very moment by reading this book. And I have no doubt you can do it. Anyone can; in fact, we all program all the time, only we aren't aware of it.

Would you like an example?

Say you want to make instant coffee. You have to get a mug, the instant coffee jar, a teaspoon, water, and the kettle. Even if you're not aware of it, you're evaluating a lot of data. You're making sure that there is water in the kettle and that the kettle is plugged in, that the mug is clean, and that there is enough coffee in the jar. Then, you boil the water and maybe, in the meantime, you put some coffee in the mug. When the water is ready, you pour it into the cup, and stir.

So, how is this programming?

Well, we gathered resources (the kettle, coffee, water, teaspoon, and mug) and we verified some conditions concerning them (the kettle is plugged in, the mug is clean, and there is enough coffee). Then we started two actions (boiling the water and putting coffee in the mug), and when both of them were completed, we finally ended the procedure by pouring water in to the mug and stirring.

Can you see it? I have just described the high-level functionality of a coffee program. It wasn't that hard because this is what the brain does all day long: evaluate conditions, decide to take actions, carry out tasks, repeat some of them, and stop at some point. Clean objects, put them back, and so on.

All you need now is to learn how to deconstruct all those actions you do automatically in real life so that a computer can actually make some sense of them. And you need to learn a language as well, to instruct it.

So this is what this book is for. I'll tell you how to do it and I'll try to do that by means of many simple but focused examples (my favorite kind).

In this chapter, we are going to cover the following:

- Python's characteristics and ecosystem
- Guidelines on how to get up and running with Python and virtual environments
- How to run Python programs
- How to organize Python code and Python's execution model

A proper introduction

I love to make references to the real world when I teach coding; I believe they help people retain the concepts better. However, now is the time to be a bit more rigorous and see what coding is from a more technical perspective.

When we write code, we're instructing a computer about the things it has to do. Where does the action happen? In many places: the computer memory, hard drives, network cables, the CPU, and so on. It's a whole *world*, which most of the time is the representation of a subset of the real world.

If you write a piece of software that allows people to buy clothes online, you will have to represent real people, real clothes, real brands, sizes, and so on and so forth, within the boundaries of a program.

In order to do so, you will need to create and handle objects in the program you're writing. A person can be an object. A car is an object. A pair of socks is an object. Luckily, Python understands objects very well.

The two main features any object has are properties and methods. Let's take a person object as an example. Typically in a computer program, you'll represent people as customers or employees. The properties that you store against them are things like the name, the SSN, the age, if they have a driving license, their email, gender, and so on. In a computer program, you store all the data you need in order to use an object for the purpose you're serving. If you are coding a website to sell clothes, you probably want to store the heights and weights as well as other measures of your customers so that you can suggest the appropriate clothes for them. So, properties are characteristics of an object. We use them all the time: *Could you pass me that pen?—Which one?—The black one*. Here, we used the *black* property of a pen to identify it (most likely among a blue and a red one).

Methods are things that an object can do. As a person, I have methods such as *speak, walk, sleep, wake up, eat, dream, write, read*, and so on. All the things that I can do could be seen as methods of the objects that represent me.

So, now that you know what objects are and that they expose methods that you can run and properties that you can inspect, you're ready to start coding. Coding in fact is simply about managing those objects that live in the subset of the world that we're reproducing in our software. You can create, use, reuse, and delete objects as you please.

According to the *Data Model* chapter on the official Python documentation (`https://docs.python.org/3/reference/datamodel.html`):

> *"Objects are Python's abstraction for data. All data in a Python program is represented by objects or by relations between objects."*

We'll take a closer look at Python objects in `Chapter 6`, *OOP, Decorators, and Iterators*. For now, all we need to know is that every object in Python has an ID (or identity), a type, and a value.

Once created, the ID of an object is never changed. It's a unique identifier for it, and it's used behind the scenes by Python to retrieve the object when we want to use it.

The type, as well, never changes. The type tells what operations are supported by the object and the possible values that can be assigned to it.

We'll see Python's most important data types in `Chapter 2`, *Built-in Data Types*.

The value can either change or not. If it can, the object is said to be **mutable**, while when it cannot, the object is said to be **immutable**.

How do we use an object? We give it a name, of course! When you give an object a name, then you can use the name to retrieve the object and use it.

In a more generic sense, objects such as numbers, strings (text), collections, and so on are associated with a name. Usually, we say that this name is the name of a variable. You can see the variable as being like a box, which you can use to hold data.

So, you have all the objects you need; what now? Well, we need to use them, right? We may want to send them over a network connection or store them in a database. Maybe display them on a web page or write them into a file. In order to do so, we need to react to a user filling in a form, or pressing a button, or opening a web page and performing a search. We react by running our code, evaluating conditions to choose which parts to execute, how many times, and under which circumstances.

And to do all this, basically we need a language. That's what Python is for. Python is the language we'll use together throughout this book to instruct the computer to do something for us.

Now, enough of this theoretical stuff; let's get started.

Enter the Python

Python is the marvelous creation of Guido Van Rossum, a Dutch computer scientist and mathematician who decided to gift the world with a project he was playing around with over Christmas 1989. The language appeared to the public somewhere around 1991, and since then has evolved to be one of the leading programming languages used worldwide today.

I started programming when I was 7 years old, on a Commodore VIC-20, which was later replaced by its bigger brother, the Commodore 64. Its language was *BASIC*. Later on, I landed on Pascal, Assembly, C, C++, Java, JavaScript, Visual Basic, PHP, ASP, ASP .NET, C#, and other minor languages I cannot even remember, but only when I landed on Python did I finally have that feeling that you have when you find the right couch in the shop. When all of your body parts are yelling, *Buy this one! This one is perfect for us!*

It took me about a day to get used to it. Its syntax is a bit different from what I was used to, but after getting past that initial feeling of discomfort (like having new shoes), I just fell in love with it. Deeply. Let's see why.

About Python

Before we get into the gory details, let's get a sense of why someone would want to use Python (I would recommend you to read the Python page on Wikipedia to get a more detailed introduction).

To my mind, Python epitomizes the following qualities.

Portability

Python runs everywhere, and porting a program from Linux to Windows or Mac is usually just a matter of fixing paths and settings. Python is designed for portability and it takes care of specific **operating system** (**OS**) quirks behind interfaces that shield you from the pain of having to write code tailored to a specific platform.

Coherence

Python is extremely logical and coherent. You can see it was designed by a brilliant computer scientist. Most of the time, you can just guess how a method is called, if you don't know it.

You may not realize how important this is right now, especially if you are at the beginning, but this is a major feature. It means less cluttering in your head, as well as less skimming through the documentation, and less need for mappings in your brain when you code.

Developer productivity

According to Mark Lutz (*Learning Python, 5th Edition, O'Reilly Media*), a Python program is typically one-fifth to one-third the size of equivalent Java or C++ code. This means the job gets done faster. And faster is good. Faster means a faster response on the market. Less code not only means less code to write, but also less code to read (and professional coders read much more than they write), less code to maintain, to debug, and to refactor.

Another important aspect is that Python runs without the need for lengthy and time-consuming compilation and linkage steps, so you don't have to wait to see the results of your work.

An extensive library

Python has an incredibly wide standard library (it's said to come with *batteries included*). If that wasn't enough, the Python community all over the world maintains a body of third-party libraries, tailored to specific needs, which you can access freely at the **Python Package Index** (**PyPI**). When you code Python and you realize that you need a certain feature, in most cases, there is at least one library where that feature has already been implemented for you.

Software quality

Python is heavily focused on readability, coherence, and quality. The language uniformity allows for high readability and this is crucial nowadays where coding is more of a collective effort than a solo endeavor. Another important aspect of Python is its intrinsic multiparadigm nature. You can use it as a scripting language, but you also can exploit object-oriented, imperative, and functional programming styles. It is versatile.

Software integration

Another important aspect is that Python can be extended and integrated with many other languages, which means that even when a company is using a different language as their mainstream tool, Python can come in and act as a glue agent between complex applications that need to talk to each other in some way. This is kind of an advanced topic, but in the real world, this feature is very important.

Satisfaction and enjoyment

Last, but not least, there is the fun of it! Working with Python is fun. I can code for 8 hours and leave the office happy and satisfied, alien to the struggle other coders have to endure because they use languages that don't provide them with the same amount of well-designed data structures and constructs. Python makes coding fun, no doubt about it. And fun promotes motivation and productivity.

These are the major aspects of why I would recommend Python to everyone. Of course, there are many other technical and advanced features that I could have talked about, but they don't really pertain to an introductory section like this one. They will come up naturally, chapter after chapter, in this book.

What are the drawbacks?

Probably, the only drawback that one could find in Python, which is not due to personal preferences, is its *execution speed*. Typically, Python is slower than its compiled brothers. The standard implementation of Python produces, when you run an application, a compiled version of the source code called byte code (with the extension `.pyc`), which is then run by the Python interpreter. The advantage of this approach is portability, which we pay for with a slowdown due to the fact that Python is not compiled down to machine level as are other languages.

However, Python speed is rarely a problem today, hence its wide use regardless of this suboptimal feature. What happens is that, in real life, hardware cost is no longer a problem, and usually it's easy enough to gain speed by parallelizing tasks. Moreover, many programs spend a great proportion of the time waiting for IO operations to complete; therefore, the raw execution speed is often a secondary factor to the overall performance. When it comes to number crunching though, one can switch to faster Python implementations, such as PyPy, which provides an average five-fold speedup by implementing advanced compilation techniques (check `http://pypy.org/` for reference).

When doing data science, you'll most likely find that the libraries that you use with Python, such as **Pandas** and **NumPy**, achieve native speed due to the way they are implemented.

If that wasn't a good-enough argument, you can always consider that Python has been used to drive the backend of services such as Spotify and Instagram, where performance is a concern. Nonetheless, Python has done its job perfectly adequately.

Who is using Python today?

Not yet convinced? Let's take a very brief look at the companies that are using Python today: Google, YouTube, Dropbox, Yahoo!, Zope Corporation, Industrial Light & Magic, Walt Disney Feature Animation, Blender 3D, Pixar, NASA, the NSA, Red Hat, Nokia, IBM, Netflix, Yelp, Intel, Cisco, HP, Qualcomm, and JPMorgan Chase, to name just a few.

Even games such as *Battlefield 2*, *Civilization IV*, and *QuArK* are implemented using Python.

Python is used in many different contexts, such as system programming, web programming, GUI applications, gaming and robotics, rapid prototyping, system integration, data science, database applications, and much more. Several prestigious universities have also adopted Python as their main language in computer science courses.

Setting up the environment

Before we talk about installing Python on your system, let me tell you about which Python version I'll be using in this book.

Python 2 versus Python 3

Python comes in two main versions: Python 2, which is the past, and Python 3, which is the present. The two versions, though very similar, are incompatible in some respects.

In the real world, Python 2 is actually quite far from being the past. In short, even though Python 3 has been out since 2008, the transition phase from Version 2 is still far from being over. This is mostly due to the fact that Python 2 is widely used in the industry, and of course, companies aren't so keen on updating their systems just for the sake of updating them, following the *if it ain't broke, don't fix it* philosophy. You can read all about the transition between the two versions on the web.

Another issue that has hindered the transition is the availability of third-party libraries. Usually, a Python project relies on tens of external libraries, and of course, when you start a new project, you need to be sure that there is already a Version-3-compatible library for any business requirement that may come up. If that's not the case, starting a brand-new project in Python 3 means introducing a potential risk, which many companies are not happy to take.

At the time of writing, though, the majority of the most widely used libraries have been ported to Python 3, and it's quite safe to start a project in Python 3 for most cases. Many of the libraries have been rewritten so that they are compatible with both versions, mostly harnessing the power of the `six` library (the name comes from the multiplication 2 x 3, due to the porting from Version 2 to 3), which helps introspecting and adapting the behavior according to the version used. According to PEP 373 (`https://legacy.python.org/dev/peps/pep-0373/`), the **end of life** (**EOL**) of Python 2.7 has been set to 2020, and there won't be a Python 2.8, so this is the time when companies that have projects running in Python 2 need to start devising an upgrade strategy to move to Python 3 before it's too late.

On my box (MacBook Pro), this is the latest Python version I have:

```
>>> import sys
>>> print(sys.version)
3.7.0a3 (default, Jan 27 2018, 00:46:45)
[Clang 9.0.0 (clang-900.0.39.2)]
```

So you can see that the version is an alpha release of Python 3.7, which will be released in June 2018. The preceding text is a little bit of Python code that I typed into my console. We'll talk about it in a moment.

All the examples in this book will be run using Python 3.7. Even though at the moment the final version might still be slightly different than what I have, I will make sure that all the code and examples are up to date with 3.7 by the time the book is published.

Some of the code can also run in Python 2.7, either as it is or with minor tweaks, but at this point in time, I think it's better to learn Python 3, and then, if you need to, learn the differences it has with Python 2, rather than going the other way around.

Don't worry about this version thing though; it's not that big an issue in practice.

Installing Python

I never really got the point of having a *setup* section in a book, regardless of what it is that you have to set up. Most of the time, between the time the author writes the instructions and the time you actually try them out, months have passed. That is, if you're lucky. One version change and things may not work in the way that is described in the book. Luckily, we have the web now, so in order to help you get up and running, I'll just give you pointers and objectives.

I am conscious that the majority of readers would probably have preferred to have guidelines in the book. I doubt it would have made their life much easier, as I strongly believe that if you want to get started with Python you have to put in that initial effort in order to get familiar with the ecosystem. It is very important, and it will boost your confidence to face the material in the chapters ahead. If you get stuck, remember that Google is your friend.

Setting up the Python interpreter

First of all, let's talk about your OS. Python is fully integrated and most likely already installed in basically almost every Linux distribution. If you have a macOS, it's likely that Python is already there as well (however, possibly only Python 2.7), whereas if you're using Windows, you probably need to install it.

Getting Python and the libraries you need up and running requires a bit of handiwork. Linux and macOS seem to be the most user-friendly OSes for Python programmers; Windows, on the other hand, is the one that requires the biggest effort.

My current system is a MacBook Pro, and this is what I will use throughout the book, along with Python 3.7.

The place you want to start is the official Python website: `https://www.python.org`. This website hosts the official Python documentation and many other resources that you will find very useful. Take the time to explore it.

 Another excellent, resourceful website on Python and its ecosystem is `http://docs.python-guide.org`. You can find instructions to set up Python on different operating systems, using different methods.

Find the download section and choose the installer for your OS. If you are on Windows, make sure that when you run the installer, you check the option `install pip` (actually, I would suggest to make a complete installation, just to be safe, of all the components the installer holds). We'll talk about `pip` later.

Now that Python is installed in your system, the objective is to be able to open a console and run the Python interactive shell by typing `python`.

Please note that I usually refer to the **Python interactive shell** simply as the **Python console**.

To open the console in Windows, go to the **Start** menu, choose **Run**, and type `cmd`. If you encounter anything that looks like a permission problem while working on the examples in this book, please make sure you are running the console with administrator rights.

On the macOS X, you can start a Terminal by going to **Applications | Utilities | Terminal**.

If you are on Linux, you know all that there is to know about the console.

I will use the term *console* interchangeably to indicate the Linux console, the Windows Command Prompt, and the Macintosh Terminal. I will also indicate the command-line prompt with the Linux default format, like this:

```
$ sudo apt-get update
```

If you're not familiar with that, please take some time to learn the basics on how a console works. In a nutshell, after the `$` sign, you normally find an instruction that you have to type. Pay attention to capitalization and spaces, as they are very important.

Whatever console you open, type `python` at the prompt, and make sure the Python interactive shell shows up. Type `exit()` to quit. Keep in mind that you may have to specify `python3` if your OS comes with Python 2.* preinstalled.

This is roughly what you should see when you run Python (it will change in some details according to the version and OS):

```
$ python3.7
Python 3.7.0a3 (default, Jan 27 2018, 00:46:45)
[Clang 9.0.0 (clang-900.0.39.2)] on darwin
Type "help", "copyright", "credits" or "license" for more information.
>>>
```

Now that Python is set up and you can run it, it's time to make sure you have the other tool that will be indispensable to follow the examples in the book: virtualenv.

About virtualenv

As you probably have guessed by its name, **virtualenv** is all about virtual environments. Let me explain what they are and why we need them and let me do it by means of a simple example.

You install Python on your system and you start working on a website for Client X. You create a project folder and start coding. Along the way, you also install some libraries; for example, the Django framework, which we'll see in depth in `Chapter 14`, *Web Development*. Let's say the Django version you install for Project X is 1.7.1.

Now, your website is so good that you get another client, Y. She wants you to build another website, so you start Project Y and, along the way, you need to install Django again. The only issue is that now the Django version is 1.8 and you cannot install it on your system because this would replace the version you installed for Project X. You don't want to risk introducing incompatibility issues, so you have two choices: either you stick with the version you have currently on your machine, or you upgrade it and make sure the first project is still fully working correctly with the new version.

Let's be honest, neither of these options is very appealing, right? Definitely not. So, here's the solution: virtualenv!

virtualenv is a tool that allows you to create a virtual environment. In other words, it is a tool to create isolated Python environments, each of which is a folder that contains all the necessary executables to use the packages that a Python project would need (think of packages as libraries for the time being).

So you create a virtual environment for Project X, install all the dependencies, and then you create a virtual environment for Project Y, installing all its dependencies without the slightest worry because every library you install ends up within the boundaries of the appropriate virtual environment. In our example, Project X will hold Django 1.7.1, while Project Y will hold Django 1.8.

It is of vital importance that you never install libraries directly at the system level. Linux, for example, relies on Python for many different tasks and operations, and if you fiddle with the system installation of Python, you risk compromising the integrity of the whole system (guess to whom this happened...). So take this as a rule, such as brushing your teeth before going to bed: *always, always create a virtual environment when you start a new project.*

To install virtualenv on your system, there are a few different ways. On a Debian-based distribution of Linux, for example, you can install it with the following command:

```
$ sudo apt-get install python-virtualenv
```

Probably, the easiest way is to follow the instructions you can find on the virtualenv official website: https://virtualenv.pypa.io.

You will find that one of the most common ways to install virtualenv is by using `pip`, a package management system used to install and manage software packages written in Python.

 As of Python 3.5, the suggested way to create a virtual environment is to use the `venv` module. Please see the `official documentation` for further information. However, at the time of writing, virtualenv is still by far the tool most used for creating virtual environments.

Your first virtual environment

It is very easy to create a virtual environment, but according to how your system is configured and which Python version you want the virtual environment to run, you need to run the command properly. Another thing you will need to do with virtualenv, when you want to work with it, is to activate it. Activating virtualenv basically produces some path juggling behind the scenes so that when you call the Python interpreter, you're actually calling the active virtual environment one, instead of the mere system one.

I'll show you a full example on my Macintosh console. We will:

1. Create a folder named `learn.pp` under your project root (which in my case is a folder called `srv`, in my home folder). Please adapt the paths according to the setup you fancy on your box.
2. Within the `learn.pp` folder, we will create a virtual environment called `learnpp`.

 Some developers prefer to call all virtual environments using the same name (for example, `.venv`). This way they can run scripts against any virtualenv by just knowing the name of the project they dwell in. The dot in `.venv` is there because in Linux/macOS prepending a name with a dot makes that file or folder invisible.

3. After creating the virtual environment, we will activate it. The methods are slightly different between Linux, macOS, and Windows.
4. Then, we'll make sure that we are running the desired Python version (3.7.*) by running the Python interactive shell.
5. Finally, we will deactivate the virtual environment using the `deactivate` command.

These five simple steps will show you all you have to do to start and use a project.

Here's an example of how those steps might look (note that you might get a slightly different result, according to your OS, Python version, and so on) on the macOS (commands that start with a # are comments, spaces have been introduced for readability, and ⤳ indicates where the line has wrapped around due to lack of space):

```
fabmp:srv fab$ # step 1 - create folder
fabmp:srv fab$ mkdir learn.pp
fabmp:srv fab$ cd learn.pp

fabmp:learn.pp fab$ # step 2 - create virtual environment
fabmp:learn.pp fab$ which python3.7
/Users/fab/.pyenv/shims/python3.7
fabmp:learn.pp fab$ virtualenv -p
⤳ /Users/fab/.pyenv/shims/python3.7 learnpp
Running virtualenv with interpreter /Users/fab/.pyenv/shims/python3.7
Using base prefix '/Users/fab/.pyenv/versions/3.7.0a3'
New python executable in /Users/fab/srv/learn.pp/learnpp/bin/python3.7
Also creating executable in /Users/fab/srv/learn.pp/learnpp/bin/python
Installing setuptools, pip, wheel...done.

fabmp:learn.pp fab$ # step 3 - activate virtual environment
```

```
fabmp:learn.pp fab$ source learnpp/bin/activate

(learnpp) fabmp:learn.pp fab$ # step 4 - verify which python
(learnpp) fabmp:learn.pp fab$ which python
/Users/fab/srv/learn.pp/learnpp/bin/python

(learnpp) fabmp:learn.pp fab$ python
Python 3.7.0a3 (default, Jan 27 2018, 00:46:45)
[Clang 9.0.0 (clang-900.0.39.2)] on darwin
Type "help", "copyright", "credits" or "license" for more information.
>>> exit()

(learnpp) fabmp:learn.pp fab$ # step 5 - deactivate
(learnpp) fabmp:learn.pp fab$ deactivate
fabmp:learn.pp fab$
```

Notice that I had to tell virtualenv explicitly to use the Python 3.7 interpreter because on my box Python 2.7 is the default one. Had I not done that, I would have had a virtual environment with Python 2.7 instead of Python 3.7.

You can combine the two instructions for step 2 in one single command like this:

```
$ virtualenv -p $( which python3.7 ) learnpp
```

I chose to be explicitly verbose in this instance, to help you understand each bit of the procedure.

Another thing to notice is that in order to activate a virtual environment, we need to run the `/bin/activate` script, which needs to be sourced. When a script is **sourced**, it means that it is executed in the current shell, and therefore its effects last after the execution. This is very important. Also notice how the prompt changes after we activate the virtual environment, showing its name on the left (and how it disappears when we deactivate it). On Linux, the steps are the same so I won't repeat them here. On Windows, things change slightly, but the concepts are the same. Please refer to the official virtualenv website for guidance.

At this point, you should be able to create and activate a virtual environment. Please try and create another one without me guiding you. Get acquainted with this procedure because it's something that you will always be doing: **we never work system-wide with Python**, remember? It's extremely important.

So, with the scaffolding out of the way, we're ready to talk a bit more about Python and how you can use it. Before we do that though, allow me to speak a few words about the console.

Your friend, the console

In this era of GUIs and touchscreen devices, it seems a little ridiculous to have to resort to a tool such as the console, when everything is just about one click away.

But the truth is every time you remove your right hand from the keyboard (or the left one, if you're a lefty) to grab your mouse and move the cursor over to the spot you want to click on, you're losing time. Getting things done with the console, counter-intuitive as it may be, results in higher productivity and speed. I know, you have to trust me on this.

Speed and productivity are important and, personally, I have nothing against the mouse, but there is another very good reason for which you may want to get well-acquainted with the console: when you develop code that ends up on some server, the console might be the only available tool. If you make friends with it, I promise you, you will never get lost when it's of utmost importance that you don't (typically, when the website is down and you have to investigate very quickly what's going on).

So it's really up to you. If you're undecided, please grant me the benefit of the doubt and give it a try. It's easier than you think, and you'll never regret it. There is nothing more pitiful than a good developer who gets lost within an SSH connection to a server because they are used to their own custom set of tools, and only to that.

Now, let's get back to Python.

How you can run a Python program

There are a few different ways in which you can run a Python program.

Running Python scripts

Python can be used as a scripting language. In fact, it always proves itself very useful. Scripts are files (usually of small dimensions) that you normally execute to do something like a task. Many developers end up having their own arsenal of tools that they fire when they need to perform a task. For example, you can have scripts to parse data in a format and render it into another different format. Or you can use a script to work with files and folders. You can create or modify configuration files, and much more. Technically, there is not much that cannot be done in a script.

It's quite common to have scripts running at a precise time on a server. For example, if your website database needs cleaning every 24 hours (for example, the table that stores the user sessions, which expire pretty quickly but aren't cleaned automatically), you could set up a Cron job that fires your script at 3:00 A.M. every day.

 According to Wikipedia, the software utility Cron is a time-based job scheduler in Unix-like computer operating systems. People who set up and maintain software environments use Cron to schedule jobs (commands or shell scripts) to run periodically at fixed times, dates, or intervals.

I have Python scripts to do all the menial tasks that would take me minutes or more to do manually, and at some point, I decided to automate. We'll devote half of Chapter 12, *GUIs and Scripts*, on scripting with Python.

Running the Python interactive shell

Another way of running Python is by calling the interactive shell. This is something we already saw when we typed python on the command line of our console.

So, open a console, activate your virtual environment (which by now should be second nature to you, right?), and type python. You will be presented with a couple of lines that should look like this:

```
$ python
Python 3.7.0a3 (default, Jan 27 2018, 00:46:45)
[Clang 9.0.0 (clang-900.0.39.2)] on darwin
Type "help", "copyright", "credits" or "license" for more information.
>>>
```

Those >>> are the prompt of the shell. They tell you that Python is waiting for you to type something. If you type a simple instruction, something that fits in one line, that's all you'll see. However, if you type something that requires more than one line of code, the shell will change the prompt to . . ., giving you a visual clue that you're typing a multiline statement (or anything that would require more than one line of code).

Go on, try it out; let's do some basic math:

```
>>> 2 + 4
6
>>> 10 / 4
2.5
>>> 2 ** 1024
17976931348623159077293051907890247336179769789423065727343008115773267580
```

```
500963132708477322407536021120113879871393357658789768814416622492847430639
474124377767893424865485276302219601246094119453082952085005768838150682342
462881473913110540827237163350510684586298239947245938479716304835356329624
224137216
```

The last operation is showing you something incredible. We raise 2 to the power of 1024, and Python is handling this task with no trouble at all. Try to do it in Java, C++, or C#. It won't work, unless you use special libraries to handle such big numbers.

I use the interactive shell every day. It's extremely useful to debug very quickly, for example, to check if a data structure supports an operation. Or maybe to inspect or run a piece of code.

When you use Django (a web framework), the interactive shell is coupled with it and allows you to work your way through the framework tools, to inspect the data in the database, and many more things. You will find that the interactive shell will soon become one of your dearest friends on the journey you are embarking on.

Another solution, which comes in a much nicer graphic layout, is to use **Integrated DeveLopment Environment (IDLE)**. It's quite a simple IDE, which is intended mostly for beginners. It has a slightly larger set of capabilities than the naked interactive shell you get in the console, so you may want to explore it. It comes for free in the Windows Python installer and you can easily install it in any other system. You can find information about it on the Python website.

Guido Van Rossum named Python after the British comedy group, Monty Python, so it's rumored that the name IDLE has been chosen in honor of Eric Idle, one of Monty Python's founding members.

Running Python as a service

Apart from being run as a script, and within the boundaries of a shell, Python can be coded and run as an application. We'll see many examples throughout the book about this mode. And we'll understand more about it in a moment, when we'll talk about how Python code is organized and run.

Running Python as a GUI application

Python can also be run as a **graphical user interface** (**GUI**). There are several frameworks available, some of which are cross-platform and some others are platform-specific. In Chapter 12, *GUIs and Scripts*, we'll see an example of a GUI application created using Tkinter, which is an object-oriented layer that lives on top of **Tk** (Tkinter means Tk interface).

 Tk is a GUI toolkit that takes desktop application development to a higher level than the conventional approach. It is the standard GUI for **Tool Command Language** (**Tcl**), but also for many other dynamic languages, and it can produce rich native applications that run seamlessly under Windows, Linux, macOS X, and more.

Tkinter comes bundled with Python; therefore, it gives the programmer easy access to the GUI world, and for these reasons, I have chosen it to be the framework for the GUI examples that I'll present in this book.

Among the other GUI frameworks, we find that the following are the most widely used:

- PyQt
- wxPython
- PyGTK

Describing them in detail is outside the scope of this book, but you can find all the information you need on the Python website (https://docs.python.org/3/faq/gui.html) in the *What platform-independent GUI toolkits exist for Python?* section. If GUIs are what you're looking for, remember to choose the one you want according to some principles. Make sure they:

- Offer all the features you may need to develop your project
- Run on all the platforms you may need to support
- Rely on a community that is as wide and active as possible
- Wrap graphic drivers/tools that you can easily install/access

How is Python code organized?

Let's talk a little bit about how Python code is organized. In this section, we'll start going down the rabbit hole a little bit more and introduce more technical names and concepts.

Starting with the basics, how is Python code organized? Of course, you write your code into files. When you save a file with the extension .py, that file is said to be a Python module.

 If you're on Windows or macOS that typically hide file extensions from the user, please make sure you change the configuration so that you can see the complete names of the files. This is not strictly a requirement, but a suggestion.

It would be impractical to save all the code that it is required for software to work within one single file. That solution works for scripts, which are usually not longer than a few hundred lines (and often they are quite shorter than that).

A complete Python application can be made of hundreds of thousands of lines of code, so you will have to scatter it through different modules, which is better, but not nearly good enough. It turns out that even like this, it would still be impractical to work with the code. So Python gives you another structure, called **package**, which allows you to group modules together. A package is nothing more than a folder, which must contain a special file, __init__.py, that doesn't need to hold any code but whose presence is required to tell Python that the folder is not just some folder, but it's actually a package (note that as of Python 3.3, the __init__.py module is not strictly required any more).

As always, an example will make all of this much clearer. I have created an example structure in my book project, and when I type in my console:

```
$ tree -v example
```

I get a tree representation of the contents of the ch1/example folder, which holds the code for the examples of this chapter. Here's what the structure of a really simple application could look like:

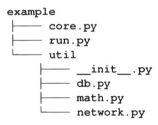

```
example
├── core.py
├── run.py
└── util
    ├── __init__.py
    ├── db.py
    ├── math.py
    └── network.py
```

You can see that within the root of this example, we have two modules, `core.py` and `run.py`, and one package: `util`. Within `core.py`, there may be the core logic of our application. On the other hand, within the `run.py` module, we can probably find the logic to start the application. Within the `util` package, I expect to find various utility tools, and in fact, we can guess that the modules there are named based on the types of tools they hold: `db.py` would hold tools to work with databases, `math.py` would, of course, hold mathematical tools (maybe our application deals with financial data), and `network.py` would probably hold tools to send/receive data on networks.

As explained before, the `__init__.py` file is there just to tell Python that `util` is a package and not just a mere folder.

Had this software been organized within modules only, it would have been harder to infer its structure. I put a *module only* example under the `ch1/files_only` folder; see it for yourself:

```
$ tree -v files_only
```

This shows us a completely different picture:

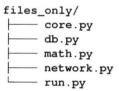

```
files_only/
├── core.py
├── db.py
├── math.py
├── network.py
└── run.py
```

It is a little harder to guess what each module does, right? Now, consider that this is just a simple example, so you can guess how much harder it would be to understand a real application if we couldn't organize the code in packages and modules.

How do we use modules and packages?

When a developer is writing an application, it is likely that they will need to apply the same piece of logic in different parts of it. For example, when writing a parser for the data that comes from a form that a user can fill in a web page, the application will have to validate whether a certain field is holding a number or not. Regardless of how the logic for this kind of validation is written, it's likely that it will be needed in more than one place.

For example, in a poll application, where the user is asked many questions, it's likely that several of them will require a numeric answer. For example:

- What is your age?
- How many pets do you own?
- How many children do you have?
- How many times have you been married?

It would be very bad practice to copy/paste (or, more properly said: duplicate) the validation logic in every place where we expect a numeric answer. This would violate the **don't repeat yourself** (**DRY**) principle, which states that you should never repeat the same piece of code more than once in your application. I feel the need to stress the importance of this principle: *you should never repeat the same piece of code more than once in your application* (pun intended).

There are several reasons why repeating the same piece of logic can be very bad, the most important ones being:

- There could be a bug in the logic, and therefore, you would have to correct it in every place that the logic is applied.
- You may want to amend the way you carry out the validation, and again you would have to change it in every place it is applied.
- You may forget to fix/amend a piece of logic because you missed it when searching for all its occurrences. This would leave wrong/inconsistent behavior in your application.
- Your code would be longer than needed, for no good reason.

Python is a wonderful language and provides you with all the tools you need to apply all the coding best practices. For this particular example, we need to be able to reuse a piece of code. To be able to reuse a piece of code, we need to have a construct that will hold the code for us so that we can call that construct every time we need to repeat the logic inside it. That construct exists, and it's called a **function**.

I'm not going too deep into the specifics here, so please just remember that a function is a block of organized, reusable code that is used to perform a task. Functions can assume many forms and names, according to what kind of environment they belong to, but for now this is not important. We'll see the details when we are able to appreciate them, later on, in the book. Functions are the building blocks of modularity in your application, and they are almost indispensable. Unless you're writing a super-simple script, you'll use functions all the time. We'll explore functions in Chapter 4, *Functions, the Building Blocks of Code*.

Python comes with a very extensive library, as I have already said a few pages ago. Now, maybe it's a good time to define what a library is: a **library** is a collection of functions and objects that provide functionalities that enrich the abilities of a language.

For example, within Python's `math` library, we can find a plethora of functions, one of which is the `factorial` function, which of course calculates the factorial of a number.

> In mathematics, the **factorial** of a non-negative integer number N, denoted as $N!$, is defined as the product of all positive integers less than or equal to N. For example, the factorial of 5 is calculated as:
> `5! = 5 * 4 * 3 * 2 * 1 = 120`
> The factorial of 0 is `0! = 1`, to respect the convention for an empty product.

So, if you wanted to use this function in your code, all you would have to do is to import it and call it with the right input values. Don't worry too much if input values and the concept of calling is not very clear for now; please just concentrate on the import part. We use a library by importing what we need from it, and then we use it.

In Python, to calculate the factorial of number 5, we just need the following code:

```
>>> from math import factorial
>>> factorial(5)
120
```

> Whatever we type in the shell, if it has a printable representation, will be printed on the console for us (in this case, the result of the function call: `120`).

So, let's go back to our example, the one with `core.py`, `run.py`, `util`, and so on.

In our example, the package `util` is our utility library. Our custom utility belt that holds all those reusable tools (that is, functions), which we need in our application. Some of them will deal with databases (`db.py`), some with the network (`network.py`), and some will perform mathematical calculations (`math.py`) that are outside the scope of Python's standard `math` library and, therefore, we have to code them for ourselves.

We will see in detail how to import functions and use them in their dedicated chapter. Let's now talk about another very important concept: *Python's execution model*.

Python's execution model

In this section, I would like to introduce you to a few very important concepts, such as scope, names, and namespaces. You can read all about Python's execution model in the official language reference, of course, but I would argue that it is quite technical and abstract, so let me give you a less formal explanation first.

Names and namespaces

Say you are looking for a book, so you go to the library and ask someone for the book you want to fetch. They tell you something like *Second Floor, Section X, Row Three*. So you go up the stairs, look for Section X, and so on.

It would be very different to enter a library where all the books are piled together in random order in one big room. No floors, no sections, no rows, no order. Fetching a book would be extremely hard.

When we write code, we have the same issue: we have to try and organize it so that it will be easy for someone who has no prior knowledge about it to find what they're looking for. When software is structured correctly, it also promotes code reuse. On the other hand, disorganized software is more likely to expose scattered pieces of duplicated logic.

First of all, let's start with the book. We refer to a book by its title and in Python lingo, that would be a name. Python names are the closest abstraction to what other languages call variables. Names basically refer to objects and are introduced by name-binding operations. Let's make a quick example (notice that anything that follows a # is a comment):

```
>>> n = 3  # integer number
>>> address = "221b Baker Street, NW1 6XE, London"  # Sherlock Holmes'
address
>>> employee = {
...     'age': 45,
...     'role': 'CTO',
...     'SSN': 'AB1234567',
... }
>>> # let's print them
>>> n
3
>>> address
'221b Baker Street, NW1 6XE, London'
>>> employee
{'age': 45, 'role': 'CTO', 'SSN': 'AB1234567'}
>>> other_name
Traceback (most recent call last):
```

```
    File "<stdin>", line 1, in <module>
  NameError: name 'other_name' is not defined
```

We defined three objects in the preceding code (do you remember what are the three features every Python object has?):

- An integer number n (type: `int`, value: 3)
- A string `address` (type: `str`, value: Sherlock Holmes' address)
- A dictionary `employee` (type: `dict`, value: a dictionary that holds three key/value pairs)

Don't worry, I know you're not supposed to know what a dictionary is. We'll see in `Chapter 2`, *Built-in Data Types*, that it's the king of Python data structures.

 Have you noticed that the prompt changed from >>> to . . . when I typed in the definition of employee? That's because the definition spans over multiple lines.

So, what are n, `address`, and `employee`? They are **names**. Names that we can use to retrieve data within our code. They need to be kept somewhere so that whenever we need to retrieve those objects, we can use their names to fetch them. We need some space to hold them, hence: namespaces!

A **namespace** is therefore a mapping from names to objects. Examples are the set of built-in names (containing functions that are always accessible in any Python program), the global names in a module, and the local names in a function. Even the set of attributes of an object can be considered a namespace.

The beauty of namespaces is that they allow you to define and organize your names with clarity, without overlapping or interference. For example, the namespace associated with that book we were looking for in the library can be used to import the book itself, like this:

```
from library.second_floor.section_x.row_three import book
```

We start from the `library` namespace, and by means of the dot (.) operator, we walk into that namespace. Within this namespace, we look for `second_floor`, and again we walk into it with the . operator. We then walk into `section_x`, and finally within the last namespace, `row_three`, we find the name we were looking for: `book`.

Walking through a namespace will be clearer when we'll be dealing with real code examples. For now, just keep in mind that namespaces are places where names are associated with objects.

There is another concept, which is closely related to that of a namespace, which I'd like to briefly talk about: the **scope**.

Scopes

According to Python's documentation:

> " *A scope is a textual region of a Python program, where a namespace is directly accessible.*"

Directly accessible means that when you're looking for an unqualified reference to a name, Python tries to find it in the namespace.

Scopes are determined statically, but actually, during runtime, they are used dynamically. This means that by inspecting the source code, you can tell what the scope of an object is, but this doesn't prevent the software from altering that during runtime. There are four different scopes that Python makes accessible (not necessarily all of them are present at the same time, of course):

- The **local** scope, which is the innermost one and contains the local names.
- The **enclosing** scope, that is, the scope of any enclosing function. It contains non-local names and also non-global names.
- The **global** scope contains the global names.
- The **built-in** scope contains the built-in names. Python comes with a set of functions that you can use in an off-the-shelf fashion, such as `print`, `all`, `abs`, and so on. They live in the built-in scope.

The rule is the following: when we refer to a name, Python starts looking for it in the current namespace. If the name is not found, Python continues the search to the enclosing scope and this continues until the built-in scope is searched. If a name hasn't been found after searching the built-in scope, then Python raises a `NameError` **exception**, which basically means that the name hasn't been defined (you saw this in the preceding example).

The order in which the namespaces are scanned when looking for a name is therefore: **local, enclosing, global, built-in (LEGB)**.

This is all very theoretical, so let's see an example. In order to show you local and enclosing namespaces, I will have to define a few functions. Don't worry if you are not familiar with their syntax for the moment. We'll study functions in Chapter 4, *Functions, the Building Blocks of Code*. Just remember that in the following code, when you see def, it means I'm defining a function:

```
# scopes1.py
# Local versus Global

# we define a function, called local
def local():
    m = 7
    print(m)

m = 5
print(m)

# we call, or `execute` the function local
local()
```

In the preceding example, we define the same name m, both in the global scope and in the local one (the one defined by the local function). When we execute this program with the following command (have you activated your virtualenv?):

```
$ python scopes1.py
```

We see two numbers printed on the console: 5 and 7.

What happens is that the Python interpreter parses the file, top to bottom. First, it finds a couple of comment lines, which are skipped, then it parses the definition of the function local. When called, this function does two things: it sets up a name to an object representing number 7 and prints it. The Python interpreter keeps going and it finds another name binding. This time the binding happens in the global scope and the value is 5. The next line is a call to the print function, which is executed (and so we get the first value printed on the console: 5).

After this, there is a call to the function local. At this point, Python executes the function, so at this time, the binding m = 7 happens and it's printed.

One very important thing to notice is that the part of the code that belongs to the definition of the `local` function is indented by four spaces on the right. Python, in fact, defines scopes by indenting the code. You walk into a scope by indenting, and walk out of it by unindenting. Some coders use two spaces, others three, but the suggested number of spaces to use is four. It's a good measure to maximize readability. We'll talk more about all the conventions you should embrace when writing Python code later.

What would happen if we removed that `m = 7` line? Remember the LEGB rule. Python would start looking for `m` in the local scope (function `local`), and, not finding it, it would go to the next enclosing scope. The next one, in this case, is the global one because there is no enclosing function wrapped around `local`. Therefore, we would see two numbers 5 printed on the console. Let's actually see what the code would look like:

```
# scopes2.py
# Local versus Global

def local():
    # m doesn't belong to the scope defined by the local function
    # so Python will keep looking into the next enclosing scope.
    # m is finally found in the global scope
    print(m, 'printing from the local scope')

m = 5
print(m, 'printing from the global scope')

local()
```

Running `scopes2.py` will print this:

```
$ python scopes2.py
5 printing from the global scope
5 printing from the local scope
```

As expected, Python prints `m` the first time, then when the function `local` is called, `m` isn't found in its scope, so Python looks for it following the LEGB chain until `m` is found in the global scope.

Let's see an example with an extra layer, the enclosing scope:

```
# scopes3.py
# Local, Enclosing and Global

def enclosing_func():
    m = 13

    def local():
```

```
        # m doesn't belong to the scope defined by the local
        # function so Python will keep looking into the next
        # enclosing scope. This time m is found in the enclosing
        # scope
        print(m, 'printing from the local scope')

    # calling the function local
    local()

m = 5
print(m, 'printing from the global scope')

enclosing_func()
```

Running `scopes3.py` will print on the console:

```
$ python scopes3.py
(5, 'printing from the global scope')
(13, 'printing from the local scope')
```

As you can see, the `print` instruction from the function `local` is referring to m as before. m is still not defined within the function itself, so Python starts walking scopes following the LEGB order. This time m is found in the enclosing scope.

Don't worry if this is still not perfectly clear for now. It will come to you as we go through the examples in the book. The *Classes* section of the Python tutorial (`https://docs.python.org/3/tutorial/classes.html`) has an interesting paragraph about scopes and namespaces. Make sure you read it at some point if you want a deeper understanding of the subject.

Before we finish off this chapter, I would like to talk a bit more about objects. After all, basically everything in Python is an object, so I think they deserve a bit more attention.

Objects and classes

When I introduced objects previously in the *A proper introduction* section of the chapter, I said that we use them to represent real-life objects. For example, we sell goods of any kind on the web nowadays and we need to be able to handle, store, and represent them properly. But objects are actually so much more than that. Most of what you will ever do, in Python, has to do with manipulating objects.

So, without going into too much detail (we'll do that in `Chapter 6`, *OOP, Decorators, and Iterators*), I want to give you the *in a nutshell* kind of explanation about classes and objects.

We've already seen that objects are Python's abstraction for data. In fact, everything in Python is an object, infact numbers, strings (data structures that hold text), containers, collections, even functions. You can think of them as if they were boxes with at least three features: an ID (unique), a type, and a value.

But how do they come to life? How do we create them? How do we write our own custom objects? The answer lies in one simple word: **classes**.

Objects are, in fact, instances of classes. The beauty of Python is that classes are objects themselves, but let's not go down this road. It leads to one of the most advanced concepts of this language: **metaclasses**. For now, the best way for you to get the difference between classes and objects is by means of an example.

Say a friend tells you, *I bought a new bike!* You immediately understand what she's talking about. Have you seen the bike? No. Do you know what color it is? Nope. The brand? Nope. Do you know anything about it? Nope. But at the same time, you know everything you need in order to understand what your friend meant when she told you she bought a new bike. You know that a bike has two wheels attached to a frame, a saddle, pedals, handlebars, brakes, and so on. In other words, even if you haven't seen the bike itself, you know the concept of *bike*. An abstract set of features and characteristics that together form something called *bike*.

In computer programming, that is called a **class**. It's that simple. Classes are used to create objects. In fact, objects are said to be **instances of classes**.

In other words, we all know what a bike is; we know the class. But then I have my own bike, which is an instance of the bike class. And my bike is an object with its own characteristics and methods. You have your own bike. Same class, but different instance. Every bike ever created in the world is an instance of the bike class.

Let's see an example. We will write a class that defines a bike and then we'll create two bikes, one red and one blue. I'll keep the code very simple, but don't fret if you don't understand everything about it; all you need to care about at this moment is to understand the difference between a class and an object (or instance of a class):

```
# bike.py
# let's define the class Bike
class Bike:

    def __init__(self, colour, frame_material):
        self.colour = colour
```

```
        self.frame_material = frame_material

    def brake(self):
        print("Braking!")

# let's create a couple of instances
red_bike = Bike('Red', 'Carbon fiber')
blue_bike = Bike('Blue', 'Steel')

# let's inspect the objects we have, instances of the Bike class.
print(red_bike.colour)  # prints: Red
print(red_bike.frame_material)  # prints: Carbon fiber
print(blue_bike.colour)  # prints: Blue
print(blue_bike.frame_material)  # prints: Steel

# let's brake!
red_bike.brake()  # prints: Braking!
```

 I hope by now I don't need to tell you to run the file every time, right? The filename is indicated in the first line of the code block. Just run `$ python filename`, and you'll be fine. But remember to have your virtualenv activated!

So many interesting things to notice here. First things first; the definition of a class happens with the `class` statement. Whatever code comes after the `class` statement, and is indented, is called the body of the class. In our case, the last line that belongs to the class definition is the `print("Braking!")` one.

After having defined the class, we're ready to create instances. You can see that the class body hosts the definition of two methods. A method is basically (and simplistically) a function that belongs to a class.

The first method, __init__, is an **initializer**. It uses some Python magic to set up the objects with the values we pass when we create it.

 Every method that has leading and trailing double underscores, in Python, is called a **magic method**. Magic methods are used by Python for a multitude of different purposes; hence it's never a good idea to name a custom method using two leading and trailing underscores. This naming convention is best left to Python.

The other method we defined, `brake`, is just an example of an additional method that we could call if we wanted to brake the bike. It contains just a `print` statement, of course; it's an example.

We created two bikes then. One has red color and a carbon fiber frame, and the other one has blue color and a steel frame. We pass those values upon creation. After creation, we print out the color property and frame type of the red bike, and the frame type of the blue one just as an example. We also call the `brake` method of the `red_bike`.

One last thing to notice. You remember I told you that the set of attributes of an object is considered to be a namespace? I hope it's clearer what I meant now. You see that by getting to the `frame_type` property through different namespaces (`red_bike`, `blue_bike`), we obtain different values. No overlapping, no confusion.

The dot (`.`) operator is of course the means we use to walk into a namespace, in the case of objects as well.

Guidelines on how to write good code

Writing good code is not as easy as it seems. As I already said before, good code exposes a long list of qualities that is quite hard to put together. Writing good code is, to some extent, an art. Regardless of where on the path you will be happy to settle, there is something that you can embrace which will make your code instantly better: **PEP 8**.

According to Wikipedia:

> *"Python's development is conducted largely through the Python Enhancement Proposal (PEP) process. The PEP process is the primary mechanism for proposing major new features, for collecting community input on an issue, and for documenting the design decisions that have gone into Python."*

PEP 8 is perhaps the most famous of all PEPs. It lays out a simple but effective set of guidelines to define Python aesthetics so that we write beautiful Python code. If you take one suggestion out of this chapter, please let it be this: use it. Embrace it. You will thank me later.

Coding today is no longer a check-in/check-out business. Rather, it's more of a social effort. Several developers collaborate on a piece of code through tools such as Git and Mercurial, and the result is code that is fathered by many different hands.

Git and Mercurial are probably the distributed revision control systems that are most used today. They are essential tools designed to help teams of developers collaborate on the same software.

These days, more than ever, we need to have a consistent way of writing code, so that readability is maximized. When all developers of a company abide by PEP 8, it's not uncommon for any of them landing on a piece of code to think they wrote it themselves. It actually happens to me all the time (I always forget the code I write).

This has a tremendous advantage: when you read code that you could have written yourself, you read it easily. Without a convention, every coder would structure the code the way they like most, or simply the way they were taught or are used to, and this would mean having to interpret every line according to someone else's style. It would mean having to lose much more time just trying to understand it. Thanks to PEP 8, we can avoid this. I'm such a fan of it that I won't sign off a code review if the code doesn't respect it. So, please take the time to study it; it's very important.

In the examples in this book, I will try to respect it as much as I can. Unfortunately, I don't have the luxury of 79 characters (which is the maximum line length suggested by PEP 8), and I will have to cut down on blank lines and other things, but I promise you I'll try to lay out my code so that it's as readable as possible.

The Python culture

Python has been adopted widely in all coding industries. It's used by many different companies for many different purposes, and it's also used in education (it's an excellent language for that purpose, because of its many qualities and the fact that it's easy to learn).

One of the reasons Python is so popular today is that the community around it is vast, vibrant, and full of brilliant people. Many events are organized all over the world, mostly either around Python or its main web framework, Django.

Python is open, and very often so are the minds of those who embrace it. Check out the community page on the Python website for more information and get involved!

There is another aspect to Python which revolves around the notion of being **Pythonic**. It has to do with the fact that Python allows you to use some idioms that aren't found elsewhere, at least not in the same form or as easy to use (I feel quite claustrophobic when I have to code in a language which is not Python now).

Anyway, over the years, this concept of being Pythonic has emerged and, the way I understand it, is something along the lines of *doing things the way they are supposed to be done in Python.*

To help you understand a little bit more about Python's culture and about being Pythonic, I will show you the *Zen of Python*. A lovely Easter egg that is very popular. Open up a Python console and type `import this`. What follows is the result of this line:

```
>>> import this
The Zen of Python, by Tim Peters

Beautiful is better than ugly.
Explicit is better than implicit.
Simple is better than complex.
Complex is better than complicated.
Flat is better than nested.
Sparse is better than dense.
Readability counts.
Special cases aren't special enough to break the rules.
Although practicality beats purity.
Errors should never pass silently.
Unless explicitly silenced.
In the face of ambiguity, refuse the temptation to guess.
There should be one-- and preferably only one --obvious way to do it.
Although that way may not be obvious at first unless you're Dutch.
Now is better than never.
Although never is often better than *right* now.
If the implementation is hard to explain, it's a bad idea.
If the implementation is easy to explain, it may be a good idea.
Namespaces are one honking great idea -- let's do more of those!
```

There are two levels of reading here. One is to consider it as a set of guidelines that have been put down in a fun way. The other one is to keep it in mind, and maybe read it once in a while, trying to understand how it refers to something deeper: some Python characteristics that you will have to understand deeply in order to write Python the way it's supposed to be written. Start with the fun level, and then dig deeper. Always dig deeper.

A note on IDEs

Just a few words about IDEs. To follow the examples in this book, you don't need one; any text editor will do fine. If you want to have more advanced features, such as syntax coloring and auto completion, you will have to fetch yourself an IDE. You can find a comprehensive list of open source IDEs (just Google Python IDEs) on the Python website. I personally use Sublime Text editor. It's free to try out and it costs just a few dollars. I have tried many IDEs in my life, but this is the one that makes me most productive.

Two important pieces of advice:

- Whatever IDE you choose to use, try to learn it well so that you can exploit its strengths, but *don't depend on it*. Exercise yourself to work with VIM (or any other text editor) once in a while; learn to be able to do some work on any platform, with any set of tools.
- Whatever text editor/IDE you use, when it comes to writing Python, *indentation is four spaces*. Don't use tabs, don't mix them with spaces. Use four spaces, not two, not three, not five. Just use four. The whole world works like that, and you don't want to become an outcast because you were fond of the three-space layout.

Summary

In this chapter, we started to explore the world of programming and that of Python. We've barely scratched the surface, just a little, touching concepts that will be discussed later on in the book in greater detail.

We talked about Python's main features, who is using it and for what, and what are the different ways in which we can write a Python program.

In the last part of the chapter, we flew over the fundamental notions of namespaces, scopes, classes, and objects. We also saw how Python code can be organized using modules and packages.

On a practical level, we learned how to install Python on our system, how to make sure we have the tools we need, `pip` and virtualenv, and we also created and activated our first virtual environment. This will allow us to work in a self-contained environment without the risk of compromising the Python system installation.

Now you're ready to start this journey with me. All you need is enthusiasm, an activated virtual environment, this book, your fingers, and some coffee.

Try to follow the examples; I'll keep them simple and short. If you put them under your fingertips, you will retain them much better than if you just read them.

In the next chapter, we will explore Python's rich set of built-in data types. There's much to cover and much to learn!

2
Built-in Data Types

"Data! Data! Data!" he cried impatiently. "I can't make bricks without clay."

– Sherlock Holmes – The Adventure of the Copper Beeches

Everything you do with a computer is managing data. Data comes in many different shapes and flavors. It's the music you listen to, the movies you stream, the PDFs you open. Even the source of the chapter you're reading at this very moment is just a file, which is data.

Data can be simple, an integer number to represent an age, or complex, like an order placed on a website. It can be about a single object or about a collection of them. Data can even be about data, that is, metadata. Data that describes the design of other data structures or data that describes application data or its context. In Python, *objects are abstraction for data*, and Python has an amazing variety of data structures that you can use to represent data, or combine them to create your own custom data.

In this chapter, we are going to cover the following:

- Python objects' structures
- Mutability and immutability
- Built-in data types: numbers, strings, sequences, collections, and mapping types
- The collections module
- Enumerations

Everything is an object

Before we delve into the specifics, I want you to be very clear about objects in Python, so let's talk a little bit more about them. As we already said, everything in Python is an object. But what really happens when you type an instruction like `age = 42` in a Python module?

 If you go to `http://pythontutor.com/`, you can type that instruction into a text box and get its visual representation. Keep this website in mind; it's very useful to consolidate your understanding of what goes on behind the scenes.

So, what happens is that an object is created. It gets an `id`, the `type` is set to `int` (integer number), and the `value` to `42`. A name `age` is placed in the global namespace, pointing to that object. Therefore, whenever we are in the global namespace, after the execution of that line, we can retrieve that object by simply accessing it through its name: `age`.

If you were to move house, you would put all the knives, forks, and spoons in a box and label it *cutlery*. Can you see it's exactly the same concept? Here's a screenshot of what it may look like (you may have to tweak the settings to get to the same view):

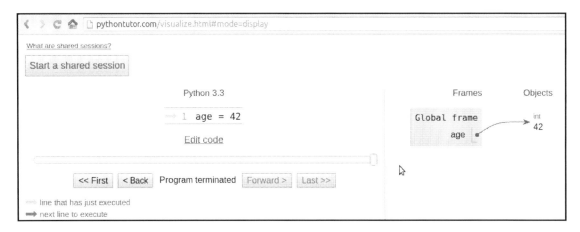

So, for the rest of this chapter, whenever you read something such as `name = some_value`, think of a name placed in the namespace that is tied to the scope in which the instruction was written, with a nice arrow pointing to an object that has an `id`, a `type`, and a `value`. There is a little bit more to say about this mechanism, but it's much easier to talk about it over an example, so we'll get back to this later.

Mutable or immutable? That is the question

A first fundamental distinction that Python makes on data is about whether or not the value of an object changes. If the value can change, the object is called **mutable**, while if the value cannot change, the object is called **immutable**.

It is very important that you understand the distinction between mutable and immutable because it affects the code you write, so here's a question:

```
>>> age = 42
>>> age
42
>>> age = 43   #A
>>> age
43
```

In the preceding code, on the line #A, have I changed the value of age? Well, no. But now it's 43 (I hear you say...). Yes, it's 43, but 42 was an integer number, of the type int, which is immutable. So, what happened is really that on the first line, age is a name that is set to point to an int object, whose value is 42. When we type age = 43, what happens is that another object is created, of the type int and value 43 (also, the id will be different), and the name age is set to point to it. So, we didn't change that 42 to 43. We actually just pointed age to a different location: the new int object whose value is 43. Let's see the same code also printing the IDs:

```
>>> age = 42
>>> id(age)
4377553168
>>> age = 43
>>> id(age)
4377553200
```

Notice that we print the IDs by calling the built-in id function. As you can see, they are different, as expected. Bear in mind that age points to one object at a time: 42 first, then 43. Never together.

Now, let's see the same example using a mutable object. For this example, let's just use a Person object, that has a property age (don't worry about the class declaration for now; it's there only for completeness):

```
>>> class Person():
...     def __init__(self, age):
...         self.age = age
...
>>> fab = Person(age=42)
```

```
>>> fab.age
42
>>> id(fab)
4380878496
>>> id(fab.age)
4377553168
>>> fab.age = 25   # I wish!
>>> id(fab)   # will be the same
4380878496
>>> id(fab.age)   # will be different
4377552624
```

In this case, I set up an object `fab` whose `type` is `Person` (a custom class). On creation, the object is given the `age` of `42`. I'm printing it, along with the object `id`, and the ID of `age` as well. Notice that, even after I change `age` to be `25`, the ID of `fab` stays the same (while the ID of `age` has changed, of course). Custom objects in Python are mutable (unless you code them not to be). Keep this concept in mind; it's very important. I'll remind you about it throughout the rest of the chapter.

Numbers

Let's start by exploring Python's built-in data types for numbers. Python was designed by a man with a master's degree in mathematics and computer science, so it's only logical that it has amazing support for numbers.

Numbers are immutable objects.

Integers

Python integers have an unlimited range, subject only to the available virtual memory. This means that it doesn't really matter how big a number you want to store is: as long as it can fit in your computer's memory, Python will take care of it. Integer numbers can be positive, negative, and 0 (zero). They support all the basic mathematical operations, as shown in the following example:

```
>>> a = 14
>>> b = 3
>>> a + b   # addition
17
>>> a - b   # subtraction
11
>>> a * b   # multiplication
```

```
42
>>> a / b  # true division
4.666666666666667
>>> a // b  # integer division
4
>>> a % b  # modulo operation (reminder of division)
2
>>> a ** b  # power operation
2744
```

The preceding code should be easy to understand. Just notice one important thing: Python has two division operators, one performs the so-called **true division** (/), which returns the quotient of the operands, and the other one, the so-called **integer division** (//), which returns the *floored* quotient of the operands. It might be worth noting that in Python 2 the division operator / behaves differently than in Python 3. See how that is different for positive and negative numbers:

```
>>> 7 / 4  # true division
1.75
>>> 7 // 4  # integer division, truncation returns 1
1
>>> -7 / 4  # true division again, result is opposite of previous
-1.75
>>> -7 // 4  # integer div., result not the opposite of previous
-2
```

This is an interesting example. If you were expecting a -1 on the last line, don't feel bad, it's just the way Python works. The result of an integer division in Python is always rounded towards minus infinity. If, instead of flooring, you want to truncate a number to an integer, you can use the built-in int function, as shown in the following example:

```
>>> int(1.75)
1
>>> int(-1.75)
-1
```

Notice that the truncation is done toward 0.

There is also an operator to calculate the remainder of a division. It's called a modulo operator, and it's represented by a percentage (%):

```
>>> 10 % 3  # remainder of the division 10 // 3
1
>>> 10 % 4  # remainder of the division 10 // 4
2
```

One nice feature introduced in Python 3.6 is the ability to add underscores within number literals (between digits or base specifiers, but not leading or trailing). The purpose is to help make some numbers more readable, like for example 1_000_000_000:

```
>>> n = 1_024
>>> n
1024
>>> hex_n = 0x_4_0_0  # 0x400 == 1024
>>> hex_n
1024
```

Booleans

Boolean algebra is that subset of algebra in which the values of the variables are the truth values: true and false. In Python, True and False are two keywords that are used to represent truth values. Booleans are a subclass of integers, and behave respectively like 1 and 0. The equivalent of the int class for Booleans is the bool class, which returns either True or False. Every built-in Python object has a value in the Boolean context, which means they basically evaluate to either True or False when fed to the bool function. We'll see all about this in Chapter 3, *Iterating and Making Decisions*.

Boolean values can be combined in Boolean expressions using the logical operators and, or, and not. Again, we'll see them in full in the next chapter, so for now let's just see a simple example:

```
>>> int(True)  # True behaves like 1
1
>>> int(False)  # False behaves like 0
0
>>> bool(1)  # 1 evaluates to True in a boolean context
True
>>> bool(-42)  # and so does every non-zero number
True
>>> bool(0)  # 0 evaluates to False
False
>>> # quick peak at the operators (and, or, not)
>>> not True
False
>>> not False
True
>>> True and True
True
>>> False or True
True
```

You can see that `True` and `False` are subclasses of integers when you try to add them. Python upcasts them to integers and performs the addition:

```
>>> 1 + True
2
>>> False + 42
42
>>> 7 - True
6
```

 Upcasting is a type conversion operation that goes from a subclass to its parent. In the example presented here, `True` and `False`, which belong to a class derived from the integer class, are converted back to integers when needed. This topic is about inheritance and will be explained in detail in `Chapter 6`, *OOP, Decorators, and Iterators*.

Real numbers

Real numbers, or floating point numbers, are represented in Python according to the IEEE 754 double-precision binary floating-point format, which is stored in 64 bits of information divided into three sections: sign, exponent, and mantissa.

 Quench your thirst for knowledge about this format on Wikipedia: `http://en.wikipedia.org/wiki/Double-precision_floating-point_format`.

Usually, programming languages give coders two different formats: single and double precision. The former takes up 32 bits of memory, and the latter 64. Python supports only the double format. Let's see a simple example:

```
>>> pi = 3.1415926536  # how many digits of PI can you remember?
>>> radius = 4.5
>>> area = pi * (radius ** 2)
>>> area
63.617251235400005
```

In the calculation of the area, I wrapped the `radius ** 2` within braces. Even though that wasn't necessary because the power operator has higher precedence than the multiplication one, I think the formula reads more easily like that. Moreover, should you get a slightly different result for the area, don't worry. It might depend on your OS, how Python was compiled, and so on. As long as the first few decimal digits are correct, you know it's a correct result.

The `sys.float_info` struct sequence holds information about how floating point numbers will behave on your system. This is what I see on my box:

```
>>> import sys
>>> sys.float_info
sys.float_info(max=1.7976931348623157e+308, max_exp=1024, max_10_exp=308,
min=2.2250738585072014e-308, min_exp=-1021, min_10_exp=-307, dig=15,
mant_dig=53, epsilon=2.220446049250313e-16, radix=2, rounds=1)
```

Let's make a few considerations here: we have 64 bits to represent float numbers. This means we can represent at most `2 ** 64 == 18,446,744,073,709,551,616` numbers with that amount of bits. Take a look at the `max` and `epsilon` values for the float numbers, and you'll realize it's impossible to represent them all. There is just not enough space, so they are approximated to the closest representable number. You probably think that only extremely big or extremely small numbers suffer from this issue. Well, think again and try the following in your console:

```
>>> 0.3 - 0.1 * 3  # this should be 0!!!
-5.551115123125783e-17
```

What does this tell you? It tells you that double precision numbers suffer from approximation issues even when it comes to simple numbers like `0.1` or `0.3`. Why is this important? It can be a big problem if you're handling prices, or financial calculations, or any kind of data that needs not to be approximated. Don't worry, Python gives you the **decimal** type, which doesn't suffer from these issues; we'll see them in a moment.

Complex numbers

Python gives you complex numbers support out of the box. If you don't know what complex numbers are, they are numbers that can be expressed in the form *a* + *ib* where *a* and *b* are real numbers, and *i* (or *j* if you're an engineer) is the imaginary unit, that is, the square root of *-1*. *a* and *b* are called, respectively, the *real* and *imaginary* part of the number.

It's actually unlikely you'll be using them, unless you're coding something scientific. Let's see a small example:

```
>>> c = 3.14 + 2.73j
>>> c.real  # real part
3.14
>>> c.imag  # imaginary part
2.73
>>> c.conjugate()  # conjugate of A + Bj is A - Bj
(3.14-2.73j)
>>> c * 2  # multiplication is allowed
(6.28+5.46j)
>>> c ** 2  # power operation as well
(2.4067000000000007+17.1444j)
>>> d = 1 + 1j  # addition and subtraction as well
>>> c - d
(2.14+1.73j)
```

Fractions and decimals

Let's finish the tour of the number department with a look at fractions and decimals. Fractions hold a rational numerator and denominator in their lowest forms. Let's see a quick example:

```
>>> from fractions import Fraction
>>> Fraction(10, 6)  # mad hatter?
Fraction(5, 3)  # notice it's been simplified
>>> Fraction(1, 3) + Fraction(2, 3)  # 1/3 + 2/3 == 3/3 == 1/1
Fraction(1, 1)
>>> f = Fraction(10, 6)
>>> f.numerator
5
>>> f.denominator
3
```

Although they can be very useful at times, it's not that common to spot them in commercial software. Much easier instead, is to see decimal numbers being used in all those contexts where precision is everything; for example, in scientific and financial calculations.

It's important to remember that arbitrary precision decimal numbers come at a price in performance, of course. The amount of data to be stored for each number is far greater than it is for fractions or floats as well as the way they are handled, which causes the Python interpreter much more work behind the scenes. Another interesting thing to note is that you can get and set the precision by accessing decimal.getcontext().prec.

Let's see a quick example with decimal numbers:

```
>>> from decimal import Decimal as D  # rename for brevity
>>> D(3.14)  # pi, from float, so approximation issues
Decimal('3.140000000000000124344978758017532527446746826171875')
>>> D('3.14')  # pi, from a string, so no approximation issues
Decimal('3.14')
>>> D(0.1) * D(3) - D(0.3)  # from float, we still have the issue
Decimal('2.775557561565156540423631668E-17')
>>> D('0.1') * D(3) - D('0.3')  # from string, all perfect
Decimal('0.0')
>>> D('1.4').as_integer_ratio()  # 7/5 = 1.4 (isn't this cool?!)
(7, 5)
```

Notice that when we construct a Decimal number from a float, it takes on all the approximation issues float may come from. On the other hand, when the Decimal has no approximation issues (for example, when we feed an int or a string representation to the constructor), then the calculation has no quirky behavior. When it comes to money, use decimals.

This concludes our introduction to built-in numeric types. Let's now look at sequences.

Immutable sequences

Let's start with immutable sequences: strings, tuples, and bytes.

Strings and bytes

Textual data in Python is handled with str objects, more commonly known as **strings**. They are immutable sequences of **Unicode code points**. Unicode code points can represent a character, but can also have other meanings, such as formatting data, for example. Python, unlike other languages, doesn't have a char type, so a single character is rendered simply by a string of length 1.

Unicode is an excellent way to handle data, and should be used for the internals of any application. When it comes to storing textual data though, or sending it on the network, you may want to encode it, using an appropriate encoding for the medium you're using. The result of an encoding produces a `bytes` object, whose syntax and behavior is similar to that of strings. String literals are written in Python using single, double, or triple quotes (both single or double). If built with triple quotes, a string can span on multiple lines. An example will clarify this:

```
>>> # 4 ways to make a string
>>> str1 = 'This is a string. We built it with single quotes.'
>>> str2 = "This is also a string, but built with double quotes."
>>> str3 = '''This is built using triple quotes,
... so it can span multiple lines.'''
>>> str4 = """This too
... is a multiline one
... built with triple double-quotes."""
>>> str4    #A
'This too\nis a multiline one\nbuilt with triple double-quotes.'
>>> print(str4)    #B
This too
is a multiline one
built with triple double-quotes.
```

In `#A` and `#B`, we print `str4`, first implicitly, and then explicitly, using the `print` function. A nice exercise would be to find out why they are different. Are you up to the challenge? (hint: look up the `str` function.)

Strings, like any sequence, have a length. You can get this by calling the `len` function:

```
>>> len(str1)
49
```

Encoding and decoding strings

Using the `encode/decode` methods, we can encode Unicode strings and decode bytes objects. **UTF-8** is a variable length character encoding, capable of encoding all possible Unicode code points. It is the dominant encoding for the web. Notice also that by adding a literal `b` in front of a string declaration, we're creating a *bytes* object:

```
>>> s = "This is üŋíc0de"    # unicode string: code points
>>> type(s)
<class 'str'>
>>> encoded_s = s.encode('utf-8')    # utf-8 encoded version of s
>>> encoded_s
b'This is \xc3\xbc\xc5\x8b\xc3\xadc0de'    # result: bytes object
```

```
>>> type(encoded_s)  # another way to verify it
<class 'bytes'>
>>> encoded_s.decode('utf-8')  # let's revert to the original
'This is üŋíc0de'
>>> bytes_obj = b"A bytes object"  # a bytes object
>>> type(bytes_obj)
<class 'bytes'>
```

Indexing and slicing strings

When manipulating sequences, it's very common to have to access them at one precise position (indexing), or to get a subsequence out of them (slicing). When dealing with immutable sequences, both operations are read-only.

While indexing comes in one form, a zero-based access to any position within the sequence, slicing comes in different forms. When you get a slice of a sequence, you can specify the start and stop positions, and the step. They are separated with a colon (:) like this: my_sequence[start:stop:step]. All the arguments are optional, start is inclusive, and stop is exclusive. It's much easier to show an example, rather than explain them further in words:

```
>>> s = "The trouble is you think you have time."
>>> s[0]  # indexing at position 0, which is the first char
'T'
>>> s[5]  # indexing at position 5, which is the sixth char
'r'
>>> s[:4]  # slicing, we specify only the stop position
'The '
>>> s[4:]  # slicing, we specify only the start position
'trouble is you think you have time.'
>>> s[2:14]  # slicing, both start and stop positions
'e trouble is'
>>> s[2:14:3]  # slicing, start, stop and step (every 3 chars)
'erb '
>>> s[:]  # quick way of making a copy
'The trouble is you think you have time.'
```

Of all the lines, the last one is probably the most interesting. If you don't specify a parameter, Python will fill in the default for you. In this case, start will be the start of the string, stop will be the end of the string, and step will be the default 1. This is an easy and quick way of obtaining a copy of the string s (same value, but different object). Can you find a way to get the reversed copy of a string using slicing (don't look it up; find it for yourself)?

String formatting

One of the features strings have is the ability to be used as a template. There are several different ways of formatting a string, and for the full list of possibilities, I encourage you to look up the documentation. Here are some common examples:

```
>>> greet_old = 'Hello %s!'
>>> greet_old % 'Fabrizio'
'Hello Fabrizio!'

>>> greet_positional = 'Hello {} {}!'
>>> greet_positional.format('Fabrizio', 'Romano')
'Hello Fabrizio Romano!'

>>> greet_positional_idx = 'This is {0}! {1} loves {0}!'
>>> greet_positional_idx.format('Python', 'Fabrizio')
'This is Python! Fabrizio loves Python!'
>>> greet_positional_idx.format('Coffee', 'Fab')
'This is Coffee! Fab loves Coffee!'

>>> keyword = 'Hello, my name is {name} {last_name}'
>>> keyword.format(name='Fabrizio', last_name='Romano')
'Hello, my name is Fabrizio Romano'
```

In the previous example, you can see four different ways of formatting stings. The first one, which relies on the `%` operator, is deprecated and shouldn't be used any more. The current, modern way to format a string is by using the `format` string method. You can see, from the different examples, that a pair of curly braces acts as a placeholder within the string. When we call `format`, we feed it data that replaces the placeholders. We can specify indexes (and much more) within the curly braces, and even names, which implies we'll have to call `format` using keyword arguments instead of positional ones.

Notice how `greet_positional_idx` is rendered differently by feeding different data to the call to `format`. Apparently, I'm into Python and coffee... big surprise!

One last feature I want to show you is a relatively new addition to Python (Version 3.6) and it's called **formatted string literals**. This feature is quite cool: strings are prefixed with `f`, and contain replacement fields surrounded by curly braces. Replacement fields are expressions evaluated at runtime, and then formatted using the `format` protocol:

```
>>> name = 'Fab'
>>> age = 42
>>> f"Hello! My name is {name} and I'm {age}"
"Hello! My name is Fab and I'm 42"
>>> from math import pi
>>> f"No arguing with {pi}, it's irrational..."
```

```
"No arguing with 3.141592653589793, it's irrational..."
```

Check out the official documentation to learn everything about string formatting and how powerful it can be.

Tuples

The last immutable sequence type we're going to see is the tuple. A **tuple** is a sequence of arbitrary Python objects. In a tuple, items are separated by commas. They are used everywhere in Python, because they allow for patterns that are hard to reproduce in other languages. Sometimes tuples are used implicitly; for example, to set up multiple variables on one line, or to allow a function to return multiple different objects (usually a function returns one object only, in many other languages), and even in the Python console, you can use tuples implicitly to print multiple elements with one single instruction. We'll see examples for all these cases:

```
>>> t = ()  # empty tuple
>>> type(t)
<class 'tuple'>
>>> one_element_tuple = (42, )  # you need the comma!
>>> three_elements_tuple = (1, 3, 5)  # braces are optional here
>>> a, b, c = 1, 2, 3 # tuple for multiple assignment
>>> a, b, c  # implicit tuple to print with one instruction
(1, 2, 3)
>>> 3 in three_elements_tuple  # membership test
True
```

Notice that the membership operator in can also be used with lists, strings, dictionaries, and, in general, with collection and sequence objects.

 Notice that to create a tuple with one item, we need to put that comma after the item. The reason is that without the comma that item is just itself wrapped in braces, kind of in a redundant mathematical expression. Notice also that on assignment, braces are optional so my_tuple = 1, 2, 3 is the same as my_tuple = (1, 2, 3).

One thing that tuple assignment allows us to do, is *one-line swaps*, with no need for a third temporary variable. Let's see first a more traditional way of doing it:

```
>>> a, b = 1, 2
>>> c = a  # we need three lines and a temporary var c
>>> a = b
>>> b = c
>>> a, b  # a and b have been swapped
```

```
(2, 1)
```

And now let's see how we would do it in Python:

```
>>> a, b = 0, 1
>>> a, b = b, a  # this is the Pythonic way to do it
>>> a, b
(1, 0)
```

Take a look at the line that shows you the Pythonic way of swapping two values. Do you remember what I wrote in Chapter 1, *A Gentle Introduction to Python*? A Python program is typically one-fifth to one-third the size of equivalent Java or C++ code, and features like one-line swaps contribute to this. Python is elegant, where elegance in this context also means economy.

Because they are immutable, tuples can be used as keys for dictionaries (we'll see this shortly). To me, tuples are Python's built-in data that most closely represent a mathematical vector. This doesn't mean that this was the reason for which they were created though. Tuples usually contain an heterogeneous sequence of elements, while on the other hand, lists are most of the times homogeneous. Moreover, tuples are normally accessed via unpacking or indexing, while lists are usually iterated over.

Mutable sequences

Mutable sequences differ from their immutable sisters in that they can be changed after creation. There are two mutable sequence types in Python: lists and byte arrays. I said before that the dictionary is the king of data structures in Python. I guess this makes the list its rightful queen.

Lists

Python lists are mutable sequences. They are very similar to tuples, but they don't have the restrictions of immutability. Lists are commonly used to storing collections of homogeneous objects, but there is nothing preventing you from store heterogeneous collections as well. Lists can be created in many different ways. Let's see an example:

```
>>> []   # empty list
[]
>>> list()  # same as []
[]
>>> [1, 2, 3]  # as with tuples, items are comma separated
[1, 2, 3]
```

```
>>> [x + 5 for x in [2, 3, 4]]  # Python is magic
[7, 8, 9]
>>> list((1, 3, 5, 7, 9))  # list from a tuple
[1, 3, 5, 7, 9]
>>> list('hello')  # list from a string
['h', 'e', 'l', 'l', 'o']
```

In the previous example, I showed you how to create a list using different techniques. I would like you to take a good look at the line that says `Python is magic`, which I am not expecting you to fully understand at this point (unless you cheated and you're not a novice!). That is called a **list comprehension**, a very powerful functional feature of Python, which we'll see in detail in `Chapter 5`, *Saving Time and Memory*. I just wanted to make your mouth water at this point.

Creating lists is good, but the real fun comes when we use them, so let's see the main methods they gift us with:

```
>>> a = [1, 2, 1, 3]
>>> a.append(13)  # we can append anything at the end
>>> a
[1, 2, 1, 3, 13]
>>> a.count(1)  # how many `1` are there in the list?
2
>>> a.extend([5, 7])  # extend the list by another (or sequence)
>>> a
[1, 2, 1, 3, 13, 5, 7]
>>> a.index(13)  # position of `13` in the list (0-based indexing)
4
>>> a.insert(0, 17)  # insert `17` at position 0
>>> a
[17, 1, 2, 1, 3, 13, 5, 7]
>>> a.pop()  # pop (remove and return) last element
7
>>> a.pop(3)  # pop element at position 3
1
>>> a
[17, 1, 2, 3, 13, 5]
>>> a.remove(17)  # remove `17` from the list
>>> a
[1, 2, 3, 13, 5]
>>> a.reverse()  # reverse the order of the elements in the list
>>> a
[5, 13, 3, 2, 1]
>>> a.sort()  # sort the list
>>> a
[1, 2, 3, 5, 13]
>>> a.clear()  # remove all elements from the list
```

```
>>> a
[]
```

The preceding code gives you a roundup of a list's main methods. I want to show you how powerful they are, using `extend` as an example. You can extend lists using any sequence type:

```
>>> a = list('hello')  # makes a list from a string
>>> a
['h', 'e', 'l', 'l', 'o']
>>> a.append(100)  # append 100, heterogeneous type
>>> a
['h', 'e', 'l', 'l', 'o', 100]
>>> a.extend((1, 2, 3))  # extend using tuple
>>> a
['h', 'e', 'l', 'l', 'o', 100, 1, 2, 3]
>>> a.extend('...')  # extend using string
>>> a
['h', 'e', 'l', 'l', 'o', 100, 1, 2, 3, '.', '.', '.']
```

Now, let's see what are the most common operations you can do with lists:

```
>>> a = [1, 3, 5, 7]
>>> min(a)  # minimum value in the list
1
>>> max(a)  # maximum value in the list
7
>>> sum(a)  # sum of all values in the list
16
>>> len(a)  # number of elements in the list
4
>>> b = [6, 7, 8]
>>> a + b  # `+` with list means concatenation
[1, 3, 5, 7, 6, 7, 8]
>>> a * 2  # `*` has also a special meaning
[1, 3, 5, 7, 1, 3, 5, 7]
```

The last two lines in the preceding code are quite interesting because they introduce us to a concept called **operator overloading**. In short, it means that operators such as +, −. *, %, and so on, may represent different operations according to the context they are used in. It doesn't make any sense to sum two lists, right? Therefore, the + sign is used to concatenate them. Hence, the * sign is used to concatenate the list to itself according to the right operand.

Now, let's take a step further and see something a little more interesting. I want to show you how powerful the `sorted` method can be and how easy it is in Python to achieve results that require a great deal of effort in other languages:

```
>>> from operator import itemgetter
>>> a = [(5, 3), (1, 3), (1, 2), (2, -1), (4, 9)]
>>> sorted(a)
[(1, 2), (1, 3), (2, -1), (4, 9), (5, 3)]
>>> sorted(a, key=itemgetter(0))
[(1, 3), (1, 2), (2, -1), (4, 9), (5, 3)]
>>> sorted(a, key=itemgetter(0, 1))
[(1, 2), (1, 3), (2, -1), (4, 9), (5, 3)]
>>> sorted(a, key=itemgetter(1))
[(2, -1), (1, 2), (5, 3), (1, 3), (4, 9)]
>>> sorted(a, key=itemgetter(1), reverse=True)
[(4, 9), (5, 3), (1, 3), (1, 2), (2, -1)]
```

The preceding code deserves a little explanation. First of all, a is a list of tuples. This means each element in a is a tuple (a 2-tuple, to be precise). When we call `sorted(some_list)`, we get a sorted version of `some_list`. In this case, the sorting on a 2-tuple works by sorting them on the first item in the tuple, and on the second when the first one is the same. You can see this behavior in the result of `sorted(a)`, which yields `[(1, 2), (1, 3), ...]`. Python also gives us the ability to control which element(s) of the tuple the sorting must be run against. Notice that when we instruct the `sorted` function to work on the first element of each tuple (by `key=itemgetter(0)`), the result is different: `[(1, 3), (1, 2), ...]`. The sorting is done only on the first element of each tuple (which is the one at position 0). If we want to replicate the default behavior of a simple `sorted(a)` call, we need to use `key=itemgetter(0, 1)`, which tells Python to sort first on the elements at position 0 within the tuples, and then on those at position 1. Compare the results and you'll see they match.

For completeness, I included an example of sorting only on the elements at position 1, and the same but in reverse order. If you have ever seen sorting in Java, I expect you to be quite impressed at this moment.

The Python sorting algorithm is very powerful, and it was written by Tim Peters (we've already seen this name, can you recall when?). It is aptly named **Timsort**, and it is a blend between **merge** and **insertion sort** and has better time performances than most other algorithms used for mainstream programming languages. Timsort is a stable sorting algorithm, which means that when multiple records have the same key, their original order is preserved. We've seen this in the result of `sorted(a, key=itemgetter(0))`, which has yielded `[(1, 3), (1, 2), ...]`, in which the order of those two tuples has been preserved because they have the same value at position 0.

Byte arrays

To conclude our overview of mutable sequence types, let's spend a couple of minutes on the `bytearray` type. Basically, they represent the mutable version of `bytes` objects. They expose most of the usual methods of mutable sequences as well as most of the methods of the `bytes` type. Items are integers in the range [0, 256).

 When it comes to intervals, I'm going to use the standard notation for open/closed ranges. A square bracket on one end means that the value is included, while a round brace means it's excluded. The granularity is usually inferred by the type of the edge elements so, for example, the interval [3, 7] means all integers between 3 and 7, inclusive. On the other hand, (3, 7) means all integers between 3 and 7 exclusive (hence 4, 5, and 6). Items in a `bytearray` type are integers between 0 and 256; 0 is included, 256 is not. One reason intervals are often expressed like this is to ease coding. If we break a range $[a, b)$ into N consecutive ranges, we can easily represent the original one as a concatenation like this:
$[a,k_1)+[k_1,k_2)+[k_2,k_3)+...+[k_{N-1},b)$
The middle points (k_i) being excluded on one end, and included on the other end, allow for easy concatenation and splitting when intervals are handled in the code.

Let's see a quick example with the `bytearray` type:

```
>>> bytearray()   # empty bytearray object
bytearray(b'')
>>> bytearray(10)   # zero-filled instance with given length
bytearray(b'\x00\x00\x00\x00\x00\x00\x00\x00\x00\x00')
>>> bytearray(range(5)) # bytearray from iterable of integers
bytearray(b'\x00\x01\x02\x03\x04')
>>> name = bytearray(b'Lina')   #A - bytearray from bytes
>>> name.replace(b'L', b'l')
bytearray(b'lina')
>>> name.endswith(b'na')
True
>>> name.upper()
bytearray(b'LINA')
>>> name.count(b'L')
1
```

As you can see in the preceding code, there are a few ways to create a `bytearray` object. They can be useful in many situations; for example, when receiving data through a socket, they eliminate the need to concatenate data while polling, hence they can prove to be very handy. On the line `#A`, I created a `bytearray` named as `name` from the bytes literal `b'Lina'` to show you how the `bytearray` object exposes methods from both sequences and strings, which is extremely handy. If you think about it, they can be considered as mutable strings.

Set types

Python also provides two set types, `set` and `frozenset`. The `set` type is mutable, while `frozenset` is immutable. They are unordered collections of immutable objects. **Hashability** is a characteristic that allows an object to be used as a set member as well as a key for a dictionary, as we'll see very soon.

 From the official documentation: *An object is hashable if it has a hash value which never changes during its lifetime, and can be compared to other objects. Hashability makes an object usable as a dictionary key and a set member, because these data structures use the hash value internally. All of Python's immutable built-in objects are hashable while mutable containers are not.*

Objects that compare equally must have the same hash value. Sets are very commonly used to test for membership, so let's introduce the `in` operator in the following example:

```
>>> small_primes = set()  # empty set
>>> small_primes.add(2)   # adding one element at a time
>>> small_primes.add(3)
>>> small_primes.add(5)
>>> small_primes
{2, 3, 5}
>>> small_primes.add(1)   # Look what I've done, 1 is not a prime!
>>> small_primes
{1, 2, 3, 5}
>>> small_primes.remove(1)   # so let's remove it
>>> 3 in small_primes # membership test
True
>>> 4 in small_primes
False
>>> 4 not in small_primes  # negated membership test
True
>>> small_primes.add(3)   # trying to add 3 again
>>> small_primes
{2, 3, 5}  # no change, duplication is not allowed
```

```
>>> bigger_primes = set([5, 7, 11, 13])  # faster creation
>>> small_primes | bigger_primes # union operator `|`
{2, 3, 5, 7, 11, 13}
>>> small_primes & bigger_primes  # intersection operator `&`
{5}
>>> small_primes - bigger_primes  # difference operator `-`
{2, 3}
```

In the preceding code, you can see two different ways to create a set. One creates an empty set and then adds elements one at a time. The other creates the set using a list of numbers as an argument to the constructor, which does all the work for us. Of course, you can create a set from a list or tuple (or any iterable) and then you can add and remove members from the set as you please.

 We'll look at iterable objects and iteration in the next chapter. For now, just know that iterable objects are objects you can iterate on in a direction.

Another way of creating a set is by simply using the curly braces notation, like this:

```
>>> small_primes = {2, 3, 5, 5, 3}
>>> small_primes
{2, 3, 5}
```

Notice I added some duplication to emphasize that the resulting set won't have any. Let's see an example about the immutable counterpart of the set type, frozenset:

```
>>> small_primes = frozenset([2, 3, 5, 7])
>>> bigger_primes = frozenset([5, 7, 11])
>>> small_primes.add(11)  # we cannot add to a frozenset
Traceback (most recent call last):
  File "<stdin>", line 1, in <module>
AttributeError: 'frozenset' object has no attribute 'add'
>>> small_primes.remove(2)  # neither we can remove
Traceback (most recent call last):
  File "<stdin>", line 1, in <module>
AttributeError: 'frozenset' object has no attribute 'remove'
>>> small_primes & bigger_primes  # intersect, union, etc. allowed
frozenset({5, 7})
```

As you can see, frozenset objects are quite limited in respect of their mutable counterpart. They still prove very effective for membership test, union, intersection, and difference operations, and for performance reasons.

Mapping types – dictionaries

Of all the built-in Python data types, the dictionary is easily the most interesting one. It's the only standard mapping type, and it is the backbone of every Python object.

A dictionary maps keys to values. Keys need to be hashable objects, while values can be of any arbitrary type. Dictionaries are mutable objects. There are quite a few different ways to create a dictionary, so let me give you a simple example of how to create a dictionary equal to {'A': 1, 'Z': -1} in five different ways:

```
>>> a = dict(A=1, Z=-1)
>>> b = {'A': 1, 'Z': -1}
>>> c = dict(zip(['A', 'Z'], [1, -1]))
>>> d = dict([('A', 1), ('Z', -1)])
>>> e = dict({'Z': -1, 'A': 1})
>>> a == b == c == d == e  # are they all the same?
True  # They are indeed
```

Have you noticed those double equals? Assignment is done with one equal, while to check whether an object is the same as another one (or five in one go, in this case), we use double equals. There is also another way to compare objects, which involves the is operator, and checks whether the two objects are the same (if they have the same ID, not just the value), but unless you have a good reason to use it, you should use the double equals instead. In the preceding code, I also used one nice function: zip. It is named after the real-life zip, which glues together two things taking one element from each at a time. Let me show you an example:

```
>>> list(zip(['h', 'e', 'l', 'l', 'o'], [1, 2, 3, 4, 5]))
[('h', 1), ('e', 2), ('l', 3), ('l', 4), ('o', 5)]
>>> list(zip('hello', range(1, 6)))  # equivalent, more Pythonic
[('h', 1), ('e', 2), ('l', 3), ('l', 4), ('o', 5)]
```

In the preceding example, I have created the same list in two different ways, one more explicit, and the other a little bit more Pythonic. Forget for a moment that I had to wrap the list constructor around the zip call (the reason is because zip returns an iterator, not a list, so if I want to see the result I need to exhaust that iterator into something—a list in this case), and concentrate on the result. See how zip has coupled the first elements of its two arguments together, then the second ones, then the third ones, and so on and so forth? Take a look at your pants (or at your purse, if you're a lady) and you'll see the same behavior in your actual zip. But let's go back to dictionaries and see how many wonderful methods they expose for allowing us to manipulate them as we want.

Let's start with the basic operations:

```
>>> d = {}
>>> d['a'] = 1  # let's set a couple of (key, value) pairs
>>> d['b'] = 2
>>> len(d)  # how many pairs?
2
>>> d['a']  # what is the value of 'a'?
1
>>> d  # how does `d` look now?
{'a': 1, 'b': 2}
>>> del d['a']  # let's remove `a`
>>> d
{'b': 2}
>>> d['c'] = 3  # let's add 'c': 3
>>> 'c' in d  # membership is checked against the keys
True
>>> 3 in d  # not the values
False
>>> 'e' in d
False
>>> d.clear()  # let's clean everything from this dictionary
>>> d
{}
```

Notice how accessing keys of a dictionary, regardless of the type of operation we're performing, is done through square brackets. Do you remember strings, lists, and tuples? We were accessing elements at some position through square brackets as well, which is yet another example of Python's consistency.

Let's see now three special objects called dictionary views: keys, values, and items. These objects provide a dynamic view of the dictionary entries and they change when the dictionary changes. keys() returns all the keys in the dictionary, values() returns all the values in the dictionary, and items() returns all the *(key, value)* pairs in the dictionary.

According to the Python documentation: "*Keys and values are iterated over in an arbitrary order which is non-random, varies across Python implementations, and depends on the dictionary's history of insertions and deletions. If keys, values and items views are iterated over with no intervening modifications to the dictionary, the order of items will directly correspond.*"

Enough with this chatter; let's put all this down into code:

```
>>> d = dict(zip('hello', range(5)))
>>> d
{'h': 0, 'e': 1, 'l': 3, 'o': 4}
>>> d.keys()
dict_keys(['h', 'e', 'l', 'o'])
>>> d.values()
dict_values([0, 1, 3, 4])
>>> d.items()
dict_items([('h', 0), ('e', 1), ('l', 3), ('o', 4)])
>>> 3 in d.values()
True
>>> ('o', 4) in d.items()
True
```

There are a few things to notice in the preceding code. First, notice how we're creating a dictionary by iterating over the zipped version of the string `'hello'` and the list `[0, 1, 2, 3, 4]`. The string `'hello'` has two `'l'` characters inside, and they are paired up with the values 2 and 3 by the `zip` function. Notice how in the dictionary, the second occurrence of the `'l'` key (the one with value 3), overwrites the first one (the one with value 2). Another thing to notice is that when asking for any view, the original order is now preserved, while before Version 3.6 there was no guarantee of that.

 As of Python 3.6, the `dict` type has been reimplemented to use a more compact representation. This resulted in dictionaries using 20% to 25% less memory when compared to Python 3.5. Moreover, in Python 3.6, as a side effect, dictionaries are natively ordered. This feature has received such a welcome from the community that in 3.7 it has become a legit feature of the language rather than an implementation side effect. A `dict` is ordered if it remembers the order in which keys were first inserted.

We'll see how these views are fundamental tools when we talk about iterating over collections. Let's take a look now at some other methods exposed by Python's dictionaries; there's plenty of them and they are very useful:

```
>>> d
{'e': 1, 'h': 0, 'o': 4, 'l': 3}
>>> d.popitem()  # removes a random item (useful in algorithms)
('o', 4)
>>> d
{'h': 0, 'e': 1, 'l': 3}
>>> d.pop('l')  # remove item with key `l`
3
>>> d.pop('not-a-key')  # remove a key not in dictionary: KeyError
```

```
Traceback (most recent call last):
  File "<stdin>", line 1, in <module>
KeyError: 'not-a-key'
>>> d.pop('not-a-key', 'default-value')  # with a default value?
'default-value'  # we get the default value
>>> d.update({'another': 'value'})  # we can update dict this way
>>> d.update(a=13)  # or this way (like a function call)
>>> d
{'h': 0, 'e': 1, 'another': 'value', 'a': 13}
>>> d.get('a')  # same as d['a'] but if key is missing no KeyError
13
>>> d.get('a', 177)  # default value used if key is missing
13
>>> d.get('b', 177)  # like in this case
177
>>> d.get('b')  # key is not there, so None is returned
```

All these methods are quite simple to understand, but it's worth talking about that None, for a moment. Every function in Python returns None, unless the return statement is explicitly used to return something else, but we'll see this when we explore functions. None is frequently used to represent the absence of a value, and it is quite commonly used as a default value for arguments in function declaration. Some inexperienced coders sometimes write code that returns either False or None. Both False and None evaluate to False in a Boolean context so it may seem there is not much difference between them. But actually, I would argue there is quite an important difference: False means that we have information, and the information we have is False. None means *no information*. And no information is very different from information that is False. In layman's terms, if you ask your mechanic, *Is my car ready?*, there is a big difference between the answer, *No, it's not* (False) and, *I have no idea* (None).

One last method I really like about dictionaries is setdefault. It behaves like get, but also sets the key with the given value if it is not there. Let's see an example:

```
>>> d = {}
>>> d.setdefault('a', 1)  # 'a' is missing, we get default value
1
>>> d
{'a': 1}  # also, the key/value pair ('a', 1) has now been added
>>> d.setdefault('a', 5)  # let's try to override the value
1
>>> d
{'a': 1}  # no override, as expected
```

So, we're now at the end of this tour. Test your knowledge about dictionaries by trying to foresee what d looks like after this line:

```
>>> d = {}
>>> d.setdefault('a', {}).setdefault('b', []).append(1)
```

Don't worry if you don't get it immediately. I just wanted to encourage you to experiment with dictionaries.

This concludes our tour of built-in data types. Before I discuss some considerations about what we've seen in this chapter, I want to take a peek briefly at the collections module.

The collections module

When Python general purpose built-in containers (tuple, list, set, and dict) aren't enough, we can find specialized container datatypes in the collections module. They are:

Data type	Description
namedtuple()	Factory function for creating tuple subclasses with named fields
deque	List-like container with fast appends and pops on either end
ChainMap	Dictionary-like class for creating a single view of multiple mappings
Counter	Dictionary subclass for counting hashable objects
OrderedDict	Dictionary subclass that remembers the order entries were added
defaultdict	Dictionary subclass that calls a factory function to supply missing values
UserDict	Wrapper around dictionary objects for easier dictionary subclassing
UserList	Wrapper around list objects for easier list subclassing
UserString	Wrapper around string objects for easier string subclassing

We don't have the room to cover all of them, but you can find plenty of examples in the official documentation, so here I'll just give a small example to show you namedtuple, defaultdict, and ChainMap.

namedtuple

A `namedtuple` is a tuple-like object that has fields accessible by attribute lookup as well as being indexable and iterable (it's actually a subclass of `tuple`). This is sort of a compromise between a full-fledged object and a tuple, and it can be useful in those cases where you don't need the full power of a custom object, but you want your code to be more readable by avoiding weird indexing. Another use case is when there is a chance that items in the tuple need to change their position after refactoring, forcing the coder to refactor also all the logic involved, which can be very tricky. As usual, an example is better than a thousand words (or was it a picture?). Say we are handling data about the left and right eyes of a patient. We save one value for the left eye (position 0) and one for the right eye (position 1) in a regular tuple. Here's how that might be:

```
>>> vision = (9.5, 8.8)
>>> vision
(9.5, 8.8)
>>> vision[0]  # left eye (implicit positional reference)
9.5
>>> vision[1]  # right eye (implicit positional reference)
8.8
```

Now let's pretend we handle `vision` objects all the time, and at some point the designer decides to enhance them by adding information for the combined vision, so that a `vision` object stores data in this format: *(left eye, combined, right eye)*.

Do you see the trouble we're in now? We may have a lot of code that depends on `vision[0]` being the left eye information (which it still is) and `vision[1]` being the right eye information (which is no longer the case). We have to refactor our code wherever we handle these objects, changing `vision[1]` to `vision[2]`, and it can be painful. We could have probably approached this a bit better from the beginning, by using a `namedtuple`. Let me show you what I mean:

```
>>> from collections import namedtuple
>>> Vision = namedtuple('Vision', ['left', 'right'])
>>> vision = Vision(9.5, 8.8)
>>> vision[0]
9.5
>>> vision.left  # same as vision[0], but explicit
9.5
>>> vision.right  # same as vision[1], but explicit
8.8
```

If within our code, we refer to the left and right eyes using `vision.left` and `vision.right`, all we need to do to fix the new design issue is to change our factory and the way we create instances. The rest of the code won't need to change:

```
>>> Vision = namedtuple('Vision', ['left', 'combined', 'right'])
>>> vision = Vision(9.5, 9.2, 8.8)
>>> vision.left  # still correct
9.5
>>> vision.right  # still correct (though now is vision[2])
8.8
>>> vision.combined  # the new vision[1]
9.2
```

You can see how convenient it is to refer to those values by name rather than by position. After all, a wise man once wrote, *Explicit is better than implicit* (can you recall where? Think *Zen* if you can't...). This example may be a little extreme; of course, it's not likely that our code designer will go for a change like this, but you'd be amazed to see how frequently issues similar to this one happen in a professional environment, and how painful it is to refactor them.

defaultdict

The `defaultdict` data type is one of my favorites. It allows you to avoid checking if a key is in a dictionary by simply inserting it for you on your first access attempt, with a default value whose type you pass on creation. In some cases, this tool can be very handy and shorten your code a little. Let's see a quick example. Say we are updating the value of `age`, by adding one year. If `age` is not there, we assume it was 0 and we update it to 1:

```
>>> d = {}
>>> d['age'] = d.get('age', 0) + 1  # age not there, we get 0 + 1
>>> d
{'age': 1}
>>> d = {'age': 39}
>>> d['age'] = d.get('age', 0) + 1  # age is there, we get 40
>>> d
{'age': 40}
```

Now let's see how it would work with a `defaultdict` data type. The second line is actually the short version of a four-lines-long `if` clause that we would have to write if dictionaries didn't have the `get` method (we'll see all about `if` clauses in Chapter 3, *Iterating and Making Decisions)*:

```
>>> from collections import defaultdict
>>> dd = defaultdict(int)  # int is the default type (0 the value)
>>> dd['age'] += 1  # short for dd['age'] = dd['age'] + 1
>>> dd
defaultdict(<class 'int'>, {'age': 1})  # 1, as expected
```

Notice how we just need to instruct the `defaultdict` factory that we want an `int` number to be used in case the key is missing (we'll get 0, which is the default for the `int` type). Also, notice that even though in this example there is no gain on the number of lines, there is definitely a gain in readability, which is very important. You can also use a different technique to instantiate a `defaultdict` data type, which involves creating a factory object. To dig deeper, please refer to the official documentation.

ChainMap

`ChainMap` is an extremely nice data type which was introduced in Python 3.3. It behaves like a normal dictionary but according to the Python documentation: *"is provided for quickly linking a number of mappings so they can be treated as a single unit"*. This is usually much faster than creating one dictionary and running multiple update calls on it. `ChainMap` can be used to simulate nested scopes and is useful in templating. The underlying mappings are stored in a list. That list is public and can be accessed or updated using the maps attribute. Lookups search the underlying mappings successively until a key is found. By contrast, writes, updates, and deletions only operate on the first mapping.

A very common use case is providing defaults, so let's see an example:

```
>>> from collections import ChainMap
>>> default_connection = {'host': 'localhost', 'port': 4567}
>>> connection = {'port': 5678}
>>> conn = ChainMap(connection, default_connection)  # map creation
>>> conn['port']  # port is found in the first dictionary
5678
>>> conn['host']  # host is fetched from the second dictionary
'localhost'
>>> conn.maps  # we can see the mapping objects
[{'port': 5678}, {'host': 'localhost', 'port': 4567}]
>>> conn['host'] = 'packtpub.com'  # let's add host
>>> conn.maps
```

```
[{'port': 5678, 'host': 'packtpub.com'},
 {'host': 'localhost', 'port': 4567}]
>>> del conn['port']  # let's remove the port information
>>> conn.maps
[{'host': 'packtpub.com'}, {'host': 'localhost', 'port': 4567}]
>>> conn['port']  # now port is fetched from the second dictionary
4567
>>> dict(conn)  # easy to merge and convert to regular dictionary
{'host': 'packtpub.com', 'port': 4567}
```

I just love how Python makes your life easy. You work on a `ChainMap` object, configure the first mapping as you want, and when you need a complete dictionary with all the defaults as well as the customized items, you just feed the `ChainMap` object to a `dict` constructor. If you have never coded in other languages, such as Java or C++, you probably won't be able to appreciate fully how precious this is, and how Python makes your life so much easier. I do, I feel claustrophobic every time I have to code in some other language.

Enums

Technically not a built-in data type, as you have to import them from the `enum` module, but definitely worth mentioning, are enumerations. They were introduced in Python 3.4, and though it is not that common to see them in professional code (yet), I thought I'd give you an example anyway.

The official definition goes like this: "*An enumeration is a set of symbolic names (members) bound to unique, constant values. Within an enumeration, the members can be compared by identity, and the enumeration itself can be iterated over.*"

Say you need to represent traffic lights. In your code, you might resort to doing this:

```
>>> GREEN = 1
>>> YELLOW = 2
>>> RED = 4
>>> TRAFFIC_LIGHTS = (GREEN, YELLOW, RED)
>>> # or with a dict
>>> traffic_lights = {'GREEN': 1, 'YELLOW': 2, 'RED': 4}
```

There's nothing special about the preceding code. It's something, in fact, that is very common to find. But, consider doing this instead:

```
>>> from enum import Enum
>>> class TrafficLight(Enum):
...     GREEN = 1
...     YELLOW = 2
```

```
...        RED = 4
...
>>> TrafficLight.GREEN
<TrafficLight.GREEN: 1>
>>> TrafficLight.GREEN.name
'GREEN'
>>> TrafficLight.GREEN.value
1
>>> TrafficLight(1)
<TrafficLight.GREEN: 1>
>>> TrafficLight(4)
<TrafficLight.RED: 4>
```

Ignoring for a moment the (relative) complexity of a class definition, you can appreciate how this might be more advantageous. The data structure is much cleaner, and the API it provides is much more powerful. I encourage you to check out the official documentation to explore all the great features you can find in the `enum` module. I think it's worth exploring, at least once.

Final considerations

That's it. Now you have seen a very good proportion of the data structures that you will use in Python. I encourage you to take a dive into the Python documentation and experiment further with each and every data type we've seen in this chapter. It's worth it, believe me. Everything you'll write will be about handling data, so make sure your knowledge about it is rock solid.

Before we leap into `Chapter 3`, *Iterating and Making Decisions*, I'd like to share some final considerations about different aspects that to my mind are important and not to be neglected.

Small values caching

When we discussed objects at the beginning of this chapter, we saw that when we assigned a name to an object, Python creates the object, sets its value, and then points the name to it. We can assign different names to the same value and we expect different objects to be created, like this:

```
>>> a = 1000000
>>> b = 1000000
>>> id(a) == id(b)
False
```

In the preceding example, a and b are assigned to two int objects, which have the same value but they are not the same object, as you can see, their id is not the same. So let's do it again:

```
>>> a = 5
>>> b = 5
>>> id(a) == id(b)
True
```

Oh, oh! Is Python broken? Why are the two objects the same now? We didn't do a = b = 5, we set them up separately. Well, the answer is performances. Python caches short strings and small numbers, to avoid having many copies of them clogging up the system memory. Everything is handled properly under the hood so you don't need to worry a bit, but make sure that you remember this behavior should your code ever need to fiddle with IDs.

How to choose data structures

As we've seen, Python provides you with several built-in data types and sometimes, if you're not that experienced, choosing the one that serves you best can be tricky, especially when it comes to collections. For example, say you have many dictionaries to store, each of which represents a customer. Within each customer dictionary, there's an 'id': 'code' unique identification code. In what kind of collection would you place them? Well, unless I know more about these customers, it's very hard to answer. What kind of access will I need? What sort of operations will I have to perform on each of them, and how many times? Will the collection change over time? Will I need to modify the customer dictionaries in any way? What is going to be the most frequent operation I will have to perform on the collection?

If you can answer the preceding questions, then you will know what to choose. If the collection never shrinks or grows (in other words, it won't need to add/delete any customer object after creation) or shuffles, then tuples are a possible choice. Otherwise, lists are a good candidate. Every customer dictionary has a unique identifier though, so even a dictionary could work. Let me draft these options for you:

```
# example customer objects
customer1 = {'id': 'abc123', 'full_name': 'Master Yoda'}
customer2 = {'id': 'def456', 'full_name': 'Obi-Wan Kenobi'}
customer3 = {'id': 'ghi789', 'full_name': 'Anakin Skywalker'}
# collect them in a tuple
customers = (customer1, customer2, customer3)
# or collect them in a list
customers = [customer1, customer2, customer3]
# or maybe within a dictionary, they have a unique id after all
```

```
customers = {
    'abc123': customer1,
    'def456': customer2,
    'ghi789': customer3,
}
```

Some customers we have there, right? I probably wouldn't go with the tuple option, unless I wanted to highlight that the collection is not going to change. I'd say usually a list is better, as it allows for more flexibility.

Another factor to keep in mind is that tuples and lists are ordered collections. If you use a dictionary (prior to Python 3.6) or a set, you lose the ordering, so you need to know if ordering is important in your application.

What about performances? For example, in a list, operations such as insertion and membership can take $O(n)$, while they are $O(1)$ for a dictionary. It's not always possible to use dictionaries though, if we don't have the guarantee that we can uniquely identify each item of the collection by means of one of its properties, and that the property in question is hashable (so it can be a key in `dict`).

> If you're wondering what $O(n)$ and $O(1)$ mean, please Google `big O notation`. In this context, let's just say that if performing an operation Op on a data structure takes $O(f(n))$, it would mean that Op takes at most a time $t \leq c * f(n)$ to complete, where c is some positive constant, n is the size of the input, and f is some function. So, think of $O(...)$ as an upper bound for the running time of an operation (it can be used also to size other measurable quantities, of course).
>
> Another way of understanding if you have chosen the right data structure is by looking at the code you have to write in order to manipulate it. If everything comes easily and flows naturally, then you probably have chosen correctly, but if you find yourself thinking your code is getting unnecessarily complicated, then you probably should try and decide whether you need to reconsider your choices. It's quite hard to give advice without a practical case though, so when you choose a data structure for your data, try to keep ease of use and performance in mind and give precedence to what matters most in the context you are in.

About indexing and slicing

At the beginning of this chapter, we saw slicing applied on strings. Slicing, in general, applies to a sequence: tuples, lists, strings, and so on. With lists, slicing can also be used for assignment. I've almost never seen this used in professional code, but still, you know you can. Could you slice dictionaries or sets? I hear you scream, *Of course not!*. Excellent; I see we're on the same page here, so let's talk about indexing.

There is one characteristic about Python indexing I haven't mentioned before. I'll show you by way of an example. How do you address the last element of a collection? Let's see:

```
>>> a = list(range(10))  # `a` has 10 elements. Last one is 9.
>>> a
[0, 1, 2, 3, 4, 5, 6, 7, 8, 9]
>>> len(a)  # its length is 10 elements
10
>>> a[len(a) - 1]  # position of last one is len(a) - 1
9
>>> a[-1]  # but we don't need len(a)! Python rocks!
9
>>> a[-2]  # equivalent to len(a) - 2
8
>>> a[-3]  # equivalent to len(a) - 3
7
```

If the list `a` has 10 elements, because of the 0-index positioning system of Python, the first one is at position 0 and the last one is at position 9. In the preceding example, the elements are conveniently placed in a position equal to their value: 0 is at position 0, 1 at position 1, and so on.

So, in order to fetch the last element, we need to know the length of the whole list (or tuple, or string, and so on) and then subtract 1. Hence: `len(a) - 1`. This is so common an operation that Python provides you with a way to retrieve elements using **negative indexing**. This proves very useful when you do data manipulation. Here's a nice diagram about how indexing works on the string `"HelloThere"` (which is Obi-Wan Kenobi sarcastically greeting General Grievous):

Trying to address indexes greater than **9** or smaller than **-10** will raise an `IndexError`, as expected.

About the names

You may have noticed that, in order to keep the examples as short as possible, I have called many objects using simple letters, like a, b, c, d, and so on. This is perfectly OK when you debug on the console or when you show that `a + b == 7`, but it's bad practice when it comes to professional coding (or any type of coding, for that matter). I hope you will indulge me if I sometimes do it; the reason is to present the code in a more compact way.

In a real environment though, when you choose names for your data, you should choose them carefully and they should reflect what the data is about. So, if you have a collection of `Customer` objects, `customers` is a perfectly good name for it. Would `customers_list`, `customers_tuple`, or `customers_collection` work as well? Think about it for a second. Is it good to tie the name of the collection to the datatype? I don't think so, at least in most cases. So I'd say if you have an excellent reason to do so, go ahead; otherwise, don't. The reason is, once that `customers_tuple` starts being used in different places of your code, and you realize you actually want to use a list instead of a tuple, you're up for some fun refactoring (also known as **wasted time**). Names for data should be nouns, and names for functions should be verbs. Names should be as expressive as possible. Python is actually a very good example when it comes to names. Most of the time you can just guess what a function is called if you know what it does. Crazy, huh?

Chapter 2 of *Meaningful Names* of *Clean Code, Robert C. Martin, Prentice Hall* is entirely dedicated to names. It's an amazing book that helped me improve my coding style in many different ways, and is a must-read if you want to take your coding to the next level.

Summary

In this chapter, we've explored the built-in data types of Python. We've seen how many there are and how much can be achieved by just using them in different combinations.

We've seen number types, sequences, sets, mappings, collections (and a special guest appearance by `Enum`), we've seen that everything is an object, we've learned the difference between mutable and immutable, and we've also learned about slicing and indexing (and, proudly, negative indexing as well).

We've presented simple examples, but there's much more that you can learn about this subject, so stick your nose into the official documentation and explore.

Most of all, I encourage you to try out all the exercises by yourself, get your fingers using that code, build some muscle memory, and experiment, experiment, experiment. Learn what happens when you divide by zero, when you combine different number types into a single expression, when you manage strings. Play with all data types. Exercise them, break them, discover all their methods, enjoy them, and learn them very, very well.

If your foundation is not rock solid, how good can your code be? And data is the foundation for everything. Data shapes what dances around it.

The more you progress with the book, the more it's likely that you will find some discrepancies or maybe a small typo here and there in my code (or yours). You will get an error message, something will break. That's wonderful! When you code, things break all the time, you debug and fix all the time, so consider errors as useful exercises to learn something new about the language you're using, and not as failures or problems. Errors will keep coming up until your very last line of code, that's for sure, so you may as well start making your peace with them now.

The next chapter is about iterating and making decisions. We'll see how actually to put those collections to use, and take decisions based on the data we're presented with. We'll start to go a little faster now that your knowledge is building up, so make sure you're comfortable with the contents of this chapter before you move to the next one. Once more, have fun, explore, break things. It's a very good way to learn.

Iterating and Making Decisions

3

"Insanity: doing the same thing over and over again and expecting different results."

– *Albert Einstein*

In the previous chapter, we looked at Python's built-in data types. Now that you're familiar with data in its many forms and shapes, it's time to start looking at how a program can use it.

According to Wikipedia:

> *In computer science, control flow (or alternatively, flow of control) refers to the specification of the order in which the individual statements, instructions or function calls of an imperative program are executed or evaluated.*

In order to control the flow of a program, we have two main weapons: **conditional programming** (also known as **branching**) and **looping**. We can use them in many different combinations and variations, but in this chapter, instead of going through all the possible forms of those two constructs in a *documentation* fashion, I'd rather give you the basics and then I'll write a couple of small scripts with you. In the first one, we'll see how to create a rudimentary prime-number generator, while in the second one, we'll see how to apply discounts to customers based on coupons. This way, you should get a better feeling for how conditional programming and looping can be used.

In this chapter, we are going to cover the following:

- Conditional programming
- Looping in Python
- A quick peek at the itertools module

Conditional programming

Conditional programming, or branching, is something you do every day, every moment. It's about evaluating conditions: *if the light is green, then I can cross; if it's raining, then I'm taking the umbrella;* and *if I'm late for work, then I'll call my manager.*

The main tool is the `if` statement, which comes in different forms and colors, but basically it evaluates an expression and, based on the result, chooses which part of the code to execute. As usual, let's look at an example:

```
# conditional.1.py
late = True
if late:
    print('I need to call my manager!')
```

This is possibly the simplest example: when fed to the `if` statement, `late` acts as a conditional expression, which is evaluated in a Boolean context (exactly like if we were calling `bool(late)`). If the result of the evaluation is `True`, then we enter the body of the code immediately after the `if` statement. Notice that the `print` instruction is indented: this means it belongs to a scope defined by the `if` clause. Execution of this code yields:

```
$ python conditional.1.py
I need to call my manager!
```

Since `late` is `True`, the `print` statement was executed. Let's expand on this example:

```
# conditional.2.py
late = False
if late:
    print('I need to call my manager!')  #1
else:
    print('no need to call my manager...')  #2
```

This time I set `late = False`, so when I execute the code, the result is different:

```
$ python conditional.2.py
no need to call my manager...
```

Depending on the result of evaluating the `late` expression, we can either enter block #1 or block #2, *but not both*. Block #1 is executed when `late` evaluates to `True`, while block #2 is executed when `late` evaluates to `False`. Try assigning `False`/`True` values to the `late` name, and see how the output for this code changes accordingly.

The preceding example also introduces the else clause, which becomes very handy when we want to provide an alternative set of instructions to be executed when an expression evaluates to False within an if clause. The else clause is optional, as is evident by comparing the preceding two examples.

A specialized else – elif

Sometimes all you need is to do something if a condition is met (a simple if clause). At other times, you need to provide an alternative, in case the condition is False (if/else clause), but there are situations where you may have more than two paths to choose from, so, since calling the manager (or not calling them) is kind of a binary type of example (either you call or you don't), let's change the type of example and keep expanding. This time, we decide on tax percentages. If my income is less than $10,000, I won't pay any taxes. If it is between $10,000 and $30,000, I'll pay 20% in taxes. If it is between $30,000 and $100,000, I'll pay 35% in taxes, and if it's over $100,000, I'll (gladly) pay 45% in taxes. Let's put this all down into beautiful Python code:

```
# taxes.py
income = 15000
if income < 10000:
    tax_coefficient = 0.0    #1
elif income < 30000:
    tax_coefficient = 0.2    #2
elif income < 100000:
    tax_coefficient = 0.35   #3
else:
    tax_coefficient = 0.45   #4

print('I will pay:', income * tax_coefficient, 'in taxes')
```

Executing the preceding code yields:

```
$ python taxes.py
I will pay: 3000.0 in taxes
```

Let's go through the example line by line: we start by setting up the income value. In the example, my income is $15,000. We enter the if clause. Notice that this time we also introduced the elif clause, which is a contraction of else-if, and it's different from a bare else clause in that it also has its own condition. So, the if expression of income < 10000 evaluates to False, therefore block #1 is not executed.

The control passes to the next condition evaluator: `elif income < 30000`. This one evaluates to `True`, therefore block #2 is executed, and because of this, Python then resumes execution after the whole `if/elif/elif/else` clause (which we can just call the `if` clause from now on). There is only one instruction after the `if` clause, the `print` call, which tells us I will pay `3000.0` in taxes this year (*15,000 * 20%*). Notice that the order is mandatory: `if` comes first, then (optionally) as many `elif` clauses as you need, and then (optionally) an `else` clause.

Interesting, right? No matter how many lines of code you may have within each block, when one of the conditions evaluates to `True`, the associated block is executed and then execution resumes after the whole clause. If none of the conditions evaluates to `True` (for example, `income = 200000`), then the body of the `else` clause would be executed (block #4). This example expands our understanding of the behavior of the `else` clause. Its block of code is executed when none of the preceding `if/elif/.../elif` expressions has evaluated to `True`.

Try to modify the value of `income` until you can comfortably execute all blocks at will (one per execution, of course). And then try the **boundaries**. This is crucial, whenever you have conditions expressed as **equalities** or **inequalities** (`==`, `!=`, `<`, `>`, `<=`, `>=`), those numbers represent boundaries. It is essential to test boundaries thoroughly. Should I allow you to drive at 18 or 17? Am I checking your age with `age < 18`, or `age <= 18`? You can't imagine how many times I've had to fix subtle bugs that stemmed from using the wrong operator, so go ahead and experiment with the preceding code. Change some `<` to `<=` and set income to be one of the boundary values (10,000, 30,000, 100,000) as well as any value in between. See how the result changes, and get a good understanding of it before proceeding.

Let's now see another example that shows us how to nest `if` clauses. Say your program encounters an error. If the alert system is the console, we print the error. If the alert system is an email, we send it according to the severity of the error. If the alert system is anything other than console or email, we don't know what to do, therefore we do nothing. Let's put this into code:

```
# errorsalert.py
alert_system = 'console'  # other value can be 'email'
error_severity = 'critical'  # other values: 'medium' or 'low'
error_message = 'OMG! Something terrible happened!'

if alert_system == 'console':
    print(error_message)   #1
elif alert_system == 'email':
    if error_severity == 'critical':
        send_email('admin@example.com', error_message)   #2
    elif error_severity == 'medium':
```

```
        send_email('support.1@example.com', error_message)   #3
    else:
        send_email('support.2@example.com', error_message)   #4
```

The preceding example is quite interesting, because of its silliness. It shows us two nested `if` clauses (**outer** and **inner**). It also shows us that the outer `if` clause doesn't have any `else`, while the inner one does. Notice how indentation is what allows us to nest one clause within another one.

If `alert_system == 'console'`, body #1 is executed, and nothing else happens. On the other hand, if `alert_system == 'email'`, then we enter into another `if` clause, which we called inner. In the inner `if` clause, according to `error_severity`, we send an email to either an admin, first-level support, or second-level support (blocks #2, #3, and #4). The `send_email` function is not defined in this example, therefore trying to run it would give you an error. In the source code of the book, which you can download from the website, I included a trick to redirect that call to a regular `print` function, just so you can experiment on the console without actually sending an email. Try changing the values and see how it all works.

The ternary operator

One last thing I would like to show you, before moving on to the next subject, is the **ternary operator** or, in layman's terms, the short version of an `if/else` clause. When the value of a name is to be assigned according to some condition, sometimes it's easier and more readable to use the ternary operator instead of a proper `if` clause. In the following example, the two code blocks do exactly the same thing:

```
# ternary.py
order_total = 247  # GBP

# classic if/else form
if order_total > 100:
    discount = 25  # GBP
else:
    discount = 0  # GBP
print(order_total, discount)

# ternary operator
discount = 25 if order_total > 100 else 0
print(order_total, discount)
```

For simple cases like this, I find it very nice to be able to express that logic in one line instead of four. Remember, as a coder, you spend much more time reading code than writing it, so Python's conciseness is invaluable.

Are you clear on how the ternary operator works? Basically, `name = something if condition else something-else`. So `name` is assigned `something` if `condition` evaluates to `True`, and `something-else` if `condition` evaluates to `False`.

Now that you know everything about controlling the path of the code, let's move on to the next subject: *looping*.

Looping

If you have any experience with looping in other programming languages, you will find Python's way of looping a bit different. First of all, what is looping? **Looping** means being able to repeat the execution of a code block more than once, according to the loop parameters we're given. There are different looping constructs, which serve different purposes, and Python has distilled all of them down to just two, which you can use to achieve everything you need. These are the `for` and `while` statements.

While it's definitely possible to do everything you need using either of them, they serve different purposes and therefore they're usually used in different contexts. We'll explore this difference thoroughly in this chapter.

The for loop

The `for` loop is used when looping over a sequence, such as a list, tuple, or a collection of objects. Let's start with a simple example and expand on the concept to see what the Python syntax allows us to do:

```
# simple.for.py
for number in [0, 1, 2, 3, 4]:
    print(number)
```

This simple snippet of code, when executed, prints all numbers from 0 to 4. The `for` loop is fed the list `[0, 1, 2, 3, 4]` and at each iteration, `number` is given a value from the sequence (which is iterated sequentially, in order), then the body of the loop is executed (the print line). The `number` value changes at every iteration, according to which value is coming next from the sequence. When the sequence is exhausted, the `for` loop terminates, and the execution of the code resumes normally with the code after the loop.

Iterating over a range

Sometimes we need to iterate over a range of numbers, and it would be quite unpleasant to have to do so by hardcoding the list somewhere. In such cases, the range function comes to the rescue. Let's see the equivalent of the previous snippet of code:

```
# simple.for.py
for number in range(5):
    print(number)
```

The range function is used extensively in Python programs when it comes to creating sequences: you can call it by passing one value, which acts as stop (counting from 0), or you can pass two values (start and stop), or even three (start, stop, and step). Check out the following example:

```
>>> list(range(10))   # one value: from 0 to value (excluded)
[0, 1, 2, 3, 4, 5, 6, 7, 8, 9]
>>> list(range(3, 8))   # two values: from start to stop (excluded)
[3, 4, 5, 6, 7]
>>> list(range(-10, 10, 4))   # three values: step is added
[-10, -6, -2, 2, 6]
```

For the moment, ignore that we need to wrap range(...) within a list. The range object is a little bit special, but in this case, we're just interested in understanding what values it will return to us. You can see that the deal is the same with slicing: start is included, stop excluded, and optionally you can add a step parameter, which by default is 1.

Try modifying the parameters of the range() call in our simple.for.py code and see what it prints. Get comfortable with it.

Iterating over a sequence

Now we have all the tools to iterate over a sequence, so let's build on that example:

```
# simple.for.2.py
surnames = ['Rivest', 'Shamir', 'Adleman']
for position in range(len(surnames)):
    print(position, surnames[position])
```

The preceding code adds a little bit of complexity to the game. Execution will show this result:

```
$ python simple.for.2.py
0 Rivest
1 Shamir
2 Adleman
```

Let's use the **inside-out** technique to break it down, OK? We start from the innermost part of what we're trying to understand, and we expand outward. So, `len(surnames)` is the length of the `surnames` list: 3. Therefore, `range(len(surnames))` is actually transformed into `range(3)`. This gives us the range [0, 3), which is basically a sequence (0, 1, 2). This means that the `for` loop will run three iterations. In the first one, `position` will take value 0, while in the second one, it will take value 1, and finally value 2 in the third and last iteration. What is (0, 1, 2), if not the possible indexing positions for the `surnames` list? At position 0, we find `'Rivest'`, at position 1, `'Shamir'`, and at position 2, `'Adleman'`. If you are curious about what these three men created together, change `print(position, surnames[position])` to `print(surnames[position][0], end='')`, add a final `print()` outside of the loop, and run the code again.

Now, this style of looping is actually much closer to languages such as Java or C++. In Python, it's quite rare to see code like this. You can just iterate over any sequence or collection, so there is no need to get the list of positions and retrieve elements out of a sequence at each iteration. It's expensive, needlessly expensive. Let's change the example into a more Pythonic form:

```
# simple.for.3.py
surnames = ['Rivest', 'Shamir', 'Adleman']
for surname in surnames:
    print(surname)
```

Now that's something! It's practically English. The `for` loop can iterate over the `surnames` list, and it gives back each element in order at each interaction. Running this code will print the three surnames, one at a time. It's much easier to read, right?

What if you wanted to print the position as well though? Or what if you actually needed it? Should you go back to the `range(len(...))` form? No. You can use the `enumerate` built-in function, like this:

```
# simple.for.4.py
surnames = ['Rivest', 'Shamir', 'Adleman']
for position, surname in enumerate(surnames):
    print(position, surname)
```

This code is very interesting as well. Notice that enumerate gives back a two-tuple (position, surname) at each iteration, but still, it's much more readable (and more efficient) than the range(len(...)) example. You can call enumerate with a start parameter, such as enumerate(iterable, start), and it will start from start, rather than 0. Just another little thing that shows you how much thought has been given in designing Python so that it makes your life easier.

You can use a for loop to iterate over lists, tuples, and in general anything that Python calls iterable. This is a very important concept, so let's talk about it a bit more.

Iterators and iterables

According to the Python documentation (https://docs.python.org/3/glossary.html), an iterable is:

> *An object capable of returning its members one at a time. Examples of iterables include all sequence types (such as list, str, and tuple) and some non-sequence types like dict, file objects, and objects of any classes you define with an __iter__() or __getitem__() method. Iterables can be used in a for loop and in many other places where a sequence is needed (zip(), map(), ...). When an iterable object is passed as an argument to the built-in function iter(), it returns an iterator for the object. This iterator is good for one pass over the set of values. When using iterables, it is usually not necessary to call iter() or deal with iterator objects yourself. The for statement does that automatically for you, creating a temporary unnamed variable to hold the iterator for the duration of the loop.*

Simply put, what happens when you write for k in sequence: ... body ..., is that the for loop asks sequence for the next element, it gets something back, it calls that something k, and then executes its body. Then, once again, the for loop asks sequence for the next element, it calls it k again, and executes the body again, and so on and so forth, until the sequence is exhausted. Empty sequences will result in zero executions of the body.

Some data structures, when iterated over, produce their elements in order, such as lists, tuples, and strings, while some others don't, such as sets and dictionaries (prior to Python 3.6). Python gives us the ability to iterate over iterables, using a type of object called an **iterator**.

According to the official documentation (`https://docs.python.org/3/glossary.html`), an iterator is:

> *An object representing a stream of data. Repeated calls to the iterator's __next__() method (or passing it to the built-in function next()) return successive items in the stream. When no more data are available a StopIteration exception is raised instead. At this point, the iterator object is exhausted and any further calls to its __next__() method just raise StopIteration again. Iterators are required to have an __iter__() method that returns the iterator object itself so every iterator is also iterable and may be used in most places where other iterables are accepted. One notable exception is code which attempts multiple iteration passes. A container object (such as a list) produces a fresh new iterator each time you pass it to the iter() function or use it in a for loop. Attempting this with an iterator will just return the same exhausted iterator object used in the previous iteration pass, making it appear like an empty container.*

Don't worry if you don't fully understand all the preceding legalese, you will in due time. I put it here as a handy reference for the future.

In practice, the whole iterable/iterator mechanism is somewhat hidden behind the code. Unless you need to code your own iterable or iterator for some reason, you won't have to worry about this too much. But it's very important to understand how Python handles this key aspect of control flow because it will shape the way you will write your code.

Iterating over multiple sequences

Let's see another example of how to iterate over two sequences of the same length, in order to work on their respective elements in pairs. Say we have a list of people and a list of numbers representing the age of the people in the first list. We want to print a pair person/age on one line for all of them. Let's start with an example and let's refine it gradually:

```
# multiple.sequences.py
people = ['Conrad', 'Deepak', 'Heinrich', 'Tom']
ages = [29, 30, 34, 36]
for position in range(len(people)):
    person = people[position]
    age = ages[position]
    print(person, age)
```

By now, this code should be pretty straightforward for you to understand. We need to iterate over the list of positions (0, 1, 2, 3) because we want to retrieve elements from two different lists. Executing it we get the following:

```
$ python multiple.sequences.py
Conrad 29
Deepak 30
Heinrich 34
Tom 36
```

This code is both inefficient and not Pythonic. It's inefficient because retrieving an element given the position can be an expensive operation, and we're doing it from scratch at each iteration. The postal worker doesn't go back to the beginning of the road each time they deliver a letter, right? They move from house to house. From one to the next one. Let's try to make it better using `enumerate`:

```
# multiple.sequences.enumerate.py
people = ['Conrad', 'Deepak', 'Heinrich', 'Tom']
ages = [29, 30, 34, 36]
for position, person in enumerate(people):
    age = ages[position]
    print(person, age)
```

That's better, but still not perfect. And it's still a bit ugly. We're iterating properly on `people`, but we're still fetching `age` using positional indexing, which we want to lose as well. Well, no worries, Python gives you the `zip` function, remember? Let's use it:

```
# multiple.sequences.zip.py
people = ['Conrad', 'Deepak', 'Heinrich', 'Tom']
ages = [29, 30, 34, 36]
for person, age in zip(people, ages):
    print(person, age)
```

Ah! So much better! Once again, compare the preceding code with the first example and admire Python's elegance. The reason I wanted to show this example is twofold. On the one hand, I wanted to give you an idea of how shorter code in Python can be compared to other languages where the syntax doesn't allow you to iterate over sequences or collections as easily. And on the other hand, and much more importantly, notice that when the `for` loop asks `zip(sequenceA, sequenceB)` for the next element, it gets back a tuple, not just a single object. It gets back a tuple with as many elements as the number of sequences we feed to the `zip` function. Let's expand a little on the previous example in two ways, using explicit and implicit assignment:

```
# multiple.sequences.explicit.py
people = ['Conrad', 'Deepak', 'Heinrich', 'Tom']
```

```
ages = [29, 30, 34, 36]
nationalities = ['Poland', 'India', 'South Africa', 'England']
for person, age, nationality in zip(people, ages, nationalities):
    print(person, age, nationality)
```

In the preceding code, we added the nationalities list. Now that we feed three sequences to the `zip` function, the for loop gets back a *three-tuple* at each iteration. Notice that the position of the elements in the tuple respects the position of the sequences in the `zip` call. Executing the code will yield the following result:

```
$ python multiple.sequences.explicit.py
Conrad 29 Poland
Deepak 30 India
Heinrich 34 South Africa
Tom 36 England
```

Sometimes, for reasons that may not be clear in a simple example such as the preceding one, you may want to explode the tuple within the body of the `for` loop. If that is your desire, it's perfectly possible to do so:

```
# multiple.sequences.implicit.py
people = ['Conrad', 'Deepak', 'Heinrich', 'Tom']
ages = [29, 30, 34, 36]
nationalities = ['Poland', 'India', 'South Africa', 'England']
for data in zip(people, ages, nationalities):
    person, age, nationality = data
    print(person, age, nationality)
```

It's basically doing what the `for` loop does automatically for you, but in some cases you may want to do it yourself. Here, the three-tuple `data` that comes from `zip(...)` is exploded within the body of the `for` loop into three variables: `person`, `age`, and `nationality`.

The while loop

In the preceding pages, we saw the `for` loop in action. It's incredibly useful when you need to loop over a sequence or a collection. The key point to keep in mind, when you need to be able to discriminate which looping construct to use, is that the `for` loop rocks when you have to iterate over a finite amount of elements. It can be a huge amount, but still, something that ends at some point.

There are other cases though, when you just need to loop until some condition is satisfied, or even loop indefinitely until the application is stopped, such as cases where we don't really have something to iterate on, and therefore the for loop would be a poor choice. But fear not, for these cases, Python provides us with the while loop.

The while loop is similar to the for loop, in that they both loop, and at each iteration they execute a body of instructions. What is different between them is that the while loop doesn't loop over a sequence (it can, but you have to write the logic manually and it wouldn't make any sense, you would just want to use a for loop), rather, it loops as long as a certain condition is satisfied. When the condition is no longer satisfied, the loop ends.

As usual, let's see an example that will clarify everything for us. We want to print the binary representation of a positive number. In order to do so, we can use a simple algorithm that collects the remainders of division by 2 (in reverse order), and that turns out to be the binary representation of the number itself:

```
6 / 2 = 3 (remainder: 0)
3 / 2 = 1 (remainder: 1)
1 / 2 = 0 (remainder: 1)
List of remainders: 0, 1, 1.
Inverse is 1, 1, 0, which is also the binary representation of 6: 110
```

Let's write some code to calculate the binary representation for the number 39: 100111_2:

```python
# binary.py
n = 39
remainders = []
while n > 0:
    remainder = n % 2  # remainder of division by 2
    remainders.insert(0, remainder)  # we keep track of remainders
    n //= 2  # we divide n by 2

print(remainders)
```

In the preceding code, I highlighted n > 0, which is the condition to keep looping. We can make the code a little shorter (and more Pythonic), by using the divmod function, which is called with a number and a divisor, and returns a tuple with the result of the integer division and its remainder. For example, divmod(13, 5) would return (2, 3), and indeed *5 * 2 + 3 = 13*:

```python
# binary.2.py
n = 39
remainders = []
while n > 0:
    n, remainder = divmod(n, 2)
```

```
        remainders.insert(0, remainder)

    print(remainders)
```

In the preceding code, we have reassigned n to the result of the division by 2, and the remainder, in one single line.

Notice that the condition in a while loop is a condition to continue looping. If it evaluates to True, then the body is executed and then another evaluation follows, and so on, until the condition evaluates to False. When that happens, the loop is exited immediately without executing its body.

If the condition never evaluates to False, the loop becomes a so-called **infinite loop**. Infinite loops are used, for example, when polling from network devices: you ask the socket whether there is any data, you do something with it if there is any, then you sleep for a small amount of time, and then you ask the socket again, over and over again, without ever stopping.

Having the ability to loop over a condition, or to loop indefinitely, is the reason why the for loop alone is not enough, and therefore Python provides the while loop.

By the way, if you need the binary representation of a number, check out the bin function.

Just for fun, let's adapt one of the examples (multiple.sequences.py) using the while logic:

```python
# multiple.sequences.while.py
people = ['Conrad', 'Deepak', 'Heinrich', 'Tom']
ages = [29, 30, 34, 36]
position = 0
while position < len(people):
    person = people[position]
    age = ages[position]
    print(person, age)
    position += 1
```

In the preceding code, I have highlighted the *initialization, condition,* and *update* of the `position` variable, which makes it possible to simulate the equivalent `for` loop code by handling the iteration variable manually. Everything that can be done with a `for` loop can also be done with a `while` loop, even though you can see there's a bit of boilerplate you have to go through in order to achieve the same result. The opposite is also true, but unless you have a reason to do so, you ought to use the right tool for the job, and 99.9% of the time you'll be fine.

So, to recap, use a `for` loop when you need to iterate over an iterable, and a `while` loop when you need to loop according to a condition being satisfied or not. If you keep in mind the difference between the two purposes, you will never choose the wrong looping construct.

Let's now see how to alter the normal flow of a loop.

The break and continue statements

According to the task at hand, sometimes you will need to alter the regular flow of a loop. You can either skip a single iteration (as many times as you want), or you can break out of the loop entirely. A common use case for skipping iterations is, for example, when you're iterating over a list of items and you need to work on each of them only if some condition is verified. On the other hand, if you're iterating over a collection of items, and you have found one of them that satisfies some need you have, you may decide not to continue the loop entirely and therefore break out of it. There are countless possible scenarios, so it's better to see a couple of examples.

Let's say you want to apply a 20% discount to all products in a basket list for those that have an expiration date of today. The way you achieve this is to use the `continue` statement, which tells the looping construct (`for` or `while`) to stop execution of the body immediately and go to the next iteration, if any. This example will take us a little deeper down the rabbit hole, so be ready to jump:

```
# discount.py
from datetime import date, timedelta

today = date.today()
tomorrow = today + timedelta(days=1)  # today + 1 day is tomorrow
products = [
    {'sku': '1', 'expiration_date': today, 'price': 100.0},
    {'sku': '2', 'expiration_date': tomorrow, 'price': 50},
    {'sku': '3', 'expiration_date': today, 'price': 20},
]
```

```
for product in products:
    if product['expiration_date'] != today:
        continue
    product['price'] *= 0.8  # equivalent to applying 20% discount
    print(
        'Price for sku', product['sku'],
        'is now', product['price'])
```

We start by importing the `date` and `timedelta` objects, then we set up our products. Those with `sku` as 1 and 3 have an expiration date of `today`, which means we want to apply a 20% discount on them. We loop over each `product` and we inspect the expiration date. If it is not (inequality operator, `!=`) `today`, we don't want to execute the rest of the body suite, so we `continue`.

Notice that it is not important where in the body suite you place the `continue` statement (you can even use it more than once). When you reach it, execution stops and goes back to the next iteration. If we run the `discount.py` module, this is the output:

```
$ python discount.py
Price for sku 1 is now 80.0
Price for sku 3 is now 16.0
```

This shows you that the last two lines of the body haven't been executed for `sku` number 2.

Let's now see an example of breaking out of a loop. Say we want to tell whether at least one of the elements in a list evaluates to `True` when fed to the `bool` function. Given that we need to know whether there is at least one, when we find it, we don't need to keep scanning the list any further. In Python code, this translates to using the `break` statement. Let's write this down into code:

```
# any.py
items = [0, None, 0.0, True, 0, 7]  # True and 7 evaluate to True

found = False  # this is called "flag"
for item in items:
    print('scanning item', item)
    if item:
        found = True  # we update the flag
        break

if found:  # we inspect the flag
    print('At least one item evaluates to True')
else:
    print('All items evaluate to False')
```

The preceding code is such a common pattern in programming, you will see it a lot. When you inspect items this way, basically what you do is to set up a `flag` variable, then start the inspection. If you find one element that matches your criteria (in this example, that evaluates to `True`), then you update the flag and stop iterating. After iteration, you inspect the flag and take action accordingly. Execution yields:

```
$ python any.py
scanning item 0
scanning item None
scanning item 0.0
scanning item True
At least one item evaluates to True
```

See how execution stopped after `True` was found? The `break` statement acts exactly like the `continue` one, in that it stops executing the body of the loop immediately, but also, prevents any other iteration from running, effectively breaking out of the loop. The `continue` and `break` statements can be used together with no limitation in their numbers, both in the `for` and `while` looping constructs.

 By the way, there is no need to write code to detect whether there is at least one element in a sequence that evaluates to `True`. Just check out the built-in `any` function.

A special else clause

One of the features I've seen only in the Python language is the ability to have `else` clauses after `while` and `for` loops. It's very rarely used, but it's definitely nice to have. In short, you can have an `else` suite after a `for` or `while` loop. If the loop ends normally, because of exhaustion of the iterator (`for` loop) or because the condition is finally not met (`while` loop), then the `else` suite (if present) is executed. In case execution is interrupted by a `break` statement, the `else` clause is not executed. Let's take an example of a `for` loop that iterates over a group of items, looking for one that would match some condition. In case we don't find at least one that satisfies the condition, we want to raise an **exception**. This means we want to arrest the regular execution of the program and signal that there was an error, or exception, that we cannot deal with. Exceptions will be the subject of Chapter 8, *Testing, Profiling, and Dealing with Exceptions*, so don't worry if you don't fully understand them now. Just bear in mind that they will alter the regular flow of the code.

Let me now show you two examples that do exactly the same thing, but one of them is using the special `for...else` syntax. Say that we want to find, among a collection of people, one that could drive a car:

```
# for.no.else.py
class DriverException(Exception):
    pass

people = [('James', 17), ('Kirk', 9), ('Lars', 13), ('Robert', 8)]
driver = None
for person, age in people:
    if age >= 18:
        driver = (person, age)
        break

if driver is None:
    raise DriverException('Driver not found.')
```

Notice the `flag` pattern again. We set the driver to be `None`, then if we find one, we update the `driver` flag, and then, at the end of the loop, we inspect it to see whether one was found. I kind of have the feeling that those kids would drive a very *metallic* car, but anyway, notice that if a driver is not found, `DriverException` is raised, signaling to the program that execution cannot continue (we're lacking the driver).

The same functionality can be rewritten a bit more elegantly using the following code:

```
# for.else.py
class DriverException(Exception):
    pass

people = [('James', 17), ('Kirk', 9), ('Lars', 13), ('Robert', 8)]
for person, age in people:
    if age >= 18:
        driver = (person, age)
        break
else:
    raise DriverException('Driver not found.')
```

Notice that we aren't forced to use the `flag` pattern any more. The exception is raised as part of the `for` loop logic, which makes good sense because the `for` loop is checking on some condition. All we need is to set up a `driver` object in case we find one, because the rest of the code is going to use that information somewhere. Notice the code is shorter and more elegant, because the logic is now correctly grouped together where it belongs.

In the *Transforming Code into Beautiful, Idiomatic Python* video, Raymond Hettinger suggests a much better name for the `else` statement associated with a for loop: `nobreak`. If you struggle remembering how the `else` works for a `for` loop, simply remembering this fact should help you.

Putting all this together

Now that you have seen all there is to see about conditionals and loops, it's time to spice things up a little, and look at those two examples I anticipated at the beginning of this chapter. We'll mix and match here, so you can see how you can use all these concepts together. Let's start by writing some code to generate a list of prime numbers up to some limit. Please bear in mind that I'm going to write a very inefficient and rudimentary algorithm to detect primes. The important thing for you is to concentrate on those bits in the code that belong to this chapter's subject.

A prime generator

According to Wikipedia:

> *A prime number (or a prime) is a natural number greater than 1 that has no positive divisors other than 1 and itself. A natural number greater than 1 that is not a prime number is called a composite number.*

Based on this definition, if we consider the first 10 natural numbers, we can see that 2, 3, 5, and 7 are primes, while 1, 4, 6, 8, 9, and 10 are not. In order to have a computer tell you whether a number, *N*, is prime, you can divide that number by all natural numbers in the range [2, *N*). If any of those divisions yields zero as a remainder, then the number is not a prime. Enough chatter, let's get down to business. I'll write two versions of this, the second of which will exploit the `for...else` syntax:

```
# primes.py
primes = []  # this will contain the primes in the end
upto = 100  # the limit, inclusive
for n in range(2, upto + 1):
    is_prime = True  # flag, new at each iteration of outer for
    for divisor in range(2, n):
        if n % divisor == 0:
            is_prime = False
            break
```

```
        if is_prime:  # check on flag
            primes.append(n)
    print(primes)
```

There are a lot of things to notice in the preceding code. First of all, we set up an empty `primes` list, which will contain the primes at the end. The limit is `100`, and you can see it's inclusive in the way we call `range()` in the outer loop. If we wrote `range(2, upto)` that would be *[2, upto)*, right? Therefore `range(2, upto + 1)` gives us *[2, upto + 1)* == *[2, upto]*.

So, there are two `for` loops. In the outer one, we loop over the candidate primes, that is, all natural numbers from 2 to upto. Inside each iteration of this outer loop, we set up a flag (which is set to `True` at each iteration), and then start dividing the current `n` by all numbers from 2 to n - 1. If we find a proper divisor for `n`, it means `n` is composite, and therefore we set the flag to `False` and break the loop. Notice that when we break the inner one, the outer one keeps on going normally. The reason why we break after having found a proper divisor for `n` is that we don't need any further information to be able to tell that `n` is not a prime.

When we check on the `is_prime` flag, if it is still `True`, it means we couldn't find any number in *[2, n)* that is a proper divisor for n, therefore n is a prime. We append n to the `primes` list, and hop! Another iteration proceeds, until n equals `100`.

Running this code yields:

```
$ python primes.py
[2, 3, 5, 7, 11, 13, 17, 19, 23, 29, 31, 37, 41, 43, 47, 53, 59, 61, 67,
71, 73, 79, 83, 89, 97]
```

Before we proceed, one question: of all the iterations of the outer loop, one of them is different from all the others. Could you tell which one, and why? Think about it for a second, go back to the code, try to figure it out for yourself, and then keep reading on.

Did you figure it out? If not, don't feel bad, it's perfectly normal. I asked you to do it as a small exercise because it's what coders do all the time. The skill to understand what the code does by simply looking at it is something you build over time. It's very important, so try to exercise it whenever you can. I'll tell you the answer now: the iteration that behaves differently from all others is the first one. The reason is because in the first iteration, n is 2. Therefore the innermost `for` loop won't even run, because it's a `for` loop that iterates over `range(2, 2)`, and what is that if not [2, 2)? Try it out for yourself, write a simple `for` loop with that iterable, put a `print` in the body suite, and see whether anything happens (it won't...).

Now, from an algorithmic point of view, this code is inefficient, so let's at least make it more beautiful:

```
# primes.else.py
primes = []
upto = 100
for n in range(2, upto + 1):
    for divisor in range(2, n):
        if n % divisor == 0:
            break
    else:
        primes.append(n)
print(primes)
```

Much nicer, right? The `is_prime` flag is gone, and we append `n` to the `primes` list when we know the inner `for` loop hasn't encountered any `break` statements. See how the code looks cleaner and reads better?

Applying discounts

In this example, I want to show you a technique I like a lot. In many programming languages, other than the `if`/`elif`/`else` constructs, in whatever form or syntax they may come, you can find another statement, usually called `switch`/`case`, that in Python is missing. It is the equivalent of a cascade of `if`/`elif`/.../`elif`/`else` clauses, with a syntax similar to this (warning! JavaScript code!):

```
/* switch.js */
switch (day_number) {
    case 1:
    case 2:
    case 3:
    case 4:
    case 5:
        day = "Weekday";
        break;
    case 6:
        day = "Saturday";
        break;
    case 0:
        day = "Sunday";
        break;
    default:
        day = "";
```

```
            alert(day_number + ' is not a valid day number.')
    }
```

In the preceding code, we `switch` on a variable called `day_number`. This means we get its value and then we decide what case it fits in (if any). From 1 to 5 there is a cascade, which means no matter the number, [1, 5] all go down to the bit of logic that sets `day` as `"Weekday"`. Then we have single cases for 0 and 6, and a `default` case to prevent errors, which alerts the system that `day_number` is not a valid day number, that is, not in [0, 6]. Python is perfectly capable of realizing such logic using `if`/`elif`/`else` statements:

```
# switch.py
if 1 <= day_number <= 5:
    day = 'Weekday'
elif day_number == 6:
    day = 'Saturday'
elif day_number == 0:
    day = 'Sunday'
else:
    day = ''
    raise ValueError(
        str(day_number) + ' is not a valid day number.')
```

In the preceding code, we reproduce the same logic of the JavaScript snippet in Python, using `if`/`elif`/`else` statements. I raised the `ValueError` exception just as an example at the end, if `day_number` is not in [0, 6]. This is one possible way of translating the `switch`/`case` logic, but there is also another one, sometimes called dispatching, which I will show you in the last version of the next example.

 By the way, did you notice the first line of the previous snippet? Have you noticed that Python can make double (actually, even multiple) comparisons? It's just wonderful!

Let's start the new example by simply writing some code that assigns a discount to customers based on their coupon value. I'll keep the logic down to a minimum here, remember that all we really care about is understanding conditionals and loops:

```
# coupons.py
customers = [
    dict(id=1, total=200, coupon_code='F20'),   # F20: fixed, £20
    dict(id=2, total=150, coupon_code='P30'),   # P30: percent, 30%
    dict(id=3, total=100, coupon_code='P50'),   # P50: percent, 50%
    dict(id=4, total=110, coupon_code='F15'),   # F15: fixed, £15
]
for customer in customers:
```

```
    code = customer['coupon_code']
    if code == 'F20':
        customer['discount'] = 20.0
    elif code == 'F15':
        customer['discount'] = 15.0
    elif code == 'P30':
        customer['discount'] = customer['total'] * 0.3
    elif code == 'P50':
        customer['discount'] = customer['total'] * 0.5
    else:
        customer['discount'] = 0.0

for customer in customers:
    print(customer['id'], customer['total'], customer['discount'])
```

We start by setting up some customers. They have an order total, a coupon code, and an ID. I made up four different types of coupons, two are fixed and two are percentage-based. You can see that in the `if`/`elif`/`else` cascade I apply the discount accordingly, and I set it as a `'discount'` key in the `customer` dictionary.

At the end, I just print out part of the data to see whether my code is working properly:

```
$ python coupons.py
1 200 20.0
2 150 45.0
3 100 50.0
4 110 15.0
```

This code is simple to understand, but all those clauses are kind of cluttering the logic. It's not easy to see what's going on at a first glance, and I don't like it. In cases like this, you can exploit a dictionary to your advantage, like this:

```
# coupons.dict.py
customers = [
    dict(id=1, total=200, coupon_code='F20'),  # F20: fixed, £20
    dict(id=2, total=150, coupon_code='P30'),  # P30: percent, 30%
    dict(id=3, total=100, coupon_code='P50'),  # P50: percent, 50%
    dict(id=4, total=110, coupon_code='F15'),  # F15: fixed, £15
]
discounts = {
    'F20': (0.0, 20.0),  # each value is (percent, fixed)
    'P30': (0.3, 0.0),
    'P50': (0.5, 0.0),
    'F15': (0.0, 15.0),
}
for customer in customers:
    code = customer['coupon_code']
```

```
        percent, fixed = discounts.get(code, (0.0, 0.0))
        customer['discount'] = percent * customer['total'] + fixed

for customer in customers:
    print(customer['id'], customer['total'], customer['discount'])
```

Running the preceding code yields exactly the same result we had from the snippet before it. We spared two lines, but more importantly, we gained a lot in readability, as the body of the `for` loop now is just three lines long, and very easy to understand. The concept here is to use a dictionary as a **dispatcher**. In other words, we try to fetch something from the dictionary based on a code (our `coupon_code`), and by using `dict.get(key, default)`, we make sure we also cater for when the `code` is not in the dictionary and we need a default value.

Notice that I had to apply some very simple linear algebra in order to calculate the discount properly. Each discount has a percentage and fixed part in the dictionary, represented by a two-tuple. By applying `percent * total + fixed`, we get the correct discount. When `percent` is 0, the formula just gives the fixed amount, and it gives `percent * total` when fixed is 0.

This technique is important because it is also used in other contexts, with functions, where it actually becomes much more powerful than what we've seen in the preceding snippet. Another advantage of using it is that you can code it in such a way that the keys and values of the `discounts` dictionary are fetched dynamically (for example, from a database). This will allow the code to adapt to whatever discounts and conditions you have, without having to modify anything.

If it's not completely clear to you how it works, I suggest you take your time and experiment with it. Change values and add print statements to see what's going on while the program is running.

A quick peek at the itertools module

A chapter about iterables, iterators, conditional logic, and looping wouldn't be complete without a few words about the `itertools` module. If you are into iterating, this is a kind of heaven.

According to the Python official documentation (`https://docs.python.org/2/library/itertools.html`), the `itertools` module is:

> *This module which implements a number of iterator building blocks inspired by constructs from APL, Haskell, and SML. Each has been recast in a form suitable for Python. The module standardizes a core set of fast, memory efficient tools that are useful by themselves or in combination. Together, they form an "iterator algebra" making it possible to construct specialized tools succinctly and efficiently in pure Python.*

By no means do I have the room here to show you all the goodies you can find in this module, so I encourage you to go check it out for yourself, I promise you'll enjoy it. In a nutshell, it provides you with three broad categories of iterators. I will give you a very small example of one iterator taken from each one of them, just to make your mouth water a little.

Infinite iterators

Infinite iterators allow you to work with a `for` loop in a different fashion, such as if it were a `while` loop:

```python
# infinite.py
from itertools import count

for n in count(5, 3):
    if n > 20:
        break
    print(n, end=', ') # instead of newline, comma and space
```

Running the code gives this:

```
$ python infinite.py
5, 8, 11, 14, 17, 20,
```

The `count` factory class makes an iterator that just goes on and on counting. It starts from 5 and keeps adding 3 to it. We need to break it manually if we don't want to get stuck in an infinite loop.

Iterators terminating on the shortest input sequence

This category is very interesting. It allows you to create an iterator based on multiple iterators, combining their values according to some logic. The key point here is that among those iterators, in case any of them are shorter than the rest, the resulting iterator won't break, it will simply stop as soon as the shortest iterator is exhausted. This is very theoretical, I know, so let me give you an example using `compress`. This iterator gives you back the data according to a corresponding item in a selector being `True` or `False`:

`compress('ABC', (1, 0, 1))` would give back `'A'` and `'C'`, because they correspond to `1`. Let's see a simple example:

```
# compress.py
from itertools import compress
data = range(10)
even_selector = [1, 0] * 10
odd_selector = [0, 1] * 10

even_numbers = list(compress(data, even_selector))
odd_numbers = list(compress(data, odd_selector))

print(odd_selector)
print(list(data))
print(even_numbers)
print(odd_numbers)
```

Notice that `odd_selector` and `even_selector` are 20 elements long, while `data` is just 10 elements long. `compress` will stop as soon as `data` has yielded its last element. Running this code produces the following:

```
$ python compress.py
[0, 1, 0, 1, 0, 1, 0, 1, 0, 1, 0, 1, 0, 1, 0, 1, 0, 1, 0, 1]
[0, 1, 2, 3, 4, 5, 6, 7, 8, 9]
[0, 2, 4, 6, 8]
[1, 3, 5, 7, 9]
```

It's a very fast and nice way of selecting elements out of an iterable. The code is very simple, just notice that instead of using a `for` loop to iterate over each value that is given back by the compress calls, we used `list()`, which does the same, but instead of executing a body of instructions, puts all the values into a list and returns it.

Combinatoric generators

Last but not least, combinatoric generators. These are really fun, if you are into this kind of thing. Let's just see a simple example on permutations.

According to Wolfram Mathworld:

> *A permutation, also called an "arrangement number" or "order", is a rearrangement of the elements of an ordered list S into a one-to-one correspondence with S itself.*

For example, there are six permutations of ABC: ABC, ACB, BAC, BCA, CAB, and CBA.

If a set has N elements, then the number of permutations of them is $N!$ (N factorial). For the ABC string, the permutations are $3! = 3 * 2 * 1 = 6$. Let's do it in Python:

```
# permutations.py
from itertools import permutations
print(list(permutations('ABC')))
```

This very short snippet of code produces the following result:

```
$ python permutations.py
[('A', 'B', 'C'), ('A', 'C', 'B'), ('B', 'A', 'C'), ('B', 'C', 'A'), ('C',
'A', 'B'), ('C', 'B', 'A')]
```

Be very careful when you play with permutations. Their number grows at a rate that is proportional to the factorial of the number of the elements you're permuting, and that number can get really big, really fast.

Summary

In this chapter, we've taken another step toward expanding our coding vocabulary. We've seen how to drive the execution of the code by evaluating conditions, and we've seen how to loop and iterate over sequences and collections of objects. This gives us the power to control what happens when our code is run, which means we are getting an idea of how to shape it so that it does what we want and it reacts to data that changes dynamically.

We've also seen how to combine everything together in a couple of simple examples, and in the end, we took a brief look at the `itertools` module, which is full of interesting iterators that can enrich our abilities with Python even more.

Now it's time to switch gears, take another step forward, and talk about functions. The next chapter is all about them because they are extremely important. Make sure you're comfortable with what has been covered up to now. I want to provide you with interesting examples, so I'll have to go a little faster. Ready? Turn the page.

4
Functions, the Building Blocks of Code

"To create architecture is to put in order. Put what in order? Functions and objects."

– Le Corbusier

In the previous chapters, we have seen that everything is an object in Python, and functions are no exception. But, what exactly is a function? A **function** is a sequence of instructions that perform a task, bundled as a unit. This unit can then be imported and used wherever it's needed. There are many advantages to using functions in your code, as we'll see shortly.

In this chapter, we are going to cover the following:

- Functions—what they are and why we should use them
- Scopes and name resolution
- Function signatures—input parameters and return values
- Recursive and anonymous functions
- Importing objects for code reuse

I believe the saying, *a picture is worth one thousand words*, is particularly true when explaining functions to someone who is new to this concept, so please take a look at the following diagram:

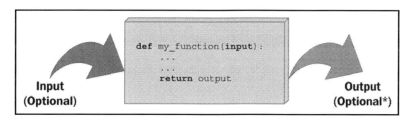

As you can see, a function is a block of instructions, packaged as a whole, like a box. Functions can accept input arguments and produce output values. Both of these are optional, as we'll see in the examples in this chapter.

A function in Python is defined by using the def keyword, after which the name of the function follows, terminated by a pair of parentheses (which may or may not contain input parameters), and a colon (:) signals the end of the function definition line. Immediately afterwards, indented by four spaces, we find the body of the function, which is the set of instructions that the function will execute when called.

 Note that the indentation by four spaces is not mandatory, but it is the amount of spaces suggested by **PEP 8**, and, in practice, it is the most widely used spacing measure.

A function may or may not return an output. If a function wants to return an output, it does so by using the return keyword, followed by the desired output. If you have an eagle eye, you may have noticed the little * after **Optional** in the output section of the preceding diagram. This is because a function always returns something in Python, even if you don't explicitly use the return clause. If the function has no return statement in its body, or no value is given to the return statement itself, the function returns None. The reasons behind this design choice are outside the scope of an introductory chapter, so all you need to know is that this behavior will make your life easier. As always, thank you, Python.

Why use functions?

Functions are among the most important concepts and constructs of any language, so let me give you a few reasons why we need them:

- They reduce code duplication in a program. By having a specific task taken care of by a nice block of packaged code that we can import and call whenever we want, we don't need to duplicate its implementation.
- They help in splitting a complex task or procedure into smaller blocks, each of which becomes a function.
- They hide the implementation details from their users.
- They improve traceability.
- They improve readability.

Let's look at a few examples to get a better understanding of each point.

Reducing code duplication

Imagine that you are writing a piece of scientific software, and you need to calculate primes up to a limit, as we did in the previous chapter. You have a nice algorithm to calculate them, so you copy and paste it to wherever you need. One day, though, your friend, *B. Riemann*, gives you a better algorithm to calculate primes, which will save you a lot of time. At this point, you need to go over your whole code base and replace the old code with the new one.

This is actually a bad way to go about it. It's error-prone, you never know what lines you are chopping out or leaving in by mistake, when you cut and paste code into other code, and you may also risk missing one of the places where prime calculation is done, leaving your software in an inconsistent state where the same action is performed in different places in different ways. What if, instead of replacing code with a better version of it, you need to fix a bug, and you miss one of the places? That would be even worse.

So, what should you do? Simple! You write a function, `get_prime_numbers(upto)`, and use it anywhere you need a list of primes. When *B. Riemann* comes to you and gives you the new code, all you have to do is replace the body of that function with the new implementation, and you're done! The rest of the software will automatically adapt, since it's just calling the function.

Your code will be shorter, it will not suffer from inconsistencies between old and new ways of performing a task, or undetected bugs due to copy-and-paste failures or oversights. Use functions, and you'll only gain from it, I promise.

Splitting a complex task

Functions are also very useful for splitting long or complex tasks into smaller ones. The end result is that the code benefits from it in several ways, for example, readability, testability, and reuse. To give you a simple example, imagine that you're preparing a report. Your code needs to fetch data from a data source, parse it, filter it, polish it, and then a whole series of algorithms needs to be run against it, in order to produce the results that will feed the `Report` class. It's not uncommon to read procedures like this that are just one big `do_report(data_source)` function. There are tens or hundreds of lines of code that end with `return report`.

These situations are slightly more common in scientific code, which tend to be brilliant from an algorithmic point of view, but sometimes lack the touch of experienced programmers when it comes to the style in which they are written. Now, picture a few hundred lines of code. It's very hard to follow through, to find the places where things are changing context (such as finishing one task and starting the next one). Do you have the picture in your mind? Good. Don't do it! Instead, look at this code:

```python
# data.science.example.py
def do_report(data_source):
    # fetch and prepare data
    data = fetch_data(data_source)
    parsed_data = parse_data(data)
    filtered_data = filter_data(parsed_data)
    polished_data = polish_data(filtered_data)

    # run algorithms on data
    final_data = analyse(polished_data)

    # create and return report
    report = Report(final_data)
    return report
```

The previous example is fictitious, of course, but can you see how easy it would be to go through the code? If the end result looks wrong, it would be very easy to debug each of the single data outputs in the `do_report` function. Moreover, it's even easier to exclude part of the process temporarily from the whole procedure (you just need to comment out the parts you need to suspend). Code like this is easier to deal with.

Hiding implementation details

Let's stay with the preceding example to talk about this point as well. You can see that, by going through the code of the `do_report` function, you can get a pretty good understanding without reading one single line of implementation. This is because functions hide the implementation details. This feature means that, if you don't need to delve into the details, you are not forced to, in the way you would if `do_report` was just one big, fat function. In order to understand what was going on, you would have to read every single line of code. With functions, you don't need to. This reduces the time you spend reading the code and since, in a professional environment, reading code takes much more time than actually writing it, it's very important to reduce it by as much as we can.

Improving readability

Coders sometimes don't see the point in writing a function with a body of one or two lines of code, so let's look at an example that shows you why you should do it.

Imagine that you need to multiply two matrices:

$$\begin{pmatrix} 1 & 2 \\ 3 & 4 \end{pmatrix} \cdot \begin{pmatrix} 5 & 1 \\ 2 & 1 \end{pmatrix} = \begin{pmatrix} 9 & 3 \\ 23 & 7 \end{pmatrix}$$

Would you prefer to have to read this code:

```
# matrix.multiplication.nofunc.py
a = [[1, 2], [3, 4]]
b = [[5, 1], [2, 1]]

c = [[sum(i * j for i, j in zip(r, c)) for c in zip(*b)]
        for r in a]
```

Or would you prefer this one:

```
# matrix.multiplication.func.py
# this function could also be defined in another module
def matrix_mul(a, b):
    return [[sum(i * j for i, j in zip(r, c)) for c in zip(*b)]
                for r in a]

a = [[1, 2], [3, 4]]
b = [[5, 1], [2, 1]]
c = matrix_mul(a, b)
```

It's much easier to understand that c is the result of the multiplication between a and b in the second example. It's much easier to read through the code and, if you don't need to modify that multiplication logic, you don't even need to go into the implementation details. Therefore, readability is improved here while, in the first snippet, you would have to spend time trying to understand what that complicated list comprehension is doing.

 Don't worry if you don't understand *list comprehensions*, we'll study them in Chapter 5, *Saving Time and Memory*.

Improving traceability

Imagine that you have written an e-commerce website. You have displayed the product prices all over the pages. Imagine that the prices in your database are stored with no VAT (sales tax), but you want to display them on the website with VAT at 20%. Here's a few ways of calculating the VAT-inclusive price from the VAT-exclusive price:

```
# vat.py
price = 100  # GBP, no VAT
final_price1 = price * 1.2
final_price2 = price + price / 5.0
final_price3 = price * (100 + 20) / 100.0
final_price4 = price + price * 0.2
```

All these four different ways of calculating a VAT-inclusive price are perfectly acceptable, and I promise you I have found them all in my colleagues' code, over the years. Now, imagine that you have started selling your products in different countries and some of them have different VAT rates, so you need to refactor your code (throughout the website) in order to make that VAT calculation dynamic.

How do you trace all the places in which you are performing a VAT calculation? Coding today is a collaborative task and you cannot be sure that the VAT has been calculated using only one of those forms. It's going to be hell, believe me.

So, let's write a function that takes the input values, `vat` and `price` (VAT-exclusive), and returns a VAT-inclusive price:

```
# vat.function.py
def calculate_price_with_vat(price, vat):
    return price * (100 + vat) / 100
```

Now you can import that function and use it in any place in your website where you need to calculate a VAT-inclusive price, and when you need to trace those calls, you can search for `calculate_price_with_vat`.

 Note that, in the preceding example, `price` is assumed to be VAT-exclusive, and `vat` is a percentage value (for example, 19, 20, or 23).

Scopes and name resolution

Do you remember when we talked about scopes and namespaces in Chapter 1, *A Gentle Introduction to Python*? We're going to expand on that concept now. Finally, we can talk about functions and this will make everything easier to understand. Let's start with a very simple example:

```python
# scoping.level.1.py
def my_function():
    test = 1  # this is defined in the local scope of the function
    print('my_function:', test)

test = 0  # this is defined in the global scope
my_function()
print('global:', test)
```

I have defined the test name in two different places in the previous example. It is actually in two different scopes. One is the global scope (test = 0), and the other is the local scope of the my_function function (test = 1). If you execute the code, you'll see this:

```
$ python scoping.level.1.py
my_function: 1
global: 0
```

It's clear that test = 1 shadows the test = 0 assignment in my_function. In the global context, test is still 0, as you can see from the output of the program, but we define the test name again in the function body, and we set it to point to an integer of value 1. Both the two test names therefore exist, one in the global scope, pointing to an int object with a value of 0, the other in the my_function scope, pointing to an int object with a value of 1. Let's comment out the line with test = 1. Python searches for the test name in the next enclosing namespace (recall the **LEGB** rule: **local, enclosing, global, built-in** described in Chapter 1, *A Gentle Introduction to Python*) and, in this case, we will see the value 0 printed twice. Try it in your code.

Now, let's raise the stakes here and level up:

```python
# scoping.level.2.py
def outer():
    test = 1  # outer scope
    def inner():
        test = 2  # inner scope
        print('inner:', test)

    inner()
    print('outer:', test)
```

```
test = 0   # global scope
outer()
print('global:', test)
```

In the preceding code, we have two levels of shadowing. One level is in the function `outer`, and the other one is in the function `inner`. It is far from rocket science, but it can be tricky. If we run the code, we get:

```
$ python scoping.level.2.py
inner: 2
outer: 1
global: 0
```

Try commenting out the `test = 1` line. Can you figure out what the result will be? Well, when reaching the `print('outer:', test)` line, Python will have to look for `test` in the next enclosing scope, therefore it will find and print `0`, instead of `1`. Make sure you comment out `test = 2` as well, to see whether you understand what happens, and whether the LEGB rule is clear, before proceeding.

Another thing to note is that Python gives you the ability to define a function in another function. The inner function's name is defined within the namespace of the outer function, exactly as would happen with any other name.

The global and nonlocal statements

Going back to the preceding example, we can alter what happens to the shadowing of the test name by using one of these two special statements: `global` and `nonlocal`. As you can see from the previous example, when we define `test = 2` in the `inner` function, we overwrite `test` neither in the `outer` function nor in the global scope. We can get read access to those names if we use them in a nested scope that doesn't define them, but we cannot modify them because, when we write an assignment instruction, we're actually defining a new name in the current scope.

How do we change this behavior? Well, we can use the `nonlocal` statement. According to the official documentation:

> "The nonlocal statement causes the listed identifiers to refer to previously bound variables in the nearest enclosing scope excluding globals."

Let's introduce it in the `inner` function, and see what happens:

```
# scoping.level.2.nonlocal.py
def outer():
    test = 1  # outer scope
    def inner():
        nonlocal test
        test = 2  # nearest enclosing scope (which is 'outer')
        print('inner:', test)

    inner()
    print('outer:', test)

test = 0  # global scope
outer()
print('global:', test)
```

Notice how in the body of the `inner` function, I have declared the `test` name to be `nonlocal`. Running this code produces the following result:

```
$ python scoping.level.2.nonlocal.py
inner: 2
outer: 2
global: 0
```

Wow, look at that result! It means that, by declaring `test` to be `nonlocal` in the `inner` function, we actually get to bind the `test` name to the one declared in the `outer` function. If we removed the `nonlocal test` line from the `inner` function and tried the same trick in the `outer` function, we would get a `SyntaxError`, because the `nonlocal` statement works on enclosing scopes excluding the global one.

Is there a way to get to that `test` = 0 in the global namespace then? Of course, we just need to use the `global` statement:

```
# scoping.level.2.global.py
def outer():
    test = 1  # outer scope
    def inner():
        global test
        test = 2  # global scope
        print('inner:', test)

    inner()
    print('outer:', test)

test = 0  # global scope
outer()
```

```
print('global:', test)
```

Note that we have now declared the `test` name to be `global`, which will basically bind it to the one we defined in the global namespace (`test = 0`). Run the code and you should get the following:

```
$ python scoping.level.2.global.py
inner: 2
outer: 1
global: 2
```

This shows that the name affected by the `test = 2` assignment is now the `global` one. This trick would also work in the `outer` function because, in this case, we're referring to the global scope. Try it for yourself and see what changes, get comfortable with scopes and name resolution, it's very important. Also, could you tell what happens if you defined `inner` outside `outer` in the preceding examples?

Input parameters

At the beginning of this chapter, we saw that a function can take input parameters. Before we delve into all possible type of parameters, let's make sure you have a clear understanding of what passing a parameter to a function means. There are three key points to keep in mind:

- Argument-passing is nothing more than assigning an object to a local variable name
- Assigning an object to an argument name inside a function doesn't affect the caller
- Changing a mutable object argument in a function affects the caller

Let's look at an example for each of these points.

Argument-passing

Take a look at the following code. We declare a name, x, in the global scope, then we declare a function, `func(y)`, and finally we call it, passing x:

```
# key.points.argument.passing.py
x = 3
def func(y):
    print(y)
```

```
func(x)   # prints: 3
```

When `func` is called with x, within its local scope, a name, y, is created, and it's pointed to the same object x is pointing to. This is better clarified by the following figure (don't worry about **Python 3.3**, this is a feature that hasn't changed):

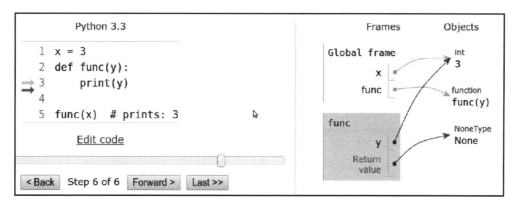

The right part of the preceding figure depicts the state of the program when execution has reached the end, after `func` has returned (None). Take a look at the **Frames** column, and note that we have two names, x and `func`, in the global namespace (**Global frame**), pointing to an `int` (with a value of **3**) and to a `function` object, respectively. Right beneath it, in the rectangle titled `func`, we can see the function's local namespace, in which only one name has been defined: y. Because we have called `func` with x (line **5** in the left part of the figure), y is pointing to the same object that x is pointing to. This is what happens under the hood when an argument is passed to a function. If we had used the name x instead of y in the function definition, things would have been exactly the same (only maybe a bit confusing at first), there would be a local x in the function, and a global x outside, as we saw in the *Scopes and name resolution* section previously in this chapter.

So, in a nutshell, what really happens is that the function creates, in its local scope, the names defined as arguments and, when we call it, we basically tell Python which objects those names must be pointed toward.

Assignment to argument names doesn't affect the caller

This is something that can be tricky to understand at first, so let's look at an example:

```python
# key.points.assignment.py
x = 3
def func(x):
    x = 7  # defining a local x, not changing the global one
func(x)
print(x)  # prints: 3
```

In the preceding code, when the `x = 7` line is executed, within the local scope of the `func` function, the name, `x`, is pointed to an integer with a value of `7`, leaving the global `x` unaltered.

Changing a mutable affects the caller

This is the final point, and it's very important because Python apparently behaves differently with mutables (just apparently, though). Let's look at an example:

```python
# key.points.mutable.py
x = [1, 2, 3]
def func(x):
    x[1] = 42  # this affects the caller!

func(x)
print(x)  # prints: [1, 42, 3]
```

Wow, we actually changed the original object! If you think about it, there is nothing weird in this behavior. The `x` name in the function is set to point to the caller object by the function call and within the body of the function, we're not changing `x`, in that we're not changing its reference, or, in other words, we are not changing the object `x` is pointing to. We're accessing that object's element at position 1, and changing its value.

Remember point #2 under the *Input parameters* section: *Assigning an object to an argument name within a function doesn't affect the caller*. If that is clear to you, the following code should not be surprising:

```python
# key.points.mutable.assignment.py
x = [1, 2, 3]
def func(x):
    x[1] = 42  # this changes the caller!
```

```
    x = 'something else'  # this points x to a new string object

func(x)
print(x)  # still prints: [1, 42, 3]
```

Take a look at the two lines I have highlighted. At first, like before, we just access the caller object again, at position 1, and change its value to number 42. Then, we reassign x to point to the 'something else' string. This leaves the caller unaltered and, in fact, the output is the same as that of the previous snippet.

Take your time to play around with this concept, and experiment with prints and calls to the id function until everything is clear in your mind. This is one of the key aspects of Python and it must be very clear, otherwise you risk introducing subtle bugs into your code. Once again, the Python Tutor website (http://www.pythontutor.com/) will help you a lot by giving you a visual representation of these concepts.

Now that we have a good understanding of input parameters and how they behave, let's see how we can specify them.

How to specify input parameters

There are five different ways of specifying input parameters:

- Positional arguments
- Keyword arguments
- Variable positional arguments
- Variable keyword arguments
- Keyword-only arguments

Let's look at them one by one.

Positional arguments

Positional arguments are read from left to right and they are the most common type of arguments:

```
# arguments.positional.py
def func(a, b, c):
    print(a, b, c)
func(1, 2, 3)  # prints: 1 2 3
```

There is not much else to say. They can be as numerous as you want and they are assigned by position. In the function call, 1 comes first, 2 comes second, and 3 comes third, therefore they are assigned to a, b, and c, respectively.

Keyword arguments and default values

Keyword arguments are assigned by keyword using the name=value syntax:

```
# arguments.keyword.py
def func(a, b, c):
    print(a, b, c)
func(a=1, c=2, b=3)   # prints: 1 3 2
```

Keyword arguments are matched by name, even when they don't respect the definition's original position (we'll see that there is a limitation to this behavior later, when we mix and match different types of arguments).

The counterpart of keyword arguments, on the definition side, is **default values**. The syntax is the same, name=value, and allows us to not have to provide an argument if we are happy with the given default:

```
# arguments.default.py
def func(a, b=4, c=88):
    print(a, b, c)

func(1)   # prints: 1 4 88
func(b=5, a=7, c=9)   # prints: 7 5 9
func(42, c=9)   # prints: 42 4 9
func(42, 43, 44)   # prints: 42, 43, 44
```

The are two things to notice, which are very important. First of all, you cannot specify a default argument on the left of a positional one. Second, note how in the examples, when an argument is passed without using the argument_name=value syntax, it must be the first one in the list, and it is always assigned to a. Notice also that passing values in a positional fashion still works, and follows the function signature order (last line of the example).

Try and scramble those arguments and see what happens. Python error messages are very good at telling you what's wrong. So, for example, if you tried something such as this:

```
# arguments.default.error.py
def func(a, b=4, c=88):
    print(a, b, c)
func(b=1, c=2, 42)   # positional argument after keyword one
```

You would get the following error:

```
$ python arguments.default.error.py
  File "arguments.default.error.py", line 4
    func(b=1, c=2, 42) # positional argument after keyword one
                 ^
SyntaxError: positional argument follows keyword argument
```

This informs you that you've called the function incorrectly.

Variable positional arguments

Sometimes you may want to pass a variable number of positional arguments to a function, and Python provides you with the ability to do it. Let's look at a very common use case, the `minimum` function. This is a function that calculates the minimum of its input values:

```
# arguments.variable.positional.py
def minimum(*n):
    # print(type(n))  # n is a tuple
    if n:  # explained after the code
        mn = n[0]
        for value in n[1:]:
            if value < mn:
                mn = value
        print(mn)

minimum(1, 3, -7, 9)    # n = (1, 3, -7, 9) - prints: -7
minimum()               # n = () - prints: nothing
```

As you can see, when we specify a parameter prepending a `*` to its name, we are telling Python that that parameter will be collecting a variable number of positional arguments, according to how the function is called. Within the function, n is a tuple. Uncomment `print(type(n))` to see for yourself and play around with it for a bit.

> Have you noticed how we checked whether n wasn't empty with a simple `if n:`? This is because collection objects evaluate to `True` when non-empty, and otherwise `False` in Python. This is true for tuples, sets, lists, dictionaries, and so on.
>
> One other thing to note is that we may want to throw an error when we call the function with no arguments, instead of silently doing nothing. In this context, we're not concerned about making this function robust, but in understanding variable positional arguments.

Let's make another example to show you two things that, in my experience, are confusing to those who are new to this:

```python
# arguments.variable.positional.unpacking.py
def func(*args):
    print(args)

values = (1, 3, -7, 9)
func(values)   # equivalent to: func((1, 3, -7, 9))
func(*values)  # equivalent to: func(1, 3, -7, 9)
```

Take a good look at the last two lines of the preceding example. In the first one, we call func with one argument, a four-elements tuple. In the second example, by using the * syntax, we're doing something called **unpacking**, which means that the four-elements tuple is unpacked, and the function is called with four arguments: 1, 3, -7, 9.

This behavior is part of the magic Python does to allow you to do amazing things when calling functions dynamically.

Variable keyword arguments

Variable keyword arguments are very similar to variable positional arguments. The only difference is the syntax (** instead of *) and that they are collected in a dictionary. Collection and unpacking work in the same way, so let's look at an example:

```python
# arguments.variable.keyword.py
def func(**kwargs):
    print(kwargs)

# All calls equivalent. They print: {'a': 1, 'b': 42}
func(a=1, b=42)
func(**{'a': 1, 'b': 42})
func(**dict(a=1, b=42))
```

All the calls are equivalent in the preceding example. You can see that adding a ** in front of the parameter name in the function definition tells Python to use that name to collect a variable number of keyword parameters. On the other hand, when we call the function, we can either pass name=value arguments explicitly, or unpack a dictionary using the same ** syntax.

The reason why being able to pass a variable number of keyword parameters is so important may not be evident at the moment, so, how about a more realistic example? Let's define a function that connects to a database. We want to connect to a default database by simply calling this function with no parameters. We also want to connect to any other database by passing the function the appropriate arguments. Before you read on, try to spend a couple of minutes figuring out a solution by yourself:

```
# arguments.variable.db.py
def connect(**options):
    conn_params = {
        'host': options.get('host', '127.0.0.1'),
        'port': options.get('port', 5432),
        'user': options.get('user', ''),
        'pwd': options.get('pwd', ''),
    }
    print(conn_params)
    # we then connect to the db (commented out)
    # db.connect(**conn_params)

connect()
connect(host='127.0.0.42', port=5433)
connect(port=5431, user='fab', pwd='gandalf')
```

Note that in the function, we can prepare a dictionary of connection parameters (conn_params) using default values as fallbacks, allowing them to be overwritten if they are provided in the function call. There are better ways to do this with fewer lines of code, but we're not concerned with that right now. Running the preceding code yields the following result:

```
$ python arguments.variable.db.py
{'host': '127.0.0.1', 'port': 5432, 'user': '', 'pwd': ''}
{'host': '127.0.0.42', 'port': 5433, 'user': '', 'pwd': ''}
{'host': '127.0.0.1', 'port': 5431, 'user': 'fab', 'pwd': 'gandalf'}
```

Note the correspondence between the function calls and the output. Notice how default values are overridden according to what was passed to the function.

Keyword-only arguments

Python 3 allows for a new type of parameter: the **keyword-only** parameter. We are going to study them only briefly as their use cases are not that frequent. There are two ways of specifying them, either after the variable positional arguments, or after a bare ⋆. Let's see an example of both:

```
# arguments.keyword.only.py
def kwo(*a, c):
    print(a, c)

kwo(1, 2, 3, c=7)  # prints: (1, 2, 3) 7
kwo(c=4)  # prints: () 4
# kwo(1, 2)  # breaks, invalid syntax, with the following error
# TypeError: kwo() missing 1 required keyword-only argument: 'c'

def kwo2(a, b=42, *, c):
    print(a, b, c)

kwo2(3, b=7, c=99)  # prints: 3 7 99
kwo2(3, c=13)  # prints: 3 42 13
# kwo2(3, 23)  # breaks, invalid syntax, with the following error
# TypeError: kwo2() missing 1 required keyword-only argument: 'c'
```

As anticipated, the function, kwo, takes a variable number of positional arguments (a) and a keyword-only one, c. The results of the calls are straightforward and you can uncomment the third call to see what error Python returns.

The same applies to the function, kwo2, which differs from kwo in that it takes a positional argument, a, a keyword argument, b, and then a keyword-only one, c. You can uncomment the third call to see the error.

Now that you know how to specify different types of input parameters, let's see how you can combine them in function definitions.

Combining input parameters

You can combine input parameters, as long as you follow these ordering rules:

- When defining a function, normal positional arguments come first (name), then any default arguments (name=value), then the variable positional arguments (*name or simply *), then any keyword-only arguments (either name or name=value form is good), and then any variable keyword arguments (**name).

- On the other hand, when calling a function, arguments must be given in the following order: positional arguments first (`value`), then any combination of keyword arguments (`name=value`), variable positional arguments (`*name`), and then variable keyword arguments (`**name`).

Since this can be a bit tricky when left hanging in the theoretical world, let's look at a couple of quick examples:

```
# arguments.all.py
def func(a, b, c=7, *args, **kwargs):
    print('a, b, c:', a, b, c)
    print('args:', args)
    print('kwargs:', kwargs)

func(1, 2, 3, *(5, 7, 9), **{'A': 'a', 'B': 'b'})
func(1, 2, 3, 5, 7, 9, A='a', B='b')  # same as previous one
```

Note the order of the parameters in the function definition, and that the two calls are equivalent. In the first one, we're using the unpacking operators for iterables and dictionaries, while in the second one we're using a more explicit syntax. The execution of this yields the following (I printed only the result of one call, the other one being the same):

```
$ python arguments.all.py
a, b, c: 1 2 3
args: (5, 7, 9)
kwargs: {'A': 'a', 'B': 'b'}
```

Let's now look at an example with keyword-only arguments:

```
# arguments.all.kwonly.py
def func_with_kwonly(a, b=42, *args, c, d=256, **kwargs):
    print('a, b:', a, b)
    print('c, d:', c, d)
    print('args:', args)
    print('kwargs:', kwargs)

# both calls equivalent
func_with_kwonly(3, 42, c=0, d=1, *(7, 9, 11), e='E', f='F')
func_with_kwonly(3, 42, *(7, 9, 11), c=0, d=1, e='E', f='F')
```

Note that I have highlighted the keyword-only arguments in the function declaration. They come after the `*args` variable positional argument, and it would be the same if they came right after a single `*` (in which case there wouldn't be a variable positional argument). The execution of this yields the following (I printed only the result of one call):

```
$ python arguments.all.kwonly.py
a, b: 3 42
c, d: 0 1
args: (7, 9, 11)
kwargs: {'e': 'E', 'f': 'F'}
```

One other thing to note is the names I gave to the variable positional and keyword arguments. You're free to choose differently, but be aware that `args` and `kwargs` are the conventional names given to these parameters, at least generically.

Additional unpacking generalizations

One of the recent new features, introduced in Python 3.5, is the ability to extend the iterable (`*`) and dictionary (`**`) unpacking operators to allow unpacking in more positions, an arbitrary number of times, and in additional circumstances. I'll present you with an example concerning function calls:

```
# additional.unpacking.py
def additional(*args, **kwargs):
    print(args)
    print(kwargs)


args1 = (1, 2, 3)
args2 = [4, 5]
kwargs1 = dict(option1=10, option2=20)
kwargs2 = {'option3': 30}
additional(*args1, *args2, **kwargs1, **kwargs2)
```

In the previous example, we defined a simple function that prints its input arguments, `args` and `kwargs`. The new feature lies in the way we call this function. Notice how we can unpack multiple iterables and dictionaries, and they are correctly coalesced under `args` and `kwargs`. The reason why this feature is important is that it allows us not to have to merge `args1` with `args2`, and `kwargs1` with `kwargs2` in the code. Running the code produces:

```
$ python additional.unpacking.py
(1, 2, 3, 4, 5)
{'option1': 10, 'option2': 20, 'option3': 30}
```

Please refer to PEP 448 (`https://www.python.org/dev/peps/pep-0448/`) to learn the full extent of this new feature and see further examples.

Avoid the trap! Mutable defaults

One thing to be very aware of with Python is that default values are created at `def` time, therefore, subsequent calls to the same function will possibly behave differently according to the mutability of their default values. Let's look at an example:

```
# arguments.defaults.mutable.py
def func(a=[], b={}):
    print(a)
    print(b)
    print('#' * 12)
    a.append(len(a))  # this will affect a's default value
    b[len(a)] = len(a)  # and this will affect b's one

func()
func()
func()
```

Both parameters have mutable default values. This means that, if you affect those objects, any modification will stick around in subsequent function calls. See if you can understand the output of those calls:

```
$ python arguments.defaults.mutable.py
[]
{}
############
[0]
{1: 1}
############
[0, 1]
{1: 1, 2: 2}
############
```

It's interesting, isn't it? While this behavior may seem very weird at first, it actually makes sense, and it's very handy, for example, when using memoization techniques (Google an example of that, if you're interested). Even more interesting is what happens when, between the calls, we introduce one that doesn't use defaults, such as this:

```
# arguments.defaults.mutable.intermediate.call.py
func()
func(a=[1, 2, 3], b={'B': 1})
func()
```

When we run this code, this is the output:

```
$ python arguments.defaults.mutable.intermediate.call.py
[]
{}
###########
[1, 2, 3]
{'B': 1}
###########
[0]
{1: 1}
###########
```

This output shows us that the defaults are retained even if we call the function with other values. One question that comes to mind is, how do I get a fresh empty value every time? Well, the convention is the following:

```
# arguments.defaults.mutable.no.trap.py
def func(a=None):
    if a is None:
        a = []
    # do whatever you want with `a` ...
```

Note that, by using the preceding technique, if a isn't passed when calling the function, you always get a brand new, empty list.

Okay, enough with the input, let's look at the other side of the coin, the output.

Return values

The return values of functions are one of those things where Python is ahead of most other languages. Functions are usually allowed to return one object (one value) but, in Python, you can return a tuple, and this implies that you can return whatever you want. This feature allows a coder to write software that would be much harder to write in any other language, or certainly more tedious. We've already said that to return something from a function we need to use the return statement, followed by what we want to return. There can be as many return statements as needed in the body of a function.

On the other hand, if within the body of a function we don't return anything, or we invoke a bare return statement, the function will return None. This behavior is harmless and, even though I don't have the room here to go into detail explaining why Python was designed like this, let me just tell you that this feature allows for several interesting patterns, and confirms Python as a very consistent language.

I say it's harmless because you are never forced to collect the result of a function call. I'll show you what I mean with an example:

```
# return.none.py
def func():
    pass
func()  # the return of this call won't be collected. It's lost.
a = func()  # the return of this one instead is collected into `a`
print(a)  # prints: None
```

Note that the whole body of the function is composed only of the `pass` statement. As the official documentation tells us, `pass` is a null operation. When it is executed, nothing happens. It is useful as a placeholder when a statement is required syntactically, but no code needs to be executed. In other languages, we would probably just indicate that with a pair of curly brackets ({ }), which define an *empty scope*, but in Python, a scope is defined by indenting code, therefore a statement such as `pass` is necessary.

Notice also that the first call of the `func` function returns a value (`None`) which we don't collect. As I said before, collecting the return value of a function call is not mandatory.

Now, that's good but not very interesting so, how about we write an interesting function? Remember that in `Chapter 1`, *A Gentle Introduction to Python*, we talked about the factorial of a function. Let's write our own here (for simplicity, I will assume the function is always called correctly with appropriate values so I won't sanity-check the input argument):

```
# return.single.value.py
def factorial(n):
    if n in (0, 1):
        return 1
    result = n
    for k in range(2, n):
        result *= k
    return result

f5 = factorial(5)  # f5 = 120
```

Note that we have two points of return. If n is either 0 or 1 (in Python it's common to use the `in` type of check, as I did instead of the more verbose `if n == 0 or n == 1:`), we return 1. Otherwise, we perform the required calculation and we return `result`. Let's try to write this function a little bit more succinctly:

```
# return.single.value.2.py
from functools import reduce
from operator import mul

def factorial(n):
```

```
        return reduce(mul, range(1, n + 1), 1)

f5 = factorial(5)   # f5 = 120
```

I know what you're thinking: one line? Python is elegant, and concise! I think this function is readable even if you have never seen `reduce` or `mul`, but if you can't read it or understand it, set aside a few minutes and do some research on the Python documentation until its behavior is clear to you. Being able to look up functions in the documentation and understand code written by someone else is a task every developer needs to be able to perform, so take this as a challenge.

To this end, make sure you look up the `help` function, which proves quite helpful when exploring with the console.

Returning multiple values

Unlike in most other languages, in Python it's very easy to return multiple objects from a function. This feature opens up a whole world of possibilities and allows you to code in a style that is hard to reproduce with other languages. Our thinking is limited by the tools we use, therefore when Python gives you more freedom than other languages, it is actually boosting your own creativity as well. To return multiple values is very easy, you just use tuples (either explicitly or implicitly). Let's look at a simple example that mimics the `divmod` built-in function:

```
# return.multiple.py
def moddiv(a, b):
    return a // b, a % b

print(moddiv(20, 7))  # prints (2, 6)
```

I could have wrapped the highlighted part in the preceding code in brackets, making it an explicit tuple, but there's no need for that. The preceding function returns both the result and the remainder of the division, at the same time.

In the source code for this example, I have left a simple example of a test function to make sure my code is doing the correct calculation.

A few useful tips

When writing functions, it's very useful to follow guidelines so that you write them well. I'll quickly point some of them out:

- **Functions should do one thing**: Functions that do one thing are easy to describe in one short sentence. Functions that do multiple things can be split into smaller functions that do one thing. These smaller functions are usually easier to read and understand. Remember the data science example we saw a few pages ago.
- **Functions should be small**: The smaller they are, the easier it is to test them and to write them so that they do one thing.
- **The fewer input parameters, the better**: Functions that take a lot of arguments quickly become harder to manage (among other issues).
- **Functions should be consistent in their return values**: Returning `False` or `None` is not the same thing, even if within a Boolean context they both evaluate to `False`. `False` means that we have information (`False`), while `None` means that there is no information. Try writing functions that return in a consistent way, no matter what happens in their body.
- **Functions shouldn't have side effects**: In other words, functions should not affect the values you call them with. This is probably the hardest statement to understand at this point, so I'll give you an example using lists. In the following code, note how `numbers` is not sorted by the `sorted` function, which actually returns a sorted copy of `numbers`. Conversely, the `list.sort()` method is acting on the `numbers` object itself, and that is fine because it is a method (a function that belongs to an object and therefore has the rights to modify it):

```
>>> numbers = [4, 1, 7, 5]
>>> sorted(numbers)  # won't sort the original `numbers` list
[1, 4, 5, 7]
>>> numbers  # let's verify
[4, 1, 7, 5]  # good, untouched
>>> numbers.sort()  # this will act on the list
>>> numbers
[1, 4, 5, 7]
```

Follow these guidelines and you'll write better functions, which will serve you well.

Chapter 3, Functions in *Clean Code* by Robert C. Martin, Prentice Hall is dedicated to functions and it's probably the best set of guidelines I've ever read on the subject.

Recursive functions

When a function calls itself to produce a result, it is said to be **recursive**. Sometimes recursive functions are very useful in that they make it easier to write code. Some algorithms are very easy to write using the recursive paradigm, while others are not. There is no recursive function that cannot be rewritten in an iterative fashion, so it's usually up to the programmer to choose the best approach for the case at hand.

The body of a recursive function usually has two sections: one where the return value depends on a subsequent call to itself, and one where it doesn't (called a base case).

As an example, we can consider the (hopefully familiar by now) `factorial` function, *N!*. The base case is when *N* is either 0 or 1. The function returns 1 with no need for further calculation. On the other hand, in the general case, *N!* returns the product *1 * 2 * ... * (N-1) * N*. If you think about it, *N!* can be rewritten like this: *N! = (N-1)! * N*. As a practical example, consider *5! = 1 * 2 * 3 * 4 * 5 = (1 * 2 * 3 * 4) * 5 = 4! * 5*.

Let's write this down in code:

```
# recursive.factorial.py
def factorial(n):
    if n in (0, 1):  # base case
        return 1
    return factorial(n - 1) * n  # recursive case
```

 When writing recursive functions, always consider how many nested calls you make, since there is a limit. For further information on this, check out `sys.getrecursionlimit()` and `sys.setrecursionlimit()`.

Recursive functions are used a lot when writing algorithms and they can be really fun to write. As an exercise, try to solve a couple of simple problems using both a recursive and an iterative approach.

Anonymous functions

One last type of functions that I want to talk about are **anonymous** functions. These functions, which are called **lambdas** in Python, are usually used when a fully-fledged function with its own name would be overkill, and all we want is a quick, simple one-liner that does the job.

Imagine that you want a list of all the numbers up to *N* that are multiples of five. Imagine that you want to filter those out using the `filter` function, which takes a function and an iterable and constructs a filter object that you can iterate on, from those elements of iterables for which the function returns `True`. Without using an anonymous function, you would do something like this:

```
# filter.regular.py
def is_multiple_of_five(n):
    return not n % 5

def get_multiples_of_five(n):
    return list(filter(is_multiple_of_five, range(n)))
```

Note how we use `is_multiple_of_five` to filter the first n natural numbers. This seems a bit excessive, the task is simple and we don't need to keep the `is_multiple_of_five` function around for anything else. Let's rewrite it using a lambda function:

```
# filter.lambda.py
def get_multiples_of_five(n):
    return list(filter(lambda k: not k % 5, range(n)))
```

The logic is exactly the same but the filtering function is now a lambda. Defining a lambda is very easy and follows this form: func_name = lambda [parameter_list]: expression. A function object is returned, which is equivalent to this: def func_name([parameter_list]): return expression.

Note that optional parameters are indicated following the common syntax of wrapping them in square brackets.

Let's look at another couple of examples of equivalent functions defined in the two forms:

```
# lambda.explained.py
# example 1: adder
def adder(a, b):
    return a + b

# is equivalent to:
adder_lambda = lambda a, b: a + b

# example 2: to uppercase
def to_upper(s):
    return s.upper()
```

```
# is equivalent to:
to_upper_lambda = lambda s: s.upper()
```

The preceding examples are very simple. The first one adds two numbers, and the second one produces the uppercase version of a string. Note that I assigned what is returned by the `lambda` expressions to a name (`adder_lambda`, `to_upper_lambda`), but there is no need for that when you use lambdas in the way we did in the `filter` example.

Function attributes

Every function is a fully-fledged object and, as such, they have many attributes. Some of them are special and can be used in an introspective way to inspect the function object at runtime. The following script is an example that shows a part of them and how to display their value for an example function:

```
# func.attributes.py
def multiplication(a, b=1):
    """Return a multiplied by b. """
    return a * b

special_attributes = [
    "__doc__", "__name__", "__qualname__", "__module__",
    "__defaults__", "__code__", "__globals__", "__dict__",
    "__closure__", "__annotations__", "__kwdefaults__",
]

for attribute in special_attributes:
    print(attribute, '->', getattr(multiplication, attribute))
```

I used the built-in `getattr` function to get the value of those attributes. `getattr(obj, attribute)` is equivalent to `obj.attribute` and comes in handy when we need to get an attribute at runtime using its string name. Running this script yields:

```
$ python func.attributes.py
__doc__ -> Return a multiplied by b.
__name__ -> multiplication
__qualname__ -> multiplication
__module__ -> __main__
__defaults__ -> (1,)
__code__ -> <code object multiplication at 0x10caf7660, file
"func.attributes.py", line 1>
__globals__ -> {...omitted...}
__dict__ -> {}
```

```
__closure__ -> None
__annotations__ -> {}
__kwdefaults__ -> None
```

I have omitted the value of the __globals__ attribute, as it was too big. An explanation of the meaning of this attribute can be found in the *Callable types* section of the *Python Data Model* documentation page (`https://docs.python.org/3/reference/datamodel.html#the-standard-type-hierarchy`). Should you want to see all the attributes of an object, just call `dir(object_name)` and you'll be given the list of all of its attributes.

Built-in functions

Python comes with a lot of built-in functions. They are available anywhere and you can get a list of them by inspecting the `builtins` module with `dir(__builtins__)`, or by going to the official Python documentation. Unfortunately, I don't have the room to go through all of them here. We've already seen some of them, such as `any`, `bin`, `bool`, `divmod`, `filter`, `float`, `getattr`, `id`, `int`, `len`, `list`, `min`, `print`, `set`, `tuple`, `type`, and `zip`, but there are many more, which you should read at least once. Get familiar with them, experiment, write a small piece of code for each of them, and make sure you have them at your finger tips so that you can use them when you need them.

One final example

Before we finish off this chapter, how about one last example? I was thinking we could write a function to generate a list of prime numbers up to a limit. We've already seen the code for this so let's make it a function and, to keep it interesting, let's optimize it a bit.

It turns out that you don't need to divide it by all numbers from 2 to *N*-1 to decide whether a number, *N*, is prime. You can stop at $\sqrt{N}$. Moreover, you don't need to test the division for all numbers from 2 to $\sqrt{N}$, you can just use the primes in that range. I'll leave it to you to figure out why this works, if you're interested. Let's see how the code changes:

```python
# primes.py
from math import sqrt, ceil

def get_primes(n):
    """Calculate a list of primes up to n (included). """
    primelist = []
    for candidate in range(2, n + 1):
        is_prime = True
        root = ceil(sqrt(candidate))  # division limit
```

```
        for prime in primelist:  # we try only the primes
            if prime > root:  # no need to check any further
                break
            if candidate % prime == 0:
                is_prime = False
                break
        if is_prime:
            primelist.append(candidate)
    return primelist
```

The code is the same as in the previous chapter. We have changed the division algorithm so that we only test divisibility using the previously calculated primes and we stopped once the testing divisor was greater than the root of the candidate. We used the `primelist` result list to get the primes for the division. We calculated the root value using a fancy formula, the integer value of the ceiling of the root of the candidate. While a simple `int(k ** 0.5) + 1` would have served our purpose as well, the formula I chose is cleaner and requires me to use a couple of imports, which I wanted to show you. Check out the functions in the `math` module, they are very interesting!

Documenting your code

I'm a big fan of code that doesn't need documentation. When you program correctly, choose the right names and take care of the details, your code should come out as self-explanatory and documentation should not be needed. Sometimes a comment is very useful though, and so is some documentation. You can find the guidelines for documenting Python in *PEP 257 - Docstring conventions* (`https://www.python.org/dev/peps/pep-0257/`), but I'll show you the basics here.

Python is documented with strings, which are aptly called **docstrings**. Any object can be documented, and you can use either one-line or multiline docstrings. One-liners are very simple. They should not provide another signature for the function, but clearly state its purpose:

```python
# docstrings.py
def square(n):
    """Return the square of a number n. """
    return n ** 2

def get_username(userid):
    """Return the username of a user given their id. """
    return db.get(user_id=userid).username
```

Using triple double-quoted strings allows you to expand easily later on. Use sentences that end in a period, and don't leave blank lines before or after.

Multiline comments are structured in a similar way. There should be a one-liner that briefly gives you the gist of what the object is about, and then a more verbose description. As an example, I have documented a fictitious `connect` function, using the Sphinx notation, in the following example:

```
def connect(host, port, user, password):
    """Connect to a database.

    Connect to a PostgreSQL database directly, using the given
    parameters.

    :param host: The host IP.
    :param port: The desired port.
    :param user: The connection username.
    :param password: The connection password.
    :return: The connection object.
    """
    # body of the function here...
    return connection
```

Sphinx is probably the most widely used tool for creating Python documentation. In fact, the official Python documentation was written with it. It's definitely worth spending some time checking it out.

Importing objects

Now that you know a lot about functions, let's look at how to use them. The whole point of writing functions is to be able to reuse them later, and in Python, this translates to importing them into the namespace where you need them. There are many different ways to import objects into a namespace, but the most common ones are `import module_name` and `from module_name import function_name`. Of course, these are quite simplistic examples, but bear with me for the time being.

The `import module_name` form finds the `module_name` module and defines a name for it in the local namespace where the `import` statement is executed. The `from module_name import identifier` form is a little bit more complicated than that, but basically does the same thing. It finds `module_name` and searches for an attribute (or a submodule) and stores a reference to `identifier` in the local namespace.

Both forms have the option to change the name of the imported object using the `as` clause:

```
from mymodule import myfunc as better_named_func
```

Just to give you a flavor of what importing looks like, here's an example from a test module of one of my projects (notice that the blank lines between blocks of imports follow the guidelines from PEP 8 at https://www.python.org/dev/peps/pep-0008/#imports: standard library, third party, and local code):

```
from datetime import datetime, timezone  # two imports on the same line
from unittest.mock import patch  # single import

import pytest  # third party library

from core.models import (  # multiline import
    Exam,
    Exercise,
    Solution,
)
```

When you have a structure of files starting in the root of your project, you can use the dot notation to get to the object you want to import into your current namespace, be it a package, a module, a class, a function, or anything else. The `from module import` syntax also allows a catch-all clause, `from module import *`, which is sometimes used to get all the names from a module into the current namespace at once, but it's frowned upon for several reasons, such as performance and the risk of silently shadowing other names. You can read all that there is to know about imports in the official Python documentation but, before we leave the subject, let me give you a better example.

Imagine that you have defined a couple of functions: `square(n)` and `cube(n)` in a module, `funcdef.py`, which is in the `lib` folder. You want to use them in a couple of modules that are at the same level of the `lib` folder, called `func_import.py` and `func_from.py`. Showing the tree structure of that project produces something like this:

```
├── func_from.py
├── func_import.py
├── lib
    ├── funcdef.py
    └── __init__.py
```

Before I show you the code of each module, please remember that in order to tell Python that it is actually a package, we need to put a `__init__.py` module in it.

There are two things to note about the __init__.py file. First of all, it is a fully-fledged Python module so you can put code into it as you would with any other module. Second, as of Python 3.3, its presence is no longer required to make a folder be interpreted as a Python package.

The code is as follows:

```
# funcdef.py
def square(n):
    return n ** 2
def cube(n):
    return n ** 3

# func_import.py
import lib.funcdef
print(lib.funcdef.square(10))
print(lib.funcdef.cube(10))

# func_from.py
from lib.funcdef import square, cube
print(square(10))
print(cube(10))
```

Both these files, when executed, print 100 and 1000. You can see how differently we then access the square and cube functions, according to how and what we imported in the current scope.

Relative imports

The imports we've seen so far are called **absolute**, that is, they define the whole path of the module that we want to import, or from which we want to import an object. There is another way of importing objects into Python, which is called a **relative import**. It's helpful in situations where we want to rearrange the structure of large packages without having to edit sub-packages, or when we want to make a module inside a package able to import itself. Relative imports are done by adding as many leading dots in front of the module as the number of folders we need to backtrack, in order to find what we're searching for. Simply put, it is something such as this:

```
from .mymodule import myfunc
```

For a complete explanation of relative imports, refer to PEP 328 (`https://www.python.org/dev/peps/pep-0328/`). In later chapters, we'll create projects using different libraries and we'll use several different types of imports, including relative ones, so make sure you take a bit of time to read up about it in the official Python documentation.

Summary

In this chapter, we explored the world of functions. They are extremely important and, from now on, we'll use them basically everywhere. We talked about the main reasons for using them, the most important of which are code reuse and implementation hiding.

We saw that a function object is like a box that takes optional inputs and produces outputs. We can feed input values to a function in many different ways, using positional and keyword arguments, and using variable syntax for both types.

Now you should know how to write a function, document it, import it into your code, and call it.

The next chapter will force me to push my foot down on the throttle even more, so I suggest you take any opportunity you get to consolidate and enrich the knowledge you've gathered so far by putting your nose into the Python official documentation.

Saving Time and Memory

5

I love this quote from Bruce Lee. He was such a wise man! Especially, the second part, *"hack away at the unessential"*, is to me what makes a computer program elegant. After all, if there is a better way of doing things so that we don't waste time or memory, why not?

Sometimes, there are valid reasons for not pushing our code up to the maximum limit: for example, sometimes to achieve a negligible improvement, we have to sacrifice on readability or maintainability. Does it make any sense to have a web page served in 1 second with unreadable, complicated code, when we can serve it in 1.05 seconds with readable, clean code? No, it makes no sense.

On the other hand, sometimes it's perfectly reasonable to try to shave off a millisecond from a function, especially when the function is meant to be called thousands of times. Every millisecond you save there means one second saved per thousands of calls, and this could be meaningful for your application.

In light of these considerations, the focus of this chapter will not be to give you the tools to push your code to the absolute limits of performance and optimization "no matter what," but rather, to enable you to write efficient, elegant code that reads well, runs fast, and doesn't waste resources in an obvious way.

In this chapter, we are going to cover the following:

- The map, zip, and filter functions
- Comprehensions
- Generators

I will perform several measurements and comparisons, and cautiously draw some conclusions. Please do keep in mind that on a different box with a different setup or a different operating system, results may vary. Take a look at this code:

```
# squares.py
def square1(n):
    return n ** 2  # squaring through the power operator

def square2(n):
    return n * n  # squaring through multiplication
```

Both functions return the square of n, but which is faster? From a simple benchmark I ran on them, it looks like the second is slightly faster. If you think about it, it makes sense: calculating the power of a number involves multiplication and therefore, whatever algorithm you may use to perform the power operation, it's not likely to beat a simple multiplication such as the one in square2.

Do we care about this result? In most cases, no. If you're coding an e-commerce website, chances are you won't ever even need to raise a number to the second power, and if you do, it's likely to be a sporadic operation. You don't need to concern yourself with saving a fraction of a microsecond on a function you call a few times.

So, when does optimization become important? One very common case is when you have to deal with huge collections of data. If you're applying the same function on a million customer objects, then you want your function to be tuned up to its best. Gaining 1/10 of a second on a function called one million times saves you 100,000 seconds, which is about 27.7 hours. That's not the same, right? So, let's focus on collections, and let's see which tools Python gives you to handle them with efficiency and grace.

 Many of the concepts we will see in this chapter are based on those of the iterator and iterable. Simply put, the ability for an object to return its next element when asked, and to raise a StopIteration exception when exhausted. We'll see how to code a custom iterator and iterable objects in Chapter 6, *OOP, Decorators, and Iterators*.

Due to the nature of the objects we're going to explore in this chapter, I was often forced to wrap the code in a list constructor. This is because passing an iterator/generator to list(...) exhausts it and puts all the generated items in a newly created list, which I can easily print to show you its content. This technique hinders readability, so let me introduce an alias for list:

```
# alias.py
>>> range(7)
range(0, 7)
```

```
>>> list(range(7))  # put all elements in a list to view them
[0, 1, 2, 3, 4, 5, 6]
>>> _ = list  # create an "alias" to list
>>> _(range(7))  # same as list(range(7))
[0, 1, 2, 3, 4, 5, 6]
```

Of the three sections I have highlighted, the first one is the call we need to do in order to show what would be generated by range(7), the second one is the moment when I create the alias to list (I chose the hopefully unobtrusive underscore), and the third one is the equivalent call, when I use the alias instead of list.

 Hopefully readability will benefit from this, and please keep in mind that I will assume this alias to have been defined for all the code in this chapter.

The map, zip, and filter functions

We'll start by reviewing map, filter, and zip, which are the main built-in functions one can employ when handling collections, and then we'll learn how to achieve the same results using two very important constructs: **comprehensions** and **generators**. Fasten your seatbelt!

map

According to the official Python documentation:

map(function, iterable, ...) returns an iterator that applies function to every item of iterable, yielding the results. If additional iterable arguments are passed, function must take that many arguments and is applied to the items from all iterables in parallel. With multiple iterables, the iterator stops when the shortest iterable is exhausted.

We will explain the concept of yielding later on in the chapter. For now, let's translate this into code—we'll use a lambda function that takes a variable number of positional arguments, and just returns them as a tuple:

```
# map.example.py
>>> map(lambda *a: a, range(3))  # 1 iterable
<map object at 0x10acf8f98>  # Not useful! Let's use alias
>>> _(map(lambda *a: a, range(3)))  # 1 iterable
[(0,), (1,), (2,)]
>>> _(map(lambda *a: a, range(3), 'abc'))  # 2 iterables
```

```
[(0, 'a'), (1, 'b'), (2, 'c')]
>>> _(map(lambda *a: a, range(3), 'abc', range(4, 7)))  # 3
[(0, 'a', 4), (1, 'b', 5), (2, 'c', 6)]
>>> # map stops at the shortest iterator
>>> _(map(lambda *a: a, (), 'abc'))  # empty tuple is shortest
[]
>>> _(map(lambda *a: a, (1, 2), 'abc'))  # (1, 2) shortest
[(1, 'a'), (2, 'b')]
>>> _(map(lambda *a: a, (1, 2, 3, 4), 'abc'))  # 'abc' shortest
[(1, 'a'), (2, 'b'), (3, 'c')]
```

In the preceding code, you can see why we have to wrap calls in `list(...)` (or its alias, `_`, in this case). Without it, I get the string representation of a `map` object, which is not really useful in this context, is it?

You can also notice how the elements of each iterable are applied to the function; at first, the first element of each iterable, then the second one of each iterable, and so on. Notice also that `map` stops when the shortest of the iterables we called it with is exhausted. This is actually a very nice behavior; it doesn't force us to level off all the iterables to a common length, and it doesn't break if they aren't all the same length.

`map` is very useful when you have to apply the same function to one or more collections of objects. As a more interesting example, let's see the **decorate-sort-undecorate** idiom (also known as **Schwartzian transform**). It's a technique that was extremely popular when Python sorting wasn't providing *key-functions*, and therefore is less used today, but it's a cool trick that still comes in handy once in a while.

Let's see a variation of it in the next example: we want to sort in descending order by the sum of credits accumulated by students, so to have the best student at position 0. We write a function to produce a decorated object, we sort, and then we undecorate. Each student has credits in three (possibly different) subjects. In this context, to decorate an object means to transform it, either adding extra data to it, or putting it into another object, in a way that allows us to be able to sort the original objects the way we want. This technique has nothing to do with Python decorators, which we will explore later on in the book.

After the sorting, we revert the decorated objects to get the original ones from them. This is called to undecorate:

```
# decorate.sort.undecorate.py
students = [
    dict(id=0, credits=dict(math=9, physics=6, history=7)),
    dict(id=1, credits=dict(math=6, physics=7, latin=10)),
    dict(id=2, credits=dict(history=8, physics=9, chemistry=10)),
    dict(id=3, credits=dict(math=5, physics=5, geography=7)),
]
```

```
def decorate(student):
    # create a 2-tuple (sum of credits, student) from student dict
    return (sum(student['credits'].values()), student)

def undecorate(decorated_student):
    # discard sum of credits, return original student dict
    return decorated_student[1]

students = sorted(map(decorate, students), reverse=True)
students = _(map(undecorate, students))
```

Let's start by understanding what each student object is. In fact, let's print the first one:

```
{'credits': {'history': 7, 'math': 9, 'physics': 6}, 'id': 0}
```

You can see that it's a dictionary with two keys: id and credits. The value of credits is also a dictionary in which there are three subject/grade key/value pairs. As I'm sure you recall from our visit in the data structures world, calling dict.values() returns an object similar to iterable, with only the values. Therefore, sum(student['credits'].values()) for the first student is equivalent to sum((9, 6, 7)).

Let's print the result of calling decorate with the first student:

```
>>> decorate(students[0])
(22, {'credits': {'history': 7, 'math': 9, 'physics': 6}, 'id': 0})
```

If we decorate all the students like this, we can sort them on their total amount of credits by just sorting the list of tuples. In order to apply the decoration to each item in students, we call map(decorate, students). Then we sort the result, and then we undecorate in a similar fashion. If you have gone through the previous chapters correctly, understanding this code shouldn't be too hard.

Printing students after running the whole code yields:

```
$ python decorate.sort.undecorate.py
[{'credits': {'chemistry': 10, 'history': 8, 'physics': 9}, 'id': 2},
 {'credits': {'latin': 10, 'math': 6, 'physics': 7}, 'id': 1},
 {'credits': {'history': 7, 'math': 9, 'physics': 6}, 'id': 0},
 {'credits': {'geography': 7, 'math': 5, 'physics': 5}, 'id': 3}]
```

And you can see, by the order of the student objects, that they have indeed been sorted by the sum of their credits.

For more on the *decorate-sort-undecorate* idiom, there's a very nice introduction in the sorting how-to section of the official Python documentation (`https://docs.python.org/3.7/howto/sorting.html#the-old-way-using-decorate-sort-undecorate`).

One thing to notice about the sorting part: what if two or more students share the same total sum? The sorting algorithm would then proceed to sort the tuples by comparing the `student` objects with each other. This doesn't make any sense, and in more complex cases, could lead to unpredictable results, or even errors. If you want to be sure to avoid this issue, one simple solution is to create a three-tuple instead of a two-tuple, having the sum of credits in the first position, the position of the `student` object in the `students` list in the second one, and the `student` object itself in the third one. This way, if the sum of credits is the same, the tuples will be sorted against the position, which will always be different and therefore enough to resolve the sorting between any pair of tuples.

zip

We've already covered `zip` in the previous chapters, so let's just define it properly and then I want to show you how you could combine it with `map`.

According to the Python documentation:

> *zip(*iterables) returns an iterator of tuples, where the i-th tuple contains the i-th element from each of the argument sequences or iterables. The iterator stops when the shortest input iterable is exhausted. With a single iterable argument, it returns an iterator of 1-tuples. With no arguments, it returns an empty iterator.*

Let's see an example:

```
# zip.grades.py
>>> grades = [18, 23, 30, 27]
>>> avgs = [22, 21, 29, 24]
>>> _(zip(avgs, grades))
[(22, 18), (21, 23), (29, 30), (24, 27)]
>>> _(map(lambda *a: a, avgs, grades))  # equivalent to zip
[(22, 18), (21, 23), (29, 30), (24, 27)]
```

In the preceding code, we're zipping together the average and the grade for the last exam, for each student. Notice how easy it is to reproduce `zip` using `map` (last two instructions of the example). Here as well, to visualize results we have to use our _ alias.

A simple example on the combined use of `map` and `zip` could be a way of calculating the element-wise maximum amongst sequences, that is, the maximum of the first element of each sequence, then the maximum of the second one, and so on:

```
# maxims.py
>>> a = [5, 9, 2, 4, 7]
>>> b = [3, 7, 1, 9, 2]
>>> c = [6, 8, 0, 5, 3]
>>> maxs = map(lambda n: max(*n), zip(a, b, c))
>>> _(maxs)
[6, 9, 2, 9, 7]
```

Notice how easy it is to calculate the max values of three sequences. `zip` is not strictly needed of course, we could just use `map`. Sometimes it's hard, when showing a simple example, to grasp why using a technique might be good or bad. We forget that we aren't always in control of the source code, we might have to use a third-party library, which we can't change the way we want. Having different ways to work with data is therefore really helpful.

filter

According to the Python documentation:

> *filter(function, iterable) construct an iterator from those elements of iterable for which function returns True. iterable may be either a sequence, a container which supports iteration, or an iterator. If function is None, the identity function is assumed, that is, all elements of iterable that are false are removed.*

Let's see a very quick example:

```
# filter.py
>>> test = [2, 5, 8, 0, 0, 1, 0]
>>> _(filter(None, test))
[2, 5, 8, 1]
>>> _(filter(lambda x: x, test))   # equivalent to previous one
[2, 5, 8, 1]
>>> _(filter(lambda x: x > 4, test))   # keep only items > 4
[5, 8]
```

In the preceding code, notice how the second call to `filter` is equivalent to the first one. If we pass a function that takes one argument and returns the argument itself, only those arguments that are `True` will make the function return `True`, therefore this behavior is exactly the same as passing `None`. It's often a very good exercise to mimic some of the built-in Python behaviors. When you succeed, you can say you fully understand how Python behaves in a specific situation.

Armed with `map`, `zip`, and `filter` (and several other functions from the Python standard library) we can massage sequences very effectively. But those functions are not the only way to do it. So let's see one of the nicest features of Python: comprehensions.

Comprehensions

Comprehensions are a concise notation, both perform some operation for a collection of elements, and/or select a subset of them that meet some condition. They are borrowed from the functional programming language Haskell (https://www.haskell.org/), and contribute to giving Python a functional flavor, together with iterators and generators.

Python offers you different types of comprehensions: `list`, `dict`, and `set`. We'll concentrate on the first one for now, and then it will be easy to explain the other two.

Let's start with a very simple example. I want to calculate a list with the squares of the first 10 natural numbers. How would you do it? There are a couple of equivalent ways:

```
# squares.map.py
# If you code like this you are not a Python dev! ;)
>>> squares = []
>>> for n in range(10):
...     squares.append(n ** 2)
...
>>> squares
[0, 1, 4, 9, 16, 25, 36, 49, 64, 81]

# This is better, one line, nice and readable
>>> squares = map(lambda n: n**2, range(10))
>>> _(squares)
[0, 1, 4, 9, 16, 25, 36, 49, 64, 81]
```

The preceding example should be nothing new for you. Let's see how to achieve the same result using a `list` comprehension:

```
# squares.comprehension.py
>>> [n ** 2 for n in range(10)]
[0, 1, 4, 9, 16, 25, 36, 49, 64, 81]
```

As simple as that. Isn't it elegant? Basically we have put a `for` loop within square brackets. Let's now filter out the odd squares. I'll show you how to do it with `map` and `filter` first, and then using a `list` comprehension again:

```
# even.squares.py
# using map and filter
sq1 = list(
    map(lambda n: n ** 2, filter(lambda n: not n % 2, range(10)))
)
# equivalent, but using list comprehensions
sq2 = [n ** 2 for n in range(10) if not n % 2]

print(sq1, sq1 == sq2)  # prints: [0, 4, 16, 36, 64] True
```

I think that now the difference in readability is evident. The `list` comprehension reads much better. It's almost English: give me all squares (`n ** 2`) for n between 0 and 9 if n is even.

According to the Python documentation:

> *A list comprehension consists of brackets containing an expression followed by a for clause, then zero or more for or if clauses. The result will be a new list resulting from evaluating the expression in the context of the for and if clauses which follow it.*

Nested comprehensions

Let's see an example of nested loops. It's very common when dealing with algorithms to have to iterate on a sequence using two placeholders. The first one runs through the whole sequence, left to right. The second one as well, but it starts from the first one, instead of 0. The concept is that of testing all pairs without duplication. Let's see the classical `for` loop equivalent:

```
# pairs.for.loop.py
items = 'ABCD'
pairs = []

for a in range(len(items)):
```

```
    for b in range(a, len(items)):
        pairs.append((items[a], items[b]))
```

If you print pairs at the end, you get:

```
$ python pairs.for.loop.py
[('A', 'A'), ('A', 'B'), ('A', 'C'), ('A', 'D'), ('B', 'B'), ('B', 'C'),
('B', 'D'), ('C', 'C'), ('C', 'D'), ('D', 'D')]
```

All the tuples with the same letter are those where b is at the same position as a. Now, let's see how we can translate this in a list comprehension:

```
# pairs.list.comprehension.py
items = 'ABCD'
pairs = [(items[a], items[b])
    for a in range(len(items)) for b in range(a, len(items))]
```

This version is just two lines long and achieves the same result. Notice that in this particular case, because the for loop over b has a dependency on a, it must follow the for loop over a in the comprehension. If you swap them around, you'll get a name error.

Filtering a comprehension

We can apply filtering to a comprehension. Let's do it first with filter. Let's find all Pythagorean triples whose short sides are numbers smaller than 10. We obviously don't want to test a combination twice, and therefore we'll use a trick similar to the one we saw in the previous example:

```
# pythagorean.triple.py
from math import sqrt
# this will generate all possible pairs
mx = 10
triples = [(a, b, sqrt(a**2 + b**2))
    for a in range(1, mx) for b in range(a, mx)]
# this will filter out all non pythagorean triples
triples = list(
    filter(lambda triple: triple[2].is_integer(), triples))

print(triples)  # prints: [(3, 4, 5.0), (6, 8, 10.0)]
```

A **Pythagorean triple** is a triple (a, b, c) of integer numbers satisfying the equation $a^2 + b^2 = c^2$.

In the preceding code, we generated a list of *three-tuples*, `triples`. Each tuple contains two integer numbers (the legs), and the hypotenuse of the Pythagorean triangle whose legs are the first two numbers in the tuple. For example, when `a` is 3 and `b` is 4, the tuple will be `(3, 4, 5.0)`, and when `a` is 5 and `b` is 7, the tuple will be `(5, 7, 8.602325267042627)`.

After having all the `triples` done, we need to filter out all those that don't have a hypotenuse that is an integer number. In order to do this, we filter based on `float_number.is_integer()` being `True`. This means that of the two example tuples I showed you before, the one with `5.0` hypotenuse will be retained, while the one with the `8.602325267042627` hypotenuse will be discarded.

This is good, but I don't like that the triple has two integer numbers and a float. They are supposed to be all integers, so let's use `map` to fix this:

```
# pythagorean.triple.int.py
from math import sqrt
mx = 10
triples = [(a, b, sqrt(a**2 + b**2))
    for a in range(1, mx) for b in range(a, mx)]
triples = filter(lambda triple: triple[2].is_integer(), triples)
# this will make the third number in the tuples integer
triples = list(
    map(lambda triple: triple[:2] + (int(triple[2]), ), triples))

print(triples)  # prints: [(3, 4, 5), (6, 8, 10)]
```

Notice the step we added. We take each element in `triples` and we slice it, taking only the first two elements in it. Then, we concatenate the slice with a one-tuple, in which we put the integer version of that float number that we didn't like. Seems like a lot of work, right? Indeed it is. Let's see how to do all this with a `list` comprehension:

```
# pythagorean.triple.comprehension.py
from math import sqrt
# this step is the same as before
mx = 10
triples = [(a, b, sqrt(a**2 + b**2))
    for a in range(1, mx) for b in range(a, mx)]
# here we combine filter and map in one CLEAN list comprehension
triples = [(a, b, int(c)) for a, b, c in triples if c.is_integer()]
print(triples)  # prints: [(3, 4, 5), (6, 8, 10)]
```

I know. It's much better, isn't it? It's clean, readable, shorter. In other words, it's elegant.

I'm going quite fast here, as anticipated in the *Summary* of Chapter 4, *Functions, the Building Blocks of Code*. Are you playing with this code? If not, I suggest you do. It's very important that you play around, break things, change things, see what happens. Make sure you have a clear understanding of what is going on. You want to become a ninja, right?

dict comprehensions

Dictionary and set comprehensions work exactly like the list ones, only there is a little difference in the syntax. The following example will suffice to explain everything you need to know:

```
# dictionary.comprehensions.py
from string import ascii_lowercase
lettermap = dict((c, k) for k, c in enumerate(ascii_lowercase, 1))
```

If you print lettermap, you will see the following (I omitted the middle results, you get the gist):

```
$ python dictionary.comprehensions.py
{'a': 1,
 'b': 2,
 ...
 'y': 25,
 'z': 26}
```

What happens in the preceding code is that we're feeding the dict constructor with a comprehension (technically, a generator expression, we'll see it in a bit). We tell the dict constructor to make *key/value* pairs from each tuple in the comprehension. We enumerate the sequence of all lowercase ASCII letters, starting from 1, using enumerate. Piece of cake. There is also another way to do the same thing, which is closer to the other dictionary syntax:

```
lettermap = {c: k for k, c in enumerate(ascii_lowercase, 1)}
```

It does exactly the same thing, with a slightly different syntax that highlights a bit more of the *key: value* part.

Dictionaries do not allow duplication in the keys, as shown in the following example:

```
# dictionary.comprehensions.duplicates.py
word = 'Hello'
swaps = {c: c.swapcase() for c in word}
print(swaps)  # prints: {'H': 'h', 'e': 'E', 'l': 'L', 'o': 'O'}
```

We create a dictionary with keys, the letters in the `'Hello'` string, and values of the same letters, but with the case swapped. Notice there is only one `'l': 'L'` pair. The constructor doesn't complain, it simply reassigns duplicates to the latest value. Let's make this clearer with another example; let's assign to each key its position in the string:

```
# dictionary.comprehensions.positions.py
word = 'Hello'
positions = {c: k for k, c in enumerate(word)}
print(positions)  # prints: {'H': 0, 'e': 1, 'l': 3, 'o': 4}
```

Notice the value associated with the letter `'l': 3`. The `'l': 2` pair isn't there; it has been overridden by `'l': 3`.

set comprehensions

The `set` comprehensions are very similar to list and dictionary ones. Python allows both the `set()` constructor to be used, or the explicit `{}` syntax. Let's see one quick example:

```
# set.comprehensions.py
word = 'Hello'
letters1 = set(c for c in word)
letters2 = {c for c in word}
print(letters1)  # prints: {'H', 'o', 'e', 'l'}
print(letters1 == letters2)  # prints: True
```

Notice how for `set` comprehensions, as for dictionaries, duplication is not allowed and therefore the resulting set has only four letters. Also, notice that the expressions assigned to `letters1` and `letters2` produce equivalent sets.

The syntax used to create `letters2` is very similar to the one we can use to create a dictionary comprehension. You can spot the difference only by the fact that dictionaries require keys and values, separated by columns, while sets don't.

Generators

Generators are very powerful tool that Python gifts us with. They are based on the concepts of *iteration*, as we said before, and they allow for coding patterns that combine elegance with efficiency.

Generators are of two types:

- **Generator functions**: These are very similar to regular functions, but instead of returning results through return statements, they use yield, which allows them to suspend and resume their state between each call
- **Generator expressions**: These are very similar to the `list` comprehensions we've seen in this chapter, but instead of returning a list they return an object that produces results one by one

Generator functions

Generator functions behave like regular functions in all respects, except for one difference. Instead of collecting results and returning them at once, they are automatically turned into iterators that yield results one at a time when you call `next` on them. Generator functions are automatically turned into their own iterators by Python.

This is all very theoretical so, let's make it clear why such a mechanism is so powerful, and then let's see an example.

Say I asked you to count out loud from 1 to 1,000,000. You start, and at some point I ask you to stop. After some time, I ask you to resume. At this point, what is the minimum information you need to be able to resume correctly? Well, you need to remember the last number you called. If I stopped you after 31,415, you will just go on with 31,416, and so on.

The point is, you don't need to remember all the numbers you said before 31,415, nor do you need them to be written down somewhere. Well, you may not know it, but you're behaving like a generator already!

Take a good look at the following code:

```
# first.n.squares.py
def get_squares(n): # classic function approach
    return [x ** 2 for x in range(n)]
print(get_squares(10))

def get_squares_gen(n):  # generator approach
    for x in range(n):
```

```
        yield x ** 2  # we yield, we don't return
print(list(get_squares_gen(10)))
```

The result of the two `print` statements will be the same: `[0, 1, 4, 9, 16, 25, 36, 49, 64, 81]`. But there is a huge difference between the two functions. `get_squares` is a classic function that collects all the squares of numbers in [0, *n*) in a list, and returns it. On the other hand, `get_squares_gen` is a generator, and behaves very differently. Each time the interpreter reaches the `yield` line, its execution is suspended. The only reason those `print` statements return the same result is because we fed `get_squares_gen` to the `list` constructor, which exhausts the generator completely by asking the next element until a `StopIteration` is raised. Let's see this in detail:

```
# first.n.squares.manual.py
def get_squares_gen(n):
    for x in range(n):
        yield x ** 2

squares = get_squares_gen(4)  # this creates a generator object
print(squares)  # <generator object get_squares_gen at 0x10dd...>
print(next(squares))  # prints: 0
print(next(squares))  # prints: 1
print(next(squares))  # prints: 4
print(next(squares))  # prints: 9
# the following raises StopIteration, the generator is exhausted,
# any further call to next will keep raising StopIteration
print(next(squares))
```

In the preceding code, each time we call `next` on the generator object, we either start it (first `next`) or make it resume from the last suspension point (any other `next`).

The first time we call `next` on it, we get `0`, which is the square of `0`, then `1`, then `4`, then `9`, and since the `for` loop stops after that (`n` is 4), then the generator naturally ends. A classic function would at that point just return `None`, but in order to comply with the iteration protocol, a generator will instead raise a `StopIteration` exception.

This explains how a `for` loop works. When you call `for k in range(n)`, what happens under the hood is that the `for` loop gets an iterator out of `range(n)` and starts calling `next` on it, until `StopIteration` is raised, which tells the `for` loop that the iteration has reached its end.

Having this behavior built into every iteration aspect of Python makes generators even more powerful because once we write them, we'll be able to plug them into whatever iteration mechanism we want.

At this point, you're probably asking yourself why you would want to use a generator instead of a regular function. Well, the title of this chapter should suggest the answer. I'll talk about performances later, so for now let's concentrate on another aspect: sometimes generators allow you to do something that wouldn't be possible with a simple list. For example, say you want to analyze all permutations of a sequence. If the sequence has a length of N, then the number of its permutations is $N!$. This means that if the sequence is 10 elements long, the number of permutations is 3,628,800. But a sequence of 20 elements would have 2,432,902,008,176,640,000 permutations. They grow factorially.

Now imagine you have a classic function that is attempting to calculate all permutations, put them in a list, and return it to you. With 10 elements, it would require probably a few dozen seconds, but for 20 elements there is simply no way that it can be done.

On the other hand, a generator function will be able to start the computation and give you back the first permutation, then the second, and so on. Of course you won't have the time to parse them all, there are too many, but at least you'll be able to work with some of them.

Remember when we were talking about the `break` statement in `for` loops? When we found a number dividing a *candidate prime* we were breaking the loop, and there was no need to go on.

Sometimes it's exactly the same, only the amount of data you have to iterate over is so huge that you cannot keep it all in memory in a list. In this case, generators are invaluable: they make possible what wouldn't be possible otherwise.

So, in order to save memory (and time), use generator functions whenever possible.

It's also worth noting that you can use the return statement in a generator function. It will produce a `StopIteration` exception to be raised, effectively ending the iteration. This is extremely important. If a `return` statement were actually to make the function return something, it would break the iteration protocol. Python's consistency prevents this, and allows us great ease when coding. Let's see a quick example:

```python
# gen.yield.return.py
def geometric_progression(a, q):
    k = 0
    while True:
        result = a * q**k
        if result <= 100000:
            yield result
```

```
        else:
            return
        k += 1

for n in geometric_progression(2, 5):
    print(n)
```

The preceding code yields all terms of the geometric progression, a, aq, aq^2, aq^3, …. When the progression produces a term that is greater than `100000`, the generator stops (with a `return` statement). Running the code produces the following result:

```
$ python gen.yield.return.py
2
10
50
250
1250
6250
31250
```

The next term would have been `156250`, which is too big.

 Speaking about `StopIteration`, as of Python 3.5, the way that exceptions are handled in generators has changed. To understand the implications of the change is probably asking too much of you at this point, so just know that you can read all about it in PEP 479 (https://legacy.python.org/dev/peps/pep-0479/).

Going beyond next

At the beginning of this chapter, I told you that generator objects are based on the iteration protocol. We'll see in `Chapter 6`, *OOP, Decorators, and Iterators* a complete example of how to write a custom iterator/iterable object. For now, I just want you to understand how `next()` works.

What happens when you call `next(generator)` is that you're calling the `generator.__next__()` method. Remember, a **method** is just a function that belongs to an object, and objects in Python can have special methods. `__next__()` is just one of these and its purpose is to return the next element of the iteration, or to raise `StopIteration` when the iteration is over and there are no more elements to return.

If you recall, in Python, an object's special methods are also called **magic methods**, or **dunder** (from "double underscore") **methods**.

When we write a generator function, Python automatically transforms it into an object that is very similar to an iterator, and when we call `next(generator)`, that call is transformed in `generator.__next__()`. Let's revisit the previous example about generating squares:

```
# first.n.squares.manual.method.py
def get_squares_gen(n):
    for x in range(n):
        yield x ** 2

squares = get_squares_gen(3)
print(squares.__next__())  # prints: 0
print(squares.__next__())  # prints: 1
print(squares.__next__())  # prints: 4
# the following raises StopIteration, the generator is exhausted,
# any further call to next will keep raising StopIteration
```

The result is exactly as the previous example, only this time instead of using the `next(squares)` proxy call, we're directly calling `squares.__next__()`.

Generator objects have also three other methods that allow us to control their behavior: `send`, `throw`, and `close`. `send` allows us to communicate a value back to the generator object, while `throw` and `close`, respectively, allow us to raise an exception within the generator and close it. Their use is quite advanced and I won't be covering them here in detail, but I want to spend a few words on `send`, with a simple example:

```
# gen.send.preparation.py
def counter(start=0):
    n = start
    while True:
        yield n
        n += 1

c = counter()
print(next(c))  # prints: 0
print(next(c))  # prints: 1
print(next(c))  # prints: 2
```

The preceding iterator creates a generator object that will run forever. You can keep calling it, and it will never stop. Alternatively, you can put it in a `for` loop, for example, `for n in counter(): ...`, and it will go on forever as well. But what if you wanted to stop it at some point? One solution is to use a variable to control the `while` loop. Something such as this:

```
# gen.send.preparation.stop.py
stop = False
def counter(start=0):
    n = start
    while not stop:
        yield n
        n += 1

c = counter()
print(next(c))   # prints: 0
print(next(c))   # prints: 1
stop = True
print(next(c))   # raises StopIteration
```

This will do it. We start with `stop = False`, and until we change it to `True`, the generator will just keep going, like before. The moment we change stop to `True` though, the `while` loop will exit, and the next call will raise a `StopIteration` exception. This trick works, but I don't like it. We depend on an external variable, and this can lead to issues: what if another function changes that `stop`? Moreover, the code is scattered. In a nutshell, this isn't good enough.

We can make it better by using `generator.send()`. When we call `generator.send()`, the value that we feed to `send` will be passed in to the generator, execution is resumed, and we can fetch it via the `yield` expression. This is all very complicated when explained with words, so let's see an example:

```
# gen.send.py
def counter(start=0):
    n = start
    while True:
        result = yield n                # A
        print(type(result), result)     # B
        if result == 'Q':
            break
        n += 1

c = counter()
print(next(c))              # C
print(c.send('Wow!'))       # D
print(next(c))              # E
```

```
print(c.send('Q'))        # F
```

Execution of the preceding code produces the following:

```
$ python gen.send.py
0
<class 'str'> Wow!
1
<class 'NoneType'> None
2
<class 'str'> Q
Traceback (most recent call last):
  File "gen.send.py", line 14, in <module>
    print(c.send('Q')) # F
StopIteration
```

I think it's worth going through this code line by line, like if we were executing it, to see whether we can understand what's going on.

We start the generator execution with a call to next (#C). Within the generator, n is set to the same value as start. The while loop is entered, execution stops (#A) and n (0) is yielded back to the caller. 0 is printed on the console.

We then call send (#D), execution resumes, and result is set to 'Wow!' (still #A), then its type and value are printed on the console (#B). result is not 'Q', therefore n is incremented by 1 and execution goes back to the while condition, which, being True, evaluates to True (that wasn't hard to guess, right?). Another loop cycle begins, execution stops again (#A), and n (1) is yielded back to the caller. 1 is printed on the console.

At this point, we call next (#E), execution is resumed again (#A), and because we are not sending anything to the generator explicitly, Python behaves exactly like functions that are not using the return statement; the yield n expression (#A) returns None. result therefore is set to None, and its type and value are yet again printed on the console (#B). Execution continues, result is not 'Q' so n is incremented by 1, and we start another loop again. Execution stops again (#A) and n (2) is yielded back to the caller. 2 is printed on the console.

And now for the grand finale: we call send again (#F), but this time we pass in 'Q', therefore when execution is resumed, result is set to 'Q' (#A). Its type and value are printed on the console (#B), and then finally the if clause evaluates to True and the while loop is stopped by the break statement. The generator naturally terminates, which means a StopIteration exception is raised. You can see the print of its traceback on the last few lines printed on the console.

This is not at all simple to understand at first, so if it's not clear to you, don't be discouraged. You can keep reading on and then you can come back to this example after some time.

Using `send` allows for interesting patterns, and it's worth noting that `send` can also be used to start the execution of a generator (provided you call it with `None`).

The yield from expression

Another interesting construct is the `yield from` expression. This expression allows you to yield values from a sub iterator. Its use allows for quite advanced patterns, so let's just see a very quick example of it:

```
# gen.yield.for.py
def print_squares(start, end):
    for n in range(start, end):
        yield n ** 2

for n in print_squares(2, 5):
    print(n)
```

The previous code prints the numbers 4, 9, 16 on the console (on separate lines). By now, I expect you to be able to understand it by yourself, but let's quickly recap what happens. The `for` loop outside the function gets an iterator from `print_squares(2, 5)` and calls `next` on it until iteration is over. Every time the generator is called, execution is suspended (and later resumed) on `yield n ** 2`, which returns the square of the current n. Let's see how we can transform this code benefiting from the `yield from` expression:

```
# gen.yield.from.py
def print_squares(start, end):
    yield from (n ** 2 for n in range(start, end))

for n in print_squares(2, 5):
    print(n)
```

This code produces the same result, but as you can see `yield from` is actually running a sub iterator, `(n ** 2 ...)`. The `yield from` expression returns to the caller each value the sub iterator is producing. It's shorter and it reads better.

Generator expressions

Let's now talk about the other techniques to generate values one at a time.

The syntax is exactly the same as `list` comprehensions, only, instead of wrapping the comprehension with square brackets, you wrap it with round brackets. That is called a **generator expression**.

In general, generator expressions behave like equivalent `list` comprehensions, but there is one very important thing to remember: generators allow for one iteration only, then they will be exhausted. Let's see an example:

```
# generator.expressions.py
>>> cubes = [k**3 for k in range(10)]  # regular list
>>> cubes
[0, 1, 8, 27, 64, 125, 216, 343, 512, 729]
>>> type(cubes)
<class 'list'>
>>> cubes_gen = (k**3 for k in range(10))  # create as generator
>>> cubes_gen
<generator object <genexpr> at 0x103fb5a98>
>>> type(cubes_gen)
<class 'generator'>
>>> _(cubes_gen)  # this will exhaust the generator
[0, 1, 8, 27, 64, 125, 216, 343, 512, 729]
>>> _(cubes_gen)  # nothing more to give
[]
```

Look at the line in which the generator expression is created and assigned the name `cubes_gen`. You can see it's a generator object. In order to see its elements, we can use a `for` loop, a manual set of calls to `next`, or simply, feed it to a `list` constructor, which is what I did (remember I'm using _ as an alias).

Notice how, once the generator has been exhausted, there is no way to recover the same elements from it again. We need to recreate it if we want to use it from scratch again.

In the next few examples, let's see how to reproduce `map` and `filter` using generator expressions:

```
# gen.map.py
def adder(*n):
    return sum(n)
s1 = sum(map(lambda *n: adder(*n), range(100), range(1, 101)))
s2 = sum(adder(*n) for n in zip(range(100), range(1, 101)))
```

In the previous example, s1 and s2 are exactly the same: they are the sum of `adder(0, 1)`, `adder(1, 2)`, `adder(2, 3)`, and so on, which translates to `sum(1, 3, 5, ...)`. The syntax is different, though I find the generator expression to be much more readable:

```
# gen.filter.py
cubes = [x**3 for x in range(10)]

odd_cubes1 = filter(lambda cube: cube % 2, cubes)
odd_cubes2 = (cube for cube in cubes if cube % 2)
```

In the previous example, `odd_cubes1` and `odd_cubes2` are the same: they generate a sequence of odd cubes. Yet again, I prefer the generator syntax. This should be evident when things get a little more complicated:

```
# gen.map.filter.py
N = 20
cubes1 = map(
    lambda n: (n, n**3),
    filter(lambda n: n % 3 == 0 or n % 5 == 0, range(N))
)
cubes2 = (
    (n, n**3) for n in range(N) if n % 3 == 0 or n % 5 == 0)
```

The preceding code creates two generators, `cubes1` and `cubes2`. They are exactly the same, and return two-tuples (n, n^3) when n is a multiple of 3 or 5.

If you print the list(cubes1), you get: `[(0, 0), (3, 27), (5, 125), (6, 216), (9, 729), (10, 1000), (12, 1728), (15, 3375), (18, 5832)]`.

See how much better the generator expression reads? It may be debatable when things are very simple, but as soon as you start nesting functions a bit, like we did in this example, the superiority of the generator syntax is evident. It's shorter, simpler, and more elegant.

Now, let me ask you a question—what is the difference between the following lines of code:

```
# sum.example.py
s1 = sum([n**2 for n in range(10**6)])
s2 = sum((n**2 for n in range(10**6)))
s3 = sum(n**2 for n in range(10**6))
```

Strictly speaking, they all produce the same sum. The expressions to get s2 and s3 are exactly the same because the brackets in s2 are redundant. They are both generator expressions inside the sum function. The expression to get s1 is different though. Inside sum, we find a list comprehension. This means that in order to calculate s1, the sum function has to call next on a list a million times.

Do you see where we're losing time and memory? Before `sum` can start calling `next` on that list, the list needs to have been created, which is a waste of time and space. It's much better for `sum` to call `next` on a simple generator expression. There is no need to have all the numbers from `range(10**6)` stored in a list.

So, *watch out for extra parentheses when you write your expressions*: sometimes it's easy to skip over these details, which makes our code very different. If you don't believe me, check out the following code:

```
# sum.example.2.py
s = sum([n**2 for n in range(10**8)])   # this is killed
# s = sum(n**2 for n in range(10**8))    # this succeeds
print(s)  # prints: 333333328333333350000000
```

Try running the preceding example. If I run the first line on my old Linux box with 8 GB RAM, this is what I get:

```
$ python sum.example.2.py
Killed
```

On the other hand, if I comment out the first line, and uncomment the second one, this is the result:

```
$ python sum.example.2.py
333333328333333350000000
```

Sweet generator expressions. The difference between the two lines is that in the first one, a list with the squares of the first hundred million numbers must be made before being able to sum them up. That list is huge, and we ran out of memory (at least, my box did, if yours doesn't try a bigger number), therefore Python kills the process for us. Sad face.

But when we remove the square brackets, we don't have a list any more. The `sum` function receives 0, 1, 4, 9, and so on until the last one, and sums them up. No problems, happy face.

Some performance considerations

So, we've seen that we have many different ways to achieve the same result. We can use any combination of `map`, `zip`, and `filter`, or choose to go with a comprehension, or maybe choose to use a generator, either function or expression. We may even decide to go with `for` loops; when the logic to apply to each running parameter isn't simple, they may be the best option.

Other than readability concerns though, let's talk about performance. When it comes to performance, usually there are two factors that play a major role: **space** and **time**.

Space means the size of the memory that a data structure is going to take up. The best way to choose is to ask yourself if you really need a list (or tuple) or if a simple generator function would work as well. If the answer is yes, go with the generator, it'll save a lot of space. The same goes for functions; if you don't actually need them to return a list or tuple, then you can transform them into generator functions as well.

Sometimes, you will have to use lists (or tuples), for example there are algorithms that scan sequences using multiple pointers or maybe they run over the sequence more than once. A generator function (or expression) can be iterated over only once and then it's exhausted, so in these situations, it wouldn't be the right choice.

Time is a bit harder than space because it depends on more variables and therefore it isn't possible to state that *X is faster than Y* with absolute certainty for all cases. However, based on tests run on Python today, we can say that on average, map exhibits performances similar to list comprehensions and generator expressions, while for loops are consistently slower.

In order to appreciate the reasoning behind these statements fully, we need to understand how Python works, and this is a bit outside the scope of this book, as it's too technical in detail. Let's just say that map and list comprehensions run at C-language speed within the interpreter, while a Python for loop is run as Python bytecode within the Python Virtual Machine, which is often much slower.

 There are several different implementations of Python. The original one, and still the most common one, is CPython (https://github.com/python/cpython), which is written in C. C is one of the most powerful and popular programming languages still used today.

How about we do a small exercise and try to find out whether the claims I made are accurate? I will write a small piece of code that collects the results of divmod(a, b) for a certain set of integer pairs, (a, b). I will use the time function from the time module to calculate the elapsed time of the operations that I will perform:

```
# performances.py
from time import time
mx = 5000

t = time()  # start time for the for loop
floop = []
for a in range(1, mx):
    for b in range(a, mx):
```

```
        floop.append(divmod(a, b))
print('for loop: {:.4f} s'.format(time() - t))   # elapsed time

t = time()  # start time for the list comprehension
compr = [
    divmod(a, b) for a in range(1, mx) for b in range(a, mx)]
print('list comprehension: {:.4f} s'.format(time() - t))

t = time()  # start time for the generator expression
gener = list(
    divmod(a, b) for a in range(1, mx) for b in range(a, mx))
print('generator expression: {:.4f} s'.format(time() - t))
```

As you can see, we're creating three lists: `floop`, `compr`, and `gener`. Running the code produces the following:

```
$ python performances.py
for loop: 4.4814 s
list comprehension: 3.0210 s
generator expression: 3.4334 s
```

The `list` comprehension runs in ~67% of the time taken by the `for` loop. That's impressive. The generator expression came quite close to that, with a good ~77%. The reason the generator expression is slower is that we need to feed it to the `list()` constructor, and this has a little bit more overhead compared to a sheer `list` comprehension. If I didn't have to retain the results of those calculations, a generator would probably have been a more suitable option.

An interesting result is to notice that, within the body of the `for` loop, we're appending data to a list. This implies that Python does the work, behind the scenes, of resizing it every now and then, allocating space for items to be appended. I guessed that creating a list of zeros, and simply filling it with the results, might have sped up the `for` loop, but I was wrong. Check it for yourself, you just need `mx * (mx - 1) // 2` elements to be preallocated.

Let's see a similar example that compares a `for` loop and a `map` call:

```
# performances.map.py
from time import time
mx = 2 * 10 ** 7

t = time()
absloop = []
for n in range(mx):
    absloop.append(abs(n))
print('for loop: {:.4f} s'.format(time() - t))
```

```
t = time()
abslist = [abs(n) for n in range(mx)]
print('list comprehension: {:.4f} s'.format(time() - t))

t = time()
absmap = list(map(abs, range(mx)))
print('map: {:.4f} s'.format(time() - t))
```

This code is conceptually very similar to the previous example. The only thing that has changed is that we're applying the `abs` function instead of the `divmod` one, and we have only one loop instead of two nested ones. Execution gives the following result:

```
$ python performances.map.py
for loop: 3.8948 s
list comprehension: 1.8594 s
map: 1.1548 s
```

And `map` wins the race: ~62% of the `list` comprehension and ~30% of the `for` loop. Take these results with a pinch of salt, as things might be different according to various factors, such as OS and Python version. But in general, I think it's safe to say that these results are good enough for having an idea when it comes to coding for performance.

Apart from the case-by-case little differences though, it's quite clear that the `for` loop option is the slowest one, so let's see why we still want to use it.

Don't overdo comprehensions and generators

We've seen how powerful `list` comprehensions and generator expressions can be. And they are, don't get me wrong, but the feeling that I have when I deal with them is that their complexity grows exponentially. The more you try to do within a single comprehension or a generator expression, the harder it becomes to read, understand, and therefore maintain or change.

If you check the Zen of Python again, there are a few lines that I think are worth keeping in mind when dealing with optimized code:

```
>>> import this
...
Explicit is better than implicit.
Simple is better than complex.
...
Readability counts.
...
If the implementation is hard to explain, it's a bad idea.
...
```

Comprehensions and generator expressions are more implicit than explicit, can be quite difficult to read and understand, and they can be hard to explain. Sometimes you have to break them apart using the inside-out technique, to understand what's going on.

To give you an example, let's talk a bit more about Pythagorean triples. Just to remind you, a Pythagorean triple is a tuple of positive integers (a, b, c) such that $a^2 + b^2 = c^2$.

We saw how to calculate them in the *Filtering a comprehension* section, but we did it in a very inefficient way because we were scanning all pairs of numbers below a certain threshold, calculating the hypotenuse, and filtering out those that were not producing a triple.

A better way to get a list of Pythagorean triples is to generate them directly. There are many different formulas you can use to do this, we'll use the **Euclidean formula**.

This formula says that any triple (a, b, c), where $a = m^2 - n^2$, $b = 2mn$, $c = m^2 + n^2$, with m and n positive integers such that $m > n$, is a Pythagorean triple. For example, when $m = 2$ and $n = 1$, we find the smallest triple: $(3, 4, 5)$.

There is one catch though: consider the triple $(6, 8, 10)$ that is just like $(3, 4, 5)$ with all the numbers multiplied by 2. This triple is definitely Pythagorean, since $6^2 + 8^2 = 10^2$, but we can derive it from $(3, 4, 5)$ simply by multiplying each of its elements by 2. Same goes for $(9, 12, 15)$, $(12, 16, 20)$, and in general for all the triples that we can write as $(3k, 4k, 5k)$, with k being a positive integer greater than 1.

A triple that cannot be obtained by multiplying the elements of another one by some factor, k, is called **primitive**. Another way of stating this is: if the three elements of a triple are **coprime**, then the triple is primitive. Two numbers are coprime when they don't share any prime factor amongst their divisors, that is, their **greatest common divisor** (GCD) is 1. For example, 3 and 5 are coprime, while 3 and 6 are not, because they are both divisible by 3.

So, the Euclidean formula tells us that if m and n are coprime, and $m - n$ is odd, the triple they generate is *primitive*. In the following example, we will write a generator expression to calculate all the primitive Pythagorean triples whose hypotenuse (c) is less than or equal to some integer, N. This means we want all triples for which $m^2 + n^2 \leq N$. When n is 1, the formula looks like this: $m^2 \leq N - 1$, which means we can approximate the calculation with an upper bound of $m \leq N^{1/2}$.

So, to recap: m must be greater than n, they must also be coprime, and their difference $m - n$ must be odd. Moreover, in order to avoid useless calculations, we'll put the upper bound for m at *floor(sqrt(N)) + 1*.

 The `floor` function for a real number, x, gives the maximum integer, n, such that $n < x$, for example, *floor(3.8) = 3, floor(13.1) = 13*.
Taking *floor(sqrt(N)) + 1* means taking the integer part of the square root of N and adding a minimal margin just to make sure we don't miss any numbers.

Let's put all of this into code, step by step. Let's start by writing a simple `gcd` function that uses **Euclid's algorithm**:

```
# functions.py
def gcd(a, b):
    """Calculate the Greatest Common Divisor of (a, b). """
    while b != 0:
        a, b = b, a % b
    return a
```

The explanation of Euclid's algorithm is available on the web, so I won't spend any time here talking about it; we need to focus on the generator expression. The next step is to use the knowledge we gathered before to generate a list of primitive Pythagorean triples:

```
# pythagorean.triple.generation.py
from functions import gcd
N = 50

triples = sorted(                                      # 1
    ((a, b, c) for a, b, c in (                        # 2
        ((m**2 - n**2), (2 * m * n), (m**2 + n**2))    # 3
        for m in range(1, int(N**.5) + 1)              # 4
        for n in range(1, m)                           # 5
        if (m - n) % 2 and gcd(m, n) == 1              # 6
    ) if c <= N), key=lambda *triple: sum(*triple)     # 7
)
```

[171]

There you go. It's not easy to read, so let's go through it line by line. At #3, we start a generator expression that is creating triples. You can see from #4 and #5 that we're looping on m in *[1, M]* with *M* being the integer part of *sqrt(N)*, plus *1*. On the other hand, n loops within *[1, m)*, to respect the *m > n* rule. It's worth noting how I calculated *sqrt(N)*, that is, N**.5, which is just another way to do it that I wanted to show you.

At #6, you can see the filtering conditions to make the triples primitive: (m - n) % 2 evaluates to True when (m - n) is odd, and gcd(m, n) == 1 means m and n are coprime. With these in place, we know the triples will be primitive. This takes care of the innermost generator expression. The outermost one starts at #2, and finishes at #7. We take the triples (*a, b, c*) in (...innermost generator...) such that c <= N.

Finally, at #1 we apply sorting, to present the list in order. At #7, after the outermost generator expression is closed, you can see that we specify the sorting key to be the sum *a + b + c*. This is just my personal preference, there is no mathematical reason behind it.

So, what do you think? Was it straightforward to read? I don't think so. And believe me, this is still a simple example; I have seen much worse in my career. This kind of code is difficult to understand, debug, and modify. It shouldn't find a place in a professional environment.

So, let's see if we can rewrite this code into something more readable:

```
# pythagorean.triple.generation.for.py
from functions import gcd

def gen_triples(N):
    for m in range(1, int(N**.5) + 1):            # 1
        for n in range(1, m):                      # 2
            if (m - n) % 2 and gcd(m, n) == 1:     # 3
                c = m**2 + n**2                      # 4
                if c <= N:                           # 5
                    a = m**2 - n**2                  # 6
                    b = 2 * m * n                    # 7
                    yield (a, b, c)                  # 8

triples = sorted(
    gen_triples(50), key=lambda *triple: sum(*triple))  # 9
```

This is so much better. Let's go through it, line by line. You'll see how much easier it is to understand.

We start looping at #1 and #2, in exactly the same way we were looping in the previous example. On line #3, we have the filtering for primitive triples. On line #4, we deviate a bit from what we were doing before: we calculate c, and on line #5, we filter on c being less than or equal to N. Only when c satisfies that condition, we do calculate a and b, and yield the resulting tuple. It's always good to delay all calculations for as much as possible so that we don't waste time and CPU. On the last line, we apply sorting with the same key we were using in the generator expression example.

I hope you agree, this example is easier to understand. And I promise you, if you have to modify the code one day, you'll find that modifying this one is easy, while to modify the other version will take much longer (and it will be more error-prone).

If you print the results of both examples (they are the same), you will get this:

```
[(3, 4, 5), (5, 12, 13), (15, 8, 17), (7, 24, 25), (21, 20, 29), (35, 12,
37), (9, 40, 41)]
```

The moral of the story is, try and use comprehensions and generator expressions as much as you can, but if the code starts to be complicated to modify or to read, you may want to refactor it into something more readable. Your colleagues will thank you.

Name localization

Now that we are familiar with all types of comprehensions and generator expression, let's talk about name localization within them. Python 3.* localizes loop variables in all four forms of comprehensions: list, dict, set, and generator expressions. This behavior is therefore different from that of the for loop. Let's see a simple example to show all the cases:

```
# scopes.py
A = 100
ex1 = [A for A in range(5)]
print(A)   # prints: 100

ex2 = list(A for A in range(5))
print(A)   # prints: 100

ex3 = dict((A, 2 * A) for A in range(5))
print(A)   # prints: 100
```

```
ex4 = set(A for A in range(5))
print(A)   # prints: 100

s = 0
for A in range(5):
    s += A
print(A)   # prints: 4
```

In the preceding code, we declare a global name, `A = 100`, and then we exercise the four comprehensions: `list`, generator expression, dictionary, and `set`. None of them alter the global name, `A`. Conversely, you can see at the end that the `for` loop modifies it. The last print statement prints `4`.

Let's see what happens if `A` wasn't there:

```
# scopes.noglobal.py
ex1 = [A for A in range(5)]
print(A)   # breaks: NameError: name 'A' is not defined
```

The preceding code would work the same with any of the four types of comprehensions. After we run the first line, `A` is not defined in the global namespace. Once again, the `for` loop behaves differently:

```
# scopes.for.py
s = 0
for A in range(5):
    s += A
print(A) # prints: 4
print(globals())
```

The preceding code shows that after a `for` loop, if the loop variable wasn't defined before it, we can find it in the global frame. To make sure of it, let's take a peek at it by calling the `globals()` built-in function:

```
$ python scopes.for.py
4
{'__name__': '__main__', '__doc__': None, ..., 's': 10, 'A': 4}
```

Together with a lot of other boilerplate stuff that I have omitted, we can spot `'A': 4`.

Generation behavior in built-ins

Among the built-in types, the generation behavior is now quite common. This is a major difference between Python 2 and Python 3. A lot of functions, such as `map`, `zip`, and `filter`, have been transformed so that they return objects that behave like iterables. The idea behind this change is that if you need to make a list of those results, you can always wrap the call in a `list()` class, and you're done. On the other hand, if you just need to iterate and want to keep the impact on memory as light as possible, you can use those functions safely.

Another notable example is the `range` function. In Python 2 it returns a list, and there is another function called `xrange` that returns an object that you can iterate on, which generates the numbers on the fly. In Python 3 this function has gone, and `range` now behaves like it.

But this concept, in general, is now quite widespread. You can find it in the `open()` function, which is used to operate on file objects (we'll see it in *Chapter 7, Files and Data Persistence*), but also in `enumerate`, in the dictionary `keys`, `values`, and `items` methods, and several other places.

It all makes sense: Python's aim is to try to reduce the memory footprint by avoiding wasting space wherever possible, especially in those functions and methods that are used extensively in most situations.

Do you remember at the beginning of this chapter? I said that it makes more sense to optimize the performances of code that has to deal with a lot of objects, rather than shaving off a few milliseconds from a function that we call twice a day.

One last example

Before we finish this chapter, I'll show you a simple problem that I used to submit to candidates for a Python developer role in a company I used to work for.

The problem is the following: given the sequence `0 1 1 2 3 5 8 13 21 ...`, write a function that would return the terms of this sequence up to some limit, `N`.

If you haven't recognized it, that is the Fibonacci sequence, which is defined as *F(0) = 0, F(1) = 1* and, for any *n > 1, F(n) = F(n-1) + F(n-2)*. This sequence is excellent to test knowledge about recursion, memoization techniques, and other technical details, but in this case, it was a good opportunity to check whether the candidate knew about generators.

Let's start from a rudimentary version of a function, and then improve on it:

```
# fibonacci.first.py
def fibonacci(N):
    """Return all fibonacci numbers up to N. """
    result = [0]
    next_n = 1
    while next_n <= N:
        result.append(next_n)
        next_n = sum(result[-2:])
    return result

print(fibonacci(0))     # [0]
print(fibonacci(1))     # [0, 1, 1]
print(fibonacci(50))    # [0, 1, 1, 2, 3, 5, 8, 13, 21, 34]
```

From the top: we set up the `result` list to a starting value of `[0]`. Then we start the iteration from the next element (`next_n`), which is `1`. While the next element is not greater than `N`, we keep appending it to the list and calculating the next. We calculate the next element by taking a slice of the last two elements in the `result` list and passing it to the `sum` function. Add some `print` statements here and there if this is not clear to you, but by now I would expect it not to be an issue.

When the condition of the `while` loop evaluates to `False`, we exit the loop and return `result`. You can see the result of those `print` statements in the comments next to each of them.

At this point, I would ask the candidate the following question: *What if I just wanted to iterate over those numbers?* A good candidate would then change the code to what you'll find here (an excellent candidate would have started with it!):

```
# fibonacci.second.py
def fibonacci(N):
    """Return all fibonacci numbers up to N. """
    yield 0
    if N == 0:
        return
    a = 0
    b = 1
    while b <= N:
        yield b
        a, b = b, a + b

print(list(fibonacci(0)))     # [0]
print(list(fibonacci(1)))     # [0, 1, 1]
print(list(fibonacci(50)))    # [0, 1, 1, 2, 3, 5, 8, 13, 21, 34]
```

This is actually one of the solutions I was given. I don't know why I kept it, but I'm glad I did so I can show it to you. Now, the `fibonacci` function is a *generator function*. First we yield 0, then if N is 0, we return (this will cause a `StopIteration` exception to be raised). If that's not the case, we start iterating, yielding `b` at every loop cycle, and then updating `a` and `b`. All we need in order to be able to produce the next element of the sequence is the past two: `a` and `b`, respectively.

This code is much better, has a lighter memory footprint and all we have to do to get a list of Fibonacci numbers is to wrap the call with `list()`, as usual. But what about elegance? I can't leave it like that, can I? Let's try the following:

```python
# fibonacci.elegant.py
def fibonacci(N):
    """Return all fibonacci numbers up to N. """
    a, b = 0, 1
    while a <= N:
        yield a
        a, b = b, a + b
```

Much better. The whole body of the function is four lines, five if you count the docstring. Notice how, in this case, using tuple assignment (`a, b = 0, 1` and `a, b = b, a + b`) helps in making the code shorter, and more readable.

Summary

In this chapter, we explored the concept of iteration and generation a bit more deeply. We looked at the `map`, `zip`, and `filter` functions in detail, and learned how to use them as an alternative to a regular `for` loop approach.

Then we covered the concept of comprehensions, for lists, dictionaries, and sets. We explored their syntax and how to use them as an alternative to both the classic `for` loop approach and also to the use of the `map`, `zip`, and `filter` functions.

Finally, we talked about the concept of generation, in two forms: generator functions and expressions. We learned how to save time and space by using generation techniques and saw how they can make possible what wouldn't normally be if we used a conventional approach based on lists.

We talked about performance, and saw that `for` loops are last in terms of speed, but they provide the best readability and flexibility to change. On the other hand, functions such as `map` and `filter`, and `list` comprehensions, can be much faster.

The complexity of the code written using these techniques grows exponentially so, in order to favor readability and ease of maintainability, we still need to use the classic `for` loop approach at times. Another difference is in the name localization, where the `for` loop behaves differently from all other types of comprehensions.

The next chapter will be all about objects and classes. It is structurally similar to this one, in that we won't explore many different subjects, just a few of them, but we'll try to dive into them a little bit more deeply.

Make sure you understand the concepts of this chapter before moving on to the next one. We're building a wall brick by brick, and if the foundation is not solid, we won't get very far.

OOP, Decorators, and Iterators

6

La classe non è acqua. (Class will out)

– Italian saying

I could probably write a whole book about **object-oriented programming** (**OOP**) and classes. In this chapter, I'm facing the hard challenge of finding the balance between breadth and depth. There are simply too many things to tell, and plenty of them would take more than this whole chapter if I described them in depth. Therefore, I will try to give you what I think is a good panoramic view of the fundamentals, plus a few things that may come in handy in the next chapters. Python's official documentation will help in filling the gaps.

In this chapter, we are going to cover the following topics:

- Decorators
- OOP with Python
- Iterators

Decorators

In Chapter 5, *Saving Time and Memory*, I measured the execution time of various expressions. If you recall, I had to initialize a variable to the start time, and subtract it from the current time after execution in order to calculate the elapsed time. I also printed it on the console after each measurement. That was very tedious.

Every time you find yourself repeating things, an alarm bell should go off. Can you put that code in a function and avoid repetition? The answer most of the time is *yes*, so let's look at an example:

```
# decorators/time.measure.start.py
from time import sleep, time

def f():
    sleep(.3)

def g():
    sleep(.5)

t = time()
f()
print('f took:', time() - t)  # f took: 0.3001396656036377

t = time()
g()
print('g took:', time() - t)  # g took: 0.5039339065551758
```

In the preceding code, I defined two functions, f and g, which do nothing but sleep (by 0.3 and 0.5 seconds, respectively). I used the sleep function to suspend the execution for the desired amount of time. Notice how the time measure is pretty accurate. Now, how do we avoid repeating that code and those calculations? One first potential approach could be the following:

```
# decorators/time.measure.dry.py
from time import sleep, time

def f():
    sleep(.3)

def g():
    sleep(.5)

def measure(func):
    t = time()
    func()
    print(func.__name__, 'took:', time() - t)

measure(f)  # f took: 0.30434322357177734
measure(g)  # g took: 0.5048270225524902
```

Ah, much better now. The whole timing mechanism has been encapsulated into a function so we don't repeat code. We print the function name dynamically and it's easy enough to code. What if we need to pass arguments to the function we measure? This code would get just a bit more complicated, so let's see an example:

```
# decorators/time.measure.arguments.py
from time import sleep, time

def f(sleep_time=0.1):
    sleep(sleep_time)

def measure(func, *args, **kwargs):
    t = time()
    func(*args, **kwargs)
    print(func.__name__, 'took:', time() - t)

measure(f, sleep_time=0.3)  # f took: 0.30056095123291016
measure(f, 0.2)  # f took: 0.2033553123474121
```

Now, f is expecting to be fed sleep_time (with a default value of 0.1), so we don't need g any more. I also had to change the measure function so that it is now accepts a function, any variable positional arguments, and any variable keyword arguments. In this way, whatever we call measure with, we redirect those arguments to the call to func we do inside.

This is very good, but we can push it a little bit further. Let's say we want to somehow have that timing behavior built-in into the f function, so that we could just call it and have that measure taken. Here's how we could do it:

```
# decorators/time.measure.deco1.py
from time import sleep, time

def f(sleep_time=0.1):
    sleep(sleep_time)

def measure(func):
    def wrapper(*args, **kwargs):
        t = time()
        func(*args, **kwargs)
        print(func.__name__, 'took:', time() - t)
    return wrapper

f = measure(f)  # decoration point
```

```
f(0.2)  # f took: 0.20372915267944336
f(sleep_time=0.3)  # f took: 0.30455899238586426
print(f.__name__)  # wrapper <- ouch!
```

The preceding code is probably not so straightforward. Let's see what happens here. The magic is in the **decoration point**. We basically reassign f with whatever is returned by measure when we call it with f as an argument. Within measure, we define another function, wrapper, and then we return it. So, the net effect is that after the decoration point, when we call f, we're actually calling wrapper. Since the wrapper inside is calling func, which is f, we are actually closing the loop like that. If you don't believe me, take a look at the last line.

wrapper is actually... a wrapper. It takes variable and positional arguments, and calls f with them. It also does the time measurement calculation around the call.

This technique is called **decoration**, and measure is, effectively, a **decorator**. This paradigm became so popular and widely used that at some point, Python added a special syntax for it (check out https://www.python.org/dev/peps/pep-0318/). Let's explore three cases: one decorator, two decorators, and one decorator that takes arguments:

```
# decorators/syntax.py
def func(arg1, arg2, ...):
    pass
func = decorator(func)

# is equivalent to the following:

@decorator
def func(arg1, arg2, ...):
    pass
```

Basically, instead of manually reassigning the function to what was returned by the decorator, we prepend the definition of the function with the special syntax, @decorator_name.

We can apply multiple decorators to the same function in the following way:

```
# decorators/syntax.py
def func(arg1, arg2, ...):
    pass
func = deco1(deco2(func))

# is equivalent to the following:

@deco1
@deco2
```

```
def func(arg1, arg2, ...):
    pass
```

When applying multiple decorators, pay attention to the order. In the preceding example, `func` is decorated with `deco2` first, and the result is decorated with `deco1`. A good rule of thumb is: *the closer the decorator is to the function, the sooner it is applied.*

Some decorators can take arguments. This technique is generally used to produce other decorators. Let's look at the syntax, and then we'll see an example of it:

```
# decorators/syntax.py
def func(arg1, arg2, ...):
    pass
func = decoarg(arg_a, arg_b)(func)

# is equivalent to the following:

@decoarg(arg_a, arg_b)
def func(arg1, arg2, ...):
    pass
```

As you can see, this case is a bit different. First, `decoarg` is called with the given arguments, and then its return value (the actual decorator) is called with `func`. Before I give you another example, let's fix one thing that is bothering me. I don't want to lose the original function name and docstring (and other attributes as well, check the documentation for the details) when I decorate it. But because inside our decorator we return `wrapper`, the original attributes from `func` are lost and `f` ends up being assigned the attributes of `wrapper`. There is an easy fix for that from the beautiful `functools` module. I will fix the last example, and I will also rewrite its syntax to use the `@` operator:

```
# decorators/time.measure.deco2.py
from time import sleep, time
from functools import wraps

def measure(func):
    @wraps(func)
    def wrapper(*args, **kwargs):
        t = time()
        func(*args, **kwargs)
        print(func.__name__, 'took:', time() - t)
    return wrapper

@measure
def f(sleep_time=0.1):
    """I'm a cat. I love to sleep! """
    sleep(sleep_time)
```

```
f(sleep_time=0.3)  # f took: 0.3010902404785156
print(f.__name__, ':', f.__doc__)  # f : I'm a cat. I love to sleep!
```

Now we're talking! As you can see, all we need to do is to tell Python that `wrapper` actually wraps `func` (by means of the `wraps` function), and you can see that the original name and docstring are now maintained.

Let's see another example. I want a decorator that prints an error message when the result of a function is greater than a certain threshold. I will also take this opportunity to show you how to apply two decorators at once:

```
# decorators/two.decorators.py
from time import sleep, time
from functools import wraps

def measure(func):
    @wraps(func)
    def wrapper(*args, **kwargs):
        t = time()
        result = func(*args, **kwargs)
        print(func.__name__, 'took:', time() - t)
        return result
    return wrapper

def max_result(func):
    @wraps(func)
    def wrapper(*args, **kwargs):
        result = func(*args, **kwargs)
        if result > 100:
            print('Result is too big ({0}). Max allowed is 100.'
                  .format(result))
        return result
    return wrapper

@measure
@max_result
def cube(n):
    return n ** 3

print(cube(2))
print(cube(5))
```

Take your time in studying the preceding example until you are sure you understand it well. If you do, I don't think there is any decorator you now won't be able to write.

I had to enhance the `measure` decorator, so that its `wrapper` now returns the result of the call to `func`. The `max_result` decorator does that as well, but before returning, it checks that `result` is not greater than `100`, which is the maximum allowed. I decorated `cube` with both of them. First, `max_result` is applied, then `measure`. Running this code yields this result:

```
$ python two.decorators.py
cube took: 3.0994415283203125e-06
8

Result is too big (125). Max allowed is 100.
cube took: 1.0013580322265625e-05
125
```

For your convenience, I have separated the results of the two calls with a blank line. In the first call, the result is 8, which passes the threshold check. The running time is measured and printed. Finally, we print the result (8).

On the second call, the result is 125, so the error message is printed, the result returned, and then it's the turn of `measure`, which prints the running time again, and finally, we print the result (125).

Had I decorated the `cube` function with the same two decorators but in a different order, the error message would have followed the line that prints the running time, instead of have preceded it.

A decorator factory

Let's simplify this example now, going back to a single decorator: `max_result`. I want to make it so that I can decorate different functions with different thresholds, as I don't want to write one decorator for each threshold. Let's amend `max_result` so that it allows us to decorate functions specifying the threshold dynamically:

```python
# decorators/decorators.factory.py
from functools import wraps

def max_result(threshold):
    def decorator(func):
```

```
        @wraps(func)
        def wrapper(*args, **kwargs):
            result = func(*args, **kwargs)
            if result > threshold:
                print(
                    'Result is too big ({0}). Max allowed is {1}.'
                    .format(result, threshold))
            return result
        return wrapper
    return decorator

@max_result(75)
def cube(n):
    return n ** 3

print(cube(5))
```

The preceding code shows you how to write a **decorator factory**. If you recall, decorating a function with a decorator that takes arguments is the same as writing func = decorator(argA, argB)(func), so when we decorate cube with max_result(75), we're doing cube = max_result(75)(cube).

Let's go through what happens, step by step. When we call max_result(75), we enter its body. A decorator function is defined inside, which takes a function as its only argument. Inside that function, the usual decorator trick is performed. We define wrapper, inside of which we check the result of the original function's call. The beauty of this approach is that from the innermost level, we can still refer to as both func and threshold, which allows us to set the threshold dynamically.

wrapper **returns** result, decorator **returns** wrapper, and max_result **returns** decorator. This means that our cube = max_result(75)(cube) call actually becomes cube = decorator(cube). Not just any decorator though, but one for which threshold has a value of 75. This is achieved by a mechanism called **closure**, which is outside of the scope of this chapter but still very interesting, so I mentioned it for you to do some research on it.

Running the last example produces the following result:

```
$ python decorators.factory.py
Result is too big (125). Max allowed is 75.
125
```

The preceding code allows me to use the `max_result` decorator with different thresholds at my own will, like this:

```
# decorators/decorators.factory.py
@max_result(75)
def cube(n):
    return n ** 3

@max_result(100)
def square(n):
    return n ** 2

@max_result(1000)
def multiply(a, b):
    return a * b
```

Note that every decoration uses a different `threshold` value.

Decorators are very popular in Python. They are used quite often and they simplify (and beautify, I dare say) the code a lot.

Object-oriented programming (OOP)

It's been quite a long and hopefully nice journey and, by now, we should be ready to explore OOP. I'll use the definition from Kindler, E.; Krivy, I. (2011). *Object-oriented simulation of systems with sophisticated control* by *International Journal of General Systems*, and adapt it to Python:

> *Object-oriented programming (OOP) is a programming paradigm based on the concept of "objects", which are data structures that contain data, in the form of attributes, and code, in the form of functions known as methods. A distinguishing feature of objects is that an object's method can access and often modify the data attributes of the object with which they are associated (objects have a notion of "self"). In OO programming, computer programs are designed by making them out of objects that interact with one another.*

Python has full support for this paradigm. Actually, as we have already said, *everything in Python is an object*, so this shows that OOP is not just supported by Python, but it's a part of its very core.

The two main players in OOP are **objects** and **classes**. Classes are used to create objects (objects are instances of the classes from which they were created), so we could see them as instance factories. When objects are created by a class, they inherit the class attributes and methods. They represent concrete items in the program's domain.

The simplest Python class

I will start with the simplest class you could ever write in Python:

```
# oop/simplest.class.py
class Simplest():  # when empty, the braces are optional
    pass

print(type(Simplest))  # what type is this object?
simp = Simplest()  # we create an instance of Simplest: simp
print(type(simp))  # what type is simp?
# is simp an instance of Simplest?
print(type(simp) == Simplest)  # There's a better way for this
```

Let's run the preceding code and explain it line by line:

```
$ python simplest.class.py
<class 'type'>
<class '__main__.Simplest'>
True
```

The `Simplest` class I defined has only the `pass` instruction in its body, which means it doesn't have any custom attributes or methods. Brackets after the name are optional if empty. I will print its type (`__main__` is the name of the scope in which top-level code executes), and I am aware that, in the comment, I wrote *object* instead of *class*. It turns out that, as you can see by the result of that `print`, *classes are actually objects*. To be precise, they are instances of `type`. Explaining this concept would lead us to a talk about **metaclasses** and **metaprogramming**, advanced concepts that require a solid grasp of the fundamentals to be understood and are beyond the scope of this chapter. As usual, I mentioned it to leave a pointer for you, for when you'll be ready to dig deeper.

Let's go back to the example: I used `Simplest` to create an instance, `simp`. You can see that the syntax to create an instance is the same as we use to call a function. Then we print what type `simp` belongs to and we verify that `simp` is in fact an instance of `Simplest`. I'll show you a better way of doing this later on in the chapter.

Up to now, it's all very simple. What happens when we write `class ClassName():` `pass`, though? Well, what Python does is create a class object and assign it a name. This is very similar to what happens when we declare a function using `def`.

Class and object namespaces

After the class object has been created (which usually happens when the module is first imported), it basically represents a namespace. We can call that class to create its instances. Each instance inherits the class attributes and methods and is given its own namespace. We already know that, to walk a namespace, all we need to do is to use the dot (.) operator.

Let's look at another example:

```
# oop/class.namespaces.py
class Person:
    species = 'Human'

print(Person.species)   # Human
Person.alive = True   # Added dynamically!
print(Person.alive)   # True

man = Person()
print(man.species)   # Human (inherited)
print(man.alive)   # True (inherited)

Person.alive = False
print(man.alive)   # False (inherited)

man.name = 'Darth'
man.surname = 'Vader'
print(man.name, man.surname)   # Darth Vader
```

In the preceding example, I have defined a class attribute called species. Any variable defined in the body of a class is an attribute that belongs to that class. In the code, I have also defined Person.alive, which is another class attribute. You can see that there is no restriction on accessing that attribute from the class. You can see that man, which is an instance of Person, inherits both of them, and reflects them instantly when they change.

man has also two attributes that belong to its own namespace and therefore are called **instance attributes**: name and surname.

 Class attributes are shared among all instances, while instance attributes are not; therefore, you should use class attributes to provide the states and behaviors to be shared by all instances, and use instance attributes for data that belongs just to one specific object.

Attribute shadowing

When you search for an attribute in an object, if it is not found, Python keeps searching in the class that was used to create that object (and keeps searching until it's either found or the end of the inheritance chain is reached). This leads to an interesting shadowing behavior. Let's look at another example:

```python
# oop/class.attribute.shadowing.py
class Point:
    x = 10
    y = 7

p = Point()
print(p.x)  # 10 (from class attribute)
print(p.y)  # 7 (from class attribute)

p.x = 12  # p gets its own `x` attribute
print(p.x)  # 12 (now found on the instance)
print(Point.x)  # 10 (class attribute still the same)

del p.x  # we delete instance attribute
print(p.x)  # 10 (now search has to go again to find class attr)

p.z = 3  # let's make it a 3D point
print(p.z)  # 3

print(Point.z)
# AttributeError: type object 'Point' has no attribute 'z'
```

The preceding code is very interesting. We have defined a class called `Point` with two class attributes, `x` and `y`. When we create an instance, `p`, you can see that we can print both `x` and `y` from the `p` namespace (`p.x` and `p.y`). What happens when we do that is Python doesn't find any `x` or `y` attributes on the instance, and therefore searches the class, and finds them there.

Then we give `p` its own `x` attribute by assigning `p.x = 12`. This behavior may appear a bit weird at first, but if you think about it, it's exactly the same as what happens in a function that declares `x = 12` when there is a global `x = 10` outside. We know that `x = 12` won't affect the global one, and for classes and instances, it is exactly the same.

After assigning `p.x = 12`, when we print it, the search doesn't need to read the class attributes, because `x` is found on the instance, therefore we get `12` printed out. We also print `Point.x`, which refers to `x` in the class namespace.

And then, we delete x from the namespace of p, which means that, on the next line, when we print it again, Python will go again and search for it in the class, because it won't be found in the instance any more.

The last three lines show you that assigning attributes to an instance doesn't mean that they will be found in the class. Instances get whatever is in the class, but the opposite is not true.

What do you think about putting the x and y coordinates as class attributes? Do you think it was a good idea? What if you added another instance of `Point`? Would that help to show why class attributes can be very useful?

Me, myself, and I – using the self variable

From within a class method, we can refer to an instance by means of a special argument, called `self` by convention. `self` is always the first attribute of an instance method. Let's examine this behavior together with how we can share, not just attributes, but methods with all instances:

```
# oop/class.self.py
class Square:
    side = 8
    def area(self):  # self is a reference to an instance
        return self.side ** 2

sq = Square()
print(sq.area())  # 64 (side is found on the class)
print(Square.area(sq))  # 64 (equivalent to sq.area())

sq.side = 10
print(sq.area())  # 100 (side is found on the instance)
```

Note how the `area` method is used by sq. The two calls, `Square.area(sq)` and `sq.area()`, are equivalent, and teach us how the mechanism works. Either you pass the instance to the method call (`Square.area(sq)`), which within the method will take the name `self`, or you can use a more comfortable syntax, `sq.area()`, and Python will translate that for you behind the scenes.

Let's look at a better example:

```
# oop/class.price.py
class Price:
    def final_price(self, vat, discount=0):
        """Returns price after applying vat and fixed discount."""
        return (self.net_price * (100 + vat) / 100) - discount
```

```
p1 = Price()
p1.net_price = 100
print(Price.final_price(p1, 20, 10))  # 110 (100 * 1.2 - 10)
print(p1.final_price(20, 10))  # equivalent
```

The preceding code shows you that nothing prevents us from using arguments when declaring methods. We can use the exact same syntax as we used with the function, but we need to remember that the first argument will always be the instance. We don't need to necessarily call it `self`, but it's the convention, and this is one of the few cases where it's very important to abide by it.

Initializing an instance

Have you noticed how, before calling `p1.final_price(...)`, we had to assign `net_price` to `p1`? There is a better way to do it. In other languages, this would be called a **constructor**, but in Python, it's not. It is actually an **initializer**, since it works on an already-created instance, and therefore it's called `__init__`. It's a *magic method*, which is run right after the object is created. Python objects also have a `__new__` method, which is the actual constructor. In practice, it's not so common to have to override it though, it's a practice that is mostly used when coding metaclasses, which as we mentioned, is a fairly advanced topic that we won't explore in the book:

```
# oop/class.init.py
class Rectangle:
    def __init__(self, side_a, side_b):
        self.side_a = side_a
        self.side_b = side_b

    def area(self):
        return self.side_a * self.side_b

r1 = Rectangle(10, 4)
print(r1.side_a, r1.side_b)  # 10 4
print(r1.area())  # 40

r2 = Rectangle(7, 3)
print(r2.area())  # 21
```

Things are finally starting to take shape. When an object is created, the __init__ method is automatically run for us. In this case, I coded it so that when we create an object (by calling the class name like a function), we pass arguments to the creation call, like we would on any regular function call. The way we pass parameters follows the signature of the __init__ method, and therefore, in the two creation statements, 10 and 7 will be side_a for r1 and r2, respectively, while 4 and 3 will be side_b. You can see that the call to area() from r1 and r2 reflects that they have different instance arguments. Setting up objects in this way is much nicer and more convenient.

OOP is about code reuse

By now it should be pretty clear: *OOP is all about code reuse*. We define a class, we create instances, and those instances use methods that are defined only in the class. They will behave differently according to how the instances have been set up by the initializer.

Inheritance and composition

But this is just half of the story, *OOP is much more powerful*. We have two main design constructs to exploit: inheritance and composition.

Inheritance means that two objects are related by means of an *Is-A* type of relationship. On the other hand, **composition** means that two objects are related by means of a *Has-A* type of relationship. It's all very easy to explain with an example:

```
# oop/class_inheritance.py
class Engine:
    def start(self):
        pass

    def stop(self):
        pass

class ElectricEngine(Engine):  # Is-A Engine
    pass

class V8Engine(Engine):  # Is-A Engine
    pass

class Car:
    engine_cls = Engine

    def __init__(self):
        self.engine = self.engine_cls()  # Has-A Engine
```

```python
    def start(self):
        print(
            'Starting engine {0} for car {1}... Wroom, wroom!'
            .format(
                self.engine.__class__.__name__,
                self.__class__.__name__)
        )
        self.engine.start()

    def stop(self):
        self.engine.stop()

class RaceCar(Car):  # Is-A Car
    engine_cls = V8Engine

class CityCar(Car):  # Is-A Car
    engine_cls = ElectricEngine

class F1Car(RaceCar):  # Is-A RaceCar and also Is-A Car
    pass  # engine_cls same as parent

car = Car()
racecar = RaceCar()
citycar = CityCar()
f1car = F1Car()
cars = [car, racecar, citycar, f1car]

for car in cars:
    car.start()

""" Prints:
Starting engine Engine for car Car... Wroom, wroom!
Starting engine V8Engine for car RaceCar... Wroom, wroom!
Starting engine ElectricEngine for car CityCar... Wroom, wroom!
Starting engine V8Engine for car F1Car... Wroom, wroom!
"""
```

The preceding example shows you both the *Is-A* and *Has-A* types of relationships between objects. First of all, let's consider `Engine`. It's a simple class that has two methods, `start` and `stop`. We then define `ElectricEngine` and `V8Engine`, which both inherit from `Engine`. You can see that by the fact that when we define them, we put `Engine` within the brackets after the class name.

This means that both `ElectricEngine` and `V8Engine` inherit attributes and methods from the `Engine` class, which is said to be their **base class**.

The same happens with cars. `Car` is a base class for both `RaceCar` and `CityCar`. `RaceCar` is also the base class for `F1Car`. Another way of saying this is that `F1Car` inherits from `RaceCar`, which inherits from `Car`. Therefore, `F1Car` *Is-A* `RaceCar` and `RaceCar` *Is-A* `Car`. Because of the transitive property, we can say that `F1Car` *Is-A* `Car` as well. `CityCar` too, *Is-A* `Car`.

When we define `class A(B): pass`, we say A is the *child* of B, and B is the *parent* of A. The *parent* and *base* classes are synonyms, are *child* and *derived*. Also, we say that a class inherits from another class, or that it extends it.

This is the inheritance mechanism.

On the other hand, let's go back to the code. Each class has a class attribute, `engine_cls`, which is a reference to the engine class we want to assign to each type of car. `Car` has a generic `Engine`, while the two race cars have a powerful V8 engine, and the city car has an electric one.

When a car is created in the initializer method, `__init__`, we create an instance of whatever engine class is assigned to the car, and set it as the `engine` instance attribute.

It makes sense to have `engine_cls` shared among all class instances because it's quite likely that the same instances of a car will have the same kind of engine. On the other hand, it wouldn't be good to have one single engine (an instance of any `Engine` class) as a class attribute, because we would be sharing one engine among all instances, which is incorrect.

The type of relationship between a car and its engine is a *Has-A* type. A car *Has-A* engine. This is called **composition**, and reflects the fact that objects can be made of many other objects. A car *Has-A* engine, gears, wheels, a frame, doors, seats, and so on.

When designing OOP code, it is of vital importance to describe objects in this way so that we can use inheritance and composition correctly to structure our code in the best way.

 Notice how I had to avoid having dots in the `class_inheritance.py` script name, as dots in module names make it imports difficult. Most modules in the source code of the book are meant to be run as standalone scripts, therefore I chose to add dots to enhance readability when possible, but in general, you want to avoid dots in your module names.

Before we leave this paragraph, let's check whether I told you the truth with another example:

```python
# oop/class.issubclass.isinstance.py
from class_inheritance import Car, RaceCar, F1Car

car = Car()
racecar = RaceCar()
f1car = F1Car()
cars = [(car, 'car'), (racecar, 'racecar'), (f1car, 'f1car')]
car_classes = [Car, RaceCar, F1Car]

for car, car_name in cars:
    for class_ in car_classes:
        belongs = isinstance(car, class_)
        msg = 'is a' if belongs else 'is not a'
        print(car_name, msg, class_.__name__)

""" Prints:
car is a Car
car is not a RaceCar
car is not a F1Car
racecar is a Car
racecar is a RaceCar
racecar is not a F1Car
f1car is a Car
f1car is a RaceCar
f1car is a F1Car
"""
```

As you can see, `car` is just an instance of `Car`, while `racecar` is an instance of `RaceCar` (and of `Car`, by extension) and `f1car` is an instance of `F1Car` (and of both `RaceCar` and `Car`, by extension). A *banana* is an instance of *banana*. But, also, it is a *Fruit*. Also, it is *Food*, right? This is the same concept. To check whether an object is an instance of a class, use the `isinstance` method. It is recommended over sheer type comparison: `(type(object) == Class)`.

Notice I have left out the prints you get when instantiating the cars. We saw them in the previous example.

Let's also check inheritance–same setup, different logic in the `for` loops:

```
# oop/class.issubclass.isinstance.py
for class1 in car_classes:
    for class2 in car_classes:
        is_subclass = issubclass(class1, class2)
        msg = '{0} a subclass of'.format(
            'is' if is_subclass else 'is not')
        print(class1.__name__, msg, class2.__name__)

""" Prints:
Car is a subclass of Car
Car is not a subclass of RaceCar
Car is not a subclass of F1Car
RaceCar is a subclass of Car
RaceCar is a subclass of RaceCar
RaceCar is not a subclass of F1Car
F1Car is a subclass of Car
F1Car is a subclass of RaceCar
F1Car is a subclass of F1Car
"""
```

Interestingly, we learn that *a class is a subclass of itself*. Check the output of the preceding example to see that it matches the explanation I provided.

One thing to notice about conventions is that class names are always written using `CapWords`, which means `ThisWayIsCorrect`, as opposed to functions and methods, which are written `this_way_is_correct`. Also, when in the code, you want to use a name that is a Python-reserved keyword or a built-in function or class, the convention is to add a trailing underscore to the name. In the first `for` loop example, I'm looping through the class names using `for class_ in ...`, because `class` is a reserved word. But you already knew all this because you have thoroughly studied PEP8, right?

To help you picture the difference between *Is-A* and *Has-A*, take a look at the following diagram:

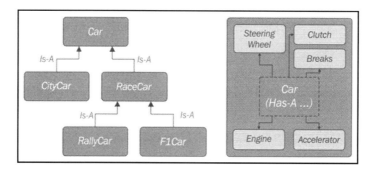

Accessing a base class

We've already seen class declarations, such as `class ClassA: pass` and `class ClassB(BaseClassName): pass`. When we don't specify a base class explicitly, Python will set the special **object** class as the base class for the one we're defining. Ultimately, all classes derive from an object. Note that, if you don't specify a base class, brackets are optional.

Therefore, writing `class A: pass` or `class A(): pass` or `class A(object): pass` is exactly the same thing. The *object* class is a special class in that it has the methods that are common to all Python classes, and it doesn't allow you to set any attributes on it.

Let's see how we can access a base class from within a class:

```
# oop/super.duplication.py
class Book:
    def __init__(self, title, publisher, pages):
        self.title = title
        self.publisher = publisher
        self.pages = pages

class Ebook(Book):
    def __init__(self, title, publisher, pages, format_):
        self.title = title
        self.publisher = publisher
        self.pages = pages
        self.format_ = format_
```

Take a look at the preceding code. Three of the input parameters are duplicated in `Ebook`. This is quite bad practice because we now have two sets of instructions that are doing the same thing. Moreover, any change in the signature of `Book.__init__` will not be reflected in `Ebook`. We know that `Ebook` *Is-A* `Book`, and therefore we would probably want changes to be reflected in the children classes.

Let's see one way to fix this issue:

```
# oop/super.explicit.py
class Book:
    def __init__(self, title, publisher, pages):
        self.title = title
        self.publisher = publisher
        self.pages = pages

class Ebook(Book):
    def __init__(self, title, publisher, pages, format_):
        Book.__init__(self, title, publisher, pages)
        self.format_ = format_

ebook = Ebook(
    'Learn Python Programming', 'Packt Publishing', 500, 'PDF')
print(ebook.title)  # Learn Python Programming
print(ebook.publisher)  # Packt Publishing
print(ebook.pages)  # 500
print(ebook.format_)  # PDF
```

Now, that's better. We have removed that nasty duplication. Basically, we tell Python to call the `__init__` method of the `Book` class, and we feed `self` to the call, making sure that we bind that call to the present instance.

If we modify the logic within the `__init__` method of `Book`, we don't need to touch `Ebook`, it will auto-adapt to the change.

This approach is good, but we can still do a bit better. Say that we change the name of `Book` to `Liber`, because we've fallen in love with Latin. We have to change the `__init__` method of `Ebook` to reflect the change. This can be avoided by using `super`:

```
# oop/super.implicit.py
class Book:
    def __init__(self, title, publisher, pages):
        self.title = title
        self.publisher = publisher
        self.pages = pages

class Ebook(Book):
```

```
    def __init__(self, title, publisher, pages, format_):
        super().__init__(title, publisher, pages)
        # Another way to do the same thing is:
        # super(Ebook, self).__init__(title, publisher, pages)
        self.format_ = format_

ebook = Ebook(
    'Learn Python Programming', 'Packt Publishing', 500, 'PDF')
print(ebook.title) # Learn Python Programming
print(ebook.publisher) # Packt Publishing
print(ebook.pages) # 500
print(ebook.format_) # PDF
```

super is a function that returns a proxy object that delegates method calls to a parent or sibling class. In this case, it will delegate that call to __init__ to the Book class, and the beauty of this method is that now we're even free to change Book to Liber without having to touch the logic in the __init__ method of Ebook.

Now that we know how to access a base class from a child, let's explore Python's multiple inheritance.

Multiple inheritance

Apart from composing a class using more than one base class, what is of interest here is how an attribute search is performed. Take a look at the following diagram:

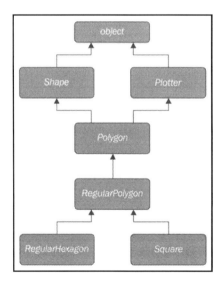

As you can see, Shape and Plotter act as base classes for all the others. Polygon inherits directly from them, RegularPolygon inherits from Polygon, and both RegularHexagon and Square inherit from RegulaPolygon. Note also that Shape and Plotter implicitly inherit from object, therefore we have what is called a **diamond** or, in simpler terms, more than one path to reach a base class. We'll see why this matters in a few moments. Let's translate it into some simple code:

```
# oop/multiple.inheritance.py
class Shape:
    geometric_type = 'Generic Shape'
    def area(self):  # This acts as placeholder for the interface
        raise NotImplementedError
    def get_geometric_type(self):
        return self.geometric_type

class Plotter:
    def plot(self, ratio, topleft):
        # Imagine some nice plotting logic here...
        print('Plotting at {}, ratio {}.'.format(
            topleft, ratio))

class Polygon(Shape, Plotter):  # base class for polygons
    geometric_type = 'Polygon'

class RegularPolygon(Polygon):  # Is-A Polygon
    geometric_type = 'Regular Polygon'
    def __init__(self, side):
        self.side = side

class RegularHexagon(RegularPolygon):  # Is-A RegularPolygon
    geometric_type = 'RegularHexagon'
    def area(self):
        return 1.5 * (3 ** .5 * self.side ** 2)

class Square(RegularPolygon):  # Is-A RegularPolygon
    geometric_type = 'Square'
    def area(self):
        return self.side * self.side

hexagon = RegularHexagon(10)
print(hexagon.area())  # 259.8076211353316
print(hexagon.get_geometric_type())  # RegularHexagon
hexagon.plot(0.8, (75, 77))  # Plotting at (75, 77), ratio 0.8.

square = Square(12)
print(square.area())   # 144
print(square.get_geometric_type())  # Square
```

```
square.plot(0.93, (74, 75))  # Plotting at (74, 75), ratio 0.93.
```

Take a look at the preceding code: the `Shape` class has one attribute, `geometric_type`, and two methods: `area` and `get_geometric_type`. It's quite common to use base classes (such as `Shape`, in our example) to define an *interface*–methods for which children must provide an implementation. There are different and better ways to do this, but I want to keep this example as simple as possible.

We also have the `Plotter` class, which adds the `plot` method, thereby providing plotting capabilities for any class that inherits from it. Of course, the `plot` implementation is just a dummy `print` in this example. The first interesting class is `Polygon`, which inherits from both `Shape` and `Plotter`.

There are many types of polygons, one of which is the regular one, which is both equiangular (all angles are equal) and equilateral (all sides are equal), so we create the `RegularPolygon` class that inherits from `Polygon`. For a regular polygon, where all sides are equal, we can implement a simple `__init__` method on `RegularPolygon`, which takes the length of the side. Finally, we create the `RegularHexagon` and `Square` classes, which both inherit from `RegularPolygon`.

This structure is quite long, but hopefully gives you an idea of how to specialize the classification of your objects when you design the code.

Now, please take a look at the last eight lines. Note that when I call the `area` method on `hexagon` and `square`, I get the correct area for both. This is because they both provide the correct implementation logic for it. Also, I can call `get_geometric_type` on both of them, even though it is not defined on their classes, and Python has to go all the way up to `Shape` to find an implementation for it. Note that, even though the implementation is provided in the `Shape` class, the `self.geometric_type` used for the return value is correctly taken from the caller instance.

The `plot` method calls are also interesting, and show you how you can enrich your objects with capabilities they wouldn't otherwise have. This technique is very popular in web frameworks such as Django (which we'll explore `Chapter 14`, *Web Development*), which provides special classes called **mixins**, whose capabilities you can just use out of the box. All you have to do is to define the desired mixin as one the base classes for your own, and that's it.

Multiple inheritance is powerful, but can also get really messy, so we need to make sure we understand what happens when we use it.

Method resolution order

By now, we know that when you ask for `someobject.attribute` and `attribute` is not found on that object, Python starts searching in the class that `someobject` was created from. If it's not there either, Python searches up the inheritance chain until either `attribute` is found or the `object` class is reached. This is quite simple to understand if the inheritance chain is only composed of single-inheritance steps, which means that classes have only one parent. However, when multiple inheritance is involved, there are cases when it's not straightforward to predict what will be the next class that will be searched for if an attribute is not found.

Python provides a way to always know the order in which classes are searched on attribute lookup: the **Method Resolution Order (MRO)**.

The MRO is the order in which base classes are searched for a member during lookup. From version 2.3, Python uses an algorithm called **C3**, which guarantees monotonicity.

In Python 2.2, *new-style classes* were introduced. The way you write a new-style class in Python 2.* is to define it with an explicit `object` base class. Classic classes were not explicitly inheriting from `object` and have been removed in Python 3. One of the differences between classic and new-style classes in Python 2.* is that new-style classes are searched with the new MRO.

With regards to the previous example, let's see the MRO for the `Square` class:

```
# oop/multiple.inheritance.py
print(square.__class__.__mro__)
# prints:
# (<class '__main__.Square'>, <class '__main__.RegularPolygon'>,
# <class '__main__.Polygon'>, <class '__main__.Shape'>,
# <class '__main__.Plotter'>, <class 'object'>)
```

To get to the MRO of a class, we can go from the instance to its `__class__` attribute, and from that to its `__mro__` attribute. Alternatively, we could have called `Square.__mro__`, or `Square.mro()` directly, but if you have to do it dynamically, it's more likely you will have an object than a class.

Note that the only point of doubt is the bisection after `Polygon`, where the inheritance chain breaks into two ways: one leads to `Shape` and the other to `Plotter`. We know by scanning the MRO for the `Square` class that `Shape` is searched before `Plotter`.

Why is this important? Well, consider the following code:

```
# oop/mro.simple.py
class A:
    label = 'a'

class B(A):
    label = 'b'

class C(A):
    label = 'c'

class D(B, C):
    pass

d = D()
print(d.label)  # Hypothetically this could be either 'b' or 'c'
```

Both B and C inherit from A, and D inherits from both B and C. This means that the lookup for the `label` attribute can reach the top (A) through either B or C. According to which is reached first, we get a different result.

So, in the preceding example, we get 'b', which is what we were expecting, since B is the leftmost one among the base classes of D. But what happens if I remove the `label` attribute from B? This would be a confusing situation: will the algorithm go all the way up to A or will it get to C first? Let's find out:

```
# oop/mro.py
class A:
    label = 'a'

class B(A):
    pass  # was: label = 'b'

class C(A):
    label = 'c'

class D(B, C):
    pass

d = D()
print(d.label)  # 'c'
print(d.__class__.mro())  # notice another way to get the MRO
# prints:
# [<class '__main__.D'>, <class '__main__.B'>,
# <class '__main__.C'>, <class '__main__.A'>, <class 'object'>]
```

So, we learn that the MRO is D-B-C-A-object, which means when we ask for d.label, we get 'c', which is correct.

In day-to-day programming, it is not common to have to deal with the MRO, but the first time you fight against some mixin from a framework, I promise you'll be glad I spent a paragraph explaining it.

Class and static methods

So far, we have coded classes with attributes in the form of data and instance methods, but there are two other types of methods that we can place inside a class: **static methods** and **class methods**.

Static methods

As you may recall, when you create a class object, Python assigns a name to it. That name acts as a namespace, and sometimes it makes sense to group functionalities under it. Static methods are perfect for this use case since, unlike instance methods, they are not passed any special argument. Let's look at an example of an imaginary StringUtil class:

```python
# oop/static.methods.py
class StringUtil:

    @staticmethod
    def is_palindrome(s, case_insensitive=True):
        # we allow only letters and numbers
        s = ''.join(c for c in s if c.isalnum())  # Study this!
        # For case insensitive comparison, we lower-case s
        if case_insensitive:
            s = s.lower()
        for c in range(len(s) // 2):
            if s[c] != s[-c -1]:
                return False
        return True

    @staticmethod
    def get_unique_words(sentence):
        return set(sentence.split())

print(StringUtil.is_palindrome(
    'Radar', case_insensitive=False))  # False: Case Sensitive
print(StringUtil.is_palindrome('A nut for a jar of tuna'))  # True
print(StringUtil.is_palindrome('Never Odd, Or Even!'))  # True
```

```
print(StringUtil.is_palindrome(
    'In Girum Imus Nocte Et Consumimur Igni')  # Latin! Show-off!
)  # True

print(StringUtil.get_unique_words(
    'I love palindromes. I really really love them!'))
# {'them!', 'really', 'palindromes.', 'I', 'love'}
```

The preceding code is quite interesting. First of all, we learn that static methods are created by simply applying the `staticmethod` decorator to them. You can see that they aren't passed any special argument so, apart from the decoration, they really just look like functions.

We have a class, `StringUtil`, that acts as a container for functions. Another approach would be to have a separate module with functions inside. It's really a matter of preference most of the time.

The logic inside `is_palindrome` should be straightforward for you to understand by now, but, just in case, let's go through it. First, we remove all characters from `s` that are neither letters nor numbers. In order to do this, we use the `join` method of a string object (an empty string object, in this case). By calling `join` on an empty string, the result is that all elements in the iterable you pass to `join` will be concatenated together. We feed `join` a generator expression that says to take any character from `s` if the character is either alphanumeric or a number. This is because, in palindrome sentences, we want to discard anything that is not a character or a number.

We then lowercase `s` if `case_insensitive` is `True`, and then we proceed to check whether it is a palindrome. In order to do this, we compare the first and last characters, then the second and the second to last, and so on. If at any point we find a difference, it means the string isn't a palindrome and therefore we can return `False`. On the other hand, if we exit the `for` loop normally, it means no differences were found, and we can therefore say the string is a palindrome.

Notice that this code works correctly regardless of the length of the string; that is, if the length is odd or even. `len(s) // 2` reaches half of `s`, and if `s` is an odd amount of characters long, the middle one won't be checked (such as in *RaDaR*, *D* is not checked), but we don't care; it would be compared with itself so it's always passing that check.

`get_unique_words` is much simpler: it just returns a set to which we feed a list with the words from a sentence. The `set` class removes any duplication for us, so we don't need to do anything else.

The `StringUtil` class provides us a nice container namespace for methods that are meant to work on strings. I could have coded a similar example with a `MathUtil` class, and some static methods to work on numbers, but I wanted to show you something different.

Class methods

Class methods are slightly different from static methods in that, like instance methods, they also take a special first argument, but in this case, it is the class object itself. A very common use case for coding class methods is to provide factory capability to a class. Let's see an example:

```
# oop/class.methods.factory.py
class Point:
    def __init__(self, x, y):
        self.x = x
        self.y = y

    @classmethod
    def from_tuple(cls, coords):  # cls is Point
        return cls(*coords)

    @classmethod
    def from_point(cls, point):  # cls is Point
        return cls(point.x, point.y)


p = Point.from_tuple((3, 7))
print(p.x, p.y)  # 3 7
q = Point.from_point(p)
print(q.x, q.y)  # 3 7
```

In the preceding code, I showed you how to use a class method to create a factory for the class. In this case, we want to create a `Point` instance by passing both coordinates (regular creation `p = Point(3, 7)`), but we also want to be able to create an instance by passing a tuple (`Point.from_tuple`) or another instance (`Point.from_point`).

Within the two class methods, the `cls` argument refers to the `Point` class. As with the instance method, which takes `self` as the first argument, the class method takes a `cls` argument. Both `self` and `cls` are named after a convention that you are not forced to follow but are strongly encouraged to respect. This is something that no Python coder would change because it is so strong a convention that parsers, linters, and any tool that automatically does something with your code would expect, so it's much better to stick to it.

Class and static methods play well together. Static methods are actually quite helpful in breaking up the logic of a class method to improve its layout. Let's see an example by refactoring the StringUtil class:

```
# oop/class.methods.split.py
class StringUtil:

    @classmethod
    def is_palindrome(cls, s, case_insensitive=True):
        s = cls._strip_string(s)
        # For case insensitive comparison, we lower-case s
        if case_insensitive:
            s = s.lower()
        return cls._is_palindrome(s)

    @staticmethod
    def _strip_string(s):
        return ''.join(c for c in s if c.isalnum())

    @staticmethod
    def _is_palindrome(s):
        for c in range(len(s) // 2):
            if s[c] != s[-c -1]:
                return False
        return True

    @staticmethod
    def get_unique_words(sentence):
        return set(sentence.split())

print(StringUtil.is_palindrome('A nut for a jar of tuna'))   # True
print(StringUtil.is_palindrome('A nut for a jar of beans'))  # False
```

Compare this code with the previous version. First of all, note that even though is_palindrome is now a class method, we call it in the same way we were calling it when it was a static one. The reason why we changed it to a class method is that after factoring out a couple of pieces of logic (_strip_string and _is_palindrome), we need to get a reference to them, and if we have no cls in our method, the only option would be to call them like this: StringUtil._strip_string(...) and StringUtil._is_palindrome(...), which is not good practice, because we would hardcode the class name in the is_palindrome method, thereby putting ourselves in the position of having to modify it whenever we want to change the class name. Using cls will act as the class name, which means our code won't need any amendments.

Notice how the new logic reads much better than the previous version. Moreover, notice that, by naming the *factored-out* methods with a leading underscore, I am hinting that those methods are not supposed to be called from outside the class, but this will be the subject of the next paragraph.

Private methods and name mangling

If you have any background with languages like Java, C#, or C++, then you know they allow the programmer to assign a privacy status to attributes (both data and methods). Each language has its own slightly different flavor for this, but the gist is that public attributes are accessible from any point in the code, while private ones are accessible only within the scope they are defined in.

In Python, there is no such thing. Everything is public; therefore, we rely on conventions and on a mechanism called **name mangling**.

The convention is as follows: if an attribute's name has no leading underscores, it is considered public. This means you can access it and modify it freely. When the name has one leading underscore, the attribute is considered private, which means it's probably meant to be used internally and you should not use it or modify it from the outside. A very common use case for private attributes are helper methods that are supposed to be used by public ones (possibly in call chains in conjunction with other methods), and internal data, such as scaling factors, or any other data that ideally we would put in a constant (a variable that cannot change, but, surprise, surprise, Python doesn't have those either).

This characteristic usually scares people from other backgrounds off; they feel threatened by the lack of privacy. To be honest, in my whole professional experience with Python, I've never heard anyone screaming "*oh my God, we have a terrible bug because Python lacks private attributes!*" Not once, I swear.

That said, the call for privacy actually makes sense because without it, you risk introducing bugs into your code for real. Let me show you what I mean:

```
# oop/private.attrs.py
class A:
    def __init__(self, factor):
        self._factor = factor

    def op1(self):
        print('Op1 with factor {}...'.format(self._factor))

class B(A):
    def op2(self, factor):
```

```
        self._factor = factor
        print('Op2 with factor {}...'.format(self._factor))


obj = B(100)
obj.op1()    # Op1 with factor 100...
obj.op2(42)  # Op2 with factor 42...
obj.op1()    # Op1 with factor 42... <- This is BAD
```

In the preceding code, we have an attribute called `_factor`, and let's pretend it's so important that it isn't modified at runtime after the instance is created, because `op1` depends on it to function correctly. We've named it with a leading underscore, but the issue here is that when we call `obj.op2(42)`, we modify it, and this is reflected in subsequent calls to `op1`.

Let's fix this undesired behavior by adding another leading underscore:

```
# oop/private.attrs.fixed.py
class A:
    def __init__(self, factor):
        self.__factor = factor

    def op1(self):
        print('Op1 with factor {}...'.format(self.__factor))

class B(A):
    def op2(self, factor):
        self.__factor = factor
        print('Op2 with factor {}...'.format(self.__factor))


obj = B(100)
obj.op1()    # Op1 with factor 100...
obj.op2(42)  # Op2 with factor 42...
obj.op1()    # Op1 with factor 100... <- Wohoo! Now it's GOOD!
```

Wow, look at that! Now it's working as desired. Python is kind of magic and in this case, what is happening is that the name-mangling mechanism has kicked in.

Name mangling means that any attribute name that has at least two leading underscores and at most one trailing underscore, such as `__my_attr`, is replaced with a name that includes an underscore and the class name before the actual name, such as `_ClassName__my_attr`.

This means that when you inherit from a class, the mangling mechanism gives your private attribute two different names in the base and child classes so that name collision is avoided. Every class and instance object stores references to their attributes in a special attribute called __dict__, so let's inspect obj.__dict__ to see name mangling in action:

```
# oop/private.attrs.py
print(obj.__dict__.keys())
# dict_keys(['_factor'])
```

This is the _factor attribute that we find in the problematic version of this example. But look at the one that is using __factor:

```
# oop/private.attrs.fixed.py
print(obj.__dict__.keys())
# dict_keys(['_A__factor', '_B__factor'])
```

See? obj has two attributes now, _A__factor (mangled within the A class), and _B__factor (mangled within the B class). This is the mechanism that ensures that when you do obj.__factor = 42, __factor in A isn't changed, because you're actually touching _B__factor, which leaves _A__factor safe and sound.

If you're designing a library with classes that are meant to be used and extended by other developers, you will need to keep this in mind in order to avoid the unintentional overriding of your attributes. Bugs like these can be pretty subtle and hard to spot.

The property decorator

Another thing that would be a crime not to mention is the property decorator. Imagine that you have an age attribute in a Person class and at some point you want to make sure that when you change its value, you're also checking that age is within a proper range, such as [18, 99]. You can write accessor methods, such as get_age() and set_age(...) (also called **getters** and **setters**), and put the logic there. get_age() will most likely just return age, while set_age(...) will also do the range check. The problem is that you may already have a lot of code accessing the age attribute directly, which means you're now up to some tedious refactoring. Languages like Java overcome this problem by using the accessor pattern basically by default. Many Java **Integrated Development Environments (IDEs)** autocomplete an attribute declaration by writing getter and setter accessor method stubs for you on the fly.

Python is smarter, and does this with the `property` decorator. When you decorate a method with `property`, you can use the name of the method as if it were a data attribute. Because of this, it's always best to refrain from putting logic that would take a while to complete in such methods because, by accessing them as attributes, we are not expecting to wait.

Let's look at an example:

```
# oop/property.py
class Person:
    def __init__(self, age):
        self.age = age  # anyone can modify this freely

class PersonWithAccessors:
    def __init__(self, age):
        self._age = age

    def get_age(self):
        return self._age

    def set_age(self, age):
        if 18 <= age <= 99:
            self._age = age
        else:
            raise ValueError('Age must be within [18, 99]')

class PersonPythonic:
    def __init__(self, age):
        self._age = age

    @property
    def age(self):
        return self._age

    @age.setter
    def age(self, age):
        if 18 <= age <= 99:
            self._age = age
        else:
            raise ValueError('Age must be within [18, 99]')

person = PersonPythonic(39)
print(person.age)   # 39 - Notice we access as data attribute
person.age = 42     # Notice we access as data attribute
print(person.age)   # 42
person.age = 100    # ValueError: Age must be within [18, 99]
```

The `Person` class may be the first version we write. Then we realize we need to put the range logic in place so, with another language, we would have to rewrite `Person` as the `PersonWithAccessors` class, and refactor all the code that was using `Person.age`. In Python, we rewrite `Person` as `PersonPythonic` (you normally wouldn't change the name, of course) so that the age is stored in a private _age variable, and we define property getters and setters using that decoration, which allows us to keep using the `person` instances as we were before. A getter is a method that is called when we access an attribute for reading. On the other hand, a setter is a method that is called when we access an attribute to write it. In other languages, such as Java, it's customary to define them as `get_age()` and `set_age(int value)`, but I find the Python syntax much neater. It allows you to start writing simple code and refactor later on, only when you need it, there is no need to pollute your code with accessors only because they may be helpful in the future.

The `property` decorator also allows for read-only data (no setter) and for special actions when the attribute is deleted. Please refer to the official documentation to dig deeper.

Operator overloading

I find Python's approach to **operator overloading** to be brilliant. To overload an operator means to give it a meaning according to the context in which it is used. For example, the + operator means addition when we deal with numbers, but concatenation when we deal with sequences.

In Python, when you use operators, you're most likely calling the special methods of some objects behind the scenes. For example, the `a[k]` call roughly translates to `type(a).__getitem__(a, k)`.

As an example, let's create a class that stores a string and evaluates to `True` if `'42'` is part of that string, and `False` otherwise. Also, let's give the class a length property that corresponds to that of the stored string:

```
# oop/operator.overloading.py
class Weird:
    def __init__(self, s):
        self._s = s

    def __len__(self):
        return len(self._s)

    def __bool__(self):
        return '42' in self._s
```

```
weird = Weird('Hello! I am 9 years old!')
print(len(weird))  # 24
print(bool(weird))  # False

weird2 = Weird('Hello! I am 42 years old!')
print(len(weird2))  # 25
print(bool(weird2))  # True
```

That was fun, wasn't it? For the complete list of magic methods that you can override in order to provide your custom implementation of operators for your classes, please refer to the Python data model in the official documentation.

Polymorphism – a brief overview

The word **polymorphism** comes from the Greek *polys* (many, much) and *morphē* (form, shape), and its meaning is the provision of a single interface for entities of different types.

In our car example, we call `engine.start()`, regardless of what kind of engine it is. As long as it exposes the start method, we can call it. That's polymorphism in action.

In other languages, such as Java, in order to give a function the ability to accept different types and call a method on them, those types need to be coded in such a way that they share an interface. In this way, the compiler knows that the method will be available regardless of the type of the object the function is fed (as long as it extends the proper interface, of course).

In Python, things are different. Polymorphism is implicit, nothing prevents you from calling a method on an object; therefore, technically, there is no need to implement interfaces or other patterns.

There is a special kind of polymorphism called **ad hoc polymorphism**, which is what we saw in the last paragraph: operator overloading. This is the ability of an operator to change shape, according to the type of data it is fed.

Polymorphism also allows Python programmers to simply use the interface (methods and properties) exposed from an object rather than having to check which class it was instantiated from. This allows the code to be more compact and feel more natural.

I cannot spend too much time on polymorphism, but I encourage you to check it out by yourself, it will expand your understanding of OOP. Good luck!

Data classes

Before we leave the OOP realm, there is one last thing I want to mention: data classes. Introduced in Python 3.7 by PEP557 (`https://www.python.org/dev/peps/pep-0557/`), they can be described as *mutable named tuples with defaults*. Let's dive into an example:

```
# oop/dataclass.py
from dataclasses import dataclass

@dataclass
class Body:
    '''Class to represent a physical body.'''
    name: str
    mass: float = 0.  # Kg
    speed: float = 1.  # m/s

    def kinetic_energy(self) -> float:
        return (self.mass * self.speed ** 2) / 2


body = Body('Ball', 19, 3.1415)
print(body.kinetic_energy())  # 93.755711375 Joule
print(body)  # Body(name='Ball', mass=19, speed=3.1415)
```

In the previous code, I have created a class to represent a physical body, with one method that allows me to calculate its kinetic energy (using the renowned formula $E_k = \frac{1}{2}mv^2$). Notice that `name` is supposed to be a string, while `mass` and `speed` are both floats, and both are given a default value. It's also interesting that I didn't have to write any `__init__` method, it's done for me by the `dataclass` decorator, along with methods for comparison and for producing the string representation of the object (implicitly called on the last line by `print`).

You can read all the specifications in PEP557 if you are curious, but for now just remember that data classes might offer a nicer, slightly more powerful alternative to named tuples, in case you need it.

Writing a custom iterator

Now we have all the tools to appreciate how we can write our own custom iterator. Let's first define an iterable and an iterator:

- **Iterable**: An object is said to be iterable if it's capable of returning its members one at a time. Lists, tuples, strings, and dictionaries are all iterables. Custom objects that define either of the __iter__ or __getitem__ methods are also iterables.
- **Iterator**: An object is said to be an iterator if it represents a stream of data. A custom iterator is required to provide an implementation for __iter__ that returns the object itself, and an implementation for __next__ that returns the next item of the data stream until the stream is exhausted, at which point all successive calls to __next__ simply raise the StopIteration exception. Built-in functions, such as iter and next, are mapped to call __iter__ and __next__ on an object, behind the scenes.

Let's write an iterator that returns all the odd characters from a string first, and then the even ones:

```
# iterators/iterator.py
class OddEven:

    def __init__(self, data):
        self._data = data
        self.indexes = (list(range(0, len(data), 2)) +
            list(range(1, len(data), 2)))

    def __iter__(self):
        return self

    def __next__(self):
        if self.indexes:
            return self._data[self.indexes.pop(0)]
        raise StopIteration

oddeven = OddEven('ThIsIsCoOl!')
print(''.join(c for c in oddeven))  # TIICO!hssol

oddeven = OddEven('HoLa')  # or manually...
it = iter(oddeven)  # this calls oddeven.__iter__ internally
print(next(it))  # H
```

```
print(next(it))    # L
print(next(it))    # o
print(next(it))    # a
```

So, we needed to provide an implementation for __iter__ that returned the object itself, and then one for __next__. Let's go through it. What needed to happen was the return of _data[0], _data[2], _data[4], ..., _data[1], _data[3], _data[5], ... until we had returned every item in the data. In order to do that, we prepared a list and indexes, such as [0, 2, 4, 6, ..., 1, 3, 5, ...], and while there was at least an element in it, we popped the first one and returned the element from the data that was at that position, thereby achieving our goal. When indexes was empty, we raised StopIteration, as required by the iterator protocol.

There are other ways to achieve the same result, so go ahead and try to code a different one yourself. Make sure the end result works for all edge cases, empty sequences, sequences of lengths of 1, 2, and so on.

Summary

In this chapter, we looked at decorators, discovered the reasons for having them, and covered a few examples using one or more at the same time. We also saw decorators that take arguments, which are usually used as decorator factories.

We scratched the surface of object-oriented programming in Python. We covered all the basics, so you should now be able to understand the code that will come in future chapters. We talked about all kinds of methods and attributes that one can write in a class, we explored inheritance versus composition, method overriding, properties, operator overloading, and polymorphism.

At the end, we very briefly touched base on iterators, so now you understand generators more deeply.

In the next chapter, we're going to see how to deal with files and how to persist data in several different ways and formats.

Files and Data Persistence

7

"Persistence is the key to the adventure we call life."

– Torsten Alexander Lange

In the previous chapters, we have explored several different aspects of Python. As the examples have a didactic purpose, we've run them in a simple Python shell, or in the form of a Python module. They ran, maybe printed something on the console, and then they terminated, leaving no trace of their brief existence.

Real-world applications though are generally much different. Naturally, they still run in memory, but they interact with networks, disks, and databases. They also exchange information with other applications and devices, using formats that are suitable for the situation.

In this chapter, we are going to start closing in to the real world by exploring the following:

- Files and directories
- Compression
- Networks and streams
- The JSON data-interchange format
- Data persistence with pickle and shelve, from the standard library
- Data persistence with SQLAlchemy

As usual, I will try to balance breadth and depth, so that by the end of the chapter, you will have a solid grasp of the fundamentals and will know how to fetch further information on the web.

Working with files and directories

When it comes to files and directories, Python offers plenty of useful tools. In particular, in the following examples, we will leverage the os and shutil modules. As we'll be reading and writing on the disk, I will be using a file, fear.txt, which contains an excerpt from *Fear*, by Thich Nhat Hanh, as a guinea pig for some of our examples.

Opening files

Opening a file in Python is very simple and intuitive. In fact, we just need to use the open function. Let's see a quick example:

```
# files/open_try.py
fh = open('fear.txt', 'rt')  # r: read, t: text

for line in fh.readlines():
    print(line.strip())  # remove whitespace and print

fh.close()
```

The previous code is very simple. We call open, passing the filename, and telling open that we want to read it in text mode. There is no path information before the filename; therefore, open will assume the file is in the same folder the script is run from. This means that if we run this script from outside the files folder, then fear.txt won't be found.

Once the file has been opened, we obtain a file object back, fh, which we can use to work on the content of the file. In this case, we use the readlines() method to iterate over all the lines in the file, and print them. We call strip() on each line to get rid of any extra spaces around the content, including the line termination character at the end, since print will already add one for us. This is a quick and dirty solution that works in this example, but should the content of the file contain meaningful spaces that need to be preserved, you will have to be slightly more careful in how you sanitize the data. At the end of the script, we flush and close the stream.

Closing a file is very important, as we don't want to risk failing to release the handle we have on it. Therefore, we need to apply some precaution, and wrap the previous logic in a try/finally block. This has the effect that, whatever error might occur while we try to open and read the file, we can rest assured that close() will be called:

```
# files/open_try.py
try:
    fh = open('fear.txt', 'rt')
```

```
    for line in fh.readlines():
        print(line.strip())
finally:
    fh.close()
```

The logic is exactly the same, but now it is also safe.

 Don't worry if you don't understand `try`/`finally` for now. We will explore how to deal with exceptions in the next chapter. For now, suffice to say that putting code within the body of a `try` block adds a mechanism around that code that allows us to detect errors (which are called *exceptions*) and decide what to do if they happen. In this case, we don't really do anything in case of errors, but by closing the file within the `finally` block, we make sure that line is executed whether or not any error has happened.

We can simplify the previous example this way:

```
# files/open_try.py
try:
    fh = open('fear.txt')  # rt is default
    for line in fh:  # we can iterate directly on fh
        print(line.strip())
finally:
    fh.close()
```

As you can see, `rt` is the default mode for opening files, so we don't need to specify it. Moreover, we can simply iterate on `fh`, without explicitly calling `readlines()` on it. Python is very nice and gives us shorthands to make our code shorter and simpler to read.

All the previous examples produce a print of the file on the console (check out the source code to read the whole content):

```
An excerpt from Fear - By Thich Nhat Hanh

The Present Is Free from Fear

When we are not fully present, we are not really living. We're not really
there, either for our loved ones or for ourselves. If we're not there, then
where are we? We are running, running, running, even during our sleep. We
run because we're trying to escape from our fear.
...
```

Using a context manager to open a file

Let's admit it: the prospect of having to disseminate our code with `try`/`finally` blocks is not one of the best. As usual, Python gives us a much nicer way to open a file in a secure fashion: by using a *context manager*. Let's see the code first:

```
# files/open_with.py
with open('fear.txt') as fh:
    for line in fh:
        print(line.strip())
```

The previous example is equivalent to the one before it, but reads so much better. The `with` statement supports the concept of a runtime context defined by a context manager. This is implemented using a pair of methods, `__enter__` and `__exit__`, that allow user-defined classes to define a runtime context that is entered before the statement body is executed and exited when the statement ends. The `open` function is capable of producing a file object when invoked by a context manager, but the true beauty of it lies in the fact that `fh.close()` will be called automatically for us, even in case of errors.

Context managers are used in several different scenarios, such as thread synchronization, closure of files or other objects, and management of network and database connections. You can find information about them in the `contextlib` documentation page (`https://docs.python.org/3.7/library/contextlib.html`).

Reading and writing to a file

Now that we know how to open a file, let's see a couple of different ways that we have to read and write to it:

```
# files/print_file.py
with open('print_example.txt', 'w') as fw:
    print('Hey I am printing into a file!!!', file=fw)
```

A first approach uses the `print` function, which you've seen plenty of times in the previous chapters. After obtaining a file object, this time specifying that we intend to write to it ("w"), we can tell the call to `print` to direct its effects on the file, instead of the default `sys.stdout`, which, when executed on a console, is mapped to it.

The previous code has the effect of creating the `print_example.txt` file if it doesn't exist, or truncate it in case it does, and writes the line `Hey I am printing into a file!!!` to it.

This is all nice and easy, but not what we typically do when we want to write to a file. Let's see a much more common approach:

```
# files/read_write.py
with open('fear.txt') as f:
    lines = [line.rstrip() for line in f]

with open('fear_copy.txt', 'w') as fw:
    fw.write('\n'.join(lines))
```

In the previous example, we first open `fear.txt` and collect its content into a list, line by line. Notice that this time, I'm calling a more precise method, `rstrip()`, as an example, to make sure I only strip the whitespace on the right-hand side of every line.

In the second part of the snippet, we create a new file, `fear_copy.txt`, and we write to it all the lines from the original file, joined by a newline, \n. Python is gracious and works by default with *universal newlines*, which means that even though the original file might have a newline that is different than \n, it will be translated automatically for us before the line is returned. This behavior is, of course, customizable, but normally it is exactly what you want. Speaking of newlines, can you think of one of them that might be missing in the copy?

Reading and writing in binary mode

Notice that by opening a file passing `t` in the options (or omitting it, as it is the default), we're opening the file in text mode. This means that the content of the file is treated and interpreted as text. If you wish to write bytes to a file, you can open it in binary mode. This is a common requirement when you deal with files that don't just contain raw text, such as images, audio/video, and, in general, any other proprietary format.

In order to handle files in binary mode, simply specify the `b` flag when opening them, as in the following example:

```
# files/read_write_bin.py
with open('example.bin', 'wb') as fw:
    fw.write(b'This is binary data...')

with open('example.bin', 'rb') as f:
    print(f.read())  # prints: b'This is binary data...'
```

In this example, I'm still using text as binary data, but it could be anything you want. You can see it's treated as a binary by the fact that you get the `b'This ...'` prefix in the output.

Protecting against overriding an existing file

Python gives us the ability to open files for writing. By using the w flag, we open a file and truncate its content. This means the file is overwritten with an empty file, and the original content is lost. If you wish to only open a file for writing in case it doesn't exist, you can use the x flag instead, in the following example:

```
# files/write_not_exists.py
with open('write_x.txt', 'x') as fw:
    fw.write('Writing line 1')  # this succeeds

with open('write_x.txt', 'x') as fw:
    fw.write('Writing line 2')  # this fails
```

If you run the previous snippet, you will find a file called write_x.txt in your directory, containing only one line of text. The second part of the snippet, in fact, fails to execute. This is the output I get on my console:

```
$ python write_not_exists.py
Traceback (most recent call last):
  File "write_not_exists.py", line 6, in <module>
    with open('write_x.txt', 'x') as fw:
FileExistsError: [Errno 17] File exists: 'write_x.txt'
```

Checking for file and directory existence

If you want to make sure a file or directory exists (or it doesn't), the os.path module is what you need. Let's see a small example:

```
# files/existence.py
import os

filename = 'fear.txt'
path = os.path.dirname(os.path.abspath(filename))

print(os.path.isfile(filename))  # True
print(os.path.isdir(path))  # True
print(path)  # /Users/fab/srv/lpp/ch7/files
```

The preceding snippet is quite interesting. After declaring the filename with a relative reference (in that it is missing the path information), we use `abspath` to calculate the full, absolute path of the file. Then, we get the path information (by removing the filename at the end) by calling `dirname` on it. The result, as you can see, is printed on the last line. Notice also how we check for existence, both for a file and a directory, by calling `isfile` and `isdir`. In the `os.path` module, you find all the functions you need to work with pathnames.

 Should you ever need to work with paths in a different way, you can check out `pathlib`. While `os.path` works with strings, `pathlib` offers classes representing filesystem paths with semantics appropriate for different operating systems. It is beyond the scope of this chapter, but if you're interested, check out PEP428 (`https://www.python.org/dev/peps/pep-0428/`), and its page in the standard library.

Manipulating files and directories

Let's see a couple of quick examples on how to manipulate files and directories. The first example manipulates the content:

```
# files/manipulation.py
from collections import Counter
from string import ascii_letters

chars = ascii_letters + ' '

def sanitize(s, chars):
    return ''.join(c for c in s if c in chars)

def reverse(s):
    return s[::-1]

with open('fear.txt') as stream:
    lines = [line.rstrip() for line in stream]

with open('raef.txt', 'w') as stream:
    stream.write('\n'.join(reverse(line) for line in lines))

# now we can calculate some statistics
lines = [sanitize(line, chars) for line in lines]
whole = ' '.join(lines)
cnt = Counter(whole.lower().split())
print(cnt.most_common(3))
```

The previous example defines two functions: sanitize and reverse. They are simple functions whose purpose is to remove anything that is not a letter or space from a string, and produce the reversed copy of a string, respectively.

We open fear.txt and we read its content into a list. Then we create a new file, raef.txt, which will contain the horizontally-mirrored version of the original one. We write all the content of lines with a single operation, using join on a new line character. Maybe more interesting, is the bit in the end. First, we reassign lines to a sanitized version of itself, by means of list comprehension. Then we put them together in the whole string, and finally, we pass the result to Counter. Notice that we split the string and put it in lowercase. This way, each word will be counted correctly, regardless of its case, and, thanks to split, we don't need to worry about extra spaces anywhere. When we print the three most common words, we realize that truly Thich Nhat Hanh's focus is on others, as we is the most common word in the text:

```
$ python manipulation.py
[('we', 17), ('the', 13), ('were', 7)]
```

Let's now see an example of manipulation more oriented to disk operations, in which we put the shutil module to use:

```
# files/ops_create.py
import shutil
import os

BASE_PATH = 'ops_example'  # this will be our base path
os.mkdir(BASE_PATH)

path_b = os.path.join(BASE_PATH, 'A', 'B')
path_c = os.path.join(BASE_PATH, 'A', 'C')
path_d = os.path.join(BASE_PATH, 'A', 'D')

os.makedirs(path_b)
os.makedirs(path_c)

for filename in ('ex1.txt', 'ex2.txt', 'ex3.txt'):
    with open(os.path.join(path_b, filename), 'w') as stream:
        stream.write(f'Some content here in {filename}\n')

shutil.move(path_b, path_d)

shutil.move(
    os.path.join(path_d, 'ex1.txt'),
    os.path.join(path_d, 'ex1d.txt')
)
```

In the previous code, we start by declaring a base path, which will safely contain all the files and folders we're going to create. We then use `makedirs` to create two directories: `ops_example/A/B` and `ops_example/A/C`. (Can you think of a way of creating the two directories by using `map`?).

We use `os.path.join` to concatenate directory names, as using / would specialize the code to run on a platform where the directory separator is /, but then the code would fail on platforms with a different separator. Let's delegate to `join` the task to figure out which is the appropriate separator.

After creating the directories, within a simple `for` loop, we put some code that creates three files in directory B. Then, we move the folder B and its content to a different name: D. And finally, we rename `ex1.txt` to `ex1d.txt`. If you open that file, you'll see it still contains the original text from the `for` loop. Calling `tree` on the result produces the following:

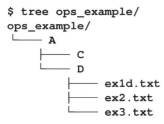

```
$ tree ops_example/
ops_example/
└── A
    ├── C
    └── D
        ├── ex1d.txt
        ├── ex2.txt
        └── ex3.txt
```

Manipulating pathnames

Let's explore a little more the abilities of `os.path` by means of a simple example:

```python
# files/paths.py
import os

filename = 'fear.txt'
path = os.path.abspath(filename)

print(path)
print(os.path.basename(path))
print(os.path.dirname(path))
print(os.path.splitext(path))
print(os.path.split(path))

readme_path = os.path.join(
    os.path.dirname(path), '..', '..', 'README.rst')
```

```
print(readme_path)
print(os.path.normpath(readme_path))
```

Reading the result is probably a good enough explanation for this simple example:

```
/Users/fab/srv/lpp/ch7/files/fear.txt          # path
fear.txt                                        # basename
/Users/fab/srv/lpp/ch7/files                    # dirname
('/Users/fab/srv/lpp/ch7/files/fear', '.txt')   # splitext
('/Users/fab/srv/lpp/ch7/files', 'fear.txt')    # split
/Users/fab/srv/lpp/ch7/files/../../README.rst   # readme_path
/Users/fab/srv/lpp/README.rst                   # normalized
```

Temporary files and directories

Sometimes, it's very useful to be able to create a temporary directory or file when running some code. For example, when writing tests that affect the disk, you can use temporary files and directories to run your logic and assert that it's correct, and to be sure that at the end of the test run, the test folder has no leftovers. Let's see how you do it in Python:

```python
# files/tmp.py
import os
from tempfile import NamedTemporaryFile, TemporaryDirectory

with TemporaryDirectory(dir='.') as td:
    print('Temp directory:', td)
    with NamedTemporaryFile(dir=td) as t:
        name = t.name
        print(os.path.abspath(name))
```

The preceding example is quite straightforward: we create a temporary directory in the current one ("."), and we create a named temporary file in it. We print the filename, as well as its full path:

```
$ python tmp.py
Temp directory: ./tmpwa9bdwgo
/Users/fab/srv/lpp/ch7/files/tmpwa9bdwgo/tmp3d45hm46
```

Running this script will produce a different result every time. After all, it's a temporary random name we're creating here, right?

Directory content

With Python, you can also inspect the content of a directory. I'll show you two ways of doing this:

```
# files/listing.py
import os

with os.scandir('.') as it:
    for entry in it:
        print(
            entry.name, entry.path,
            'File' if entry.is_file() else 'Folder'
        )
```

This snippet uses `os.scandir`, called on the current directory. We iterate on the results, each of which is an instance of `os.DirEntry`, a nice class that exposes useful properties and methods. In the code, we access a subset of those: `name`, `path`, and `is_file()`. Running the code yields the following (I omitted a few results for brevity):

```
$ python listing.py
fixed_amount.py ./fixed_amount.py File
existence.py ./existence.py File
...
ops_example ./ops_example Folder
...
```

A more powerful way to scan a directory tree is given to us by `os.walk`. Let's see an example:

```
# files/walking.py
import os

for root, dirs, files in os.walk('.'):
    print(os.path.abspath(root))
    if dirs:
        print('Directories:')
        for dir_ in dirs:
            print(dir_)
        print()
    if files:
        print('Files:')
        for filename in files:
            print(filename)
        print()
```

Running the preceding snippet will produce a list of all files and directories in the current one, and it will do the same for each sub-directory.

File and directory compression

Before we leave this section, let me give you an example of how to create a compressed file. In the source code of the book, I have two examples: one creates a ZIP file, while the other one creates a `tar.gz` file. Python allows you to create compressed files in several different ways and formats. Here, I am going to show you how to create the most common one, ZIP:

```
# files/compression/zip.py
from zipfile import ZipFile

with ZipFile('example.zip', 'w') as zp:
    zp.write('content1.txt')
    zp.write('content2.txt')
    zp.write('subfolder/content3.txt')
    zp.write('subfolder/content4.txt')

with ZipFile('example.zip') as zp:
    zp.extract('content1.txt', 'extract_zip')
    zp.extract('subfolder/content3.txt', 'extract_zip')
```

In the preceding code, we import `ZipFile`, and then, within a context manager, we write into it four dummy context files (two of which are in a sub-folder, to show ZIP preserves the full path). Afterwards, as an example, we open the compressed file and extract a couple of files from it, into the `extract_zip` directory. If you are interested in learning more about data compression, make sure you check out the *Data Compression and Archiving* section on the standard library (`https://docs.python.org/3.7/library/archiving.html`), where you'll be able to learn all about this topic.

Data interchange formats

Modern software architecture tends to split an application into several components. Whether you embrace the service-oriented architecture paradigm, or you push it even further into the microservices realm, these components will have to exchange data. But even if you are coding a monolithic application, whose code base is contained in one project, chances are that you have to still exchange data with APIs, other programs, or simply handle the data flow between the frontend and the backend part of your website, which very likely won't speak the same language.

Choosing the right format in which to exchange information is crucial. A language-specific format has the advantage that the language itself is very likely to provide you with all the tools to make serialization and deserialization a breeze. However, you will lose the ability to talk to other components that have been written in different versions of the same language, or in different languages altogether. Regardless of what the future looks like, going with a language-specific format should only be done if it is the only possible choice for the given situation.

A much better approach is to choose a format that is language agnostic, and can be spoken by all (or at least most) languages. In the team I lead, we have people from England, Poland, South Africa, Spain, Greece, India, Italy, to mention just a few. We all speak English, so regardless of our native tongue, we can all understand each other (well... mostly!).

In the software world, some popular formats have become the de facto standard over recent years. The most famous ones probably are XML, YAML, and JSON. The Python standard library features the `xml` and `json` modules, and, on PyPI (`https://docs.python.org/3.7/library/archiving.html`), you can find a few different packages to work with YAML.

In the Python environment, JSON is probably the most commonly used one. It wins over the other two because of being part of the standard library, and for its simplicity. If you have ever worked with XML, you know what a nightmare it can be.

Working with JSON

JSON is the acronym of **JavaScript Object Notation**, and it is a subset of the JavaScript language. It has been there for almost two decades now, so it is well known and widely adopted by basically all languages, even though it is actually language independent. You can read all about it on its website (`https://www.json.org/`), but I'm going to give you a quick introduction to it now.

JSON is based on two structures: a collection of name/value pairs, and an ordered list of values. You will immediately realize that these two objects map to the dictionary and list data types in Python, respectively. As data types, it offers strings, numbers, objects, and values, such as true, false, and null. Let's see a quick example to get us started:

```
# json_examples/json_basic.py
import sys
import json

data = {
    'big_number': 2 ** 3141,
    'max_float': sys.float_info.max,
```

```
        'a_list': [2, 3, 5, 7],
    }

json_data = json.dumps(data)
data_out = json.loads(json_data)
assert data == data_out  # json and back, data matches
```

We begin by importing the `sys` and `json` modules. Then we create a simple dictionary with some numbers inside and a list. I wanted to test serializing and deserializing using very big numbers, both `int` and `float`, so I put 2^{3141} and whatever is the biggest floating point number my system can handle.

We serialize with `json.dumps`, which takes data and converts it into a JSON formatted string. That data is then fed into `json.loads`, which does the opposite: from a JSON formatted string, it reconstructs the data into Python. On the last line, we make sure that the original data and the result of the serialization/deserialization through JSON match.

Let's see, in the next example, what JSON data would look like if we printed it:

```
# json_examples/json_basic.py
import json

info = {
    'full_name': 'Sherlock Holmes',
    'address': {
        'street': '221B Baker St',
        'zip': 'NW1 6XE',
        'city': 'London',
        'country': 'UK',
    }
}

print(json.dumps(info, indent=2, sort_keys=True))
```

In this example, we create a dictionary with Sherlock Holmes' data in it. If, like me, you're a fan of Sherlock Holmes, and are in London, you'll find his museum at that address (which I recommend visiting, it's small but very nice).

Notice how we call `json.dumps`, though. We have told it to indent with two spaces, and sort keys alphabetically. The result is this:

```
$ python json_basic.py
{
  "address": {
    "city": "London",
    "country": "UK",
    "street": "221B Baker St",
```

```
        "zip": "NW1 6XE"
    },
    "full_name": "Sherlock Holmes"
}
```

The similarity with Python is huge. The one difference is that if you place a comma on the last element in a dictionary, like I've done in Python (as it is customary), JSON will complain.

Let me show you something interesting:

```
# json_examples/json_tuple.py
import json

data_in = {
    'a_tuple': (1, 2, 3, 4, 5),
}

json_data = json.dumps(data_in)
print(json_data)  # {"a_tuple": [1, 2, 3, 4, 5]}
data_out = json.loads(json_data)
print(data_out)  # {'a_tuple': [1, 2, 3, 4, 5]}
```

In this example, we have put a tuple, instead of a list. The interesting bit is that, conceptually, a tuple is also an ordered list of items. It doesn't have the flexibility of a list, but still, it is considered the same from the perspective of JSON. Therefore, as you can see by the first `print`, in JSON a tuple is transformed into a list. Naturally then, the information that it was a tuple is lost, and when deserialization happens, what we have in `data_out`, `a_tuple` is actually a list. It is important that you keep this in mind when dealing with data, as going through a transformation process that involves a format that only comprises a subset of the data structures you can use implies there will be information loss. In this case, we lost the information about the type (tuple versus list).

This is actually a common problem. For example, you can't serialize all Python objects to JSON, as it is not clear if JSON should revert that (or how). Think about `datetime`, for example. An instance of that class is a Python object that JSON won't allow serializing. If we transform it into a string such as `2018-03-04T12:00:30Z`, which is the ISO 8601 representation of a date with time and time zone information, what should JSON do when deserializing? Should it say *this is actually deserializable into a datetime object, so I'd better do it*, or should it simply consider it as a string and leave it as it is? What about data types that can be interpreted in more than one way?

The answer is that when dealing with data interchange, we often need to transform our objects into a simpler format prior to serializing them with JSON. This way, we will know how to reconstruct them correctly when we deserialize them.

In some cases, though, and mostly for internal use, it is useful to be able to serialize custom objects, so, just for fun, I'm going to show you how with two examples: complex numbers (because I love math) and *datetime* objects.

Custom encoding/decoding with JSON

In the JSON world, we can consider terms like encoding/decoding as synonyms to serializing/deserializing. They basically all mean transforming to and back from JSON. In the following example, I'm going to show you how to encode complex numbers:

```python
# json_examples/json_cplx.py
import json

class ComplexEncoder(json.JSONEncoder):
    def default(self, obj):
        if isinstance(obj, complex):
            return {
                '_meta': '_complex',
                'num': [obj.real, obj.imag],
            }
        return json.JSONEncoder.default(self, obj)

data = {
    'an_int': 42,
    'a_float': 3.14159265,
    'a_complex': 3 + 4j,
}

json_data = json.dumps(data, cls=ComplexEncoder)
print(json_data)

def object_hook(obj):
    try:
        if obj['_meta'] == '_complex':
            return complex(*obj['num'])
    except (KeyError, TypeError):
        return obj

data_out = json.loads(json_data, object_hook=object_hook)
print(data_out)
```

We start by defining a `ComplexEncoder` class, which needs to implement the `default` method. This method is passed to all the objects that have to be serialized, one at a time, in the `obj` variable. At some point, `obj` will be our complex number, *3+4j*. When that is true, we return a dictionary with some custom meta information, and a list that contains both the real and the imaginary part of the number. That is all we need to do to avoid losing information for a complex number.

We then call `json.dumps`, but this time we use the `cls` argument to specify our custom encoder. The result is printed:

```
{"an_int": 42, "a_float": 3.14159265, "a_complex": {"_meta": "_complex",
"num": [3.0, 4.0]}}
```

Half the job is done. For the deserialization part, we could have written another class that would inherit from `JSONDecoder`, but, just for fun, I've used a different technique that is simpler and uses a small function: `object_hook`.

Within the body of `object_hook`, we find another `try` block, but don't worry about it for now. I'll explain it in detail in the next chapter. The important part is the two lines within the body of the `try` block itself. The function receives an object (notice, the function is only called when `obj` is a dictionary), and if the metadata matches our convention for complex numbers, we pass the real and imaginary parts to the `complex` function. The `try/except` block is there only to prevent malformed JSON from ruining the party (and if that happens, we simply return the object as it is).

The last print returns:

```
{'an_int': 42, 'a_float': 3.14159265, 'a_complex': (3+4j)}
```

You can see that `a_complex` has been correctly deserialized.

Let's see a slightly more complex (no pun intended) example now: dealing with `datetime` objects. I'm going to split the code into two blocks, the serializing part, and the deserializing afterwards:

```
# json_examples/json_datetime.py
import json
from datetime import datetime, timedelta, timezone

now = datetime.now()
now_tz = datetime.now(tz=timezone(timedelta(hours=1)))

class DatetimeEncoder(json.JSONEncoder):
    def default(self, obj):
        if isinstance(obj, datetime):
```

```
                    try:
                        off = obj.utcoffset().seconds
                    except AttributeError:
                        off = None

                    return {
                        '_meta': '_datetime',
                        'data': obj.timetuple()[:6] + (obj.microsecond, ),
                        'utcoffset': off,
                    }
                return json.JSONEncoder.default(self, obj)

        data = {
            'an_int': 42,
            'a_float': 3.14159265,
            'a_datetime': now,
            'a_datetime_tz': now_tz,
        }

        json_data = json.dumps(data, cls=DatetimeEncoder)
        print(json_data)
```

The reason why this example is slightly more complex lies in the fact that `datetime` objects in Python can be time zone aware or not; therefore, we need to be more careful. The flow is basically the same as before, only it is dealing with a different data type. We start by getting the current date and time information, and we do it both without (`now`) and with (`now_tz`) time zone awareness, just to make sure our script works. We then proceed to define a custom encoder as before, and we implement once again the `default` method. The important bits in that method are how we get the time zone offset (`off`) information, in seconds, and how we structure the dictionary that returns the data. This time, the metadata says it's a *datetime* information, and then we save the first six items in the time tuple (year, month, day, hour, minute, and second), plus the microseconds in the `data` key, and the offset after that. Could you tell that the value of `data` is a concatenation of tuples? Good job if you could!

When we have our custom encoder, we proceed to create some data, and then we serialize. The `print` statement returns (after I've done some prettifying):

```
{
  "a_datetime": {
    "_meta": "_datetime",
    "data": [2018, 3, 18, 17, 57, 27, 438792],
    "utcoffset": null
  },
  "a_datetime_tz": {
    "_meta": "_datetime",
```

```
    "data": [2018, 3, 18, 18, 57, 27, 438810],
    "utcoffset": 3600
  },
  "a_float": 3.14159265,
  "an_int": 42
}
```

Interestingly, we find out that `None` is translated to `null`, its JavaScript equivalent.
Moreover, we can see our data seems to have been encoded properly. Let's proceed to the
second part of the script:

```python
# json_examples/json_datetime.py
def object_hook(obj):
    try:
        if obj['_meta'] == '_datetime':
            if obj['utcoffset'] is None:
                tz = None
            else:
                tz = timezone(timedelta(seconds=obj['utcoffset']))
            return datetime(*obj['data'], tzinfo=tz)
    except (KeyError, TypeError):
        return obj

data_out = json.loads(json_data, object_hook=object_hook)
```

Once again, we first verify that the metadata is telling us it's a `datetime`, and then we
proceed to fetch the time zone information. Once we have that, we pass the 7-tuple (using *
to unpack its values in the call) and the time zone information to the `datetime` call, getting
back our original object. Let's verify it by printing `data_out`:

```
{
  'a_datetime': datetime.datetime(2018, 3, 18, 18, 1, 46, 54693),
  'a_datetime_tz': datetime.datetime(
    2018, 3, 18, 19, 1, 46, 54711,
    tzinfo=datetime.timezone(datetime.timedelta(seconds=3600))),
  'a_float': 3.14159265,
  'an_int': 42
}
```

As you can see, we got everything back correctly. As an exercise, I'd like to challenge you to
write the same logic, but for a `date` object, which should be simpler.

Before we move on to the next topic, a word of caution. Perhaps it is counter-intuitive, but working with `datetime` objects can be one of the trickiest things to do, so, although I'm pretty sure this code is doing what it is supposed to do, I want to stress that I only tested it very lightly. So if you intend to grab it and use it, please do test it thoroughly. Test for different time zones, test for daylight saving time being on and off, test for dates before the epoch, and so on. You might find that the code in this section then would need some modifications to suit your cases.

Let's now move to the next topic, IO.

IO, streams, and requests

IO stands for **input/output**, and it broadly refers to the communication between a computer and the outside world. There are several different types of IO, and it is outside the scope of this chapter to explain all of them, but I still want to offer you a couple of examples.

Using an in-memory stream

The first will show you the `io.StringIO` class, which is an in-memory stream for text IO. The second one instead will escape the locality of our computer, and show you how to perform an HTTP request. Let's see the first example:

```
# io_examples/string_io.py
import io

stream = io.StringIO()
stream.write('Learning Python Programming.\n')
print('Become a Python ninja!', file=stream)

contents = stream.getvalue()
print(contents)

stream.close()
```

In the preceding code snippet, we import the `io` module from the standard library. This is a very interesting module that features many tools related to streams and IO. One of them is `StringIO`, which is an in-memory buffer in which we're going to write two sentences, using two different methods, as we did with files in the first examples of this chapter. We can both call `StringIO.write` or we can use `print`, and tell it to direct the data to our stream.

By calling `getvalue`, we can get the content of the stream (and print it), and finally we close it. The call to `close` causes the text buffer to be immediately discarded.

There is a more elegant way to write the previous code (can you guess it, before you look?):

```
# io_examples/string_io.py
with io.StringIO() as stream:
    stream.write('Learning Python Programming.\n')
    print('Become a Python ninja!', file=stream)
    contents = stream.getvalue()
    print(contents)
```

Yes, it is again a context manager. Like `open`, `io.StringIO` works well within a context manager block. Notice the similarity with `open`: in this case too, we don't need to manually close the stream.

In-memory objects can be useful in a multitude of situations. Memory is much faster than a disk and, for small amounts of data, can be the perfect choice.

When running the script, the output is:

```
$ python string_io.py
Learning Python Programming.
Become a Python ninja!
```

Making HTTP requests

Let's now explore a couple of examples on HTTP requests. I will use the `requests` library for these examples, which you can install with `pip`. We're going to perform HTTP requests against the `httpbin.org` API, which, interestingly, was developed by Kenneth Reitz, the creator of the `requests` library itself. This library is amongst the most widely adopted all over the world:

```
import requests

urls = {
    'get': 'https://httpbin.org/get?title=learn+python+programming',
    'headers': 'https://httpbin.org/headers',
    'ip': 'https://httpbin.org/ip',
    'now': 'https://now.httpbin.org/',
    'user-agent': 'https://httpbin.org/user-agent',
    'UUID': 'https://httpbin.org/uuid',
}

def get_content(title, url):
```

```
    resp = requests.get(url)
    print(f'Response for {title}')
    print(resp.json())

for title, url in urls.items():
    get_content(title, url)
    print('-' * 40)
```

The preceding snippet should be simple to understand. I declare a dictionary of URLs against which I want to perform requests. I have encapsulated the code that performs the request into a tiny function: get_content. As you can see, very simply, we perform a GET request (by using requests.get), and we print the title and the JSON decoded version of the body of the response. Let me spend a word about this last bit.

When we perform a request to a website, or API, we get back a response object, which is, very simply, what was returned by the server we performed the request against. The body of all responses from httpbin.org happens to be JSON encoded, so instead of getting the body as it is (by getting resp.text) and manually decoding it, calling json.loads on it, we simply combine the two by leveraging the json method on the response object. There are plenty of reasons why the requests package has become so widely adopted, and one of them is definitely its ease of use.

Now, when you perform a request in your application, you will want to have a much more robust approach in dealing with errors and so on, but for this chapter, a simple example will do. Don't worry, I will give you a more comprehensive introduction to HTTP requests in Chapter 14, *Web Development*.

Going back to our code, in the end, we run a for loop and get all the URLs. When you run it, you will see the result of each call printed on your console, like this (prettified and trimmed for brevity):

```
$ python reqs.py
Response for get
{
  "args": {
    "title": "learn python programming"
  },
  "headers": {
    "Accept": "*/*",
    "Accept-Encoding": "gzip, deflate",
    "Connection": "close",
    "Host": "httpbin.org",
    "User-Agent": "python-requests/2.19.0"
  },
  "origin": "82.47.175.158",
```

```
    "url": "https://httpbin.org/get?title=learn+python+programming"
}
... rest of the output omitted ...
```

Notice that you might get a slightly different output in terms of version numbers and IPs, which is fine. Now, GET is only one of the HTTP verbs, and it is definitely the most commonly used. The second one is the ubiquitous POST, which is the type of request you make when you need to send data to the server. Every time you submit a form on the web, you're basically making a POST request. So, let's try to make one programmatically:

```python
# io_examples/reqs_post.py
import requests

url = 'https://httpbin.org/post'
data = dict(title='Learn Python Programming')

resp = requests.post(url, data=data)
print('Response for POST')
print(resp.json())
```

The previous code is very similar to the one we saw before, only this time we don't call `get`, but `post`, and because we want to send some data, we specify that in the call. The `requests` library offers much, much more than this, and it has been praised by the community for the beautiful API it exposes. It is a project that I encourage you to check out and explore, as you will end up using it all the time, anyway.

Running the previous script (and applying some prettifying magic to the output) yields the following:

```
$ python reqs_post.py
Response for POST
{ 'args': {},
  'data': '',
  'files': {},
  'form': {'title': 'Learn Python Programming'},
  'headers': { 'Accept': '*/*',
               'Accept-Encoding': 'gzip, deflate',
               'Connection': 'close',
               'Content-Length': '30',
               'Content-Type': 'application/x-www-form-urlencoded',
               'Host': 'httpbin.org',
               'User-Agent': 'python-requests/2.7.0 CPython/3.7.0b2 '
                             'Darwin/17.4.0'},
  'json': None,
```

```
'origin': '82.45.123.178',
'url': 'https://httpbin.org/post'}
```

Notice how the headers are now different, and we find the data we sent in the `form` key/value pair of the response body.

I hope these short examples are enough to get you started, especially with requests. The web changes every day, so it's worth learning the basics and then brush up every now and then.

Let's now move on to the last topic of this chapter: persisting data on disk in different formats.

Persisting data on disk

In the last section of this chapter, we're exploring how to persist data on disk in three different formats. We will explore `pickle`, `shelve`, and a short example that will involve accessing a database using SQLAlchemy, the most widely adopted ORM library in the Python ecosystem.

Serializing data with pickle

The `pickle` module, from the Python standard library, offers tools to convert Python objects into byte streams, and vice versa. Even though there is a partial overlap in the API that `pickle` and `json` expose, the two are quite different. As we have seen previously in this chapter, JSON is a text format, human readable, language independent, and supports only a restricted subset of Python data types. The `pickle` module, on the other hand, is not human readable, translates to bytes, is Python specific, and, thanks to the wonderful Python introspection capabilities, it supports an extremely large amount of data types.

Regardless of these differences, though, which you should know when you consider whether to use one or the other, I think that the most important concern regarding `pickle` lies in the security threats you are exposed to when you use it. *Unpickling* erroneous or malicious data from an untrusted source can be very dangerous, so if you decide to adopt it in your application, you need to be extra careful.

That said, let's see it in action, by means of a simple example:

```
# persistence/pickler.py
import pickle
from dataclasses import dataclass
```

```
@dataclass
class Person:
    first_name: str
    last_name: str
    id: int

    def greet(self):
        print(f'Hi, I am {self.first_name} {self.last_name}'
              f' and my ID is {self.id}'
        )

people = [
    Person('Obi-Wan', 'Kenobi', 123),
    Person('Anakin', 'Skywalker', 456),
]

# save data in binary format to a file
with open('data.pickle', 'wb') as stream:
    pickle.dump(people, stream)

# load data from a file
with open('data.pickle', 'rb') as stream:
    peeps = pickle.load(stream)

for person in peeps:
    person.greet()
```

In the previous example, we create a Person class using the dataclass decorator, which we have seen in Chapter 6, *OOP, Decorators, and Iterators*. The only reason I wrote this example with a data class is to show you how effortlessly pickle deals with it, with no need for us to do anything we wouldn't do for a simpler data type.

The class has three attributes: first_name, last_name, and id. It also exposes a greet method, which simply prints a hello message with the data.

We create a list of instances, and then we save it to a file. In order to do so, we use pickle.dump, to which we feed the content to be *pickled,* and the stream to which we want to write. Immediately after that, we read from that same file, and by using pickle.load, we convert back into Python the whole content of that stream. Just to make sure that the objects have been converted correctly, we call the greet method on both of them. The result is the following:

```
$ python pickler.py
Hi, I am Obi-Wan Kenobi and my ID is 123
Hi, I am Anakin Skywalker and my ID is 456
```

The `pickle` module also allows you to convert to (and from) byte objects, by means of the `dumps` and `loads` functions (note the `s` at the end of both names). In day-to-day applications, `pickle` is usually used when we need to persist Python data that is not supposed to be exchanged with another application. One example I stumbled upon recently was the session management in a `flask` plugin, which pickles the session object before sending it to Redis. In practice, though, you are unlikely to have to deal with this library very often.

Another tool that is possibly used even less, but that proves to be very useful when you are short of resources, is `shelve`.

Saving data with shelve

A `shelf`, is a persistent dictionary-like object. The beauty of it is that the values you save into a `shelf` can be any object you can `pickle`, so you're not restricted like you would be if you were using a database. Albeit interesting and useful, the `shelve` module is used quite rarely in practice. Just for completeness, let's see a quick example of how it works:

```
# persistence/shelf.py
import shelve

class Person:
    def __init__(self, name, id):
        self.name = name
        self.id = id

with shelve.open('shelf1.shelve') as db:
    db['obi1'] = Person('Obi-Wan', 123)
    db['ani'] = Person('Anakin', 456)
    db['a_list'] = [2, 3, 5]
    db['delete_me'] = 'we will have to delete this one...'

    print(list(db.keys()))  # ['ani', 'a_list', 'delete_me', 'obi1']

    del db['delete_me']  # gone!

    print(list(db.keys()))  # ['ani', 'a_list', 'obi1']

    print('delete_me' in db)  # False
    print('ani' in db)  # True

    a_list = db['a_list']
    a_list.append(7)
```

```
db['a_list'] = a_list
print(db['a_list'])  # [2, 3, 5, 7]
```

Apart from the wiring and the boilerplate around it, the previous example resembles an exercise with dictionaries. We create a simple `Person` class and then we open a `shelve` file within a context manager. As you can see, we use the dictionary syntax to store four objects: two `Person` instances, a list, and a string. If we print the `keys`, we get a list containing the four keys we used. Immediately after printing it, we delete the (aptly named) `delete_me` key/value pair from shelf. Printing the `keys` again shows the deletion has succeeded. We then test a couple of keys for membership, and finally, we append number 7 to `a_list`. Notice how we have to extract the list from the shelf, modify it, and save it again.

In case this behavior is undesired, there is something we can do:

```
# persistence/shelf.py
with shelve.open('shelf2.shelve', writeback=True) as db:
    db['a_list'] = [11, 13, 17]
    db['a_list'].append(19)  # in-place append!
    print(db['a_list'])  # [11, 13, 17, 19]
```

By opening the shelf with `writeback=True`, we enable the `writeback` feature, which allows us to simply append to `a_list` as if it actually was a value within a regular dictionary. The reason why this feature is not active by default is that it comes with a price that you pay in terms of memory consumption and slower closing of the shelf.

Now that we have paid homage to the standard library modules related to data persistence, let's take a look at the most widely adopted ORM in the Python ecosystem: *SQLAlchemy*.

Saving data to a database

For this example, we are going to work with an in-memory database, which will make things simpler for us. In the source code of the book, I have left a couple of comments to show you how to generate a SQLite file, so I hope you'll explore that option as well.

 You can find a free database browser for SQLite at `sqlitebrowser.org`. If you are not satisfied with it, you will be able to find a wide range of tools, some free, some not free, that you can use to access and manipulate a database file.

Before we dive into the code, allow me to briefly introduce the concept of a relational database.

A relational database is a database that allows you to save data following the **relational model**, invented in 1969 by Edgar F. Codd. In this model, data is stored in one or more tables. Each table has rows (also known as **records**, or **tuples**), each of which represents an entry in the table. Tables also have columns (also known as **attributes**), each of which represents an attribute of the records. Each record is identified through a unique key, more commonly known as the **primary key**, which is the union of one or more columns in the table. To give you an example: imagine a table called `Users`, with columns `id`, `username`, `password`, `name`, and `surname`. Such a table would be perfect to contain users of our system. Each row would represent a different user. For example, a row with the values `3`, `gianchub`, `my_wonderful_pwd`, `Fabrizio`, and `Romano`, would represent my user in the system.

The reason why the model is called **relational** is because you can establish relations between tables. For example, if you added a table called `PhoneNumbers` to our fictitious database, you could insert phone numbers into it, and then, through a relation, establish which phone number belongs to which user.

In order to query a relational database, we need a special language. The main standard is called **SQL**, which stands for **Structured Query Language**. It is born out of something called **relational algebra**, which is a very nice family of algebras used to model data stored according to the relational model, and performing queries on it. The most common operations you can perform usually involve filtering on the rows or columns, joining tables, aggregating the results according to some criteria, and so on. To give you an example in English, a query on our imaginary database could be: *Fetch all users (username, name, surname) whose username starts with "m", who have at most one phone number*. In this query, we are asking for a subset of the columns in the `User` table. We are filtering on users by taking only those whose username starts with the letter *m*, and even further, only those who have at most one phone number.

 Back in the days when I was a student in Padova, I spent a whole semester learning both the relational algebra semantics, and the standard SQL (amongst other things). If it wasn't for a major bicycle accident I had the day of the exam, I would say that this was one of the most fun exams I ever had to prepare.

Now, each database comes with its own *flavor* of SQL. They all respect the standard to some extent, but none fully does, and they are all different from one another in some respects. This poses an issue in modern software development. If our application contains SQL code, it is quite likely that if we decided to use a different database engine, or maybe a different version of the same engine, we would find our SQL code needs amending.

This can be quite painful, especially since SQL queries can become very, very complicated quite quickly. In order to alleviate this pain a little, computer scientists (*bless them*) have created code that maps objects of a particular language to tables of a relational database. Unsurprisingly, the name of such tools is **Object-Relational Mapping (ORMs)**.

In modern application development, you would normally start interacting with a database by using an ORM, and should you find yourself in a situation where you can't perform a query you need to perform, through the ORM, you would then resort to using SQL directly. This is a good compromise between having no SQL at all, and using no ORM, which ultimately means specializing the code that interacts with the database, with the aforementioned disadvantages.

In this section, I'd like to show an example that leverages SQLAlchemy, the most popular Python ORM. We are going to define two models (`Person` and `Address`) which map to a table each, and then we're going to populate the database and perform a few queries on it.

Let's start with the model declarations:

```
# persistence/alchemy_models.py
from sqlalchemy.ext.declarative import declarative_base
from sqlalchemy import (
    Column, Integer, String, ForeignKey, create_engine)
from sqlalchemy.orm import relationship
```

At the beginning, we import some functions and types. The first thing we need to do then is to create an engine. This engine tells SQLAlchemy about the type of database we have chosen for our example:

```
# persistence/alchemy_models.py
engine = create_engine('sqlite:///:memory:')
Base = declarative_base()

class Person(Base):
    __tablename__ = 'person'

    id = Column(Integer, primary_key=True)
    name = Column(String)
    age = Column(Integer)
```

```
        addresses = relationship(
            'Address',
            back_populates='person',
            order_by='Address.email',
            cascade='all, delete-orphan'
        )

        def __repr__(self):
            return f'{self.name}(id={self.id})'

    class Address(Base):
        __tablename__ = 'address'

        id = Column(Integer, primary_key=True)
        email = Column(String)
        person_id = Column(ForeignKey('person.id'))
        person = relationship('Person', back_populates='addresses')

        def __str__(self):
            return self.email
        __repr__ = __str__

Base.metadata.create_all(engine)
```

Each model then inherits from the `Base` table, which in this example consists of the mere default, returned by `declarative_base()`. We define `Person`, which maps to a table called `person`, and exposes the attributes `id`, `name`, and `age`. We also declare a relationship with the `Address` model, by stating that accessing the `addresses` attribute will fetch all the entries in the `address` table that are related to the particular `Person` instance we're dealing with. The `cascade` option affects how creation and deletion work, but it is a more advanced concept, so I'd suggest you glide on it for now and maybe investigate more later on.

The last thing we declare is the `__repr__` method, which provides us with the official string representation of an object. This is supposed to be a representation that can be used to completely reconstruct the object, but in this example, I simply use it to provide something in output. Python redirects `repr(obj)` to a call to `obj.__repr__()`.

We also declare the `Address` model, which will contain email addresses, and a reference to the person they belong to. You can see the `person_id` and `person` attributes are both about setting a relation between the `Address` and `Person` instances. Note how I declared the `__str__` method on `Address`, and then assigned an alias to it, called `__repr__`. This means that calling both `repr` and `str` on `Address` objects will ultimately result in calling the `__str__` method. This is quite a common technique in Python, so I took the opportunity to show it to you here.

On the last line, we tell the engine to create tables in the database according to our models.

A deeper understanding of this code would require much more space than I can afford, so I encourage you to read up on **database management systems** (**DBMS**), SQL, Relational Algebra, and SQLAlchemy.

Now that we have our models, let's use them to persist some data!

Let's take a look at the following example:

```
# persistence/alchemy.py
from alchemy_models import Person, Address, engine
from sqlalchemy.orm import sessionmaker

Session = sessionmaker(bind=engine)
session = Session()
```

First we create `session`, which is the object we use to manage the database. Next, we proceed by creating two people:

```
anakin = Person(name='Anakin Skywalker', age=32)
obi1 = Person(name='Obi-Wan Kenobi', age=40)
```

We then add email addresses to both of them, using two different techniques. One assigns them to a list, and the other one simply appends them:

```
obi1.addresses = [
    Address(email='obi1@example.com'),
    Address(email='wanwan@example.com'),
]

anakin.addresses.append(Address(email='ani@example.com'))
anakin.addresses.append(Address(email='evil.dart@example.com'))
anakin.addresses.append(Address(email='vader@example.com'))
```

We haven't touched the database yet. It's only when we use the session object that something actually happens in it:

```
session.add(anakin)
session.add(obi1)
session.commit()
```

Adding the two `Person` instances is enough to also add their addresses (this is thanks to the cascading effect). Calling `commit` is what actually tells SQLAlchemy to commit the transaction and save the data in the database. A transaction is an operation that provides something like a sandbox, but in a database context. As long as the transaction hasn't been committed, we can roll back any modification we have done to the database, and by so doing, revert to the state we were before starting the transaction itself. SQLAlchemy offers more complex and granular ways to deal with transactions, which you can study in its official documentation, as it is quite an advanced topic. We now query for all the people whose name starts with `Obi` by using `like`, which hooks to the `LIKE` operator in SQL:

```
obi1 = session.query(Person).filter(
    Person.name.like('Obi%')
).first()
print(obi1, obi1.addresses)
```

We take the first result of that query (we know we only have Obi-Wan anyway), and print it. We then fetch `anakin`, by using an exact match on his name (just to show you a different way of filtering):

```
anakin = session.query(Person).filter(
    Person.name=='Anakin Skywalker'
).first()
print(anakin, anakin.addresses)
```

We then capture Anakin's ID, and delete the `anakin` object from the global frame:

```
anakin_id = anakin.id
del anakin
```

The reason we do this is because I want to show you how to fetch an object by its ID. Before we do that, we write the `display_info` function, which we will use to display the full content of the database (fetched starting from the addresses, in order to demonstrate how to fetch objects by using a relation attribute in SQLAlchemy):

```
def display_info():
    # get all addresses first
    addresses = session.query(Address).all()

    # display results
```

```
for address in addresses:
    print(f'{address.person.name} <{address.email}>')

# display how many objects we have in total
print('people: {}, addresses: {}'.format(
    session.query(Person).count(),
    session.query(Address).count())
)
```

The `display_info` function prints all the addresses, along with the respective person's name, and, at the end, produces a final piece of information regarding the number of objects in the database. We call the function, then we fetch and delete `anakin` (think about *Darth Vader* and you won't be sad about deleting him), and then we display the info again, to verify he's actually disappeared from the database:

```
display_info()

anakin = session.query(Person).get(anakin_id)
session.delete(anakin)
session.commit()

display_info()
```

The output of all these snippets run together is the following (for your convenience, I have separated the output into four blocks, to reflect the four blocks of code that actually produce that output):

```
$ python alchemy.py
Obi-Wan Kenobi(id=2) [obi1@example.com, wanwan@example.com]

Anakin Skywalker(id=1) [ani@example.com, evil.dart@example.com,
vader@example.com]

Anakin Skywalker <ani@example.com>
Anakin Skywalker <evil.dart@example.com>
Anakin Skywalker <vader@example.com>
Obi-Wan Kenobi <obi1@example.com>
Obi-Wan Kenobi <wanwan@example.com>
people: 2, addresses: 5

Obi-Wan Kenobi <obi1@example.com>
Obi-Wan Kenobi <wanwan@example.com>
people: 1, addresses: 2
```

As you can see from the last two blocks, deleting `anakin` has deleted one `Person` object, and the three addresses associated with it. Again, this is due to the fact that cascading took place when we deleted `anakin`.

This concludes our brief introduction to data persistence. It is a vast and, at times, complex domain, which I encourage you to explore learning as much theory as possible. Lack of knowledge or proper understanding, when it comes to database systems, can really bite.

Summary

In this chapter, we have explored working with files and directories. We have learned how to open files for reading and writing and how to do that more elegantly by using context managers. We also explored directories: how to list their content, both recursively and not. We also learned about pathnames, which are the gateway to accessing both files and directories.

We then briefly saw how to create a ZIP archive, and extract its content. The source code of the book also contains an example with a different compression format: `tar.gz`.

We talked about data interchange formats, and have explored JSON in some depth. We had some fun writing custom encoders and decoders for specific Python data types.

Then we explored IO, both with in-memory streams and HTTP requests.

And finally, we saw how to persist data using `pickle`, `shelve`, and the SQLAlchemy ORM library.

You should now have a pretty good idea of how to deal with files and data persistence, and I hope you will take the time to explore these topics in much more depth by yourself.

The next chapter will look at testing, profiling, and dealing with exceptions.

8
Testing, Profiling, and Dealing with Exceptions

"Just as the wise accepts gold after testing it by heating, cutting and rubbing it, so are my words to be accepted after examining them, but not out of respect for me."

– Buddha

I love this quote by the Buddha. Within the software world, it translates perfectly into the healthy habit of never trusting code just because someone smart wrote it or because it's been working fine for a long a time. If it has not been tested, code is not to be trusted.

Why are tests so important? Well, for one, they give you predictability. Or, at least, they help you achieve high predictability. Unfortunately, there is always some bug that sneaks into the code. But we definitely want our code to be as predictable as possible. What we don't want is to have a surprise, in other words, our code behaving in an unpredictable way. Would you be happy to know that the software that checks on the sensors of the plane that is taking you on your holidays sometimes goes crazy? No, probably not.

Therefore, we need to test our code; we need to check that its behavior is correct, that it works as expected when it deals with edge cases, that it doesn't hang when the components it's talking to are broken or unreachable, that the performances are well within the acceptable range, and so on.

This chapter is all about that—making sure that your code is prepared to face the scary outside world, that it's fast enough, and that it can deal with unexpected or exceptional conditions.

In this chapter, we're going to explore the following topics:

- Testing (several aspects of it, including a brief introduction to test-driven development)
- Exception handling
- Profiling and performances

Let's start by understanding what testing is.

Testing your application

There are many different kinds of tests, so many, in fact, that companies often have a dedicated department, called **quality assurance** (**QA**), made up of individuals who spend their day testing the software the company developers produce.

To start making an initial classification, we can divide tests into two broad categories: white-box and black-box tests.

White-box tests are those that exercise the internals of the code; they inspect it down to a very fine level of detail. On the other hand, **black-box tests** are those that consider the software under test as if within a box, the internals of which are ignored. Even the technology, or the language used inside the box, is not important for black-box tests. What they do is plug input into one end of the box and verify the output at the other end—that's it.

 There is also an in-between category, called **gray-box** testing, which involves testing a system in the same way we do with the black-box approach, but having some knowledge about the algorithms and data structures used to write the software and only partial access to its source code.

There are many different kinds of tests in these categories, each of which serves a different purpose. To give you an idea, here are a few:

- **Frontend tests**: Make sure that the client side of your application is exposing the information that it should, all the links, the buttons, the advertising, everything that needs to be shown to the client. It may also verify that it is possible to walk a certain path through the user interface.
- **Scenario tests**: Make use of stories (or scenarios) that help the tester work through a complex problem or test a part of the system.

- **Integration tests**: Verify the behavior of the various components of your application when they are working together sending messages through interfaces.
- **Smoke tests**: Particularly useful when you deploy a new update on your application. They check whether the most essential, vital parts of your application are still working as they should and that they are not *on fire*. This term comes from when engineers tested circuits by making sure nothing was smoking.
- **Acceptance tests**, or **user acceptance testing** (**UAT**): What a developer does with a product owner (for example, in a SCRUM environment) to determine whether the work that was commissioned was carried out correctly.
- **Functional tests**: Verify the features or functionalities of your software.
- **Destructive tests**: Take down parts of your system, simulating a failure, to establish how well the remaining parts of the system perform. These kinds of tests are performed extensively by companies that need to provide an extremely reliable service, such as Amazon and Netflix, for example.
- **Performance tests**: Aim to verify how well the system performs under a specific load of data or traffic so that, for example, engineers can get a better understanding of the bottlenecks in the system that could bring it to its knees in a heavy-load situation, or those that prevent scalability.
- **Usability tests**, and the closely related **user experience** (**UX**) tests: Aim to check whether the user interface is simple and easy to understand and use. They aim to provide input to the designers so that the user experience is improved.
- **Security and penetration tests**: Aim to verify how well the system is protected against attacks and intrusions.
- **Unit tests**: Help the developer to write the code in a robust and consistent way, providing the first line of feedback and defense against coding mistakes, refactoring mistakes, and so on.
- **Regression tests**: Provide the developer with useful information about a feature being compromised in the system after an update. Some of the causes for a system being said to have a regression are an old bug coming back to life, an existing feature being compromised, or a new issue being introduced.

Many books and articles have been written about testing, and I have to point you to those resources if you're interested in finding out more about all the different kinds of tests. In this chapter, we will concentrate on unit tests, since they are the backbone of software-crafting and form the vast majority of tests that are written by a developer.

Testing is an *art*, an art that you don't learn from books, I'm afraid. You can learn all the definitions (and you should), and try to collect as much knowledge about testing as you can, but you will likely be able to test your software properly only when you have done it for long enough in the field.

When you are having trouble refactoring a bit of code, because every little thing you touch makes a test blow up, you learn how to write less rigid and limiting tests, which still verify the correctness of your code but, at the same time, allow you the freedom and joy to play with it, to shape it as you want.

When you are being called too often to fix unexpected bugs in your code, you learn how to write tests more thoroughly, how to come up with a more comprehensive list of edge cases, and strategies to cope with them before they turn into bugs.

When you are spending too much time reading tests and trying to refactor them to change a small feature in the code, you learn to write simpler, shorter, and better-focused tests.

I could go on with this *when you... you learn...*, but I guess you get the picture. You need to get your hands dirty and build experience. My suggestion? Study the theory as much as you can, and then experiment using different approaches. Also, try to learn from experienced coders; it's very effective.

The anatomy of a test

Before we concentrate on unit tests, let's see what a test is, and what its purpose is.

A **test** is a piece of code whose purpose is to verify something in our system. It may be that we're calling a function passing two integers, that an object has a property called `donald_duck`, or that when you place an order on some API, after a minute you can see it dissected into its basic elements, in the database.

A test is typically composed of three sections:

- **Preparation**: This is where you set up the scene. You prepare all the data, the objects, and the services you need in the places you need them so that they are ready to be used.
- **Execution**: This is where you execute the bit of logic that you're checking against. You perform an action using the data and the interfaces you have set up in the preparation phase.

- **Verification**: This is where you verify the results and make sure they are according to your expectations. You check the returned value of a function, or that some data is in the database, some is not, some has changed, a request has been made, something has happened, a method has been called, and so on.

While tests usually follow this structure, in a test suite, you will typically find some other constructs that take part in the testing game:

- **Setup**: This is something quite commonly found in several different tests. It's logic that can be customized to run for every test, class, module, or even for a whole session. In this phase usually developers set up connections to databases, maybe populate them with data that will be needed there for the test to make sense, and so on.
- **Teardown**: This is the opposite of the setup; the teardown phase takes place when the tests have been run. Like the setup, it can be customized to run for every test, class or module, or session. Typically in this phase, we destroy any artefacts that were created for the test suite, and clean up after ourselves.
- **Fixtures**: They are pieces of data used in the tests. By using a specific set of fixture, outcomes are predictable and therefore tests can perform verifications against them.

In this chapter, we will use the `pytest` Python library. It is an incredibly powerful tool that makes testing much easier and provides plenty of helpers so that the test logic can focus more on the actual testing than the wiring around it. You will see, when we get to the code, that one of the characteristics of `pytest` is that fixtures, setup, and teardown often blend into one.

Testing guidelines

Like software, tests can be good or bad, with a whole range of shades in the middle. To write good tests, here are some guidelines:

- **Keep them as simple as possible**. It's okay to violate some good coding rules, such as hardcoding values or duplicating code. Tests need, first and foremost, to be as **readable** as possible and easy to understand. When tests are hard to read or understand, you can never be confident they are actually making sure your code is performing correctly.

- **Tests should verify one thing and one thing only**. It's very important that you keep them short and contained. It's perfectly fine to write multiple tests to exercise a single object or function. Just make sure that each test has one and only one purpose.

- **Tests should not make any unnecessary assumption when verifying data**. This is tricky to understand at first, but it is important. Verifying that the result of a function call is [1, 2, 3] is not the same as saying the output is a list that contains the numbers 1, 2, and 3. In the former, we're also assuming the ordering; in the latter, we're only assuming which items are in the list. The differences sometimes are quite subtle, but they are still very important.

- **Tests should exercise the what, rather than the how**. Tests should focus on checking *what* a function is supposed to do, rather than *how* it is doing it. For example, focus on the fact that it's calculating the square root of a number (the *what*), instead of on the fact that it is calling math.sqrt to do it (the *how*). Unless you're writing performance tests or you have a particular need to verify how a certain action is performed, try to avoid this type of testing and focus on the *what*. Testing the *how* leads to restrictive tests and makes refactoring hard. Moreover, the type of test you have to write when you concentrate on the *how* is more likely to degrade the quality of your testing code base when you amend your software frequently.

- **Tests should use the minimal set of fixtures needed to do the job**. This is another crucial point. Fixtures have a tendency to grow over time. They also tend to change every now and then. If you use big amounts of fixtures and ignore redundancies in your tests, refactoring will take longer. Spotting bugs will be harder. Try to use a set of fixtures that is big enough for the test to perform correctly, but not any bigger.

- **Tests should run as fast as possible**. A good test codebase could end up being much longer than the code being tested itself. It varies according to the situation and the developer, but, whatever the length, you'll end up having hundreds, if not thousands, of tests to run, which means the faster they run, the faster you can get back to writing code. When using TDD, for example, you run tests very often, so speed is essential.

- **Tests should use up the least possible amount of resources**. The reason for this is that every developer who checks out your code should be able to run your tests, no matter how powerful their box is. It could be a skinny virtual machine or a neglected Jenkins box, your tests should run without chewing up too many resources.

A **Jenkins** box is a machine that runs Jenkins, software that is capable of, among many other things, running your tests automatically. Jenkins is frequently used in companies where developers use practices such as continuous integration and extreme programming.

Unit testing

Now that you have an idea about what testing is and why we need it, let's introduce the developer's best friend: the **unit test**.

Before we proceed with the examples, allow me to share some words of caution: I'll try to give you the fundamentals about unit testing, but I don't follow any particular school of thought or methodology to the letter. Over the years, I have tried many different testing approaches, eventually coming up with my own way of doing things, which is constantly evolving. To put it as Bruce Lee would have:

> "Absorb what is useful, discard what is useless and add what is specifically your own."

Writing a unit test

Unit tests take their name after the fact that they are used to test small units of code. To explain how to write a unit test, let's take a look at a simple snippet:

```
# data.py
def get_clean_data(source):
    data = load_data(source)
    cleaned_data = clean_data(data)
    return cleaned_data
```

The `get_clean data` function is responsible for getting data from `source`, cleaning it, and returning it to the caller. How do we test this function?

One way of doing this is to call it and then make sure that `load_data` was called once with `source` as its only argument. Then we have to verify that `clean_data` was called once, with the return value of `load_data`. And, finally, we would need to make sure that the return value of `clean_data` is what is returned by the `get_clean_data` function as well.

To do this, we need to set up the source and run this code, and this may be a problem. One of the golden rules of unit testing is that *anything that crosses the boundaries of your application needs to be simulated*. We don't want to talk to a real data source, and we don't want to actually run real functions if they are communicating with anything that is not contained in our application. A few examples would be a database, a search service, an external API, and a file in the filesystem.

We need these restrictions to act as a shield, so that we can always run our tests safely without the fear of destroying something in a real data source.

Another reason is that it may be quite difficult for a single developer to reproduce the whole architecture on their box. It may require the setting up of databases, APIs, services, files and folders, and so on and so forth, and this can be difficult, time-consuming, or sometimes not even possible.

Very simply put, an **application programming interface** (**API**) is a set of tools for building software applications. An API expresses a software component in terms of its operations, input and output, and underlying types. For example, if you create a software that needs to interface with a data provider service, it's very likely that you will have to go through their API in order to gain access to the data.

Therefore, in our unit tests, we need to simulate all those things in some way. Unit tests need to be run by any developer without the need for the whole system to be set up on their box.

A different approach, which I always favor when it's possible to do so, is to simulate entities without using fake objects, but using special-purpose test objects instead. For example, if your code talks to a database, instead of faking all the functions and methods that talk to the database and programming the fake objects so that they return what the real ones would, I'd much rather spawn a test database, set up the tables and data I need, and then patch the connection settings so that my tests are running real code, against the test database, thereby doing no harm at all. In-memory databases are excellent options for these cases.

One of the applications that allow you to spawn a database for testing is Django. Within the `django.test` package, you can find several tools that help you write your tests so that you won't have to simulate the dialog with a database. By writing tests this way, you will also be able to check on transactions, encodings, and all other database-related aspects of programming. Another advantage of this approach consists in the ability of checking against things that can change from one database to another.

Sometimes, though, it's still not possible, and we need to use fakes, so let's talk about them.

Mock objects and patching

First of all, in Python, these fake objects are called **mocks**. Up to Version 3.3, the `mock` library was a third-party library that basically every project would install via `pip` but, from Version 3.3, it has been included in the standard library under the `unittest` module, and rightfully so, given its importance and how widespread it is.

The act of replacing a real object or function (or in general, any piece of data structure) with a mock, is called **patching**. The `mock` library provides the `patch` tool, which can act as a function or class decorator, and even as a context manager that you can use to mock things out. Once you have replaced everything you don't need to run with suitable mocks, you can pass to the second phase of the test and run the code you are exercising. After the execution, you will be able to check those mocks to verify that your code has worked correctly.

Assertions

The verification phase is done through the use of assertions. An **assertion** is a function (or method) that you can use to verify equality between objects, as well as other conditions. When a condition is not met, the assertion will raise an exception that will make your test fail. You can find a list of assertions in the `unittest` module documentation; however, when using `pytest`, you will typically use the generic `assert` statement, which makes things even simpler.

Testing a CSV generator

Let's now adopt a practical approach. I will show you how to test a piece of code, and we will touch on the rest of the important concepts around unit testing, within the context of this example.

We want to write an `export` function that does the following: it takes a list of dictionaries, each of which represents a user. It creates a CSV file, puts a header in it, and then proceeds to add all the users who are deemed valid according to some rules. The `export` function takes also a filename, which will be the name for the CSV in output. And, finally, it takes an indication on whether to allow an existing file with the same name to be overwritten.

As for the users, they must abide by the following: each user has at least an email, a name, and an age. There can be a fourth field representing the role, but it's optional. The user's email address needs to be valid, the name needs to be non-empty, and the age must be an integer between 18 and 65.

This is our task, so now I'm going to show you the code, and then we're going to analyze the tests I wrote for it. But, first things first, in the following code snippets, I'll be using two third-party libraries: `marshmallow` and `pytest`. They both are in the requirements of the book's source code, so make sure you have installed them with `pip`.

`marshmallow` is a wonderful library that provides us with the ability to serialize and deserialize objects and, most importantly, gives us the ability to define a schema that we can use to validate a user dictionary. `pytest` is one of the best pieces of software I have ever seen. It is used everywhere now, and has replaced other tools such as `nose`, for example. It provides us with great tools to write beautiful short tests.

But let's get to the code. I called it `api.py` just because it exposes a function that we can use to do things. I'll show it to you in chunks:

```
# api.py
import os
import csv
from copy import deepcopy

from marshmallow import Schema, fields, pre_load
from marshmallow.validate import Length, Range

class UserSchema(Schema):
    """Represent a *valid* user. """

    email = fields.Email(required=True)
    name = fields.String(required=True, validate=Length(min=1))
```

```
    age = fields.Integer(
        required=True, validate=Range(min=18, max=65)
    )
    role = fields.String()

    @pre_load(pass_many=False)
    def strip_name(self, data):
        data_copy = deepcopy(data)

        try:
            data_copy['name'] = data_copy['name'].strip()
        except (AttributeError, KeyError, TypeError):
            pass

        return data_copy

schema = UserSchema()
```

This first part is where we import all the modules we need (`os` and `csv`), and some tools from `marshmallow`, and then we define the schema for the users. As you can see, we inherit from `marshmallow.Schema`, and then we set four fields. Notice we are using two `String` fields, `Email` and `Integer`. These will already provide us with some validation from `marshmallow`. Notice there is no `required=True` in the `role` field.

We need to add a couple of custom bits of code, though. We need to add `validate_age` to make sure the value is within the range we want. We raise `ValidationError` in case it's not. And `marshmallow` will kindly take care of raising an error should we pass anything but an integer.

Next, we add `validate_name`, because the fact that a `name` key in the dictionary is there doesn't guarantee that the name is actually non-empty. So we take its value, we strip all leading and trailing whitespace characters, and if the result is empty, we raise `ValidationError` again. Notice we don't need to add a custom validator for the `email` field. This is because `marshmallow` will validate it, and a valid email cannot be empty.

We then instantiate `schema`, so that we can use it to validate data. So let's write the `export` function:

```
# api.py
def export(filename, users, overwrite=True):
    """Export a CSV file.

    Create a CSV file and fill with valid users. If `overwrite`
    is False and file already exists, raise IOError.
```

```
    """
    if not overwrite and os.path.isfile(filename):
        raise IOError(f"'{filename}' already exists.")

    valid_users = get_valid_users(users)
    write_csv(filename, valid_users)
```

As you see, its internals are quite straightforward. If `overwrite` is `False` and the file already exists, we raise `IOError` with a message saying the file already exists. Otherwise, if we can proceed, we simply get the list of valid users and feed it to `write_csv`, which is responsible for actually doing the job. Let's see how all these functions are defined:

```
# api.py
def get_valid_users(users):
    """Yield one valid user at a time from users. """
    yield from filter(is_valid, users)

def is_valid(user):
    """Return whether or not the user is valid. """
    return not schema.validate(user)
```

Turns out I coded `get_valid_users` as a generator, as there is no need to make a potentially big list in order to put it in a file. We can validate and save them one by one. The heart of validation is simply a delegation to `schema.validate`, which uses validation engine by `marshmallow`. The way this works is by returning a dictionary, which is empty if validation succeeded, or else it will contain error information. We don't really care about collecting the error information for this task, so we simply ignore it, and within `is_valid` we basically return `True` if the return value from `schema.validate` is empty, and `False` otherwise.

One last piece is missing; here it is:

```
# api.py
def write_csv(filename, users):
    """Write a CSV given a filename and a list of users.

    The users are assumed to be valid for the given CSV structure.
    """
    fieldnames = ['email', 'name', 'age', 'role']

    with open(filename, 'x', newline='') as csvfile:
        writer = csv.DictWriter(csvfile, fieldnames=fieldnames)
        writer.writeheader()
        for user in users:
            writer.writerow(user)
```

Again, the logic is straightforward. We define the header in `fieldnames`, then we open `filename` for writing, and we specify `newline=''`, which is recommended in the documentation when dealing with CSV files. When the file has been created, we get a `writer` object by using the `csv.DictWriter` class. The beauty of this tool is that it is capable of mapping the user dictionaries to the field names, so we don't need to take care of the ordering.

We write the header first, and then we loop over the users and add them one by one. Notice, this function assumes it is fed a list of valid users, and it may break if that assumption is false (with the default values, it would break if any user dictionary had extra fields).

That's the whole code you have to keep in mind. I suggest you spend a moment to go through it again. There is no need to memorize it, and the fact that I have used small helper functions with meaningful names will enable you to follow the testing along more easily.

Let's now get to the interesting part: testing our `export` function. Once again, I'll show you the code in chunks:

```
# tests/test_api.py
import os
from unittest.mock import patch, mock_open, call
import pytest
from ..api import is_valid, export, write_csv
```

Let's start from the imports: we need `os`, temporary directories (which we already saw in `Chapter 7`, *Files and Data Persistence*), then `pytest`, and, finally, we use a relative import to fetch the three functions that we want to actually test: `is_valid`, `export`, and `write_csv`.

Before we can write tests, though, we need to make a few fixtures. As you will see, a `fixture` is a function that is decorated with the `pytest.fixture` decorator. In most cases, we expect `fixture` to return something, so that we can use it in a test. We have some requirements for a user dictionary, so let's write a couple of users: one with minimal requirements, and one with full requirements. Both need to be valid. Here is the code:

```
# tests/test_api.py
@pytest.fixture
def min_user():
    """Represent a valid user with minimal data. """
    return {
        'email': 'minimal@example.com',
        'name': 'Primus Minimus',
        'age': 18,
    }
```

```
@pytest.fixture
def full_user():
    """Represent valid user with full data. """
    return {
        'email': 'full@example.com',
        'name': 'Maximus Plenus',
        'age': 65,
        'role': 'emperor',
    }
```

In this example, the only difference is the presence of the `role` key, but it's enough to show you the point I hope. Notice that instead of simply declaring dictionaries at a module level, we actually have written two functions that return a dictionary, and we have decorated them with the `pytest.fixture` decorator. This is because when you declare a dictionary at module-level, which is supposed to be used in your tests, you need to make sure you copy it at the beginning of every test. If you don't, you may have a test that modifies it, and this will affect all tests that follow it, compromising their integrity.

By using these fixtures, `pytest` will give us a new dictionary every test run, so we don't need to go through that pain ourselves. Notice that if a fixture returns another type, instead of dict, then that is what you will get in the test. Fixtures also are *composable*, which means they can be used in one another, which is a very powerful feature of `pytest`. To show you this, let's write a fixture for a list of users, in which we put the two we already have, plus one that would fail validation because it has no age. Let's take a look at the following code:

```
# tests/test_api.py
@pytest.fixture
def users(min_user, full_user):
    """List of users, two valid and one invalid. """
    bad_user = {
        'email': 'invalid@example.com',
        'name': 'Horribilis',
    }
    return [min_user, bad_user, full_user]
```

Nice. So, now we have two users that we can use individually, but also we have a list of three users. The first round of tests will be testing how we are validating a user. We will group all the tests for this task within a class. This not only helps giving related tests a namespace, a place to be, but, as we'll see later on, it allows us to declare class-level fixtures, which are defined just for the tests belonging to the class. Take a look at this code:

```
# tests/test_api.py
class TestIsValid:
    """Test how code verifies whether a user is valid or not. """
    def test_minimal(self, min_user):
        assert is_valid(min_user)
```

```
    def test_full(self, full_user):
        assert is_valid(full_user)
```

We start very simply by making sure our fixtures are actually passing validation. This is very important, as those fixtures will be used everywhere, so we want them to be perfect. Next, we test the age. Two things to notice here: I will not repeat the class signature, so the code that follows is indented by four spaces and it's because these are all methods within the same class, okay? And, second, we're going to use parametrization quite heavily.

Parametrization is a technique that enables us to run the same test multiple times, but feeding different data to it. It is very useful, as it allows us to write the test only once with no repetition, and the result will be very intelligently handled by `pytest`, which will run all those tests as if they were actually separate, thus providing us with clear error messages when they fail. If you parametrize manually, you lose this feature, and believe me you won't be happy. Let's see how we test the age:

```
# tests/test_api.py
    @pytest.mark.parametrize('age', range(18))
    def test_invalid_age_too_young(self, age, min_user):
        min_user['age'] = age
        assert not is_valid(min_user)
```

Right, so we start by writing a test to check that validation fails when the user is too young. According to our rule, a user is too young when they are younger than 18. We check for every age between 0 and 17, by using `range`.

If you take a look at how the parametrization works, you'll see we declare the name of an object, which we then pass to the signature of the method, and then we specify which values this object will take. For each value, the test will be run once. In the case of this first test, the object's name is `age`, and the values are all those returned by `range(18)`, which means all integer numbers from `0` to `17` are included. Notice how we feed `age` to the test method, right after `self`, and then we do something else, which is also very interesting. We pass this method a fixture: `min_user`. This has the effect of activating that fixture for the test run, so that we can use it, and can refer to it from within the test. In this case, we simply change the age within the `min_user` dictionary, and then we verify that the result of `is_valid(min_user)` is `False`.

We do this last bit by asserting on the fact that `not False` is `True`. In `pytest`, this is how you check for something. You simply assert that something is truthy. If that is the case, the test has succeeded. Should it instead be the opposite, the test would fail.

Let's proceed and add all the tests needed to make validation fail on the age:

```
# tests/test_api.py
    @pytest.mark.parametrize('age', range(66, 100))
    def test_invalid_age_too_old(self, age, min_user):
        min_user['age'] = age
        assert not is_valid(min_user)

    @pytest.mark.parametrize('age', ['NaN', 3.1415, None])
    def test_invalid_age_wrong_type(self, age, min_user):
        min_user['age'] = age
        assert not is_valid(min_user)
```

So, another two tests. One takes care of the other end of the spectrum, from 66 years of age to 99. And the second one instead makes sure that age is invalid when it's not an integer number, so we pass some values, such as a string, a float, and None, just to make sure. Notice how the structure of the test is basically always the same, but, thanks to the parametrization, we feed very different input arguments to it.

Now that we have the age-failing all sorted out, let's add a test that actually checks the age is within the valid range:

```
# tests/test_api.py
    @pytest.mark.parametrize('age', range(18, 66))
    def test_valid_age(self, age, min_user):
        min_user['age'] = age
        assert is_valid(min_user)
```

It's as easy as that. We pass the correct range, from 18 to 65, and remove the not in the assertion. Notice how all tests start with the test_ prefix, and have a different name.

We can consider the age as being taken care of. Let's move on to write tests on mandatory fields:

```
# tests/test_api.py
    @pytest.mark.parametrize('field', ['email', 'name', 'age'])
    def test_mandatory_fields(self, field, min_user):
        min_user.pop(field)
        assert not is_valid(min_user)

    @pytest.mark.parametrize('field', ['email', 'name', 'age'])
    def test_mandatory_fields_empty(self, field, min_user):
        min_user[field] = ''
        assert not is_valid(min_user)
```

```
    def test_name_whitespace_only(self, min_user):
        min_user['name'] = ' \n\t'
        assert not is_valid(min_user)
```

The previous three tests still belong to the same class. The first one tests whether a user is invalid when one of the mandatory fields is missing. Notice that at every test run, the `min_user` fixture is restored, so we only have one missing field per test run, which is the appropriate way to check for mandatory fields. We simply pop the key out of the dictionary. This time the parametrization object takes the name `field`, and, by looking at the first test, you see all the mandatory fields in the parametrization decorator: `email`, `name`, and `age`.

In the second one, things are a little different. Instead of popping keys out, we simply set them (one at a time) to the empty string. Finally, in the third one, we check for the name to be made of whitespace only.

The previous tests take care of mandatory fields being there and being non-empty, and of the formatting around the `name` key of a user. Good. Let's now write the last two tests for this class. We want to check email validity, and type for email, name, and the role:

```python
# tests/test_api.py
    @pytest.mark.parametrize(
        'email, outcome',
        [
            ('missing_at.com', False),
            ('@missing_start.com', False),
            ('missing_end@', False),
            ('missing_dot@example', False),

            ('good.one@example.com', True),
            ('δοκιμή@παράδειγμα.δοκιμή', True),
            ('аджай@экзампл.рус', True),
        ]
    )
    def test_email(self, email, outcome, min_user):
        min_user['email'] = email
        assert is_valid(min_user) == outcome
```

This time, the parametrization is slightly more complex. We define two objects (`email` and `outcome`), and then we pass a list of tuples, instead of a simple list, to the decorator. What happens is that each time the test is run, one of those tuples will be unpacked so to fill the values of `email` and `outcome`, respectively. This allows us to write one test for both valid and invalid email addresses, instead of two separate ones. We define an email address, and we specify the outcome we expect from validation. The first four are invalid email addresses, but the last three are actually valid. I have used a couple of examples with Unicode, just to make sure we're not forgetting to include our friends from all over the world in the validation.

Notice how the validation is done, asserting the result of the call needs to match the outcome we have set.

Let's now write a simple test to make sure validation fails when we feed the wrong type to the fields (again, the age has been taken care of separately before):

```python
# tests/test_api.py
    @pytest.mark.parametrize(
        'field, value',
        [
            ('email', None),
            ('email', 3.1415),
            ('email', {}),

            ('name', None),
            ('name', 3.1415),
            ('name', {}),

            ('role', None),
            ('role', 3.1415),
            ('role', {}),
        ]
    )
    def test_invalid_types(self, field, value, min_user):
        min_user[field] = value
        assert not is_valid(min_user)
```

As we did before, just for fun, we pass three different values, none of which is actually a string. This test could be expanded to include more values, but, honestly, we shouldn't need to write tests such as this one. I have included it here just to show you what's possible.

Before we move to the next test class, let me talk about something we have seen when we were checking the age.

Boundaries and granularity

While checking for the age, we have written three tests to cover the three ranges: 0-17 (fail), 18-65 (success), 66-99 (fail). Why did we do this? The answer lies in the fact that we are dealing with two boundaries: 18 and 65. So our testing needs to focus on the three regions those two boundaries define: before `18`, within `18` and `65`, and after `65`. How you do it is not crucial, as long as you make sure you test the boundaries correctly. This means if someone changes the validation in the schema from `18 <= value <= 65` to `18 <= value < 65` (notice the missing =), there must be a test that fails on the `65`.

This concept is known as **boundary**, and it's very important that you recognize them in your code so that you can test against them.

Another important thing is to understand is which zoom level we want to get close to the boundaries. In other words, which unit should I use to move around it? In the case of age, we're dealing with integers, so a unit of `1` will be the perfect choice (which is why we used `16`, `17`, `18`, `19`, `20`, ...). But what if you were testing for a timestamp? Well, in that case, the correct granularity will likely be different. If the code has to act differently according to your timestamp and that timestamp represent seconds, then the granularity of your tests should zoom down to seconds. If the timestamp represents years, then years should be the unit you use. I hope you get the picture. This concept is known as **granularity**, and needs to be combined with that of boundaries, so that by going around the boundaries with the correct granularity, you can make sure your tests are not leaving anything to chance.

Let's now continue with our example, and test the `export` function.

Testing the export function

In the same test module, I have defined another class that represents a test suite for the `export` function. Here it is:

```
# tests/test_api.py
class TestExport:

    @pytest.fixture
    def csv_file(self, tmpdir):
        yield tmpdir.join("out.csv")

    @pytest.fixture
```

```
def existing_file(self, tmpdir):
    existing = tmpdir.join('existing.csv')
    existing.write('Please leave me alone...')
    yield existing
```

Let's start understanding the fixtures. We have defined them at class-level this time, which means they will be alive only for as long as the tests in the class are running. We don't need these fixtures outside of this class, so it doesn't make sense to declare them at a module level like we've done with the user ones.

So, we need two files. If you recall what I wrote at the beginning of this chapter, when it comes to interaction with databases, disks, networks, and so on, we should mock everything out. However, when possible, I prefer to use a different technique. In this case, I will employ temporary folders, which will be born within the fixture, and die within it, leaving no trace of their existence. I am much happier if I can avoid mocking. Mocking is amazing, but it can be tricky, and a source of bugs, unless it's done correctly.

Now, the first fixture, `csv_file`, defines a managed context in which we obtain a reference to a temporary folder. We can consider the logic up to and including the `yield`, as the setup phase. The fixture itself, in terms of data, is represented by the temporary filename. The file itself is not present yet. When a test runs, the fixture is created, and at the end of the test, the rest of the fixture code (the one after `yield`, if any) is executed. That part can be considered the teardown phase. In this case, it consists of exiting the context manager, which means the temporary folder is deleted (along with all its content). You can put much more in each phase of any fixture, and with experience, I'm sure you'll master the art of doing setup and teardown this way. It actually comes very naturally quite quickly.

The second fixture is very similar to the first one, but we'll use it to test that we can prevent overwriting when we call `export` with `overwrite=False`. So we create a file in the temporary folder, and we put some content into it, just to have the means to verify it hasn't been touched.

Notice how both fixtures are returning the filename with the full path information, to make sure we actually use the temporary folder in our code. Let's now see the tests:

```
# tests/test_api.py
    def test_export(self, users, csv_file):
        export(csv_file, users)

        lines = csv_file.readlines()

        assert [
            'email,name,age,role\n',
            'minimal@example.com,Primus Minimus,18,\n',
            'full@example.com,Maximus Plenus,65,emperor\n',
```

```
    ] == lines
```

This test employs the `users` and `csv_file` fixtures, and immediately calls `export` with them. We expect that a file has been created, and populated with the two valid users we have (remember the list contains three users, but one is invalid).

To verify that, we open the temporary file, and collect all its lines into a list. We then compare the content of the file with a list of the lines that we expect to be in it. Notice we only put the header, and the two valid users, in the correct order.

Now we need another test, to make sure that if there is a comma in one of the values, our CSV is still generated correctly. Being a **comma-separated values** (**CSV**) file, we need to make sure that a comma in the data doesn't break things up:

```
# tests/test_api.py
    def test_export_quoting(self, min_user, csv_file):
        min_user['name'] = 'A name, with a comma'

        export(csv_file, [min_user])

        lines = csv_file.readlines()
        assert [
            'email,name,age,role\n',
            'minimal@example.com,"A name, with a comma",18,\n',
        ] == lines
```

This time, we don't need the whole users list, we just need one as we're testing a specific thing, and we have the previous test to make sure we're generating the file correctly with all the users. Remember, always try to minimize the work you do within a test.

So, we use `min_user`, and put a nice comma in its name. We then repeat the procedure, which is very similar to that of the previous test, and finally we make sure that the name is put in the CSV file surrounded by double quotes. This is enough for any good CSV parser to understand that they don't have to break on the comma inside the double quotes.

Now I want one more test, which needs to check that whether the file exists and we don't want to override it, our code won't touch it:

```
# tests/test_api.py
    def test_does_not_overwrite(self, users, existing_file):
        with pytest.raises(IOError) as err:
            export(existing_file, users, overwrite=False)

        assert err.match(
            r"'{}' already exists\.".format(existing_file)
        )
```

```
# let's also verify the file is still intact
assert existing_file.read() == 'Please leave me alone...'
```

This is a beautiful test, because it allows me to show you how you can tell `pytest` that you expect a function call to raise an exception. We do it in the context manager given to us by `pytest.raises`, to which we feed the exception we expect from the call we make inside the body of that context manager. If the exception is not raised, the test will fail.

I like to be thorough in my test, so I don't want to stop there. I also assert on the message, by using the convenient `err.match` helper (watch out, it takes a regular expression, not a simple string–we'll see regular expressions in Chapter 14, *Web Development*).

Finally, let's make sure that the file still contains its original content (which is why I created the `existing_file` fixture) by opening it, and comparing all of its content to the string it should be.

Final considerations

Before we move on to the next topic, let me just wrap up with some considerations.

First, I hope you have noticed that I haven't tested all the functions I wrote. Specifically, I didn't test `get_valid_users`, `validate`, and `write_csv`. The reason is because these functions are implicitly tested by our test suite. We have tested `is_valid` and `export`, which is more than enough to make sure our schema is validating users correctly, and the `export` function is dealing with filtering out invalid users correctly, respecting existing files when needed, and writing a proper CSV. The functions we haven't tested are the internals, they provide logic that participates to doing something that we have thoroughly tested anyway. Would adding extra tests for those functions be good or bad? Think about it for a moment.

The answer is actually difficult. The more you test, the less you can refactor that code. As it is now, I could easily decide to call `is_valid` with another name, and I wouldn't have to change any of my tests. If you think about it, it makes sense, because as long as `is_valid` provides correct validation to the `get_valid_users` function, I don't really need to know about it. Does this make sense to you?

If instead I had tests for the `is_valid` function, then I would have to change them, if I decided to call it differently (or to somehow change its signature).

So, what is the right thing to do? Tests or no tests? It will be up to you. You have to find the right balance. My personal take on this matter is that everything needs to be thoroughly tested, either directly or indirectly. And I want the smallest possible test suite that guarantees me that. This way, I will have a great test suite in terms of coverage, but not any bigger than necessary. You need to maintain those tests!

I hope this example made sense to you, I think it has allowed me to touch on the important topics.

If you check out the source code for the book, in the `test_api.py` module, I have added a couple of extra test classes, which will show you how different testing would have been had I decided to go all the way with the mocks. Make sure you read that code and understand it well. It is quite straightforward and will offer you a good comparison with my personal approach, which I have shown you here.

Now, how about we run those tests? (The output is re-arranged to fit this book's format):

```
$ pytest tests
======================= test session starts =======================
platform darwin -- Python 3.7.0b2, pytest-3.5.0, py-1.5.3, ...
rootdir: /Users/fab/srv/lpp/ch8, inifile:
collected 132 items

tests/test_api.py .................................................
...................................................................
.................... [100%]

================== 132 passed in 0.41 seconds ==================
```

Make sure you run `$ pytest test` from within the `ch8` folder (add the `-vv` flag for a verbose output that will show you how parametrization modifies the names of your tests). As you can see, `132` tests were run in less than half a second, and they all succeeded. I strongly suggest you check out this code and play with it. Change something in the code and see whether any test is breaking. Understand why it is breaking. Is it something important that means the test isn't good enough? Or is it something silly that shouldn't cause the test to break? All these apparently innocuous questions will help you gain deep insight into the art of testing.

I also suggest you study the `unittest` module, and `pytest` too. These are tools you will use all the time, so you need to be very familiar with them.

Let's now check out test-driven development!

Test-driven development

Let's talk briefly about **test-driven development** (**TDD**). It is a methodology that was rediscovered by Kent Beck, who wrote *Test-Driven Development by Example, Addison Wesley, 2002*, which I encourage you to check out if you want to learn about the fundamentals of this subject.

> *TDD is a software development methodology that is based on the continuous repetition of a very short development cycle.*

First, the developer writes a test, and makes it run. The test is supposed to check a feature that is not yet part of the code. Maybe it is a new feature to be added, or something to be removed or amended. Running the test will make it fail and, because of this, this phase is called **Red**.

When the test has failed, the developer writes the minimal amount of code to make it pass. When running the test succeeds, we have the so-called **Green** phase. In this phase, it is okay to write code that cheats, just to make the test pass. This technique is called *fake it 'till you make it*. In a second moment, tests are enriched with different edge cases, and the cheating code then has to be rewritten with proper logic. Adding other test cases is called **triangulation**.

The last piece of the cycle is where the developer takes care of both the code and the tests (in separate times) and refactors them until they are in the desired state. This last phase is called **Refactor**.

The **TDD** mantra therefore is **Red-Green-Refactor**.

At first, it feels really weird to write tests before the code, and I must confess it took me a while to get used to it. If you stick to it, though, and force yourself to learn this slightly counter-intuitive way of working, at some point something almost magical happens, and you will see the quality of your code increase in a way that wouldn't be possible otherwise.

When you write your code before the tests, you have to take care of *what* the code has to do and *how* it has to do it, both at the same time. On the other hand, when you write tests before the code, you can concentrate on the *what* part alone, while you write them. When you write the code afterward, you will mostly have to take care of *how* the code has to implement *what* is required by the tests. This shift in focus allows your mind to concentrate on the *what* and *how* parts in separate moments, yielding a brain power boost that will surprise you.

There are several other benefits that come from the adoption of this technique:

- **You will refactor with much more confidence**: Tests will break if you introduce bugs. Moreover, the architectural refactor will also benefit from having tests that act as guardians.
- **The code will be more readable**: This is crucial in our time, when coding is a social activity and every professional developer spends much more time reading code than writing it.
- **The code will be more loosely coupled and easier to test and maintain**: Writing the tests first forces you to think more deeply about code structure.
- **Writing tests first requires you to have a better understanding of the business requirements**: If your understanding of the requirements is lacking information, you'll find writing a test extremely challenging and this situation acts as a sentinel for you.
- **Having everything unit tested means the code will be easier to debug**: Moreover, small tests are perfect for providing alternative documentation. English can be misleading, but five lines of Python in a simple test are very hard to misunderstand.
- **Higher speed**: It's faster to write tests and code than it is to write the code first and then lose time debugging it. If you don't write tests, you will probably deliver the code sooner, but then you will have to track the bugs down and solve them (and, rest assured, there will be bugs). The combined time taken to write the code and then debug it is usually longer than the time taken to develop the code with TDD, where having tests running before the code is written, ensuring that the amount of bugs in it will be much lower than in the other case.

On the other hand, the main shortcomings of this technique are the following ones:

- **The whole company needs to believe in it**: Otherwise, you will have to constantly argue with your boss, who will not understand why it takes you so long to deliver. The truth is, it may take you a bit longer to deliver in the short-term, but in the long-term, you gain a lot with TDD. However, it is quite hard to see the long-term because it's not under our noses like the short-term is. I have fought battles with stubborn bosses in my career, to be able to code using TDD. Sometimes it has been painful, but always well worth it, and I have never regretted it because, in the end, the quality of the result has always been appreciated.

- **If you fail to understand the business requirements, this will reflect in the tests you write, and therefore it will reflect in the code too**: This kind of problem is quite hard to spot until you do UAT, but one thing that you can do to reduce the likelihood of it happening is to pair with another developer. Pairing will inevitably require discussions about the business requirements, and discussion will bring clarification, which will help writing correct tests.

- **Badly written tests are hard to maintain:** This is a fact. Tests with too many mocks or with extra assumptions or badly-structured data will soon become a burden. Don't let this discourage you; just keep experimenting and change the way you write them until you find a way that doesn't require you a huge amount of work every time you touch your code.

I'm quite passionate about TDD. When I interview for a job, I always ask whether the company adopts it. I encourage you to check it out and use it. Use it until you feel something clicking in your mind. You won't regret it, I promise.

Exceptions

Even though I haven't formally introduced them to you, by now I expect you to at least have a vague idea of what an exception is. In the previous chapters, we've seen that when an iterator is exhausted, calling `next` on it raises a `StopIteration` exception. We met `IndexError` when we tried accessing a list at a position that was outside the valid range. We also met `AttributeError` when we tried accessing an attribute on an object that didn't have it, and `KeyError` when we did the same with a key and a dictionary.

Now the time has come for us to talk about exceptions.

Sometimes, even though an operation or a piece of code is correct, there are conditions in which something may go wrong. For example, if we're converting user input from `string` to `int`, the user could accidentally type a letter in place of a digit, making it impossible for us to convert that value into a number. When dividing numbers, we may not know in advance whether we're attempting a division by zero. When opening a file, it could be missing or corrupted.

When an error is detected during execution, it is called an **exception**. Exceptions are not necessarily lethal; in fact, we've seen that `StopIteration` is deeply integrated in the Python generator and iterator mechanisms. Normally, though, if you don't take the necessary precautions, an exception will cause your application to break. Sometimes, this is the desired behavior, but in other cases, we want to prevent and control problems such as these. For example, we may alert the user that the file they're trying to open is corrupted or that it is missing so that they can either fix it or provide another file, without the need for the application to die because of this issue. Let's see an example of a few exceptions:

```
# exceptions/first.example.py
>>> gen = (n for n in range(2))
>>> next(gen)
0
>>> next(gen)
1
>>> next(gen)
Traceback (most recent call last):
  File "<stdin>", line 1, in <module>
StopIteration
>>> print(undefined_name)
Traceback (most recent call last):
  File "<stdin>", line 1, in <module>
NameError: name 'undefined_name' is not defined
>>> mylist = [1, 2, 3]
>>> mylist[5]
Traceback (most recent call last):
  File "<stdin>", line 1, in <module>
IndexError: list index out of range
>>> mydict = {'a': 'A', 'b': 'B'}
>>> mydict['c']
Traceback (most recent call last):
  File "<stdin>", line 1, in <module>
KeyError: 'c'
>>> 1 / 0
Traceback (most recent call last):
  File "<stdin>", line 1, in <module>
ZeroDivisionError: division by zero
```

As you can see, the Python shell is quite forgiving. We can see `Traceback`, so that we have information about the error, but the program doesn't die. This is a special behavior, a regular program or a script would normally die if nothing were done to handle exceptions.

To handle an exception, Python gives you the `try` statement. When you enter the `try` clause, Python will watch out for one or more different types of exceptions (according to how you instruct it), and if they are raised, it will allow you to react. The `try` statement is composed of the `try` clause, which opens the statement, one or more `except` clauses (all optional) that define what to do when an exception is caught, an `else` clause (optional), which is executed when the `try` clause is exited without any exception raised, and a `finally` clause (optional), whose code is executed regardless of whatever happened in the other clauses. The `finally` clause is typically used to clean up resources (we saw this in `Chapter 7`, *Files and Data Persistence*, when we were opening files without using a context manager).

Mind the order—it's important. Also, `try` must be followed by at least one `except` clause or a `finally` clause. Let's see an example:

```
# exceptions/try.syntax.py
def try_syntax(numerator, denominator):
    try:
        print(f'In the try block: {numerator}/{denominator}')
        result = numerator / denominator
    except ZeroDivisionError as zde:
        print(zde)
    else:
        print('The result is:', result)
        return result
    finally:
        print('Exiting')

print(try_syntax(12, 4))
print(try_syntax(11, 0))
```

The preceding example defines a simple `try_syntax` function. We perform the division of two numbers. We are prepared to catch a `ZeroDivisionError` exception if we call the function with `denominator = 0`. Initially, the code enters the `try` block. If `denominator` is not 0, `result` is calculated and the execution, after leaving the `try` block, resumes in the `else` block. We print `result` and return it. Take a look at the output and you'll notice that just before returning `result`, which is the exit point of the function, Python executes the `finally` clause.

When `denominator` is 0, things change. We enter the `except` block and print `zde`. The `else` block isn't executed because an exception was raised in the `try` block. Before (implicitly) returning `None`, we still execute the `finally` block. Take a look at the output and see whether it makes sense to you:

```
$ python try.syntax.py
In the try block: 12/4      # try
The result is: 3.0          # else
Exiting                     # finally
3.0                         # return within else


In the try block: 11/0      # try
division by zero            # except
Exiting                     # finally
None                        # implicit return end of function
```

When you execute a `try` block, you may want to catch more than one exception. For example, when trying to decode a JSON object, you may incur into `ValueError` for malformed JSON, or `TypeError` if the type of the data you're feeding to `json.loads()` is not a string. In this case, you may structure your code like this:

```python
# exceptions/json.example.py
import json
json_data = '{}'

try:
    data = json.loads(json_data)
except (ValueError, TypeError) as e:
    print(type(e), e)
```

This code will catch both `ValueError` and `TypeError`. Try changing `json_data = '{}'` to `json_data = 2` or `json_data = '{{'`, and you'll see the different output.

If you want to handle multiple exceptions differently, you can just add more `except` clauses, like this:

```python
# exceptions/multiple.except.py
try:
    # some code
except Exception1:
    # react to Exception1
except (Exception2, Exception3):
    # react to Exception2 or Exception3
except Exception4:
    # react to Exception4
...
```

Keep in mind that an exception is handled in the first block that defines that exception class or any of its bases. Therefore, when you stack multiple except clauses like we've just done, make sure that you put specific exceptions at the top and generic ones at the bottom. In OOP terms, children on top, grandparents at the bottom. Moreover, remember that only one except handler is executed when an exception is raised.

You can also write **custom exceptions**. To do that, you just have to inherit from any other exception class. Python's built-in exceptions are too many to be listed here, so I have to point you to the official documentation. One important thing to know is that every Python exception derives from BaseException, but your custom exceptions should never inherit directly from it. The reason is because handling such an exception will also trap **system-exiting exceptions**, such as SystemExit and KeyboardInterrupt, which derive from BaseException, and this could lead to severe issues. In the case of disaster, you want to be able to *Ctrl + C* your way out of an application.

You can easily solve the problem by inheriting from Exception, which inherits from BaseException but doesn't include any system-exiting exception in its children because they are siblings in the built-in exceptions hierarchy (see https://docs.python.org/3/library/exceptions.html#exception-hierarchy).

Programming with exceptions can be very tricky. You could inadvertently silence out errors, or trap exceptions that aren't meant to be handled. Play it safe by keeping in mind a few guidelines: always put in the try clause only the code that may cause the exception(s) that you want to handle. When you write except clauses, be as specific as you can, don't just resort to except Exception because it's easy. Use tests to make sure your code handles edge cases in a way that requires the least possible amount of exception handling. Writing an except statement without specifying any exception would catch any exception, therefore exposing your code to the same risks you incur when you derive your custom exceptions from BaseException.

You will find information about exceptions almost everywhere on the web. Some coders use them abundantly, others sparingly. Find your own way of dealing with them by taking examples from other people's source code. There are plenty of interesting open source projects on websites such as GitHub (https://github.com) and Bitbucket (https://bitbucket.org/).

Before we talk about profiling, let me show you an unconventional use of exceptions, just to give you something to help you expand your views on them. They are not just simply errors:

```
# exceptions/for.loop.py
n = 100
found = False
for a in range(n):
    if found: break
    for b in range(n):
        if found: break
        for c in range(n):
            if 42 * a + 17 * b + c == 5096:
                found = True
                print(a, b, c)   # 79 99 95
```

The preceding code is quite a common idiom if you deal with numbers. You have to iterate over a few nested ranges and look for a particular combination of a, b, and c that satisfies a condition. In the example, condition is a trivial linear equation, but imagine something much cooler than that. What bugs me is having to check whether the solution has been found at the beginning of each loop, in order to break out of them as fast as we can when it is. The breakout logic interferes with the rest of the code and I don't like it, so I came up with a different solution for this. Take a look at it, and see whether you can adapt it to other cases too:

```
# exceptions/for.loop.py
class ExitLoopException(Exception):
    pass

try:
    n = 100
    for a in range(n):
        for b in range(n):
            for c in range(n):
                if 42 * a + 17 * b + c == 5096:
                    raise ExitLoopException(a, b, c)
except ExitLoopException as ele:
    print(ele)   # (79, 99, 95)
```

Can you see how much more elegant it is? Now the breakout logic is entirely handled with a simple exception whose name even hints at its purpose. As soon as the result is found, we raise it, and immediately the control is given to the except clause that handles it. This is food for thought. This example indirectly shows you how to raise your own exceptions. Read up on the official documentation to dive into the beautiful details of this subject.

Moreover, if you are up for a challenge, you might want to try to make this last example into a context manager for nested `for` loops. Good luck!

Profiling Python

There are a few different ways to profile a Python application. Profiling means having the application run while keeping track of several different parameters, such as the number of times a function is called and the amount of time spent inside it. Profiling can help us find the bottlenecks in our application, so that we can improve only what is really slowing us down.

If you take a look at the profiling section in the standard library official documentation, you will see that there are a couple of different implementations of the same profiling interface—`profile` and `cProfile`:

- `cProfile` is recommended for most users, it's a C extension with reasonable overhead that makes it suitable for profiling long-running programs
- `profile` is a pure Python module whose interface is imitated by `cProfile`, but which adds significant overhead to profiled programs

This interface does **determinist profiling**, which means that all function calls, function returns, and exception events are monitored, and precise timings are made for the intervals between these events. Another approach, called **statistical profiling**, randomly samples the effective instruction pointer, and deduces where time is being spent.

The latter usually involves less overhead, but provides only approximate results. Moreover, because of the way the Python interpreter runs the code, deterministic profiling doesn't add as much overhead as one would think, so I'll show you a simple example using `cProfile` from the command line.

We're going to calculate Pythagorean triples (I know, you've missed them...) using the following code:

```
# profiling/triples.py
def calc_triples(mx):
    triples = []
    for a in range(1, mx + 1):
        for b in range(a, mx + 1):
            hypotenuse = calc_hypotenuse(a, b)
            if is_int(hypotenuse):
                triples.append((a, b, int(hypotenuse)))
    return triples
```

```
def calc_hypotenuse(a, b):
    return (a**2 + b**2) ** .5

def is_int(n):  # n is expected to be a float
    return n.is_integer()

triples = calc_triples(1000)
```

The script is extremely simple; we iterate over the interval [1, mx] with a and b (avoiding repetition of pairs by setting b >= a) and we check whether they belong to a right triangle. We use `calc_hypotenuse` to get `hypotenuse` for a and b, and then, with `is_int`, we check whether it is an integer, which means (*a*, *b*, *c*) is a Pythagorean triple. When we profile this script, we get information in a tabular form. The columns are `ncalls`, `tottime`, `percall`, `cumtime`, `percall`, and `filename:lineno(function)`. They represent the amount of calls we made to a function, how much time we spent in it, and so on. I'll trim a couple of columns to save space, so if you run the profiling yourself—don't worry if you get a different result. Here is the code:

```
$ python -m cProfile triples.py
1502538 function calls in 0.704 seconds
Ordered by: standard name

ncalls tottime percall filename:lineno(function)
500500   0.393   0.000 triples.py:17(calc_hypotenuse)
500500   0.096   0.000 triples.py:21(is_int)
     1   0.000   0.000 triples.py:4(<module>)
     1   0.176   0.176 triples.py:4(calc_triples)
     1   0.000   0.000 {built-in method builtins.exec}
  1034   0.000   0.000 {method 'append' of 'list' objects}
     1   0.000   0.000 {method 'disable' of '_lsprof.Profil...
500500   0.038   0.000 {method 'is_integer' of 'float' objects}
```

Even with this limited amount of data, we can still infer some useful information about this code. First, we can see that the time complexity of the algorithm we have chosen grows with the square of the input size. The amount of times we get inside the inner loop body is exactly *mx (mx + 1) / 2*. We run the script with mx = 1000, which means we get 500500 times inside the inner `for` loop. Three main things happen inside that loop: we call `calc_hypotenuse`, we call `is_int`, and, if the condition is met, we append it to the `triples` list.

Taking a look at the profiling report, we notice that the algorithm has spent 0.393 seconds inside calc_hypotenuse, which is way more than the 0.096 seconds spent inside is_int, given that they were called the same number of times, so let's see whether we can boost calc_hypotenuse a little.

As it turns out, we can. As I mentioned earlier in this book, the ** power operator is quite expensive, and in calc_hypotenuse, we're using it three times. Fortunately, we can easily transform two of those into simple multiplications, like this:

```
def calc_hypotenuse(a, b):
    return (a*a + b*b) ** .5
```

This simple change should improve things. If we run the profiling again, we see that 0.393 is now down to 0.137. Not bad! This means now we're spending only about 37% of the time inside calc_hypotenuse that we were before.

Let's see whether we can improve is_int as well, by changing it, like this:

```
def is_int(n):
    return n == int(n)
```

This implementation is different, and the advantage is that it also works when n is an integer. Alas, when we run the profiling against it, we see that the time taken inside the is_int function has gone up to 0.135 seconds, so, in this case, we need to revert to the previous implementation. You will find the three versions in the source code for the book.

This example was trivial, of course, but enough to show you how one could profile an application. Having the amount of calls that are performed against a function helps us better understand the time complexity of our algorithms. For example, you wouldn't believe how many coders fail to see that those two for loops run proportionally to the square of the input size.

One thing to mention: depending on what system you're using, results may be different. Therefore, it's quite important to be able to profile software on a system that is as close as possible to the one the software is deployed on, if not actually on that one.

When to profile?

Profiling is super cool, but we need to know when it is appropriate to do it, and in what measure we need to address the results we get from it.

Donald Knuth once said, *"premature optimization is the root of all evil"*, and, although I wouldn't have put it down so drastically, I do agree with him. After all, who am I to disagree with the man who gave us *The Art of Computer Programming, TeX*, and some of the coolest algorithms I have ever studied when I was a university student?

So, first and foremost: *correctness*. You want your code to deliver the correct results, therefore write tests, find edge cases, and stress your code in every way you think makes sense. Don't be protective, don't put things in the back of your brain for later because you think they're not likely to happen. Be thorough.

Second, take care of coding *best practices*. Remember the following—readability, extensibility, loose coupling, modularity, and design. Apply OOP principles: encapsulation, abstraction, single responsibility, open/closed, and so on. Read up on these concepts. They will open horizons for you, and they will expand the way you think about code.

Third, *refactor like a beast!* The Boy Scouts rule says:

> *"Always leave the campground cleaner than you found it."*

Apply this rule to your code.

And, finally, when all of this has been taken care of, then and only then, take care of optimizing and profiling.

Run your profiler and identify bottlenecks. When you have an idea of the bottlenecks you need to address, start with the worst one first. Sometimes, fixing a bottleneck causes a ripple effect that will expand and change the way the rest of the code works. Sometimes this is only a little, sometimes a bit more, according to how your code was designed and implemented. Therefore, start with the biggest issue first.

One of the reasons Python is so popular is that it is possible to implement it in many different ways. So, if you find yourself having trouble boosting up some part of your code using sheer Python, nothing prevents you from rolling up your sleeves, buying 200 liters of coffee, and rewriting the slow piece of code in C—guaranteed to be fun!

Summary

In this chapter, we explored the world of testing, exceptions, and profiling.

I tried to give you a fairly comprehensive overview of testing, especially unit testing, which is the kind of testing that a developer mostly does. I hope I have succeeded in channeling the message that testing is not something that is perfectly defined that you can learn from a book. You need to experiment with it a lot before you get comfortable. Of all the efforts a coder must make in terms of study and experimentation, I'd say testing is the one that is the most important.

We briefly saw how we can prevent our program from dying because of errors, called exceptions, that happen at runtime. And, to steer away from the usual ground, I have given you an example of a somewhat unconventional use of exceptions to break out of nested `for` loops. That's not the only case, and I'm sure you'll discover others as you grow as a coder.

At the end, we very briefly touched on profiling, with a simple example and a few guidelines. I wanted to talk about profiling for the sake of completeness, so at least you can play around with it.

In the next chapter, we're going to explore the wonderful world of secrets, hashing, and creating tokens.

 I am aware that I gave you a lot of pointers in this chapter, with no links or directions. I'm afraid this was by choice. As a coder, there won't be a single day at work when you won't have to look something up in a documentation page, in a manual, on a website, and so on. I think it's vital for a coder to be able to search effectively for the information they need, so I hope you'll forgive me for this extra training. After all, it's all for your benefit.

Cryptography and Tokens **9**

"Three may keep a Secret, if two of them are dead."

– *Benjamin Franklin, Poor Richard's Almanack*

In this short chapter, I am going to give you a brief overview of the cryptographic services offered by the Python standard library. I am also going to touch upon something called JSON Web Token, which is a very interesting standard to represent claims securely between two parties.

In particular, we are going to explore the following:

- Hashlib
- Secrets
- HMAC
- JSON Web Tokens with PyJWT, which seems to be the most popular Python library for dealing with JWTs

Let's start by spending a moment talking about cryptography and why it is so important.

The need for cryptography

According to the statistics you can find all over the web, the estimated amount of smartphone users in 2019 will be around 2.5 billion. Each of those people know the PIN to unlock their phone, the credentials to log in to applications we all use to do, well, basically everything, from buying food to finding a street, from sending a message to a friend, to seeing if our bitcoin wallet has increased in value since we last checked 10 seconds ago.

If you are an application developer, you have to take security very, very seriously. It doesn't matter how small or apparently insignificant your application is: security should always be a concern for you.

Security in information technology is achieved by employing several different means, but by far, the most important one is cryptography. Everything you do with your computer or phone should include a layer where cryptography takes place (and if not, that's really bad). It is used to pay online with a credit card, to transfer messages over the network in a way that even if someone intercepts them, they won't be able to read them, and it is used to encrypt your files when you back them up in the cloud (because you do, right?). Lists of examples are endless.

Now, the purpose of this chapter is not that of teaching you the difference between hashing and encryption, as I could write a whole other book on the subject. Rather, it is that of showing you how you can use the tools that Python offers you to create digests, tokens, and in general, to be on the safe(r) side when you need to implement something cryptography-related.

Useful guidelines

Always remember the following rules:

- **Rule number one**: Do not attempt to create your own hash or encryption functions. Simply don't. Use tools and functions that are there already. It is incredibly tough to come up with a good, solid, robust algorithm to do hashing or encryption, so it's best to leave it to professional cryptographers.
- **Rule number two**: Follow rule number one.

Those are the only two rules you need. Apart from them, it is very useful to understand cryptography, so you need to try and learn as much as you can about this subject. There is plenty of information on the web, but for your convenience, I'll put some useful references at the end of this chapter.

Now, let's dig into the first of the standard library modules I want to show you: `hashlib`.

Hashlib

This module exposes a common interface to many different secure hash and message digest algorithms. The difference in those two terms is simply historical: older algorithms were called **digests**, while the modern algorithms are called **hashes**.

In general, a hash function is any function that can be used to map data of an arbitrary size to data of a fixed size. It is a one-way type of encryption, in that it is not expected to be able to recover the message given its hash.

There are several algorithms that can be used to calculate a hash, so let's see how to find out which ones are supported by your system (note, your results might be different than mine):

```
>>> import hashlib
>>> hashlib.algorithms_available
{'SHA512', 'SHA256', 'shake_256', 'sha3_256', 'ecdsa-with-SHA1',
 'DSA-SHA', 'sha1', 'sha384', 'sha3_224', 'whirlpool', 'mdc2',
 'RIPEMD160', 'shake_128', 'MD4', 'dsaEncryption', 'dsaWithSHA',
 'SHA1', 'blake2s', 'md5', 'sha', 'sha224', 'SHA', 'MD5',
 'sha256', 'SHA384', 'sha3_384', 'md4', 'SHA224', 'MDC2',
 'sha3_512', 'sha512', 'blake2b', 'DSA', 'ripemd160'}
>>> hashlib.algorithms_guaranteed
{'blake2s', 'md5', 'sha224', 'sha3_512', 'shake_256', 'sha3_256',
 'shake_128', 'sha256', 'sha1', 'sha512', 'blake2b', 'sha3_384',
 'sha384', 'sha3_224'}
```

By opening a Python shell, we can get the list of available algorithms for our system. If our application has to talk to third-party applications, it's always best to pick an algorithm out of those guaranteed, though, as that means every platform actually supports them. Notice that a lot of them start with **sha**, which means **secure hash algorithm**. Let's keep going in the same shell: we are going to create a hash for the binary string b'Hash me now!', and we're going to do it in two ways:

```
>>> h = hashlib.blake2b()
>>> h.update(b'Hash me')
>>> h.update(b' now!')
>>> h.hexdigest()
'56441b566db9aafcf8cdad3a4729fa4b2bfaab0ada36155ece29f52ff70e1e9d'
'7f54cacfe44bc97c7e904cf79944357d023877929430bc58eb2dae168e73cedf'
>>> h.digest()
b'VD\x1bVm\xb9\xaa\xfc\xf8\xcd\xad:G)\xfaK+\xfa\xab\n\xda6\x15^'
b'\xce)\xf5/\xf7\x0e\x1e\x9d\x7fT\xca\xcf\xe4K\xc9|~\x90L\xf7'
b'\x99D5}\x028w\x92\x940\xbcX\xeb-\xae\x16\x8es\xce\xdf'
>>> h.block_size
128
>>> h.digest_size
```

```
64
>>> h.name
'blake2b'
```

We have used the `blake2b` cryptographic function, which is quite sophisticated and was added in Python 3.6. After creating the hash object `h`, we update its message in two steps. Not that we need to, but sometimes we need to hash data that is not available all at once, so it's good to know we can do it in steps.

When the message is like we want it to be, we get the hex representation of the digest. This will use two characters per byte (as each character represents 4 bits, which is half a byte). We also get the byte representation of the digest, and then we inspect its details: it has a block size (the internal block size of the hash algorithm in bytes) of 128 bytes, a digest size (the size of the resulting hash in bytes) of 64 bytes, and a name. Could all this be done in one simpler line? Yes, of course:

```
>>> hashlib.blake2b(b'Hash me now!').hexdigest()
'56441b566db9aafcf8cdad3a4729fa4b2bfaab0ada36155ece29f52ff70e1e9d'
'7f54cacfe44bc97c7e904cf79944357d023877929430bc58eb2dae168e73cedf'
```

Notice how the same message produces the same hash, which of course is expected.

Let's see what we get if, instead of the `blake2b` function, we use `sha256`:

```
>>> hashlib.sha256(b'Hash me now!').hexdigest()
'10d561fa94a89a25ea0c7aa47708bdb353bbb062a17820292cd905a3a60d6783'
```

The resulting hash is shorter (and therefore less secure).

Hashing is a very interesting topic, and of course the simple examples we've seen so far are just the start. The `blake2b` function allows us a great deal of flexibility in terms of customization. This is extremely useful to prevent some kinds of attacks (for the full explanation of those threats, please do refer to the standard documentation at: https:// docs.python.org/3.7/library/hashlib.html for the `hashlib` module). Let's see another example where we customize a hash by adding a `key`, a `salt`, and a `person`. All of this extra information will cause the hash to be different than the one we would get if we didn't provide them, and are crucial in adding extra security to the data handled in our system:

```
>>> h = hashlib.blake2b(
...     b'Important payload', digest_size=16, key=b'secret-key',
...     salt=b'random-salt', person=b'fabrizio'
... )
>>> h.hexdigest()
'c2d63ead796d0d6d734a5c3c578b6e41'
```

The resulting hash is only 16 bytes long. Among the customization parameters, `salt` is probably the most famous one. It is random data that is used as an additional input to a one-way function that hashes data. It is commonly stored alongside the resulting hash, in order to provide the means to recover the same hash given the same message.

If you want to make sure you hash a password properly, you can use `pbkdf2_hmac`, a key derivation algorithm that allows you to specify a `salt` and also the number of iterations used by the algorithm itself. As computers get more and more powerful, it is important to increase the amount of iterations we do over time, otherwise the likelihood of a successful brute-force attack on our data increases as time passes. Here's how you would use such an algorithm:

```
>>> import os
>>> dk = hashlib.pbkdf2_hmac(
...     'sha256', b'Password123', os.urandom(16), 100000
... )
>>> dk.hex()
'f8715c37906df067466ce84973e6e52a955be025a59c9100d9183c4cbec27a9e'
```

Notice I have used `os.urandom` to provide a 16 byte random salt, as recommended by the documentation.

I encourage you to explore and experiment with this module, as sooner or later you will have to use it. Now, let's move on to the `secrets` one.

Secrets

This nice, small module is used for generating cryptographically strong, random numbers suitable for managing data such as passwords, account authentication, security tokens, and related secrets. It was added in Python 3.6, and basically deals with three things: random numbers, tokens, and digest comparison. Let's explore them very quickly.

Random numbers

We can use three functions in order to deal with random numbers:

```
# secrs/secr_rand.py
import secrets
print(secrets.choice('Choose one of these words'.split()))
print(secrets.randbelow(10 ** 6))
print(secrets.randbits(32))
```

The first one, `choice`, picks an element at random from a non-empty sequence. The second one, `randbelow`, generates a random integer between `0` and the argument you call it with, and the third one, `randbits`, generates an integer with n random bits in it. Running that code produces the following output (which is always different):

```
$ python secr_rand.py
one
504156
3172492450
```

You should use these functions instead of those from the `random` module whenever you need randomness in the context of cryptography, as these are specially designed for this task. Let's see what the module gives us for tokens.

Token generation

Again, we have three functions that all produce a token, albeit in different formats. Let's see the example:

```
# secrs/secr_rand.py
print(secrets.token_bytes(16))
print(secrets.token_hex(32))
print(secrets.token_urlsafe(32))
```

The first one, `token_bytes`, simply returns a random byte string containing n bytes (`16`, in this example). The other two do the same, but `token_hex` returns a token in hexadecimal format, and `token_urlsafe` returns a token that only contains characters suitable for being included in a URL. Let's see the output (which is a continuation from the previous run):

```
b'\xda\x863\xeb\xbb|\x8fk\x9b\xbd\x14Q\xd4\x8d\x15}'
9f90fd042229570bf633e91e92505523811b45e1c3a72074e19bbeb2e5111bf7
bl4qz_Av7QNvPEqZtKsLuTOUsNLFmXW3O03pn50leiY
```

This is all nice, so why don't we have some fun and write a random password generator using these tools?

```
# secrs/secr_gen.py
import secrets
from string import digits, ascii_letters

def generate_pwd(length=8):
    chars = digits + ascii_letters
    return ''.join(secrets.choice(chars) for c in range(length))
```

```
def generate_secure_pwd(length=16, upper=3, digits=3):
    if length < upper + digits + 1:
        raise ValueError('Nice try!')
    while True:
        pwd = generate_pwd(length)
        if (any(c.islower() for c in pwd)
            and sum(c.isupper() for c in pwd) >= upper
            and sum(c.isdigit() for c in pwd) >= digits):
            return pwd

print(generate_secure_pwd())
print(generate_secure_pwd(length=3, upper=1, digits=1))
```

In the previous code, we defined two functions. generate_pwd simply generates a random string of given length by joining together length characters picked at random from a string that contains all the letters of the alphabet (lowercase and uppercase), and the 10 decimal digits.

Then, we define another function, generate_secure_pwd, that simply keeps calling generate_pwd until the random string we get matches the requirements, which are quite simple. The password must have at least one lowercase character, upper uppercase characters, digits digits, and length length.

Before we dive into the while loop, it's worth noting that if we sum together the requirements (uppercase, lowercase, and digits) and that sum is greater than the overall length of the password, there is no way we can ever satisfy the condition within the loop. So, in order to avoid getting stuck in an infinite loop, I have put a check clause in the first line of the body, and I raise a ValueError in case I need it. Could you think of how to write a test for this edge case?

The body of the while loop is straightforward: first we generate the random password, and then we verify the conditions by using any and sum. any returns True if any of the items in the iterable it's called with evaluate to True. The use of sum is actually slightly more tricky here, in that it exploits polymorphism. Can you see what I'm talking about before you read on?

Well, it's very simple: True and False in Python are subclasses of integer numbers, therefore when summing on an iterable of True/False values, they will automatically be interpreted like integers by the sum function. That is called **polymorphism**, and we've briefly talked about it in Chapter 6, *OOP, Decorators, and Iterators*.

Running the example produces the following result:

```
$ python secr_gen.py
nsL5voJnCi7Ote3F
J5e
```

The second password is probably not too secure...

One last example, before we move on to the next module. Let's generate a reset password URL:

```
# secrs/secr_reset.py
import secrets

def get_reset_pwd_url(token_length=16):
    token = secrets.token_urlsafe(token_length)
    return f'https://fabdomain.com/reset-pwd/{token}'

print(get_reset_pwd_url())
```

This function is so easy I will only show you the output:

```
$ python secr_reset.py
https://fabdomain.com/reset-pwd/m4jb7aKgzTGuyjs9lTIspw
```

Digest comparison

This is probably quite surprising, but within `secrets`, you can find the `compare_digest(a, b)` function, which is the equivalent of comparing two digests by simply doing `a == b`. So, why do we need that function? It's because it has been designed to prevent timing attacks. These kind of attacks can infer information about where the two digests start being different, according to the time it takes for the comparison to fail. So, `compare_digest` prevents this attack by removing the correlation between time and failures. I think this is a brilliant example of how sophisticated attacking methods can be. If you raised your eyebrows in astonishment, maybe now it's clearer why I said to never implement cryptography functions by yourself.

And that's it! Now, let's check out `hmac`.

HMAC

This module implements the HMAC algorithm, as described by RFC 2104 (`https://tools.ietf.org/html/rfc2104.html`). Since it is very small, but nonetheless important, I will provide you with a simple example:

```
# hmc.py
import hmac
import hashlib

def calc_digest(key, message):
    key = bytes(key, 'utf-8')
    message = bytes(message, 'utf-8')
    dig = hmac.new(key, message, hashlib.sha256)
    return dig.hexdigest()

digest = calc_digest('secret-key', 'Important Message')
```

As you can see, the interface is always the same or similar. We first convert the key and the message into bytes, and then create a `digest` instance that we will use to get a hexadecimal representation of the hash. Not much else to say, but I thought to add this module anyway, for completeness.

Now, let's move on to a different type of token: JWTs.

JSON Web Tokens

A **JSON Web Token**, or **JWT**, is a JSON-based open standard for creating tokens that assert some number of claims. You can learn all about this technology on the website (`https://jwt.io/`). In a nutshell, this type of token is comprised of three sections, separated by a dot, in the format *A.B.C*. *B* is the payload, which is where we put the data and the claims. *C* is the signature, which is used to verify the validity of the token, and *A* is the algorithm used to compute the signature. *A*, *B*, and *C* are all encoded with a URL safe Base64 encoding (which I'll refer to as Base64URL).

Base64 is a very popular binary-to-text encoding scheme that represents binary data in an ASCII string format by translating it into a radix-64 representation. The radix-64 representation uses the letters *A-Z*, *a-z*, and the digits *0-9*, plus the two symbols + and / for a grand total of 64 symbols altogether. Therefore, not surprisingly, the Base64 alphabet is made up of these 64 symbols. Base64 is used, for example, to encode images attached in an email. It happens seamlessly, so the vast majority of people are completely oblivious of this fact.

The reason why a JWT is encoded using Base64URL is because of the characters + and /, which in a URL context mean space, and path separator, respectively. Therefore in the URL safe version, they are replaced with – and _. Moreover, any padding character (=), which is normally used in Base64, is stripped out, as this too has a specific meaning within a URL.

The way this type of token works is therefore slightly different than what we are used to when we work with hashes. In fact, the information that the token carries is always visible. You just need to decode *A* and *B* to get the algorithm and the payload. However, the security lies in part *C*, which is a HMAC hash of the token. If you try to modify the *B* part by editing the payload, encoding it back to Base64, and replacing it in the token, the signature won't match any more, and therefore the token will be invalid.

This means that we can build a payload with claims such as *logged in as admin*, or something along those lines, and as long as the token is valid, we know we can trust that that user is actually logged in as an admin.

When dealing with JWTs, you want to make sure you have researched how to handle them safely. Things like not accepting unsigned tokens, or restricting the list of algorithms you use to encode and decode, as well as other security measures, are very important and you should take the time to investigate and learn them.

For this part of the code, you will have to have the `PyJWT` and `cryptography` Python packages installed. As always, you will find them in the requirements of the source code of this book.

Let's start with a simple example:

```
# tok.py
import jwt

data = {'payload': 'data', 'id': 123456789}

token = jwt.encode(data, 'secret-key')
data_out = jwt.decode(token, 'secret-key')
print(token)
print(data_out)
```

We define the `data` payload, which contains an ID and some payload data. Then, we create a token using the `jwt.encode` function, which takes at least the payload and a secret key, which is used to compute the signature. The default algorithm used to calculate the token is `HS256`. Let's see the output:

```
$ python tok.py
b'eyJ0eXAiOiJKV1QiLCJhbGciOiJIUzI1NiJ9.eyJwYXlsb2FkIjoiZGF0YSIsImlkIjoxMjM0
NTY3ODI9.WFRY-uoACMoNYX97PXXjEfXFQO1rCyFCyiwxzOVMn40'
{'payload': 'data', 'id': 123456789}
```

So, as you can see, the token is a binary string of Base64URL-encoded pieces of data. We have called `jwt.decode`, providing the correct secret key. Had we done otherwise, the decoding would have broken.

Sometimes, you might want to be able to inspect the content of the token without verifying it. You can do so by simply calling `decode` this way:

```
# tok.py
jwt.decode(token, verify=False)
```

This is useful, for example, when values in the token payload are needed to recover the secret key, but that technique is quite advanced so I won't be spending time on it in this context. Instead, let's see how we can specify a different algorithm for computing the signature:

```
# tok.py
token512 = jwt.encode(data, 'secret-key', algorithm='HS512')
data_out = jwt.decode(token512, 'secret-key', algorithm='HS512')
print(data_out)
```

The output is our original payload dictionary. In case you want to allow more than one algorithm in the decoding phase, you can even specify a list of them, instead of only one.

Now, while you are free to put whatever you want in the token payload, there are some claims that have been standardized, and they enable you to have a great deal of control over the token.

Registered claims

At the time of writing this book, these are the registered claims:

- `iss`: The *issuer* of the token
- `sub`: The *subject* information about the party this token is carrying information about
- `aud`: The *audience* for the token
- `exp`: The *expiration time*, after which the token is considered to be invalid
- `nbf`: The *not before (time)*, or the time before which the token is considered to be not valid yet
- `iat`: The time at which the token was *issued*
- `jti`: The token *ID*

Claims can also be categorized as public or private:

- **Private**: Are those that are defined by users (consumers and producers) of the JWTs. In other words, these are ad hoc claims used for a particular case. As such, care must be taken to prevent collisions.
- **Public**: Are claims that are either registered with the IANA JSON Web Token Claims Registry (a registry where users can register their claims and thus prevent collisions), or named using a collision resistant name (for instance, by prepending a namespace to its name).

To learn all about claims, please refer to the official website. Now, let's see a couple of code examples involving a subset of these claims.

Time-related claims

Let's see how we might use the claims related to time:

```
# claims_time.py
from datetime import datetime, timedelta
from time import sleep
import jwt

iat = datetime.utcnow()
nfb = iat + timedelta(seconds=1)
exp = iat + timedelta(seconds=3)
data = {'payload': 'data', 'nbf': nfb, 'exp': exp, 'iat': iat}

def decode(token, secret):
```

```
        print(datetime.utcnow().time().isoformat())
        try:
            print(jwt.decode(token, secret))
        except (
            jwt.ImmatureSignatureError, jwt.ExpiredSignatureError
        ) as err:
            print(err)
            print(type(err))

secret = 'secret-key'
token = jwt.encode(data, secret)

decode(token, secret)
sleep(2)
decode(token, secret)
sleep(2)
decode(token, secret)
```

In this example, we set the issued at (`iat`) claim to the current UTC time (**UTC** stands for **Universal Time Coordinated**). We then set the not before (`nbf`) and expire time (`exp`) at 1 and 3 seconds from now, respectively. We then defined a decode helper function that reacts to a token not being valid yet, or being expired, by trapping the appropriate exceptions, and then we call it three times, interspersed by two calls to sleep. This way, we will try to decode the token when it's not valid yet, then when it's valid, and finally when it's already expired. This function also prints a useful timestamp before attempting decryption. Let's see how it goes (blank lines have been added for readability):

```
$ python claims_time.py
14:04:13.469778
The token is not yet valid (nbf)
<class 'jwt.exceptions.ImmatureSignatureError'>

14:04:15.475362
{'payload': 'data', 'nbf': 1522591454, 'exp': 1522591456, 'iat':
1522591453}

14:04:17.476948
Signature has expired
<class 'jwt.exceptions.ExpiredSignatureError'>
```

As you can see, it all executed as expected. We get nice, descriptive messages from the exceptions, and get the original payload back when the token is actually valid.

Auth-related claims

Let's see another quick example involving the issuer (`iss`) and audience (`aud`) claims. The code is conceptually very similar to the previous example, and we're going to exercise it in the same way:

```python
# claims_auth.py
import jwt

data = {'payload': 'data', 'iss': 'fab', 'aud': 'learn-python'}
secret = 'secret-key'
token = jwt.encode(data, secret)

def decode(token, secret, issuer=None, audience=None):
    try:
        print(jwt.decode(
            token, secret, issuer=issuer, audience=audience))
    except (
        jwt.InvalidIssuerError, jwt.InvalidAudienceError
    ) as err:
        print(err)
        print(type(err))

decode(token, secret)
# not providing the issuer won't break
decode(token, secret, audience='learn-python')
# not providing the audience will break
decode(token, secret, issuer='fab')
# both will break
decode(token, secret, issuer='wrong', audience='learn-python')
decode(token, secret, issuer='fab', audience='wrong')

decode(token, secret, issuer='fab', audience='learn-python')
```

As you can see, this time, we have specified `issuer` and `audience`. It turns out that if we don't provide the issuer when decoding the token, it won't cause the decoding to break. However, providing the wrong issuer will actually break decoding. On the other hand, both failing to provide the audience, or providing the wrong audience, will break decoding.

As in the previous example, I have written a custom decode function that reacts to the appropriate exceptions. See if you can follow along with the calls and the relative output that follows (I'll help with some blank lines):

```
$ python claims_auth.py
Invalid audience
<class 'jwt.exceptions.InvalidAudienceError'>
```

```
{'payload': 'data', 'iss': 'fab', 'aud': 'learn-python'}

Invalid audience
<class 'jwt.exceptions.InvalidAudienceError'>

Invalid issuer
<class 'jwt.exceptions.InvalidIssuerError'>

Invalid audience
<class 'jwt.exceptions.InvalidAudienceError'>

{'payload': 'data', 'iss': 'fab', 'aud': 'learn-python'}
```

Now, let's see one final example for a more complex use case.

Using asymmetric (public-key) algorithms

Sometimes, using a shared secret is not the best option. In those cases, it might be useful to adopt a different technique. In this example, we are going to create a token (and decode it) using a pair of RSA keys.

Public key cryptography, or asymmetrical cryptography, is any cryptographic system that uses pairs of keys: public keys which may be disseminated widely, and private keys which are known only to the owner. If you are interested in learning more about this topic, please see the end of this chapter for recommendations.

Now, let's create two pairs of keys. One pair will have no password, and one will. To create them, I'm going to use the `ssh-keygen` utils from OpenSSH (https://www.ssh.com/ssh/keygen/). In the folder where my scripts for this chapter are, I created an `rsa` subfolder. Within it, run the following:

```
$ ssh-keygen -t rsa
```

Give the name `key` to the path (it will be saved in the current folder), and simply hit the *Enter* key when asked for the password. When done, do the same again, but this time use the name `keypwd` for the key, and give it a password. The one I chose is the classic `Password123`. When you are done, change back to the `ch9` folder, and run this code:

```
# token_rsa.py
import jwt
from cryptography.hazmat.backends import default_backend
from cryptography.hazmat.primitives import serialization

data = {'payload': 'data'}
```

```python
def encode(data, priv_filename, priv_pwd=None, algorithm='RS256'):
    with open(priv_filename, 'rb') as key:
        private_key = serialization.load_pem_private_key(
            key.read(),
            password=priv_pwd,
            backend=default_backend()
        )
    return jwt.encode(data, private_key, algorithm=algorithm)

def decode(data, pub_filename, algorithm='RS256'):
    with open(pub_filename, 'rb') as key:
        public_key = key.read()
    return jwt.decode(data, public_key, algorithm=algorithm)

# no pwd
token = encode(data, 'rsa/key')
data_out = decode(token, 'rsa/key.pub')
print(data_out)

# with pwd
token = encode(data, 'rsa/keypwd', priv_pwd=b'Password123')
data_out = decode(token, 'rsa/keypwd.pub')
print(data_out)
```

In the previous example, we defined a couple of custom functions to encode and decode tokens using private/public keys. As you can see in the signature of the `encode` function, we are using the `RS256` algorithm this time. We need to open the private key file by using the special `load_pem_private_key` function, which allows us to specify a content, password, and backend. `.pem` is the name of the format in which our keys have been created. If you take a look at those files, you will probably recognize them, since they are quite popular.

The logic is pretty straightforward, and I would encourage you to think about at least one use case where this technique might be more suitable than using a shared key.

Useful references

Here, you can find a list of useful references if you want to dig deeper in to the fascinating world of cryptography:

- Cryptography: `https://en.wikipedia.org/wiki/Cryptography`
- JSON Web Tokens: `https://jwt.io`

- Hash functions: `https://en.wikipedia.org/wiki/Cryptographic_hash_function`
- HMAC: `https://en.wikipedia.org/wiki/HMAC`
- Cryptography services (Python STD library): `https://docs.python.org/3.7/library/crypto.html`
- IANA JSON Web Token Claims Registry: `https://www.iana.org/assignments/jwt/jwt.xhtml`
- PyJWT library: `https://pyjwt.readthedocs.io/`
- Cryptography library: `https://cryptography.io/`

There is way more on the web, and plenty of books you can also study, but I'd recommend that you start with the main concepts and then gradually dive into the specifics you want to understand more thoroughly.

Summary

In this short chapter, we explored the world of cryptography in the Python standard library. We learned how to create a hash (or digest) for a message using different cryptographic functions. We also learned how to create tokens and deal with random data when it comes to the cryptography context.

We then took a small tour outside the standard library to learn about JSON Web Tokens, which are used intensively today in authentication and claims-related functionalities by modern systems and applications.

The most important thing is to understand that doing things manually can be very risky when it comes to cryptography, so it's always best to leave it to the professionals and simply use the tools we have available.

The next chapter will be all about moving away from one line of software execution. We're going to learn how software works in the real world, explore concurrent execution, and learn about threads, processes, and the tools Python gives us to do *more than one thing at a time*, so to speak.

10
Concurrent Execution

"What do we want? Now! When do we want it? Fewer race conditions!"

– Anna Melzer

In this chapter, I'm going to up the game a little bit, both in terms of the concepts I'll present, and in the complexity of the code snippets I'll show you. If you don't feel up to the task, or as you are reading through you realize it is getting too difficult, feel free to skip it. You can always come back to it when you feel ready.

The plan is to take a detour from the familiar single-threaded execution paradigm, and deep dive into what can be described as concurrent execution. I will only be able to scratch the surface of this complex topic, so I won't expect you to be a master of concurrency by the time you're done reading, but I will, as usual, try to give you enough information so that you can then proceed by *walking the path*, so to speak.

We will learn about all the important concepts that apply to this area of programming, and I will try to show you examples coded in different styles, to give you a solid understanding of the basics of these topics. To dig deep into this challenging and interesting branch of programming, you will have to refer to the *Concurrent Execution* section in the Python documentation (`https://docs.python.org/3.7/library/concurrency.html`), and maybe supplement your knowledge by studying books on the subject.

In particular, we are going to explore the following:

- The theory behind threads and processes
- Writing multithreaded code
- Writing multiprocessing code
- Using executors to spawn threads and processes
- A brief example of programming with `asyncio`

Let's start by getting the theory out of the way.

Concurrency versus parallelism

Concurrency and parallelism are often mistaken for the same thing, but there is a distinction between them. **Concurrency** is the ability to run multiple things at the same time, not necessarily in parallel. **Parallelism** is the ability to do a number of things at the same time.

Imagine you take your other half to the theater. There are two lines: that is, for VIP and regular tickets. There is only one functionary checking tickets and so, in order to avoid blocking either of the two queues, they check one ticket from the VIP line, then one from the regular line. Over time, both queues are processed. This is an example of concurrency.

Now imagine that another functionary joins, so now we have one functionary per queue. This way, both queues will be processed each by its own functionary. This is an example of parallelism.

Modern laptop processors feature multiple cores (normally two to four). A **core** is an independent processing unit that belongs to a processor. Having more than one core means that the CPU in question has the physical ability to actually execute tasks in parallel. Within each core, normally there is a constant alternation of streams of work, which is concurrent execution.

Bear in mind that I'm keeping the discussion generic on purpose here. According to which system you are using, there will be differences in how execution is handled, so I will concentrate on the concepts that are common to all, or at least most, systems.

Threads and processes – an overview

A **thread** can be defined as a sequence of instructions that can be run by a scheduler, which is that part of the operating system that decides which chunk of work will receive the necessary resources to be carried out. Typically, a thread lives within a process. A process can be defined as an instance of a computer program that is being executed.

In previous chapters, we have run our own modules and scripts with commands similar to $ `python my_script.py`. What happens when a command like that is run, is that a Python process is created. Within it, a main thread of execution is spawned. The instructions in the script are what will be run within that thread.

This is just one way of working though, and Python can actually use more than one thread within the same process, and can even spawn multiple processes. Unsurprisingly, these branches of computer science are called **multithreading** and **multiprocessing**.

In order to understand the difference, let's take a moment to explore threads and processes in slightly more depth.

Quick anatomy of a thread

Generally speaking, there are two different types of threads:

- **User-level threads**: Threads that we can create and manage in order to perform a task
- **Kernel-level threads**: Low-level threads that run in kernel mode and act on behalf of the operating system

Given that Python works at the user level, we're not going to deep dive into kernel threads at this time. Instead, we will explore several examples of user-level threads in this chapter's examples.

A thread can be in any of the following states:

- **New thread**: A thread that hasn't started yet, and hasn't been allocated any resources.
- **Runnable**: The thread is waiting to run. It has all the resources needed to run, and as soon as the scheduler gives it the green light, it will be run.
- **Running**: A thread whose stream of instructions is being executed. From this state, it can go back to a non-running state, or die.
- **Not-running**: A thread that has been paused. This could be due to another thread taking precedence over it, or simply because the thread is waiting for a long-running IO operation to finish.
- **Dead**: A thread that has died because it has reached the natural end of its stream of execution, or it has been killed.

Transitions between states are provoked either by our actions or by the scheduler. There is one thing to bear in mind, though; it is best not to interfere with the death of a thread.

Killing threads

Killing threads is not considered to be good practice. Python doesn't provide the ability to kill a thread by calling a method or function, and this should be a hint that killing threads isn't something you want to be doing.

One reason is that a thread might have children—threads spawned from within the thread itself—which would be orphaned when their parent dies. Another reason could be that if the thread you're killing is holding a resource that needs to be closed properly, you might prevent that from happening and that could potentially lead to problems.

Later, we will see an example of how we can work around these issues.

Context-switching

We have said that the scheduler can decide when a thread can run, or is paused, and so on. Any time a running thread needs to be suspended so that another can be run, the scheduler saves the state of the running thread in a way that it will be possible, at a later time, to resume execution exactly where it was paused.

This act is called **context-switching**. People do that all the time too. We are doing some paperwork, and we hear *bing!* on our phone. We stop the paperwork and check our phone. When we're done dealing with what was probably the umpteenth picture of a funny cat, we go back to our paperwork. We don't start the paperwork from the beginning, though; we simply continue where we had left off.

Context-switching is a marvelous ability of modern computers, but it can become troublesome if you generate too many threads. The scheduler then will try to give each of them a chance to run for a little time, and there will be a lot of time spent saving and recovering the state of the threads that are respectively paused and restarted.

In order to avoid this problem, it is quite common to limit the amount of threads (the same consideration applies to processes) that can be run at any given point in time. This is achieved by using a structure called a pool, the size of which can be decided by the programmer. In a nutshell, we create a pool and then assign tasks to its threads. When all the threads of the pool are busy, the program won't be able to spawn a new thread until one of them terminates (and goes back to the pool). Pools are also great for saving resources, in that they provide recycling features to the thread ecosystem.

When you write multithreaded code, it is useful to have information about the machine our software is going to run on. That information, coupled with some profiling (we'll learn about it in Chapter 11, *Debugging and Troubleshooting*), should enable us to calibrate the size of our pools correctly.

The Global Interpreter Lock

In July 2015, I attended the EuroPython conference in Bilbao, where I gave a talk about test-driven development. The camera operator unfortunately lost the first half of it, but I've since been able to give that talk another couple of times, so you can find a complete version of it on the web. At the conference, I had the great pleasure of meeting Guido van Rossum and talking to him, and I also attended his keynote speech.

One of the topics he addressed was the infamous **Global Interpreter Lock (GIL)**. The GIL is a mutex that protects access to Python objects, preventing multiple threads from executing Python bytecodes at once. This means that even though you can write multithreaded code in Python, there is only one thread running at any point in time (per process, of course).

 In computer programming, a mutual exclusion object (mutex) is a program object that allows multiple program threads to share the same resource, such as file access, but not simultaneously.

This is normally seen as an undesired limitation of the language, and many developers take pride in cursing this great villain. The truth lies somewhere else though, as was beautifully explained by Raymond Hettinger in his Keynote on Concurrency, at PyBay 2017 (`https://bit.ly/2KcijOB`). About 10 minutes in, Raymond explains that it is actually quite simple to remove the GIL from Python. It takes about a day of work. The price you pay for this *GIL-ectomy* though, is that you then have to apply locks yourself wherever they are needed in your code. This leads to a more expensive footprint, as multitudes of individual locks take more time to be acquired and released, and most importantly, it introduces the risk of bugs, as writing robust multithreaded code is not easy and you might end up having to write dozens or hundreds of locks.

In order to understand what a lock is, and why you might want to use it, we first need to talk about one of the perils of multithreaded programming: race conditions.

Race conditions and deadlocks

When it comes to writing multithreaded code, you need to be aware of the dangers that come when your code is no longer executed linearly. By that, I mean that multithreaded code is exposed to the risk of being paused at any point in time by the scheduler, because it has decided to give some CPU time to another stream of instructions.

This behavior exposes you to different types of risks, the two most famous being race conditions and deadlocks. Let's talk about them briefly.

Race conditions

A **race condition** is a behavior of a system where the output of a procedure depends on the sequence or timing of other uncontrollable events. When these events don't unfold in the order intended by the programmer, a race condition becomes a bug.

It's much easier to explain this with an example.

Imagine you have two threads running. Both are performing the same task, which consists of reading a value from a location, performing an action with that value, incrementing the value by *1* unit, and saving it back. Say that the action is to post that value to an API.

Scenario A – race condition not happening

Thread *A* reads the value (*1*), posts *1* to the API, then increments it to *2*, and saves it back. Right after this, the scheduler pauses Thread *A*, and runs Thread *B*. Thread *B* reads the value (now *2*), posts *2* to the API, increments it to *3*, and saves it back.

At this point, after the operation has happened twice, the value stored is correct: *1 + 2 = 3*. Moreover, the API has been called with both *1* and *2*, correctly.

Scenario B – race condition happening

Thread *A* reads the value (*1*), posts it to the API, increments it to *2*, but before it can save it back, the scheduler decides to pause thread *A* in favor of Thread *B*.

Thread *B* reads the value (still *1*!), posts it to the API, increments it to *2*, and saves it back. The scheduler then switches over to Thread *A* again. Thread *A* resumes its stream of work by simply saving the value it was holding after incrementing, which is *2*.

After this scenario, even though the operation has happened twice as in Scenario *A*, the value saved is *2*, and the API has been called twice with *1*.

In a real-life situation, with multiple threads and real code performing several operations, the overall behavior of the program explodes into a myriad of possibilities. We'll see an example of this later on, and we'll fix it using locks.

The main problem with race conditions is that they make our code non-deterministic, which is bad. There are areas in computer science where non-determinism is used to achieve things, and that's fine, but in general you want to be able to predict how your code will behave, and race conditions make it impossible to do so.

Locks to the rescue

Locks come to the rescue when dealing with race conditions. For example, in order to fix the preceding example, all you need is a lock around the procedure. A lock is like a guardian that will allow only one thread to take hold of it (we say *to acquire* a lock), and until that thread releases the lock, no other thread can acquire it. They will have to sit and wait until the lock is available again.

Scenario C – using a lock

Thread *A* acquires the lock, reads the value (*1*), posts to the API, increases to *2*, and the scheduler suspends it. Thread *B* is given some CPU time, so it tries to acquire the lock. But the lock hasn't been released yet by Thread *A*, so Thread *B* sits and waits. The scheduler might notice this, and quickly decide to switch back to Thread *A*.

Thread *A* saves 2, and releases the lock, making it available to all other threads.

At this point, whether the lock is acquired again by Thread *A*, or by Thread *B* (because the scheduler might have decided to switch again), is not important. The procedure will always be carried out correctly, since the lock makes sure that when a thread reads a value, it has to complete the procedure (ping API, increment, and save) before any other thread can read the value as well.

There are a multitude of different locks available in the standard library. I definitely encourage you to read up on them to understand all the perils you might encounter when coding multithreaded code, and how to solve them.

Let's now talk about deadlocks.

Deadlocks

A **deadlock** is a state in which each member of a group is waiting for some other member to take action, such as sending a message or, more commonly, releasing a lock, or a resource.

A simple example will help you get the picture. Imagine two little kids playing together. Find a toy that is made of two parts, and give each of them one part. Naturally, neither of them will want to give the other one their part, and they will want the other one to release the part they have. So neither of them will be able to play with the toy, as they each hold half of it, and will indefinitely wait for the other kid to release the other half.

> Don't worry, no kids were harmed during the making of this example. It all happened in my mind.

Another example could be having two threads execute the same procedure again. The procedure requires acquiring two resources, *A* and *B*, both guarded by a separate lock. Thread *1* acquires *A*, and Thread *2* acquires *B*, and then they will wait indefinitely until the other one releases the resource it has. But that won't happen, as they both are instructed to wait and acquire the second resource in order to complete the procedure. Threads can be much more stubborn than kids.

You can solve this problem in several ways. The easiest one might be simply to apply an order to the resources acquisition, which means that the thread that gets *A*, will also get all the rest: *B*, *C*, and so on.

Another way is to put a lock around the whole resources acquisition procedure, so that even if it might happen out of order, it will still be within the context of a lock, which means only one thread at a time can actually gather all the resources.

Let's now pause our talk on threads for a moment, and explore processes.

Quick anatomy of a process

Processes are normally more complex than threads. In general, they contain a main thread, but can also be multithreaded if you choose. They are capable of spawning multiple sub-threads, each of which contains its own set of registers and a stack. Each process provides all the resources that the computer needs in order to execute the program.

Similarly to using multiple threads, we can design our code to take advantage of a multiprocessing design. Multiple processes are likely to run over multiple cores, therefore with multiprocessing, you can truly parallelize computation. Their memory footprints, though, are slightly heavier than those of threads, and another drawback to using multiple processes is that **inter-process communication** (**IPC**) tends to be more expensive than communication between threads.

Properties of a process

A UNIX process is created by the operating system. It typically contains the following:

- A process ID, process group ID, user ID, or group ID
- An environment and working directory
- Program instructions
- Registers, a stack, and a heap
- File descriptors
- Signal actions
- Shared libraries
- Inter-process communication tools (pipes, message queues, semaphores, or shared memory)

If you are curious about processes, open up a shell and type `$ top`. This command displays and updates sorted information about the processes that are running in your system. When I run it on my machine, the first line tells me the following:

```
$ top
Processes: 477 total, 4 running, 473 sleeping, 2234 threads
...
```

This gives you an idea about how much work our computers are doing without us being really aware of it.

Multithreading or multiprocessing?

Given all this information, deciding which approach is the best means having an understanding of the type of work that needs to be carried out, and knowledge about the system that will be dedicated to doing that work.

There are advantages to both approaches, so let's try to clarify the main differences.

Here are some advantages of using multithreading:

- Threads are all born within the same process. They share resources and can communicate with one another very easily. Communication between processes requires more complex structures and techniques.
- The overhead of spawning a thread is smaller than that of a process. Moreover, their memory footprint is also smaller.

- Threads can be very effective at blocking IO-bound applications. For example, while one thread is blocked waiting for a network connection to give back some data, work can be easily and effectively switched to another thread.
- Because there aren't any shared resources between processes, we need to use IPC techniques, and they require more memory than communication between threads.

Here are some advantages of using multiprocessing:

- We can avoid the limitations of the GIL by using processes.
- Sub-processes that fail won't kill the main application.
- Threads suffer from issues such as race conditions and deadlocks; while using processes the likelihood of having to deal with them is greatly reduced.
- Context-switching of threads can become quite expensive when their amount is above a certain threshold.
- Processes can make better use of multicore processors.
- Processes are better than multiple threads at handling CPU-intensive tasks.

In this chapter, I'll show you both approaches for multiple examples, so hopefully you'll gain a good understanding of the various different techniques. Let's get to the code then!

Concurrent execution in Python

Let's start by exploring the basics of Python multithreading and multiprocessing with some simple examples.

 Keep in mind that several of the following examples will produce an output that depends on a particular run. When dealing with threads, things can get non-deterministic, as I mentioned earlier. So, if you experience different results, it is absolutely fine. You will probably notice that some of your results will vary from run to run too.

Starting a thread

First things first, let's start a thread:

```
# start.py
import threading

def sum_and_product(a, b):
    s, p = a + b, a * b
    print(f'{a}+{b}={s}, {a}*{b}={p}')

t = threading.Thread(
    target=sum_and_product, name='SumProd', args=(3, 7)
)
t.start()
```

After importing `threading`, we define a function: `sum_and_product`. This function calculates the sum and the product of two numbers, and prints the results. The interesting bit is after the function. We instantiate `t` from `threading.Thread`. This is our thread. We passed the name of the function that will be run as the thread body, we gave it a name, and passed the arguments 3 and 7, which will be fed into the function as `a` and `b`, respectively.

After having created the thread, we start it with the homonymous method.

At this point, Python will start executing the function in a new thread, and when that operation is done, the whole program will be done as well, and exit. Let's run it:

```
$ python start.py
3+7=10, 3*7=21
```

Starting a thread is therefore quite simple. Let's see a more interesting example where we display more information:

```
# start_with_info.py
import threading
from time import sleep

def sum_and_product(a, b):
    sleep(.2)
    print_current()
    s, p = a + b, a * b
    print(f'{a}+{b}={s}, {a}*{b}={p}')

def status(t):
    if t.is_alive():
        print(f'Thread {t.name} is alive.')
    else:
```

```
            print(f'Thread {t.name} has terminated.')

    def print_current():
        print('The current thread is {}.'.format(
            threading.current_thread()
        ))
        print('Threads: {}'.format(list(threading.enumerate())))

    print_current()
    t = threading.Thread(
        target=sum_and_product, name='SumPro', args=(3, 7)
    )
    t.start()
    status(t)
    t.join()
    status(t)
```

In this example, the thread logic is exactly the same as in the previous one, so you don't need to sweat on it and can concentrate on the (insane!) amount of logging information I added. We use two functions to display information: status and print_current. The first one takes a thread in input and displays its name and whether or not it's alive by calling its is_alive method. The second one prints the current thread, and then enumerates all the threads in the process. This information comes from threading.current_thread and threading.enumerate.

There is a reason why I put .2 seconds of sleeping time within the function. When the thread starts, its first instruction is to sleep for a moment. The sneaky scheduler will catch that, and switch execution back to the main thread. You can verify this by the fact that in the output, you will see the result of status(t) before that of print_current from within the thread. This means that that call happens while the thread is sleeping.

Finally, notice I called t.join() at the end. That instructs Python to block until the thread has completed. The reason for that is because I want the last call to status(t) to tell us that the thread is gone. Let's peek at the output (slightly rearranged for readability):

```
$ python start_with_info.py
The current thread is
    <_MainThread(MainThread, started 140735733822336)>.
Threads: [<_MainThread(MainThread, started 140735733822336)>]
Thread SumProd is alive.
The current thread is <Thread(SumProd, started 123145375604736)>.
Threads: [
    <_MainThread(MainThread, started 140735733822336)>,
    <Thread(SumProd, started 123145375604736)>
]
3+7=10, 3*7=21
```

Thread SumProd has terminated.

As you can see, at first the current thread is the main thread. The enumeration shows only one thread. Then we create and start `SumProd`. We print its status and we learn it is alive. Then, and this time from within `SumProd`, we display information about the current thread again. Of course, now the current thread is `SumProd`, and we can see that enumerating all threads returns both of them. After the result is printed, we verify, with one last call to `status`, that the thread has terminated, as predicted. Should you get different results (apart from the IDs of the threads, of course), try increasing the sleeping time and see whether anything changes.

Starting a process

Let's now see an equivalent example, but instead of using a thread, we'll use a process:

```
# start_proc.py
import multiprocessing

...

p = multiprocessing.Process(
    target=sum_and_product, name='SumProdProc', args=(7, 9)
)
p.start()
```

The code is exactly the same as for the first example, but instead of using a `Thread`, we actually instantiate `multiprocessing.Process`. The `sum_and_product` function is the same as before. The output is also the same, except the numbers are different.

Stopping threads and processes

As mentioned before, in general, stopping a thread is a bad idea, and the same goes for a process. Being sure you've taken care to dispose and close everything that is open can be quite difficult. However, there are situations in which you might want to be able to stop a thread, so let me show you how to do it:

```
# stop.py
import threading
from time import sleep

class Fibo(threading.Thread):
    def __init__(self, *a, **kwa):
        super().__init__(*a, **kwa)
```

```
            self._running = True

        def stop(self):
            self._running = False

        def run(self):
            a, b = 0, 1
            while self._running:
                print(a, end=' ')
                a, b = b, a + b
                sleep(0.07)
            print()

    fibo = Fibo()
    fibo.start()
    sleep(1)
    fibo.stop()
    fibo.join()
    print('All done.')
```

For this example, we use a Fibonacci generator. We've seen it before so I won't explain it. The important bit to focus on is the _running attribute. First of all, notice the class inherits from Thread. By overriding the __init__ method, we can set the _running flag to True. When you write a thread this way, instead of giving it a target function, you simply override the run method in the class. Our run method calculates a new Fibonacci number, and then sleeps for about 0.07 seconds.

In the last block of code, we create and start an instance of our class. Then we sleep for one second, which should give the thread time to produce about 14 Fibonacci numbers. When we call fibo.stop(), we aren't actually stopping the thread. We simply set our flag to False, and this allows the code within run to reach its natural end. This means that the thread will die organically. We call join to make sure the thread is actually done before we print All done. on the console. Let's check the output:

```
$ python stop.py
0 1 1 2 3 5 8 13 21 34 55 89 144 233
All done.
```

Check how many numbers were printed: 14, as predicted.

This is basically a workaround technique that allows you to stop a thread. If you design your code correctly according to multithreading paradigms, you shouldn't have to kill threads all the time, so let that need become your alarm bell that something could be designed better.

Stopping a process

When it comes to stopping a process, things are different, and fuss-free. You can use either the `terminate` or `kill` method, but please make sure you know what you're doing, as all the preceding considerations about open resources left hanging are still true.

Spawning multiple threads

Just for fun, let's play with two threads now:

```
# starwars.py
import threading
from time import sleep
from random import random

def run(n):
    t = threading.current_thread()
    for count in range(n):
        print(f'Hello from {t.name}! ({count})')
        sleep(0.2 * random())

obi = threading.Thread(target=run, name='Obi-Wan', args=(4, ))
ani = threading.Thread(target=run, name='Anakin', args=(3, ))
obi.start()
ani.start()
obi.join()
ani.join()
```

The `run` function simply prints the current thread, and then enters a loop of n cycles, in which it prints a greeting message, and sleeps for a random amount of time, between 0 and 0.2 seconds (`random()` returns a float between 0 and 1).

The purpose of this example is to show you how a scheduler might jump between threads, so it helps to make them sleep a little. Let's see the output:

```
$ python starwars.py
Hello from Obi-Wan! (0)
Hello from Anakin! (0)
Hello from Obi-Wan! (1)
Hello from Obi-Wan! (2)
Hello from Anakin! (1)
Hello from Obi-Wan! (3)
Hello from Anakin! (2)
```

As you can see, the output alternates randomly between the two. Every time that happens, you know a context switch has been performed by the scheduler.

Dealing with race conditions

Now that we have the tools to start threads and run them, let's simulate a race condition such as the one we discussed earlier:

```python
# race.py
import threading
from time import sleep
from random import random

counter = 0
randsleep = lambda: sleep(0.1 * random())

def incr(n):
    global counter
    for count in range(n):
        current = counter
        randsleep()
        counter = current + 1
        randsleep()

n = 5
t1 = threading.Thread(target=incr, args=(n, ))
t2 = threading.Thread(target=incr, args=(n, ))
t1.start()
t2.start()
t1.join()
t2.join()
print(f'Counter: {counter}')
```

In this example, we define the `incr` function, which gets a number n in input, and loops over n. In each cycle, it reads the value of the counter, sleeps for a random amount of time (between 0 and 0.1 seconds) by calling `randsleep`, a tiny Lambda function I wrote to improve readability, then increases the value of the `counter` by 1.

I chose to use `global` in order to have read/write access to `counter`, but it could be anything really, so feel free to experiment with that yourself.

The whole script basically starts two threads, each of which runs the same function, and gets n = 5. Notice how we need to join on both threads at the end to make sure that when we print the final value of the counter (last line), both threads are done doing their work.

When we print the final value, we would expect the counter to be 10, right? Two threads, five loops each, that makes 10. However, we almost never get 10 if we run this script. I ran it myself many times, and it seems to always hit somewhere between 5 and 7. The reason this happens is that there is a race condition in this code, and those random sleeps I added are there to exacerbate it. If you removed them, there would still be a race condition, because the counter is increased in a non-atomic way (which means an operation that can be broken down in multiple steps, and therefore paused in between). However, the likelihood of that race condition showing is really low, so adding the random sleep helps.

Let's analyze the code. t1 gets the current value of the counter, say, 3. t1 then sleeps for a moment. If the scheduler switches context in that moment, pausing t1 and starting t2, t2 will read the same value, 3. Whatever happens afterward, we know that both threads will update the counter to be 4, which will be incorrect as after two readings it should have gone up to 5. Adding the second random sleep call, after the update, helps the scheduler switch more frequently, and makes it easier to show the race condition. Try commenting out one of them, and see how the result changes (it will do so, dramatically).

Now that we have identified the issue, let's fix it by using a lock. The code is basically the same, so I'll show you only what changes:

```
# race_with_lock.py
incr_lock = threading.Lock()

def incr(n):
    global counter
    for count in range(n):
        with incr_lock:
            current = counter
            randsleep()
            counter = current + 1
            randsleep()
```

This time we have created a lock, from the `threading.Lock` class. We could call its `acquire` and `release` methods manually, or we can be Pythonic and use it within a context manager, which looks much nicer, and does the whole acquire/release business for us. Notice I left the random sleeps in the code. However, every time you run it, it will now return `10`.

The difference is this: when the first thread acquires that lock, it doesn't matter that when it's sleeping, a moment later, the scheduler switches the context. The second thread will try to acquire the lock, and Python will answer with a resounding *no*. So, the second thread will just sit and wait until that lock is released. As soon as the scheduler switches back to the first thread, and the lock is released, then the other thread will have a chance (if it gets there first, which is not necessarily guaranteed), to acquire the lock and update the counter. Try adding some prints into that logic to see whether the threads alternate perfectly or not. My guess is that they won't, at least not every time. Remember the `threading.current_thread` function, to be able to see which thread is actually printing the information.

Python offers several data structures in the `threading` module: Lock, RLock, Condition, Semaphore, Event, Timer, and Barrier. I won't be able to show you all of them, because unfortunately I don't have the room to explain all the use cases, but reading the documentation of the `threading` module (https://docs.python.org/3.7/library/threading.html) will be a good place to start understanding them.

Let's now see an example about thread's local data.

A thread's local data

The `threading` module offers a way to implement local data for threads. Local data is an object that holds thread-specific data. Let me show you an example, and allow me to sneak in a `Barrier` too, so I can tell you how it works:

```
# local.py
import threading
from random import randint

local = threading.local()

def run(local, barrier):
    local.my_value = randint(0, 10**2)
    t = threading.current_thread()
    print(f'Thread {t.name} has value {local.my_value}')
    barrier.wait()
    print(f'Thread {t.name} still has value {local.my_value}')
```

```
count = 3
barrier = threading.Barrier(count)
threads = [
    threading.Thread(
        target=run, name=f'T{name}', args=(local, barrier)
    ) for name in range(count)
]
for t in threads:
    t.start()
```

We start by defining `local`. That is the special object that holds thread-specific data. We run three threads. Each of them will assign a random value to `local.my_value`, and print it. Then the thread reaches a `Barrier` object, which is programmed to hold three threads in total. When the barrier is hit by the third thread, they all can pass. It's basically a nice way to make sure that *N* amount of threads reach a certain point and they all wait until every single one of them has arrived.

Now, if `local` was a normal, dummy object, the second thread would override the value of `local.my_value`, and the third would do the same. This means that we would see them printing different values in the first set of prints, but they would show the same value (the last one) in the second round of prints. But that doesn't happen, thanks to `local`. The output shows the following:

```
$ python local.py
Thread T0 has value 61
Thread T1 has value 52
Thread T2 has value 38
Thread T2 still has value 38
Thread T0 still has value 61
Thread T1 still has value 52
```

Notice the wrong order, due to the scheduler switching context, but the values are all correct.

Thread and process communication

We have seen quite a lot of examples so far. So, let's explore how to make threads and processes talk to one another by employing a queue. Let's start with threads.

Thread communication

For this example, we will be using a normal `Queue`, from the `queue` module:

```python
# comm_queue.py
import threading
from queue import Queue

SENTINEL = object()

def producer(q, n):
    a, b = 0, 1
    while a <= n:
        q.put(a)
        a, b = b, a + b
    q.put(SENTINEL)

def consumer(q):
    while True:
        num = q.get()
        q.task_done()
        if num is SENTINEL:
            break
        print(f'Got number {num}')

q = Queue()
cns = threading.Thread(target=consumer, args=(q, ))
prd = threading.Thread(target=producer, args=(q, 35))
cns.start()
prd.start()
q.join()
```

The logic is very basic. We have a `producer` function that generates Fibonacci numbers and puts them in a queue. When the next number is greater than a given n, the producer exits the `while` loop, and puts one last thing in the queue: a `SENTINEL`. A `SENTINEL` is any object that is used to signal something, and in our case, it signals to the consumer that the producer is done.

The interesting bit of logic is in the `consumer` function. It loops indefinitely, reading values out of the queue and printing them out. There are a couple of things to notice here. First, see how we are calling `q.task_done()`? That is to acknowledge that the element in the queue has been processed. The purpose of this is to allow the final instruction in the code, `q.join()`, to unblock when all elements have been acknowledged, so that the execution can end.

Second, notice how we use the `is` operator to compare against the items in order to find the sentinel. We'll see shortly that when using a `multiprocessing.Queue` this won't be possible any more. Before we get there, would you be able to guess why?

Running this example produces a series of lines, such as Got number 0, Got number 1, and so on, until 34, since the limit we put is 35, and the next Fibonacci number would be 55.

Sending events

Another way to make threads communicate is to fire events. Let me quickly show you an example of that:

```
# evt.py
import threading

def fire():
    print('Firing event...')
    event.set()

def listen():
    event.wait()
    print('Event has been fired')

event = threading.Event()
t1 = threading.Thread(target=fire)
t2 = threading.Thread(target=listen)
t2.start()
t1.start()
```

Here we have two threads that run `fire` and `listen`, respectively firing and listening for an event. To fire an event, call the `set` method on it. The `t2` thread, which is started first, is already listening to the event, and will sit there until the event is fired. The output from the previous example is the following:

```
$ python evt.py
Firing event...
Event has been fired
```

Events are great in some situations. Think about having threads that are waiting on a connection object to be ready, before they can actually start using it. They could be waiting on an event, and one thread could be checking that connection, and firing the event when it's ready. Events are fun to play with, so make sure you experiment and think about use cases for them.

Inter-process communication with queues

Let's now see how to communicate between processes using a queue. This example is very very similar to the one for threads:

```python
# comm_queue_proc.py
import multiprocessing

SENTINEL = 'STOP'

def producer(q, n):
    a, b = 0, 1
    while a <= n:
        q.put(a)
        a, b = b, a + b
    q.put(SENTINEL)

def consumer(q):
    while True:
        num = q.get()
        if num == SENTINEL:
            break
        print(f'Got number {num}')

q = multiprocessing.Queue()
cns = multiprocessing.Process(target=consumer, args=(q, ))
prd = multiprocessing.Process(target=producer, args=(q, 35))
cns.start()
prd.start()
```

As you can see, in this case, we have to use a queue that is an instance of `multiprocessing.Queue`, which doesn't expose a `task_done` method. However, because of the way this queue is designed, it automatically joins the main thread, therefore we only need to start the two processes and all will work. The output of this example is the same as the one before.

When it comes to IPC, be careful. Objects are pickled when they enter the queue, so IDs get lost, and there are a few other subtle things to take care of. This is why in this example I can no longer use an object as a sentinel, and compare using `is`, like I did in the multi-threaded version. That sentinel object would be pickled in the queue (because this time the `Queue` comes from `multiprocessing` and not from `queue` like before), and would assume a new ID after unpickling, failing to compare correctly. The string `"STOP"` in this case does the trick, and it will be up to you to find a suitable value for a sentinel, which needs to be something that could never clash with any of the items that could be in the same queue. I leave it up to you to refer to the documentation, and learn as much as you can on this topic.

Queues aren't the only way to communicate between processes. You can also use pipes (`multiprocessing.Pipe`), which provide a connection (as in, a pipe, clearly) from one process to another, and vice versa. You can find plenty of examples in the documentation; they aren't that different from what we've seen here.

Thread and process pools

As mentioned before, pools are structures designed to hold *N* objects (threads, processes, and so on). When the usage reaches capacity, no work is assigned to a thread (or process) until one of those currently working becomes available again. Pools, therefore, are a great way to limit the number of threads (or processes) that can be alive at the same time, preventing the system from starving due to resource exhaustion, or the computation time from being affected by too much context switching.

In the following examples, I will be tapping into the `concurrent.futures` module to use the `ThreadPoolExecutor` and `ProcessPoolExecutor` executors. These two classes, use a pool of threads (and processes, respectively), to execute calls asynchronously. They both accept a parameter, `max_workers`, which sets the upper limit to how many threads (or processes) can be used at the same time by the executor.

Let's start from the multithreaded example:

```
# pool.py
from concurrent.futures import ThreadPoolExecutor, as_completed
from random import randint
import threading

def run(name):
    value = randint(0, 10**2)
    tname = threading.current_thread().name
    print(f'Hi, I am {name} ({tname}) and my value is {value}')
    return (name, value)
```

```
with ThreadPoolExecutor(max_workers=3) as executor:
    futures = [
        executor.submit(run, f'T{name}') for name in range(5)
    ]
    for future in as_completed(futures):
        name, value = future.result()
        print(f'Thread {name} returned {value}')
```

After importing the necessary bits, we define the `run` function. It gets a random value, prints it, and returns it, along with the `name` argument it was called with. The interesting bit comes right after the function.

As you can see, we're using a context manager to call `ThreadPoolExecutor`, to which we pass `max_workers=3`, which means the pool size is `3`. This means only three threads at any time will be alive.

We define a list of future objects by making a list comprehension, in which we call `submit` on our executor object. We instruct the executor to run the `run` function, with a name that will go from `T0` to `T4`. A `future` is an object that encapsulates the asynchronous execution of a callable.

Then we loop over the `future` objects, as they are are done. To do this, we use `as_completed` to get an iterator of the `future` instances that returns them as soon as they complete (finish or were cancelled). We grab the result of each `future` by calling the homonymous method, and simply print it. Given that `run` returns a tuple `name, value`, we expect the result to be a two-tuple containing `name` and `value`. If we print the output of a `run` (bear in mind each `run` can potentially be slightly different), we get:

```
$ python pool.py
Hi, I am T0 (ThreadPoolExecutor-0_0) and my value is 5
Hi, I am T1 (ThreadPoolExecutor-0_0) and my value is 23
Hi, I am T2 (ThreadPoolExecutor-0_1) and my value is 58
Thread T1 returned 23
Thread T0 returned 5
Hi, I am T3 (ThreadPoolExecutor-0_0) and my value is 93
Hi, I am T4 (ThreadPoolExecutor-0_1) and my value is 62
Thread T2 returned 58
Thread T3 returned 93
Thread T4 returned 62
```

Before reading on, can you tell why the output looks like this? Could you explain what happened? Spend a moment thinking about it.

So, what goes on is that three threads start running, so we get three `Hi, I am...` messages printed out. Once all three of them are running, the pool is at capacity, so we need to wait for at least one thread to complete before anything else can happen. In the example run, `T0` and `T2` complete (which is signaled by the printing of what they returned), so they return to the pool and can be used again. They get run with names `T3` and `T4`, and finally all three, `T1`, `T3`, and `T4` complete. You can see from the output how the threads are actually reused, and how the first two are reassigned to `T3` and `T4` after they complete.

Let's now see the same example, but with the multiprocess design:

```
# pool_proc.py
from concurrent.futures import ProcessPoolExecutor, as_completed
from random import randint
from time import sleep

def run(name):
    sleep(.05)
    value = randint(0, 10**2)
    print(f'Hi, I am {name} and my value is {value}')
    return (name, value)

with ProcessPoolExecutor(max_workers=3) as executor:
    futures = [
        executor.submit(run, f'P{name}') for name in range(5)
    ]
    for future in as_completed(futures):
        name, value = future.result()
        print(f'Process {name} returned {value}')
```

The difference is truly minimal. We use `ProcessPoolExecutor` this time, and the `run` function is exactly the same, with one small addition: we sleep for 50 milliseconds at the beginning of each `run`. This is to exacerbate the behavior and have the output clearly show the size of the pool, which is still three. If we run the example, we get:

```
$ python pool_proc.py
Hi, I am P0 and my value is 19
Hi, I am P1 and my value is 97
Hi, I am P2 and my value is 74
Process P0 returned 19
Process P1 returned 97
Process P2 returned 74
Hi, I am P3 and my value is 80
Hi, I am P4 and my value is 68
Process P3 returned 80
Process P4 returned 68
```

This output clearly shows the pool size being three. It is very interesting to notice that if we remove that call to `sleep`, most of the time the output will have five prints of `Hi, I am...`, followed by five prints of `Process Px returned....` How can we explain that? Well it's simple. By the time the first three processes are done, and returned by `as_completed`, all three are asked for their result, and whatever is returned, is printed. While this happens, the executor can already start recycling two processes to run the final two tasks, and they happen to print their `Hi, I am...` messages, before the prints in the `for` loop are allowed to take place.

This basically means `ProcessPoolExecutor` is quite fast and aggressive (in terms of getting the scheduler's attention), and it's worth noting that this behavior doesn't happen with the thread counterpart, in which, if you recall, we didn't need to use any artificial sleeping.

The important thing to keep in mind though, is being able to appreciate that even simple examples such as these can already be slightly tricky to understand or explain. Let this be a lesson to you, so that you raise your attention to 110% when you code for multithreaded or multiprocess designs.

Let's now move on to a more interesting example.

Using a process to add a timeout to a function

Most, if not all, libraries that expose functions to make HTTP requests, provide the ability to specify a timeout when performing the request. This means that if after *X* seconds (*X* being the timeout), the request hasn't completed, the whole operation is aborted and execution resumes from the next instruction. Not all functions expose this feature though, so, when a function doesn't provide the ability to being interrupted, we can use a process to simulate that behavior. In this example, we'll be trying to translate a hostname into an IPv4 address. The `gethostbyname` function, from the `socket` module, doesn't allow us to put a timeout on the operation though, so we use a process to do that artificially. The code that follows might not be so straightforward, so I encourage you to spend some time going through it before you read on for the explanation:

```
# hostres/util.py
import socket
from multiprocessing import Process, Queue

def resolve(hostname, timeout=5):
    exitcode, ip = resolve_host(hostname, timeout)
    if exitcode == 0:
        return ip
```

```
        else:
            return hostname

def resolve_host(hostname, timeout):
    queue = Queue()
    proc = Process(target=gethostbyname, args=(hostname, queue))
    proc.start()
    proc.join(timeout=timeout)

    if queue.empty():
        proc.terminate()
        ip = None
    else:
        ip = queue.get()
    return proc.exitcode, ip

def gethostbyname(hostname, queue):
    ip = socket.gethostbyname(hostname)
    queue.put(ip)
```

Let's start from `resolve`. It simply takes a `hostname` and a `timeout`, and calls `resolve_host` with them. If the exit code is 0 (which means the process terminated correctly), it returns the IPv4 that corresponds to that host. Otherwise, it returns the `hostname` itself, as a fallback mechanism.

Next, let's talk about `gethostbyname`. It takes a `hostname` and a `queue`, and calls `socket.gethostbyname` to resolve the `hostname`. When the result is available, it is put into the `queue`. Now, this is where the issue lies. If the call to `socket.gethostbyname` takes longer than the timeout we want to assign, we need to kill it.

The `resolve_host` function does exactly this. It receives the `hostname` and the `timeout`, and, at first, it simply creates a `queue`. Then it spawns a new process that takes `gethostbyname` as the `target`, and passes the appropriate arguments. Then the process is started and joined on, but with a timeout.

Now, the successful scenario is this: the call to `socket.gethostbyname` succeeds quickly, the IP is in the queue, the process terminates well before its timeout time, and when we get to the `if` part, the queue will not be empty. We fetch the IP from it, and return it, alongside the process exit code.

In the unsuccessful scenario, the call to `socket.gethostbyname` takes too long, and the process is killed after its timeout has expired. Because the call failed, no IP has been inserted in the `queue`, and therefore it will be empty. In the `if` logic, we therefore set the IP to `None`, and return as before. The `resolve` function will find that the exit code is not `0` (as the process didn't terminate happily, but was killed instead), and will correctly return the hostname instead of the IP, which we couldn't get anyway.

In the source code of the book, in the `hostres` folder of this chapter, I have added some tests to make sure this behavior is actually correct. You can find instructions on how to run them in the `README.md` file in the folder. Make sure you check the test code too, it should be quite interesting.

Case examples

In this final part of the chapter, I am going to show you three case examples in which we'll see how to do the same thing by employing different approaches (single-thread, multithread, and multiprocess). Finally, I'll dedicate a few words to `asyncio`, a module that introduces yet another way of doing asynchronous programming in Python.

Example one – concurrent mergesort

The first example will revolve around the mergesort algorithm. This sorting algorithm is based on the *divide et impera* (divide and conquer) design paradigm. The way it works is very simple. You have a list of numbers you want to sort. The first step is to divide the list into two parts, sort them, and merge the results back into one sorted list. Let me give you a simple example with six numbers. Imagine we have a list, `v=[8, 5, 3, 9, 0, 2]`. The first step would be to divide the list, `v`, into two sublists of three numbers: `v1=[8, 5, 3]` and `v2=[9, 0, 2]`. Then we sort `v1` and `v2` by recursively calling mergesort on them. The result would be `v1=[3, 5, 8]` and `v2=[0, 2, 9]`. In order to combine `v1` and `v2` back into a sorted `v`, we simply consider the first item in both lists, and pick the minimum of those. The first iteration would compare 3 and 0. We pick 0, leaving `v2=[2, 9]`. Then we rinse and repeat: we compare 3 and 2, we pick 2, so now `v2=[9]`. Then we compare 3 and 9. This time we pick 3, leaving `v1=[5, 8]`, and so on and so forth. Next we would pick 5 (5 versus 9), then 8 (8 versus 9), and finally 9. This would give us a new, sorted version of `v`: `v=[0, 2, 3, 5, 8, 9]`.

The reason why I chose this algorithm as an example is twofold. First, it is easy to parallelize. You split the list in two, have two processes work on them, and then collect the results. Second, it is possible to amend the algorithm so that it splits the initial list into any $N \geq 2$, and assigns those parts to N processes. Recombination is as simple as dealing with just two parts. This characteristic makes it a good candidate for a concurrent implementation.

Single-thread mergesort

Let's see how all this translates into code, starting by learning how to code our own homemade `mergesort`:

```
# ms/algo/mergesort.py
def sort(v):
    if len(v) <= 1:
        return v
    mid = len(v) // 2
    v1, v2 = sort(v[:mid]), sort(v[mid:])
    return merge(v1, v2)

def merge(v1, v2):
    v = []
    h = k = 0
    len_v1, len_v2 = len(v1), len(v2)
    while h < len_v1 or k < len_v2:
        if k == len_v2 or (h < len_v1 and v1[h] < v2[k]):
            v.append(v1[h])
            h += 1
        else:
            v.append(v2[k])
            k += 1
    return v
```

Let's start from the `sort` function. First we encounter the base of the recursion, which says that if the list has `0` or `1` elements, we don't need to sort it, we can simply return it as it is. If that is not the case, then we calculate the midpoint (`mid`), and recursively call sort on `v[:mid]` and `v[mid:]`. I hope you are by now very familiar with the slicing syntax, but just in case you need a refresher, the first one is all elements in `v` up to the `mid` index (excluded), and the second one is all elements from `mid` to the end. The results of sorting them are assigned respectively to `v1` and `v2`. Finally, we call `merge`, passing `v1` and `v2`.

The logic of `merge` uses two pointers, `h` and `k`, to keep track of which elements in `v1` and `v2` we have already compared. If we find that the minimum is in `v1`, we append it to `v`, and increase `h`. On the other hand, if the minimum is in `v2`, we append it to `v` but increase `k` this time. The procedure is running in a `while` loop whose condition, combined with the inner `if`, makes sure we don't get errors due to indexes out of bounds. It's a pretty standard algorithm that you can find in many different variations on the web.

In order to make sure this code is solid, I have written a test suite that resides in the `ch10/ms` folder. I encourage you to check it out.

Now that we have the building blocks, let's see how we modify this to make it so that it works with an arbitrary number of parts.

Single-thread multipart mergesort

The code for the multipart version of the algorithm is quite simple. We can reuse the `merge` function, but we'll have to rewrite the `sort` one:

```
# ms/algo/multi_mergesort.py
from functools import reduce
from .mergesort import merge

def sort(v, parts=2):
    assert parts > 1, 'Parts need to be at least 2.'
    if len(v) <= 1:
        return v

    chunk_len = max(1, len(v) // parts)
    chunks = (
        sort(v[k: k + chunk_len], parts=parts)
        for k in range(0, len(v), chunk_len)
    )
    return multi_merge(*chunks)

def multi_merge(*v):
    return reduce(merge, v)
```

We saw `reduce` in Chapter 4, *Functions, the Building Blocks of Code*, when we coded our own factorial function. The way it works within `multi_merge` is to merge the first two lists in `v`. Then the result is merged with the third one, after which the result is merged with the fourth one, and so on.

Take a look at the new version of `sort`. It takes the `v` list, and the number of parts we want to split it into. The first thing we do is check that we passed a correct number for `parts`, which needs to be at least two. Then, like before, we have the base of the recursion. And finally we get into the main logic of the function, which is simply a multipart version of the one we saw in the previous example. We calculate the length of each `chunk` using the `max` function, just in case there are fewer elements in the list than parts. And then we write a generator expression that calls `sort` recursively on each `chunk`. Finally, we merge all the results by calling `multi_merge`.

I am aware that in explaining this code, I haven't been as exhaustive as I usually am, and I'm afraid it is on purpose. The example that comes after the mergesort will be much more complex, so I would like to encourage you to really try to understand the previous two snippets as thoroughly as you can.

Now, let's take this example to the next step: multithreading.

Multithreaded mergesort

In this example, we amend the `sort` function once again, so that, after the initial division into chunks, it spawns a thread per part. Each thread uses the single-threaded version of the algorithm to sort its part, and then at the end we use the multi-merge technique to calculate the final result. Translating into Python:

```
# ms/algo/mergesort_thread.py
from functools import reduce
from math import ceil
from concurrent.futures import ThreadPoolExecutor, as_completed
from .mergesort import sort as _sort, merge

def sort(v, workers=2):
    if len(v) == 0:
        return v
    dim = ceil(len(v) / workers)
    chunks = (v[k: k + dim] for k in range(0, len(v), dim))
    with ThreadPoolExecutor(max_workers=workers) as executor:
        futures = [
            executor.submit(_sort, chunk) for chunk in chunks
        ]
        return reduce(
            merge,
            (future.result() for future in as_completed(futures))
        )
```

We import all the required tools, including executors, the `ceiling` function, and `sort` and `merge` from the single-threaded version of the algorithm. Notice how I changed the name of the single-threaded `sort` into `_sort` upon importing it.

In this version of `sort`, we check whether `v` is empty first, and if not we proceed. We calculate the dimension of each `chunk` using the `ceil` function. It's basically doing what we were doing with `max` in the previous snippet, but I wanted to show you another way to solve the issue.

When we have the dimension, we calculate the `chunks` and prepare a nice generator expression to serve them to the executor. The rest is straightforward: we define a list of future objects, each of which is the result of calling `submit` on the executor. Each future object runs the single-threaded `_sort` algorithm on the `chunk` it has been assigned to.

Finally as they are returned by the `as_completed` function, the results are merged using the same technique we saw in the earlier multipart example.

Multiprocess mergesort

To perform the final step, we need to amend only two lines in the previous code. If you have paid attention in the introductory examples, you will know which of the two lines I am referring to. In order to save some space, I'll just give you the diff of the code:

```
# ms/algo/mergesort_proc.py
...
from concurrent.futures import ProcessPoolExecutor, as_completed
...

def sort(v, workers=2):
    ...
    with ProcessPoolExecutor(max_workers=workers) as executor:
    ...
```

That's it! Basically all you have to do is use `ProcessPoolExecutor` instead of `ThreadPoolExecutor`, and instead of spawning threads, you are spawning processes.

Do you recall when I was saying that processes can actually run on different cores, while threads run within the same process so they are not actually running in parallel? This is a good example to show you a consequence of choosing one approach or the other. Because the code is CPU-intensive, and there is no IO going on, splitting the list and having threads working the chunks doesn't add any advantage. On the other hand, using processes does. I have run some performance tests (run the `ch10/ms/performance.py` module by yourself and you will see how your machine performs) and the results prove my expectations:

```
$ python performance.py

Testing Sort
Size: 100000
Elapsed time: 0.492s
Size: 500000
Elapsed time: 2.739s

Testing Sort Thread
Size: 100000
Elapsed time: 0.482s
Size: 500000
Elapsed time: 2.818s

Testing Sort Proc
Size: 100000
Elapsed time: 0.313s
Size: 500000
Elapsed time: 1.586s
```

The two tests are run on two lists of 100,000 and 500,000 items, respectively. And I am using four workers for the multithreaded and multiprocessing versions. Using different sizes is quite useful when looking for patterns. As you can see, the time elapsed is basically the same for the first two versions (single-threaded, and multithreaded), but they are reduced by about 50% for the multiprocessing version. It's slightly more than 50% because having to spawn processes, and handle them, comes at a price. But still, you can definitely appreciate that I have a processor with two cores on my machine.

This also tells you that even though I used four workers in the multiprocessing version, I can still only parallelize proportionately to the amount of cores my processor has. Therefore, two or more workers makes very little difference.

Now that you are all warmed up, let's move on to the next example.

Example two – batch sudoku-solver

In this example, we are going to explore a sudoku-solver. We are not going to go into much detail with it, as the point is not that of understanding how to solve sudoku, but rather to show you how to use multi-processing to solve a batch of sudoku puzzles.

What is interesting in this example, is that instead of making the comparison between single and multithreaded versions again, we're going to skip that and compare the single-threaded version with two different multiprocess versions. One will assign one puzzle per worker, so if we solve 1,000 puzzles, we'll use 1,000 workers (well, we will use a pool of *N* workers, each of which is constantly recycled). The other version will instead divide the initial batch of puzzles by the pool size, and batch-solve each chunk within one process. This means, assuming a pool size of four, dividing those 1,000 puzzles into chunks of 250 puzzles each, and giving each chunk to one worker, for a total of four of them.

The code I will present to you for the sudoku-solver (without the multiprocessing part), comes from a solution designed by Peter Norvig, which has been distributed under the MIT license. His solution is so efficient that, after trying to re-implement my own for a few days, and getting to the same result, I simply gave up and decided to go with his design. I did do a lot of refactoring though, because I wasn't happy with his choice of function and variable names, so I made those more *book friendly*, so to speak. You can find the original code, a link to the original page from which I got it, and the original MIT license, in the `ch10/sudoku/norvig` folder. If you follow the link, you'll find a very thorough explanation of the sudoku-solver by Norvig himself.

What is Sudoku?

First things first. What is a sudoku puzzle? Sudoku is a number-placement puzzle based on logic that originated in Japan. The objective is to fill a *9x9* grid with digits so that each row, column, and box (*3x3* subgrids that compose the grid) contains all of the digits from *1* to *9*. You start from a partially populated grid, and add number after number using logic considerations.

Sudoku can be interpreted, from a computer science perspective, as a problem that fits in the *exact cover* category. Donald Knuth, the author of *The Art of Computer Programming* (and many other wonderful books), has devised an algorithm, called **Algorithm X**, to solve problems in this category. A beautiful and efficient implementation of Algorithm X, called **Dancing Links**, which harnesses the power of circular doubly-linked lists, can be used to solve sudoku. The beauty of this approach is that all it requires is a mapping between the structure of the sudoku, and the Dancing Links algorithm, and without having to do any of the logic deductions normally needed to solve the puzzle, it gets to the solution at the speed of light.

Many years ago, when my free time was a number greater than zero, I wrote a Dancing Links sudoku-solver in C#, which I still have archived somewhere, which was great fun to design and code. I definitely encourage you to check out the literature and code your own solver, it's a great exercise, if you can spare the time.

In this example's solution though, we're going to use a **search** algorithm used in conjunction with a process that, in artificial intelligence, is known as **constraint propagation**. The two are quite commonly used together to make a problem simpler to solve. We'll see that in our example, they are enough for us to be able to solve a difficult sudoku in a matter of milliseconds.

Implementing a sudoku-solver in Python

Let's now explore my refactored implementation of the solver. I'm going to present the code to you in steps, as it is quite involved (also, I won't repeat the source name at the top of each snippet, until I move to another module):

```
# sudoku/algo/solver.py
import os
from itertools import zip_longest, chain
from time import time

def cross_product(v1, v2):
    return [w1 + w2 for w1 in v1 for w2 in v2]

def chunk(iterable, n, fillvalue=None):
    args = [iter(iterable)] * n
    return zip_longest(*args, fillvalue=fillvalue)
```

We start with some imports, and then we define a couple of useful functions: `cross_product` and `chunk`. They do exactly what the names hint at. The first one returns the cross-product between two iterables, while the second one returns a list of chunks from `iterable`, each of which has n elements, and the last of which might be padded with a given `fillvalue`, should the length of `iterable` not be a multiple of n. Then we proceed to define a few structures, which will be used by the solver:

```
digits = '123456789'
rows = 'ABCDEFGHI'
cols = digits
squares = cross_product(rows, cols)
all_units = (
    [cross_product(rows, c) for c in cols]
    + [cross_product(r, cols) for r in rows]
    + [cross_product(rs, cs)
        for rs in chunk(rows, 3) for cs in chunk(cols, 3)]
)
units = dict(
    (square, [unit for unit in all_units if square in unit])
    for square in squares
)
peers = dict(
    (square, set(chain(*units[square])) - set([square]))
    for square in squares
)
```

Without going too much into detail, let's hover over these objects. `squares` is a list of all squares in the grid. Squares are represented by a string such as *A3* or *C7*. Rows are numbered with letters, and columns with numbers, so *A3* will indicate the square in the first row, and third column.

`all_units` is a list of all possible rows, columns, and blocks. Each of those elements is represented as a list of the squares that belong to the row/column/block. `units` is a more complex structure. It is a dictionary with 81 keys. Each key represents a square, and the corresponding value is a list with three elements in it: a row, a column, and a block. Of course, those are the row, column, and block that the square belongs to.

Finally, `peers` is a dictionary very similar to `units`, but the value of each key (which still represents a square), is a set containing all peers for that square. Peers are defined as all the squares belonging to the row, column, and block the square in the key belongs to. These structures will be used in the calculation of the solution, when attempting to solve a puzzle.

Before we take a look at the function that parses the input lines, let me give you an example of what an input puzzle looks like:

```
1..3.......75...3..3.4.8.2...47....9.........689....4..5..178.4.....2.75...
....1.
```

The first nine characters represent the first row, then another nine for the second row, and so on. Empty squares are represented by dots:

```
def parse_puzzle(puzzle):
    assert set(puzzle) <= set('.0123456789')
    assert len(puzzle) == 81

    grid = dict((square, digits) for square in squares)
    for square, digit in zip(squares, puzzle):
        if digit in digits and not place(grid, square, digit):
            return False  # Incongruent puzzle
    return grid

def solve(puzzle):
    grid = parse_puzzle(puzzle)
    return search(grid)
```

This simple `parse_puzzle` function is used to parse an input puzzle. We do a little bit of sanity checking at the beginning, asserting that the input puzzle has to shrink into a set that is a subset of the set of all numbers plus a dot. Then we make sure we have 81 input characters, and finally we define `grid`, which initially is simply a dictionary with 81 keys, each of which is a square, all with the same value, which is a string of all possible digits. This is because a square in a completely empty grid has the potential to become any number from 1 to 9.

The `for` loop is definitely the most interesting part. We parse each of the 81 characters in the input puzzle, coupling them with the corresponding square in the grid, and we try to "*place*" them. I put that in double quotes because, as we'll see in a moment, the `place` function does much more than simply setting a given number in a given square. If we find that we cannot place a digit from the input puzzle, it means the input is invalid, and we return `False`. Otherwise, we're good to go and we return the `grid`.

`parse_puzzle` is used in the `solve` function, which simply parses the input puzzle, and unleashes `search` on it. What follows is therefore the heart of the algorithm:

```
def search(grid):
    if not grid:
        return False
    if all(len(grid[square]) == 1 for square in squares):
        return grid  # Solved
    values, square = min(
        (len(grid[square]), square) for square in squares
        if len(grid[square]) > 1
    )
    for digit in grid[square]:
        result = search(place(grid.copy(), square, digit))
        if result:
            return result
```

This simple function first checks whether the grid is actually non-empty. Then it tries to see whether the grid is solved. A solved grid will have one value per square. If that is not the case, it loops through each square and finds the square with the minimum amount of candidates. If a square has a string value of only one digit, it means a number has been placed in that square. But if the value is more than one digit, then those are possible candidates, so we need to find the square with the minimum amount of candidates, and try them. Trying a square with "23" candidates is much better than trying one with "23589". In the first case, we have a 50% chance of getting the right value, while in the second one, we only have 20%. Choosing the square with the minimum amount of candidates therefore maximizes the chances for us to place good numbers in the grid.

Once the candidates have been found, we try them in order and if any of them results in being successful, we have solved the grid and we return. You might have noticed the use of the `place` function in the search too. So let's explore its code:

```
def place(grid, square, digit):
    """Eliminate all the other values (except digit) from
    grid[square] and propagate.
    Return grid, or False if a contradiction is detected.
    """
    other_vals = grid[square].replace(digit, '')
    if all(eliminate(grid, square, val) for val in other_vals):
        return grid
    return False
```

This function takes a work-in-progress grid, and tries to place a given digit in a given square. As I mentioned before, *"placing"* is not that straightforward. In fact, when we place a number, we have to propagate the consequences of that action throughout the grid. We do that by calling the `eliminate` function, which applies two strategies of the sudoku game:

- If a square has only one possible value, eliminate that value from the square's peers
- If a unit has only one place for a value, place the value there

Let me briefly offer an example of both points. For the first one, if you place, say, number 7 in a square, then you can eliminate 7 from the list of candidates for all the squares that belong to the row, column, and block that square belongs to.

For the second point, say you're examining the fourth row and, of all the squares that belong to it, only one of them has number 7 in its candidates. This means that number 7 can only go in that precise square, so you should go ahead and place it there.

The following function, `eliminate`, applies these two rules. Its code is quite involved, so instead of going line by line and offering an excruciating explanation, I have added some comments, and will leave you with the task of understanding it:

```
def eliminate(grid, square, digit):
    """Eliminate digit from grid[square]. Propagate when candidates
    are <= 2.
    Return grid, or False if a contradiction is detected.
    """
    if digit not in grid[square]:
        return grid  # already eliminated
    grid[square] = grid[square].replace(digit, '')

    ## (1) If a square is reduced to one value, eliminate value
    ## from peers.
    if len(grid[square]) == 0:
        return False  # nothing left to place here, wrong solution
    elif len(grid[square]) == 1:
        value = grid[square]
        if not all(
            eliminate(grid, peer, value) for peer in peers[square]
        ):
            return False

    ## (2) If a unit is reduced to only one place for a value,
    ## then put it there.
    for unit in units[square]:
        places = [sqr for sqr in unit if digit in grid[sqr]]
```

```
        if len(places) == 0:
            return False  # No place for this value
        elif len(places) == 1:
            # digit can only be in one place in unit,
            # assign it there
            if not place(grid, places[0], digit):
                return False
    return grid
```

The rest of the functions in the module aren't important for the rest of this example, so I will skip them. You can run this module by itself; it will first perform a series of checks on its data structures, and then it will solve all the sudoku puzzles I have placed in the `sudoku/puzzles` folder. But that is not what we're interested in, right? We want to see how to solve sudoku using multiprocessing techniques, so let's get to it.

Solving sudoku with multiprocessing

In this module, we're going to implement three functions. The first one simply solves a batch of sudoku puzzles, with no multiprocessing involved. We will use the results for benchmarking. The second and the third ones will use multiprocessing, with and without batch-solving, so we can appreciate the differences. Let's start:

```
# sudoku/process_solver.py
import os
from functools import reduce
from operator import concat
from math import ceil
from time import time
from contextlib import contextmanager
from concurrent.futures import ProcessPoolExecutor, as_completed
from unittest import TestCase
from algo.solver import solve

@contextmanager
def timer():
    t = time()
    yield
    tot = time() - t
    print(f'Elapsed time: {tot:.3f}s')
```

After a long list of imports, we define a context manager that we're going to use as a timer device. It takes a reference to the current time (`t`), and then it yields. After having yielded, that's when the body of the managed context is executed. Finally, on exiting the managed context, we calculate `tot`, which is the total amount of time elapsed, and print it. It's a simple and elegant context manager written with the decoration technique, and it's super fun. Let's now see the three functions I mentioned earlier:

```
def batch_solve(puzzles):
    # Single thread batch solve.
    return [solve(puzzle) for puzzle in puzzles]
```

This one is a single-threaded simple batch solver, which will give us a time to compare against. It simply returns a list of all solved grids. Boring. Now, check out the following code:

```
def parallel_single_solver(puzzles, workers=4):
    # Parallel solve - 1 process per each puzzle
    with ProcessPoolExecutor(max_workers=workers) as executor:
        futures = (
            executor.submit(solve, puzzle) for puzzle in puzzles
        )
        return [
            future.result() for future in as_completed(futures)
        ]
```

This one is much better. It uses `ProcessPoolExecutor` to use a pool of `workers`, each of which is used to solve roughly one-fourth of the puzzles. This is because we are spawning one future object per puzzle. The logic is extremely similar to any multiprocessing example we have already seen in the chapter. Let's see the third function:

```
def parallel_batch_solver(puzzles, workers=4):
    # Parallel batch solve - Puzzles are chunked into `workers`
    # chunks. A process for each chunk.
    assert len(puzzles) >= workers
    dim = ceil(len(puzzles) / workers)
    chunks = (
        puzzles[k: k + dim] for k in range(0, len(puzzles), dim)
    )
    with ProcessPoolExecutor(max_workers=workers) as executor:
        futures = (
            executor.submit(batch_solve, chunk) for chunk in chunks
        )
        results = (
            future.result() for future in as_completed(futures)
        )
        return reduce(concat, results)
```

This last function is slightly different. Instead of spawning one `future` object per puzzle, it splits the total list of puzzles into `workers` chunks, and then creates one `future` object per chunk. This means that if `workers` is eight, we're going to spawn eight `future` objects. Notice that instead of passing `solve` to `executor.submit`, we're passing `batch_solve`, which does the trick. The reason why I coded the last two functions so differently is because I was curious to see the severity of the impact of the overhead we incur into when we recycle processes from a pool a non-negligible amount of times.

Now that we have the functions defined, let's use them:

```
puzzles_file = os.path.join('puzzles', 'sudoku-topn234.txt')
with open(puzzles_file) as stream:
    puzzles = [puzzle.strip() for puzzle in stream]

# single thread solve
with timer():
    res_batch = batch_solve(puzzles)

# parallel solve, 1 process per puzzle
with timer():
    res_parallel_single = parallel_single_solver(puzzles)

# parallel batch solve, 1 batch per process
with timer():
    res_parallel_batch = parallel_batch_solver(puzzles)

# Quick way to verify that the results are the same, but
# possibly in a different order, as they depend on how the
# processes have been scheduled.
assert_items_equal = TestCase().assertCountEqual
assert_items_equal(res_batch, res_parallel_single)
assert_items_equal(res_batch, res_parallel_batch)
print('Done.')
```

We use a set of 234 very hard sudoku puzzles for this benchmarking session. As you can see, we simply run the three functions, `batch_solve`, `parallel_single_solver`, and `parallel_batch_solver`, all within a timed context. We collect the results, and, just to make sure, we verify that all the runs have produced the same results.

Of course, in the second and third runs, we have used multiprocessing, so we cannot guarantee that the order in the results will be the same as that of the single-threaded `batch_solve`. This minor issue is brilliantly solved with the aid of `assertCountEqual`, one of the worst-named methods in the Python standard library. We find it in the `TestCase` class, which we can instantiate just to take a reference to the method we need. We're not actually running unit tests, but this is a cool trick, and I wanted to show it to you. Let's see the output of running this module:

```
$ python process_solver.py
Elapsed time: 5.368s
Elapsed time: 2.856s
Elapsed time: 2.818s
Done.
```

Wow. That is quite interesting. First of all, you can once again see that my machine has a two-core processor, as the time elapsed for the multiprocessing runs is about half the time taken by the single-threaded solver. However, what is actually much more interesting is the fact that there is basically no difference in the time taken by the two multiprocessing functions. Multiple runs sometimes end in favor of one approach, and sometimes in favor of the other. Understanding why requires a deep understanding of all the components that are taking part in the game, not just the processes, and therefore is not something we can discuss here. It is fairly safe to say though, that the two approaches are comparable in terms of performance.

In the source code for the book, you can find tests in the `sudoku` folder, with instructions on how to run them. Take the time to check them out!

And now, let's get to the final example.

Example three – downloading random pictures

This example has been fun to code. We are going to download random pictures from a website. I'll show you three versions: a serial one, a multiprocessing one, and finally a solution coded using `asyncio`. In these examples, we are going to use a website called `http://lorempixel.com`, which provides you with an API that you can call to get random images. If you find that the website is down or slow, you can use an excellent alternative to it: `https://lorempizza.com/`.

It may be something of a *cliché* for a book written by an Italian, but the pictures are gorgeous. You can search for another alternative on the web, if you want to have some fun. Whatever website you choose, please be sensible and try not to hammer it by making a million requests to it. The multiprocessing and `asyncio` versions of this code can be quite aggressive!

Let's start by exploring the single-threaded version of the code:

```
# aio/randompix_serial.py
import os
from secrets import token_hex
import requests

PICS_FOLDER = 'pics'
URL = 'http://lorempixel.com/640/480/'

def download(url):
    resp = requests.get(URL)
    return save_image(resp.content)

def save_image(content):
    filename = '{}.jpg'.format(token_hex(4))
    path = os.path.join(PICS_FOLDER, filename)
    with open(path, 'wb') as stream:
        stream.write(content)
    return filename

def batch_download(url, n):
    return [download(url) for _ in range(n)]

if __name__ == '__main__':
    saved = batch_download(URL, 10)
    print(saved)
```

This code should be straightforward to you by now. We define a `download` function, which makes a request to the given URL, saves the result by calling `save_image`, and feeds it the body of the response from the website. Saving the image is very simple: we create a random filename with `token_hex`, just because it's fun, then we calculate the full path of the file, create it in binary mode, and write into it the content of the response. We return the `filename` to be able to print it on screen. Finally `batch_download` simply runs the n requests we want to run and returns the filenames as a result.

You can leapfrog the `if __name__ . . .` line for now, it will be explained in `Chapter 12`, *GUIs and Scripts* and it's not important here. All we do is call `batch_download` with the URL and we tell it to download `10` images. If you have an editor, open the `pics` folder, and you can see it getting populated in a few seconds (also notice: the script assumes the `pics` folder exists).

Let's spice things up a bit. Let's introduce multiprocessing (the code is vastly similar, so I will not repeat it):

```
# aio/randompix_proc.py
...
from concurrent.futures import ProcessPoolExecutor, as_completed
...

def batch_download(url, n, workers=4):
    with ProcessPoolExecutor(max_workers=workers) as executor:
        futures = (executor.submit(download, url) for _ in range(n))
        return [future.result() for future in as_completed(futures)]

...
```

The technique should be familiar to you by now. We simply submit jobs to the executor, and collect the results as they become available. Because this is IO bound code, the processes work quite fast and there is heavy context-switching while the processes are waiting for the API response. If you have a view over the `pics` folder, you will notice that it's not getting populated in a linear fashion any more, but rather, in batches.

Let's now look at the `asyncio` version of this example.

Downloading random pictures with asyncio

The code is probably the most challenging of the whole chapter, so don't feel bad if it is too much for you at this moment in time. I have added this example just as a mouthwatering device, to encourage you to dig deeper into the heart of Python asynchronous programming. Another thing worth knowing is that there are probably several other ways to write this same logic, so please bear in mind that this is just one of the possible examples.

The `asyncio` module provides infrastructure for writing single-threaded, concurrent code using coroutines, multiplexing IO access over sockets and other resources, running network clients and servers, and other related primitives. It was added to Python in version 3.4, and some claim it will become the *de facto* standard for writing Python code in the future. I don't know whether that's true, but I know it is definitely worth seeing an example:

```
# aio/randompix_corout.py
import os
from secrets import token_hex
import asyncio
import aiohttp
```

First of all, we cannot use `requests` any more, as it is not suitable for `asyncio`. We have to use `aiohttp`, so please make sure you have installed it (it's in the requirements for the book):

```
PICS_FOLDER = 'pics'
URL = 'http://lorempixel.com/640/480/'

async def download_image(url):
    async with aiohttp.ClientSession() as session:
        async with session.get(url) as resp:
            return await resp.read()
```

The previous code does not look too friendly, but it's not so bad, once you know the concepts behind it. We define the async coroutine `download_image`, which takes a URL as parameter.

 In case you don't know, a coroutine is a computer program component that generalizes subroutines for non-preemptive multitasking, by allowing multiple entry points for suspending and resuming execution at certain locations. A subroutine is a sequence of program instructions that performs a specific task, packaged as a unit.

Inside `download_image`, we create a session object using the `ClientSession` context manager, and then we get the response by using another context manager, this time from `session.get`. The fact that these managers are defined as asynchronous simply means that they are able to suspend execution in their enter and exit methods. We return the content of the response by using the `await` keyword, which allows suspension. Notice that creating a session for each request is not optimal, but I felt that for the purpose of this example I would keep the code as straightforward as possible, so I leave its optimization to you, as an exercise.

Let's proceed with the next snippet:

```
async def download(url, semaphore):
    async with semaphore:
        content = await download_image(url)
    filename = save_image(content)
    return filename

def save_image(content):
    filename = '{}.jpg'.format(token_hex(4))
    path = os.path.join(PICS_FOLDER, filename)
    with open(path, 'wb') as stream:
        stream.write(content)
    return filename
```

Another coroutine, download, gets a URL and a semaphore. All it does is fetch the content of the image, by calling download_image, saving it, and returning the filename. The interesting bit here is the use of that semaphore. We use it as an asynchronous context manager, so that we can suspend this coroutine as well, and allow a switch to something else, but more than *how*, it is important to understand *why* we want to use a semaphore. The reason is simple, this semaphore is kind of the equivalent of a pool of threads. We use it to allow at most *N* coroutines to be active at the same time. We instantiate it in the next function, and we pass 10 as the initial value. Every time a coroutine acquires the semaphore, its internal counter is decreased by 1, therefore when 10 coroutines have acquired it, the next one will sit and wait, until the semaphore is released by a coroutine that has completed. This is a nice way to try to limit how aggressively we are fetching images from the website API.

The save_image function is not a coroutine, and its logic has already been discussed in the previous examples. Let's now get to the part of the code where execution takes place:

```
def batch_download(images, url):
    loop = asyncio.get_event_loop()
    semaphore = asyncio.Semaphore(10)
    cors = [download(url, semaphore) for _ in range(images)]
    res, _ = loop.run_until_complete(asyncio.wait(cors))
    loop.close()
    return [r.result() for r in res]

if __name__ == '__main__':
    saved = batch_download(20, URL)
    print(saved)
```

We define the `batch_download` function, which takes a number, `images`, and the URL of where to fetch them. The first thing it does is create an event loop, which is necessary to run any asynchronous code. The event loop is the central execution device provided by `asyncio`. It provides multiple facilities, including:

- Registering, executing, and cancelling delayed calls (timeouts)
- Creating client and server transports for various kinds of communication
- Launching subprocesses and the associated transports for communication with an external program
- Delegating costly function calls to a pool of threads

After the event loop is created, we instantiate the semaphore, and then we proceed to create a list of futures, `cors`. By calling `loop.run_until_complete`, we make sure the event loop will run until the whole task has been completed. We feed it the result of a call to `asyncio.wait`, which waits for the futures to complete.

When done, we close the event loop, and return a list of the results yielded by each future object (the filenames of the saved images). Notice how we capture the results of the call to `loop.run_until_complete`. We don't really care for the errors, so we assign _ to the second item in the tuple. This is a common Python idiom used when we want to signal that we're not interested in that object.

At the end of the module, we call `batch_download` and we get 20 images saved. They come in batches, and the whole process is limited by a semaphore with only 10 available spots.

And that's it! To learn more about `asyncio`, please refer to the documentation page (`https://docs.python.org/3.7/library/asyncio.html`) for the `asyncio` module on the standard library. This example was fun to code, and hopefully it will motivate you to study hard and understand the intricacies of this wonderful side of Python.

Summary

In this chapter, we learned about concurrency and parallelism. We saw how threads and processes help in achieving one and the other. We explored the nature of threads and the issues that they expose us to: race conditions and deadlocks.

We learned how to solve those issues by using locks and careful resource management. We also learned how to make threads communicate and share data, and we talked about the scheduler, which is that part of the operating system that decides which thread will run at any given time. We then moved to processes, and explored a bunch of their properties and characteristics.

Following the initial theoretical part, we learned how to implement threads and processes in Python. We dealt with multiple threads and processes, fixed race conditions, and learned workarounds to stop threads without leaving any resource open by mistake. We also explored IPC, and used queues to exchange messages between processes and threads. We also played with events and barriers, which are some of the tools provided by the standard library to control the flow of execution in a non-deterministic environment.

After all these introductory examples, we deep dived into three case examples, which showed how to solve the same problem using different approaches: single-thread, multithread, multiprocess, and `asyncio`.

We learned about mergesort and how, in general, *divide and conquer* algorithms are easy to parallelize.

We learned about sudoku, and explored a nice solution that uses a little bit of artificial intelligence to run an efficient algorithm, which we then ran in different serial and parallel modes.

Finally, we saw how to download random pictures from a website, using serial, multiprocess, and `asyncio` code. The latter was by far the hardest piece of code in the whole book, and its presence in the chapter serves as a reminder, or some sort of milestone that will encourage the reader to learn Python well, and deeply.

Now we'll move on to much simpler, and mostly project-oriented chapters, where we get a taste of different real-world applications in different contexts.

11
Debugging and Troubleshooting

"If debugging is the process of removing software bugs, then programming must be the process of putting them in."

– Edsger W. Dijkstra

In the life of a professional coder, debugging and troubleshooting take up a significant amount of time. Even if you work on the most beautiful code base ever written by a human, there will still be bugs in it; that is guaranteed.

We spend an awful lot of time reading other people's code and, in my opinion, a good software developer is someone who keeps their attention high, even when they're reading code that is not reported to be wrong or buggy.

Being able to debug code efficiently and quickly is a skill that every coder needs to keep improving. Some think that because they have read the manual, they're fine, but the reality is, the number of variables in the game is so great that there is no manual. There are guidelines one can follow, but there is no magic book that will teach you everything you need to know in order to become good at this.

I feel that on this particular subject, I have learned the most from my colleagues. It amazes me to observe someone very skilled attacking a problem. I enjoy seeing the steps they take, the things they verify to exclude possible causes, and the way they consider the suspects that eventually lead them to a solution.

Every colleague we work with can teach us something, or surprise us with a fantastic guess that turns out to be the right one. When that happens, don't just remain in wonderment (or worse, in envy), but seize the moment and ask them how they got to that guess and why. The answer will allow you to see whether there is something you can study in-depth later on so that, maybe next time, you'll be the one who will catch the bug.

Some bugs are very easy to spot. They come out of coarse mistakes and, once you see the effects of those mistakes, it's easy to find a solution that fixes the problem.

But there are other bugs that are much more subtle, much more slippery, and require true expertise, and a great deal of creativity and out-of-the-box thinking, to be dealt with.

The worst of all, at least for me, are the nondeterministic ones. These sometimes happen, and sometimes don't. Some happen only in environment A but not in environment B, even though A and B are supposed to be exactly the same. Those bugs are the truly evil ones, and they can drive you crazy.

And of course, bugs don't just happen in the sandbox, right? With your boss telling you, *"Don't worry! Take your time to fix this. Have lunch first!"* Nope. They happen on a Friday at half past five, when your brain is cooked and you just want to go home. It's in those moments when everyone is getting upset in a split second, when your boss is breathing down your neck, that you have to be able to keep calm. And I do mean it. That's the most important skill to have if you want to be able to fight bugs effectively. If you allow your mind to get stressed, say goodbye to creative thinking, to logical deduction, and to everything you need at that moment. So take a deep breath, sit properly, and focus.

In this chapter, I will try to demonstrate some useful techniques that you can employ according to the severity of the bug, and a few suggestions that will hopefully boost your weapons against bugs and issues.

Specifically, we're going to look at the following:

- Debugging techniques
  - Profiling
  - Assertions
- Troubleshooting guidelines

Debugging techniques

In this part, I'll present you with the most common techniques, the ones I use most often; however, please don't consider this list to be exhaustive.

Debugging with print

This is probably the easiest technique of all. It's not very effective, it cannot be used everywhere, and it requires access to both the source code and a Terminal that will run it (and therefore show the results of the `print` function calls).

However, in many situations, this is still a quick and useful way to debug. For example, if you are developing a Django website and what happens in a page is not what you would expect, you can fill the view with prints and keep an eye on the console while you reload the page. When you scatter calls to `print` in your code, you normally end up in a situation where you duplicate a lot of debugging code, either because you're printing a timestamp (like we did when we were measuring how fast list comprehensions and generators were), or because you have somehow to build a string of some sort that you want to display.

Another issue is that it's extremely easy to forget calls to `print` in your code.

So, for these reasons, rather than using a bare call to `print`, I sometimes prefer to code a custom function. Let's see how.

Debugging with a custom function

Having a custom function in a snippet that you can quickly grab and paste into the code, and then use to debug, can be very useful. If you're fast, you can always code one on the fly. The important thing is to code it in a way that it won't leave stuff around when you eventually remove the calls and its definition. Therefore *it's important to code it in a way that is completely self-contained*. Another good reason for this requirement is that it will avoid potential name clashes with the rest of the code.

Let's see an example of such a function:

```
# custom.py
def debug(*msg, print_separator=True):
    print(*msg)
    if print_separator:
        print('-' * 40)
```

```
debug('Data is ...')
debug('Different', 'Strings', 'Are not a problem')
debug('After while loop', print_separator=False)
```

In this case, I am using a keyword-only argument to be able to print a separator, which is a line of 40 dashes.

The function is very simple. I just redirect whatever is in `msg` to a call to `print` and, if `print_separator` is `True`, I print a line separator. Running the code will show the following:

```
$ python custom.py
Data is ...
----------------------------------------
Different Strings Are not a problem
----------------------------------------
After while loop
```

As you can see, there is no separator after the last line.

This is just one easy way to somehow augment a simple call to the `print` function. Let's see how we can calculate a time difference between calls, using one of Python's tricky features to our advantage:

```
# custom_timestamp.py
from time import sleep

def debug(*msg, timestamp=[None]):
    print(*msg)
    from time import time  # local import
    if timestamp[0] is None:
        timestamp[0] = time()  #1
    else:
        now = time()
        print(
            ' Time elapsed: {:.3f}s'.format(now - timestamp[0])
        )
        timestamp[0] = now  #2

debug('Entering nasty piece of code...')
sleep(.3)
debug('First step done.')
sleep(.5)
debug('Second step done.')
```

This is a bit trickier, but still quite simple. First, notice we import the `time` function from the `time` module from inside the `debug` function. This allows us to avoid having to add that import outside of the function, and maybe forget it there.

Take a look at how I defined `timestamp`. It's a list, of course, but what's important here is that it is a **mutable** object. This means that it will be set up when Python parses the function and it will retain its value throughout different calls. Therefore, if we put a timestamp in it after each call, we can keep track of time without having to use an external global variable. I borrowed this trick from my studies on **closures**, a technique that I encourage you to read about because it's very interesting.

Right, so, after having printed whatever message we had to print and some importing time, we then inspect the content of the only item in `timestamp`. If it is `None`, we have no previous reference, therefore we set the value to the current time (#1).

On the other hand, if we have a previous reference, we can calculate a difference (which we nicely format to three decimal digits) and then we finally put the current time again in `timestamp` (#2). It's a nice trick, isn't it?

Running this code shows this result:

```
$ python custom_timestamp.py
Entering nasty piece of code...
First step done.
 Time elapsed: 0.304s
Second step done.
 Time elapsed: 0.505s
```

Whatever your situation, having a self-contained function like this can be very useful.

Inspecting the traceback

We briefly talked about the traceback in Chapter 8, *Testing, Profiling, and Dealing with Exceptions*, when we saw several different kinds of exceptions. The traceback gives you information about what went wrong in your application. It's helpful to read it, so let's see a small example:

```
# traceback_simple.py
d = {'some': 'key'}
key = 'some-other'
print(d[key])
```

We have a dictionary and we try to access a key that isn't in it. You should remember that this will raise a `KeyError` exception. Let's run the code:

```
$ python traceback_simple.py
Traceback (most recent call last):
  File "traceback_simple.py", line 3, in <module>
    print(d[key])
KeyError: 'some-other'
```

You can see that we get all the information we need: the module name, the line that caused the error (both the number and the instruction), and the error itself. With this information, you can go back to the source code and try to understand what's going on.

Let's now create a more interesting example that builds on top of this, and exercises a feature that is only available in Python 3. Imagine that we're validating a dictionary, working on mandatory fields, therefore we expect them to be there. If not, we need to raise a custom `ValidationError` that we will trap further upstream in the process that runs the validator (which is not shown here, so it could be anything, really). It should be something like this:

```
# traceback_validator.py
class ValidatorError(Exception):
    """Raised when accessing a dict results in KeyError. """

d = {'some': 'key'}
mandatory_key = 'some-other'
try:
    print(d[mandatory_key])
except KeyError as err:
    raise ValidatorError(
        f'`{mandatory_key}` not found in d.'
    ) from err
```

We define a custom exception that is raised when the mandatory key isn't there. Note that its body consists of its documentation string, so we don't need to add any other statements.

Very simply, we define a dummy dict and try to access it using `mandatory_key`. We trap `KeyError` and raise `ValidatorError` when that happens. And we do it by using the `raise ... from ...` syntax, which was introduced in Python 3 by PEP 3134 (`https://www.python.org/dev/peps/pep-3134/`), to chain exceptions. The purpose of doing this is that we may also want to raise `ValidatorError` in other circumstances, not necessarily as a consequence of a mandatory key being missing. This technique allows us to run the validation in a simple `try/except` that only cares about `ValidatorError`.

Without being able to chain exceptions, we would lose information about `KeyError`. The code produces this result:

```
$ python traceback_validator.py
Traceback (most recent call last):
  File "traceback_validator.py", line 7, in <module>
    print(d[mandatory_key])
KeyError: 'some-other'

The above exception was the direct cause of the following exception:

Traceback (most recent call last):
  File "traceback_validator.py", line 10, in <module>
    '`{}` not found in d.'.format(mandatory_key)) from err
__main__.ValidatorError: `some-other` not found in d.
```

This is brilliant, because we can see the traceback of the exception that led us to raise `ValidationError`, as well as the traceback for the `ValidationError` itself.

I had a nice discussion with one of my reviewers about the traceback you get from the `pip` installer. He was having trouble setting everything up in order to review the code for `Chapter 13`, *Data Science*. His fresh Ubuntu installation was missing a few libraries that were needed by the `pip` packages in order to run correctly.

The reason he was blocked was that he was trying to fix the errors displayed in the traceback starting from the top one. I suggested that he started from the bottom one instead, and fix that. The reason was that, if the installer had gotten to that last line, I guess that before that, whatever error may have occurred, it was still possible to recover from it. Only after the last line, `pip` decided it wasn't possible to continue any further, and therefore I started fixing that one. Once the libraries required to fix that error had been installed, everything else went smoothly.

Reading a traceback can be tricky, and my friend was lacking the necessary experience to address this problem correctly. Therefore, if you end up in the same situation. Don't be discouraged, and try to shake things up a bit, don't take anything for granted.

Python has a huge and wonderful community and it's very unlikely that, when you encounter a problem, you're the first one to see it, so open a browser and search. By doing so, your searching skills will also improve because you will have to trim the error down to the minimum but essential set of details that will make your search effective.

If you want to play and understand the traceback a bit better, in the standard library there is a module you can use called, surprise surprise, `traceback`. It provides a standard interface to extract, format, and print stack traces of Python programs, mimicking the behavior of the Python interpreter when it prints a stack trace.

Using the Python debugger

Another very effective way of debugging Python is to use the Python debugger: `pdb`. Instead of using it directly though, you should definitely check out the `pdbpp` library. `pdbpp` augments the standard `pdb` interface by providing some convenient tools, my favorite of which is the **sticky mode**, which allows you to see a whole function while you step through its instructions.

There are several different ways to use this debugger (whichever version, it's not important), but the most common one consists of simply setting a breakpoint and running the code. When Python reaches the breakpoint, execution is suspended and you get console access to that point so that you can inspect all the names, and so on. You can also alter data on the fly to change the flow of the program.

As a toy example, let's pretend we have a parser that is raising `KeyError` because a key is missing in a dictionary. The dictionary is from a JSON payload that we cannot control, and we just want, for the time being, to cheat and pass that control, since we're interested in what comes afterward. Let's see how we could intercept this moment, inspect the data, fix it, and get to the bottom of it, with `pdbpp`:

```
# pdebugger.py
# d comes from a JSON payload we don't control
d = {'first': 'v1', 'second': 'v2', 'fourth': 'v4'}
# keys also comes from a JSON payload we don't control
keys = ('first', 'second', 'third', 'fourth')

def do_something_with_value(value):
    print(value)

for key in keys:
    do_something_with_value(d[key])

print('Validation done.')
```

As you can see, this code will break when `key` gets the `'third'` value, which is missing in the dictionary. Remember, we're pretending that both `d` and `keys` come dynamically from a JSON payload we don't control, so we need to inspect them in order to fix `d` and pass the `for` loop. If we run the code as it is, we get the following:

```
$ python pdebugger.py
v1
v2
Traceback (most recent call last):
  File "pdebugger.py", line 10, in <module>
    do_something_with_value(d[key])
KeyError: 'third'
```

So we see that that `key` is missing from the dictionary, but since every time we run this code we may get a different dictionary or `keys` tuple, this information doesn't really help us. Let's inject a call to `pdb` just before the `for` loop. You have two options:

```
import pdb
pdb.set_trace()
```

This is the most common way of doing it. You import `pdb` and call its `set_trace` method. Many developers have macros in their editor to add this line with a keyboard shortcut. As of Python 3.7 though, we can simplify things even further, to this:

```
breakpoint()
```

The new `breakpoint` built-in function calls `sys.breakpointhook()` under the hood, which is programmed by default to call `pdb.set_trace()`. However, you can reprogram `sys.breakpointhook()` to call whatever you want, and therefore `breakpoint` will point to that too, which is very convenient.

The code for this example is in the `pdebugger_pdb.py` module. If we now run this code, things get interesting (note that your output may vary a little and that all the comments in this output were added by me):

```
$ python pdebugger_pdb.py
(Pdb++) l
 16
 17 -> for key in keys:  # breakpoint comes in
 18 do_something_with_value(d[key])
 19

(Pdb++) keys  # inspecting the keys tuple
('first', 'second', 'third', 'fourth')
(Pdb++) d.keys()  # inspecting keys of `d`
dict_keys(['first', 'second', 'fourth'])
```

```
(Pdb++) d['third'] = 'placeholder'   # add tmp placeholder
(Pdb++) c  # continue
v1
v2
placeholder
v4
Validation done.
```

First, note that when you reach a breakpoint, you're served a console that tells you where you are (the Python module) and which line is the next one to be executed. You can, at this point, perform a bunch of exploratory actions, such as inspecting the code before and after the next line, printing a stack trace, and interacting with the objects. Please consult the official Python documentation (https://docs.python.org/3.7/library/pdb.html) on pdb to learn more about this. In our case, we first inspect the keys tuple. After that, we inspect the keys of d. We see that 'third' is missing, so we put it in ourselves (could this be dangerous—think about it). Finally, now that all the keys are in, we type c, which means (c)ontinue.

pdb also gives you the ability to proceed with your code one line at a time using (n)ext, to (s)tep into a function for deeper analysis, or to handle breaks with (b)reak. For a complete list of commands, please refer to the documentation or type (h)elp in the console.

You can see, from the output of the preceding run, that we could finally get to the end of the validation.

pdb (or pdbpp) is an invaluable tool that I use every day. So, go and have fun, set a breakpoint somewhere, and try to inspect it, follow the official documentation and try the commands in your code to see their effect and learn them well.

 Notice that in this example I have assumed you installed pdbpp. If that is not the case, then you might find that some commands don't work the same in pdb. One example is the letter d, which would be interpreted from pdb as the *down* command. In order to get around that, you would have to add a ! in front of d, to tell pdb that it is meant to be interpreted literally, and not as a command.

Inspecting log files

Another way of debugging a misbehaving application is to inspect its log files. **Log files** are special files in which an application writes down all sorts of things, normally related to what's going on inside of it. If an important procedure is started, I would typically expect a corresponding line in the logs. It is the same when it finishes, and possibly for what happens inside of it.

Errors need to be logged so that when a problem happens, we can inspect what went wrong by taking a look at the information in the log files.

There are many different ways to set up a logger in Python. Logging is very malleable and you can configure it. In a nutshell, there are normally four players in the game: loggers, handlers, filters, and formatters:

- **Loggers**: Expose the interface that the application code uses directly
- **Handlers**: Send the log records (created by loggers) to the appropriate destination
- **Filters**: Provide a finer-grained facility for determining which log records to output
- **Formatters**: Specify the layout of the log records in the final output

Logging is performed by calling methods on instances of the `Logger` class. Each line you log has a level. The levels normally used are: `DEBUG`, `INFO`, `WARNING`, `ERROR`, and `CRITICAL`. You can import them from the `logging` module. They are in order of severity and it's very important to use them properly because they will help you filter the contents of a log file based on what you're searching for. Log files usually become extremely big so it's very important to have the information in them written properly so that you can find it quickly when it matters.

You can log to a file but you can also log to a network location, to a queue, to a console, and so on. In general, if you have an architecture that is deployed on one machine, logging to a file is acceptable, but when your architecture spans over multiple machines (such as in the case of service-oriented or microservice architectures), it's very useful to implement a centralized solution for logging so that all log messages coming from each service can be stored and investigated in a single place. It helps a lot, otherwise trying to correlate giant files from several different sources to figure out what went wrong can become truly challenging.

A **service-oriented architecture (SOA)** is an architectural pattern in software design in which application components provide services to other components via a communications protocol, typically over a network. The beauty of this system is that, when coded properly, each service can be written in the most appropriate language to serve its purpose. The only thing that matters is the communication with the other services, which needs to happen via a common format so that data exchange can be done.

Microservice architectures are an evolution of SOAs, but follow a different set of architectural patterns.

Here, I will present you with a very simple logging example. We will log a few messages to a file:

```python
# log.py
import logging

logging.basicConfig(
    filename='ch11.log',
    level=logging.DEBUG,  # minimum level capture in the file
    format='[%(asctime)s] %(levelname)s: %(message)s',
    datefmt='%m/%d/%Y %I:%M:%S %p')

mylist = [1, 2, 3]
logging.info('Starting to process `mylist`...')

for position in range(4):
    try:
        logging.debug(
            'Value at position %s is %s', position, mylist[position]
        )
    except IndexError:
        logging.exception('Faulty position: %s', position)

logging.info('Done parsing `mylist`.')
```

Let's go through it line by line. First, we import the `logging` module, then we set up a basic configuration. In general, a production-logging configuration is much more complicated than this, but I wanted to keep things as easy as possible. We specify a filename, the minimum logging level we want to capture in the file, and the message format. We'll log the date and time information, the level, and the message.

I will start by logging an `info` message that tells me we're about to process our list. Then, I will log (this time using the `DEBUG` level, by using the `debug` function) which is the value at some position. I'm using `debug` here because I want to be able to filter out these logs in the future (by setting the minimum level to `logging.INFO` or more), because I might have to handle very big lists and I don't want to log all the values.

If we get `IndexError` (and we do, since I'm looping over `range(4)`), we call `logging.exception()`, which is the same as `logging.error()`, but it also prints the traceback.

At the end of the code, I log another `info` message saying we're done. The result is this:

```
# ch11.log
[05/06/2018 11:13:48 AM] INFO:Starting to process `mylist`...
[05/06/2018 11:13:48 AM] DEBUG:Value at position 0 is 1
[05/06/2018 11:13:48 AM] DEBUG:Value at position 1 is 2
[05/06/2018 11:13:48 AM] DEBUG:Value at position 2 is 3
[05/06/2018 11:13:48 AM] ERROR:Faulty position: 3
Traceback (most recent call last):
  File "log.py", line 15, in <module>
    position, mylist[position]))
IndexError: list index out of range
[05/06/2018 11:13:48 AM] INFO:Done parsing `mylist`.
```

This is exactly what we need to be able to debug an application that is running on a box, and not on our console. We can see what went on, the traceback of any exception raised, and so on.

 The example presented here only scratches the surface of logging. For a more in-depth explanation, you can find information in the *Python HOWTOs* section of the official Python documentation: *Logging HOWTO*, and *Logging Cookbook*.

Logging is an art. You need to find a good balance between logging everything and logging nothing. Ideally, you should log anything that you need to make sure your application is working correctly, and possibly all errors or exceptions.

Other techniques

In this final section, I'd like to demonstrate briefly a couple of techniques that you may find useful.

Profiling

We talked about profiling in Chapter 8, *Testing, Profiling, and Dealing with Exceptions*, and I'm only mentioning it here because profiling can sometimes explain weird errors that are due to a component being too slow. Especially when networking is involved, having an idea of the timings and latencies your application has to go through is very important in order to understand what may be going on when problems arise, therefore I suggest you get acquainted with profiling techniques and also for a troubleshooting perspective.

Assertions

Assertions are a nice way to make your code ensure your assumptions are verified. If they are, all proceeds regularly but, if they are not, you get a nice exception that you can work with. Sometimes, instead of inspecting, it's quicker to drop a couple of assertions in the code just to exclude possibilities. Let's see an example:

```
# assertions.py
mylist = [1, 2, 3]  # this ideally comes from some place
assert 4 == len(mylist)  # this will break
for position in range(4):
    print(mylist[position])
```

This code simulates a situation in which mylist isn't defined by us like that, of course, but we're assuming it has four elements. So we put an assertion there, and the result is this:

```
$ python assertions.py
Traceback (most recent call last):
  File "assertions.py", line 3, in <module>
    assert 4 == len(mylist)  # this will break
AssertionError
```

This tells us exactly where the problem is.

Where to find information

In the Python official documentation, there is a section dedicated to debugging and profiling, where you can read up about the bdb debugger framework, and about modules such as faulthandler, timeit, trace, tracemallock, and of course pdb. Just head to the standard library section in the documentation and you'll find all this information very easily.

Troubleshooting guidelines

In this short section, I'd like to give you a few tips that come from my troubleshooting experience.

Using console editors

First, get comfortable using **Vim** or **nano** as an editor, and learn the basics of the console. When things break, you don't have the luxury of your editor with all the bells and whistles there. You have to connect to a box and work from there. So it's a very good idea to be comfortable browsing your production environment with console commands, and be able to edit files using console-based editors, such as vi, Vim, or nano. Don't let your usual development environment spoil you.

Where to inspect

My second suggestion concerns where to place your debugging breakpoints. It doesn't matter if you are using `print`, a custom function, or `pdb`, you still have to choose where to place the calls that provide you with the information, right?

Well, some places are better than others, and there are ways to handle the debugging progression that are better than others.

I normally avoid placing a breakpoint in an `if` clause because, if that clause is not exercised, I lose the chance of getting the information I wanted. Sometimes it's not easy or quick to get to the breakpoint, so think carefully before placing them.

Another important thing is where to start. Imagine that you have 100 lines of code that handle your data. Data comes in at line 1, and somehow it's wrong at line 100. You don't know where the bug is, so what do you do? You can place a breakpoint at line 1 and patiently go through all the lines, checking your data. In the worst case scenario, 99 lines (and many cups of coffee) later, you spot the bug. So, consider using a different approach.

You start at line 50, and inspect. If the data is good, it means the bug happens later, in which case you place your next breakpoint at line 75. If the data at line 50 is already bad, you go on by placing a breakpoint at line 25. Then, you repeat. Each time, you move either backward or forward, by half the jump you did last time.

In our worst-case scenario, your debugging would go from 1, 2, 3, ..., 99, in a linear fashion, to a series of jumps such as 50, 75, 87, 93, 96, ..., 99 which is way faster. In fact, it's logarithmic. This searching technique is called **binary search**, it's based on a divide-and-conquer approach, and it's very effective, so try to master it.

Using tests to debug

Do you remember `Chapter 8`, *Testing, Profiling, and Dealing with Exceptions*, about tests? Well, if we have a bug and all tests are passing, it means something is wrong or missing in our test code base. So, one approach is to modify the tests in such a way that they cater for the new edge case that has been spotted, and then work your way through the code. This approach can be very beneficial, because it makes sure that your bug will be covered by a test when it's fixed.

Monitoring

Monitoring is also very important. Software applications can go completely crazy and have non-deterministic hiccups when they encounter edge-case situations such as the network being down, a queue being full, or an external component being unresponsive. In these cases, it's important to have an idea of what the big picture was when the problem occurred and be able to correlate it to something related to it in a subtle, perhaps mysterious way.

You can monitor API endpoints, processes, web pages availability and load times, and basically almost everything that you can code. In general, when starting an application from scratch, it can be very useful to design it keeping in mind how you want to monitor it.

Summary

In this short chapter, we looked at different techniques and suggestions for debugging and troubleshooting our code. Debugging is an activity that is always part of a software developer's work, so it's important to be good at it.

If approached with the correct attitude, it can be fun and rewarding.

We explored techniques to inspect our code base on functions, logging, debuggers, traceback information, profiling, and assertions. We saw simple examples of most of them and we also talked about a set of guidelines that will help when it comes to facing the fire.

Just remember always to *stay calm and focused*, and debugging will be much easier. This too, is a skill that needs to be learned and it's the most important. An agitated and stressed mind cannot work properly, logically, and creatively, therefore, if you don't strengthen it, it will be hard for you to put all of your knowledge to good use.

In the next chapter, we are going to explore GUIs and scripts, taking an interesting detour from the more common web-application scenario.

12
GUIs and Scripts

"A user interface is like a joke. If you have to explain it, it's not that good."

– Martin LeBlanc

In this chapter, we're going to work on a project together. We are going to write a simple scraper that finds and saves images from a web page. We'll focus on three parts:

- A simple HTTP webserver in Python
- A script that scrapes a given URL
- A GUI application that scrapes a given URL

 A **graphical user interface** (**GUI**) is a type of interface that allows the user to interact with an electronic device through graphical icons, buttons, and widgets, as opposed to text-based or command-line interfaces, which require commands or text to be typed on the keyboard. In a nutshell, any browser, any office suite such as LibreOffice, and, in general, anything that pops up when you click on an icon, is a GUI application.

So, if you haven't already done so, this would be the perfect time to start a console and position yourself in a folder called `ch12` in the root of your project for this book. Within that folder, we'll create two Python modules (`scrape.py` and `guiscrape.py`) and a folder (`simple_server`). Within `simple_server`, we'll write our HTML page: `index.html`. Images will be stored in `simple_server/img`.

The structure in `ch12` should look like this:

```
$ tree -A
.
├── guiscrape.py
├── scrape.py
└── simple_server
    ├── img
    │   ├── owl-alcohol.png
    │   ├── owl-book.png
    │   ├── owl-books.png
    │   ├── owl-ebook.jpg
    │   └── owl-rose.jpeg
    ├── index.html
    └── serve.sh
```

If you're using either Linux or macOS, you can do what I do and put the code to start the HTTP server in a `serve.sh` file. On Windows, you'll probably want to use a batch file.

The HTML page we're going to scrape has the following structure:

```
# simple_server/index.html
<!DOCTYPE html>
<html lang="en">
  <head><title>Cool Owls!</title></head>
  <body>
    <h1>Welcome to my owl gallery</h1>
    <div>
      <img src="img/owl-alcohol.png" height="128" />
      <img src="img/owl-book.png" height="128" />
      <img src="img/owl-books.png" height="128" />
      <img src="img/owl-ebook.jpg" height="128" />
      <img src="img/owl-rose.jpeg" height="128" />
    </div>
    <p>Do you like my owls?</p>
  </body>
</html>
```

It's an extremely simple page, so let's just note that we have five images, three of which are PNGs and two of which are JPGs (note that even though they are both JPGs, one ends with `.jpg` and the other with `.jpeg`, which are both valid extensions for this format).

So, Python gives you a very simple HTTP server for free that you can start with the following command (in the `simple_server` folder):

```
$ python -m http.server 8000
Serving HTTP on 0.0.0.0 port 8000 (http://0.0.0.0:8000/) ...
127.0.0.1 - - [06/May/2018 16:54:30] "GET / HTTP/1.1" 200 -
...
```

The last line is the log you get when you access `http://localhost:8000`, where our beautiful page will be served. Alternatively, you can put that command in a file called `serve.sh`, and just run that with this command (make sure it's executable):

```
$ ./serve.sh
```

It will have the same effect. If you have the code for this book, your page should look something like this:

Feel free to use any other set of images, as long as you use at least one PNG and one JPG, and that in the `src` tag you use relative paths, not absolute ones. I got these lovely owls from `https://openclipart.org/`.

First approach – scripting

Now, let's start writing the script. I'll go through the source in three steps: imports, arguments parsing, and business logic.

The imports

Here's how the script starts:

```
# scrape.py
import argparse
import base64
import json
import os
from bs4 import BeautifulSoup
import requests
```

Going through them from the top, you can see that we'll need to parse the arguments, which we'll feed to the script itself (`argparse`). We will need the `base64` library to save the images within a JSON file (`json`), and we'll need to open files for writing (`os`). Finally, we'll need `BeautifulSoup` for scraping the web page easily, and `requests` to fetch its content. I assume you're familiar with `requests` as we have used it in previous chapters.

 We will explore the HTTP protocol and the `requests` mechanism in *Chapter 14*, *Web Development*, so for now, let's just (simplistically) say that we perform an HTTP request to fetch the content of a web page. We can do it programmatically using a library, such as `requests`, and it's more or less the equivalent of typing a URL in your browser and pressing *Enter* (the browser then fetches the content of a web page and displays it to you).

Of all these imports, only the last two don't belong to the Python standard library, so make sure you have them installed:

```
$ pip freeze | egrep -i "soup|requests"
beautifulsoup4==4.6.0
requests==2.18.4
```

Of course, the version numbers might be different for you. If they're not installed, use this command to do so:

```
$ pip install beautifulsoup4==4.6.0 requests==2.18.4
```

At this point, the only thing that I reckon might confuse you is the `base64`/`json` couple, so allow me to spend a few words on that.

As we saw in the previous chapter, JSON is one of the most popular formats for data exchange between applications. It's also widely used for other purposes too, for example, to save data in a file. In our script, we're going to offer the user the ability to save images as image files, or as a JSON single file. Within the JSON, we'll put a dictionary with keys as the image names and values as their content. The only issue is that saving images in the binary format is tricky, and this is where the `base64` library comes to the rescue.

The `base64` library is actually quite useful. For example, every time you send an email with an image attached to it, the image gets encoded with `base64` before the email is sent. On the recipient side, images are automatically decoded into their original binary format so that the email client can display them.

Parsing arguments

Now that the technicalities are out of the way, let's see the second section of our script (it should be at the end of the `scrape.py` module):

```
if __name__ == "__main__":
    parser = argparse.ArgumentParser(
        description='Scrape a webpage.')
    parser.add_argument(
        '-t',
        '--type',
        choices=['all', 'png', 'jpg'],
        default='all',
        help='The image type we want to scrape.')
    parser.add_argument(
        '-f',
        '--format',
        choices=['img', 'json'],
        default='img',
        help='The format images are _saved to.')
    parser.add_argument(
        'url',
        help='The URL we want to scrape for images.')
    args = parser.parse_args()
    scrape(args.url, args.format, args.type)
```

Look at that first line; it is a very common idiom when it comes to scripting. According to the official Python documentation, the '__main__' string is the name of the scope in which top-level code executes. A module's __name__ is set equal to '__main__' when read from standard input, a script, or from an interactive prompt.

Therefore, if you put the execution logic under that `if`, it will be run only when you run the script directly, as its __name__ will be '__main__'. On the other hand, should you import from this module, then its name will be set to something else, so the logic under the `if` won't run.

The first thing we do is define our parser. I would recommend using the standard library module, `argparse`, which is simple enough and quite powerful. There are other options out there, but in this case, `argparse` will provide us with all we need.

We want to feed our script three different pieces of data: the types of images we want to save, the format in which we want to save them, and the URL for the page to be scraped.

The types can be PNGs, JPGs, or both (default), while the format can be either image or JSON, image being the default. URL is the only mandatory argument.

So, we add the `-t` option, allowing also the long version, `--type`. The choices are 'all', 'png', and 'jpg'. We set the default to 'all' and we add a `help` message.

We do a similar procedure for the `format` argument, allowing both the short and long syntax (`-f` and `--format`), and finally we add the `url` argument, which is the only one that is specified differently so that it won't be treated as an option, but rather as a positional argument.

In order to parse all the arguments, all we need is `parser.parse_args()`. Very simple, isn't it?

The last line is where we trigger the actual logic, by calling the `scrape` function, passing all the arguments we just parsed. We will see its definition shortly. The nice thing about `argparse` is that if you call the script by passing `-h`, it will print a nice usage text for you automatically. Let's try it out:

```
$ python scrape.py -h
usage: scrape.py [-h] [-t {all,png,jpg}] [-f {img,json}] url

Scrape a webpage.

positional arguments:
  url The URL we want to scrape for images.
```

```
optional arguments:
  -h, --help show this help message and exit
  -t {all,png,jpg}, --type {all,png,jpg}
                        The image type we want to scrape.
  -f {img,json}, --format {img,json}
                        The format images are _saved to.
```

If you think about it, the one true advantage of this is that we just need to specify the arguments and we don't have to worry about the usage text, which means we won't have to keep it in sync with the arguments' definition every time we change something. This is precious.

Here are a few different ways to call our `scrape.py` script, which demonstrate that `type` and `format` are optional, and how you can use the short and long syntaxes to employ them:

```
$ python scrape.py http://localhost:8000
$ python scrape.py -t png http://localhost:8000
$ python scrape.py --type=jpg -f json http://localhost:8000
```

The first one is using default values for `type` and `format`. The second one will save only PNG images, and the third one will save only JPGs, but in JSON format.

The business logic

Now that we've seen the scaffolding, let's deep dive into the actual logic (if it looks intimidating, don't worry; we'll go through it together). Within the script, this logic lies after the imports and before the parsing (before the `if __name__` clause):

```python
def scrape(url, format_, type_):
    try:
        page = requests.get(url)
    except requests.RequestException as err:
        print(str(err))
    else:
        soup = BeautifulSoup(page.content, 'html.parser')
        images = _fetch_images(soup, url)
        images = _filter_images(images, type_)
        _save(images, format_)
```

Let's start with the `scrape` function. The first thing it does is fetch the page at the given `url` argument. Whatever error may happen while doing this, we trap it in `RequestException` (`err`) and print it. `RequestException` is the base exception class for all the exceptions in the `requests` library.

However, if things go well, and we have a page back from the `GET` request, then we can proceed (`else` branch) and feed its content to the `BeautifulSoup` parser. The `BeautifulSoup` library allows us to parse a web page in no time, without having to write all the logic that would be needed to find all the images in a page, which we really don't want to do. It's not as easy as it seems, and reinventing the wheel is never good. To fetch images, we use the `_fetch_images` function and we filter them with `_filter_images`. Finally, we call `_save` with the result.

Splitting the code into different functions with meaningful names allows us to read it more easily. Even if you haven't seen the logic of the `_fetch_images`, `_filter_images`, and `_save` functions, it's not hard to predict what they do, right? Check out the following:

```python
def _fetch_images(soup, base_url):
    images = []
    for img in soup.findAll('img'):
        src = img.get('src')
        img_url = f'{base_url}/{src}'
        name = img_url.split('/')[-1]
        images.append(dict(name=name, url=img_url))
    return images
```

`_fetch_images` takes a `BeautifulSoup` object and a base URL. All it does is loop through all of the images found on the page and fill in the `name` and `url` information about them in a dictionary (one per image). All dictionaries are added to the `images` list, which is returned at the end.

There is some trickery going on when we get the name of an image. We split the `img_url` (`http://localhost:8000/img/my_image_name.png`) string using `'/'` as a separator, and we take the last item as the image name. There is a more robust way of doing this, but for this example it would be overkill. If you want to see the details of each step, try to break this logic down into smaller steps, and print the result of each of them to help yourself understand. Toward the end of the book, I'll show you another technique for debugging in a much more efficient way.

Anyway, by just adding `print(images)` at the end of the `_fetch_images` function, we get this:

```
[{'url': 'http://localhost:8000/img/owl-alcohol.png', 'name': 'owl-
alcohol.png'}, {'url': 'http://localhost:8000/img/owl-book.png', 'name':
'owl-book.png'}, ...]
```

I truncated the result for brevity. You can see each dictionary has a `url` and `name` key/value pair, which we can use to fetch, identify, and save our images as we like. At this point, I hear you asking what would happen if the images on the page were specified with an absolute path instead of a relative one, right? Good question!

The answer is that the script will fail to download them because this logic expects relative paths. I was about to add a bit of logic to solve this issue when I thought that, at this stage, it would be a nice exercise for you to do it, so I'll leave it up to you to fix it.

 Hint: Inspect the start of that `src` variable. If it starts with `'http'`, it's probably an absolute path. You might also want to checkout `urllib.parse` to do that.

I hope the body of the `_filter_images` function is interesting to you. I wanted to show you how to check on multiple extensions using a mapping technique:

```python
def _filter_images(images, type_):
    if type_ == 'all':
        return images
    ext_map = {
        'png': ['.png'],
        'jpg': ['.jpg', '.jpeg'],
    }
    return [
        img for img in images
        if _matches_extension(img['name'], ext_map[type_])
    ]

def _matches_extension(filename, extension_list):
    name, extension = os.path.splitext(filename.lower())
    return extension in extension_list
```

In this function, if `type_` is `all`, then no filtering is required, so we just return all the images. On the other hand, when `type_` is not `all`, we get the allowed extensions from the `ext_map` dictionary, and use it to filter the images in the list comprehension that ends the function body. You can see that by using another helper function, `_matches_extension`, I have made the list comprehension simpler and more readable.

All `_matches_extension` does is split the name of the image getting its extension and check whether it is within the list of allowed ones. Can you find one micro-improvement (speed-wise) that could be made to this function?

I'm sure you're wondering why I have collected all the images in the list and then removed them, instead of checking whether I wanted to save them before adding them to the list. The first reason is that I needed `_fetch_images` in the GUI application as it is now. The second reason is that combining, fetching, and filtering would produce a longer and more complicated function, and I'm trying to keep the complexity level down. The third reason is that this could be a nice exercise for you to do:

```
def _save(images, format_):
    if images:
        if format_ == 'img':
            _save_images(images)
        else:
            _save_json(images)
        print('Done')
    else:
        print('No images to save.')

def _save_images(images):
    for img in images:
        img_data = requests.get(img['url']).content
        with open(img['name'], 'wb') as f:
            f.write(img_data)

def _save_json(images):
    data = {}
    for img in images:
        img_data = requests.get(img['url']).content
        b64_img_data = base64.b64encode(img_data)
        str_img_data = b64_img_data.decode('utf-8')
        data[img['name']] = str_img_data
    with open('images.json', 'w') as ijson:
        ijson.write(json.dumps(data))
```

Let's keep going through the code and inspect the _save function. You can see that, when images isn't empty, this basically acts as a dispatcher. We either call _save_images or _save_json, depending on what information is stored in the format_ variable.

We are almost done. Let's jump to _save_images. We loop on the images list and for each dictionary we find there, we perform a GET request on the image URL and save its content in a file, which we name as the image itself.

Finally, let's now step into the _save_json function. It's very similar to the previous one. We basically fill in the data dictionary. The image name is the *key*, and the Base64 representation of its binary content is the *value*. When we're done populating our dictionary, we use the json library to dump it in the images.json file. I'll give you a small preview of that:

```
# images.json (truncated)
{
  "owl-alcohol.png": "iVBORw0KGgoAAAANSUhEUgAAASwAAAAEICA...
  "owl-book.png": "iVBORw0KGgoAAAANSUhEUgAAASwAAAAEbCAYAA...
  "owl-books.png": "iVBORw0KGgoAAAANSUhEUgAAASwAAAAElCAYA...
  "owl-ebook.jpg": "/9j/4AAQSkZJRgABAQEAMQAxAAD/2wBDAAEB...
  "owl-rose.jpeg": "/9j/4AAQSkZJRgABAQEANAA0AAD/2wBDAAEB...
}
```

And that's it! Now, before proceeding to the next section, make sure you play with this script and understand how it works. Try to modify something, print out intermediate results, add a new argument or functionality, or scramble the logic. We're going to migrate it into a GUI application now, which will add a layer of complexity simply because we'll have to build the GUI interface, so it's important that you're well acquainted with the business logic—it will allow you to concentrate on the rest of the code.

Second approach – a GUI application

There are several libraries that write GUI applications in Python. The most famous ones are **Tkinter**, **wxPython**, **PyGTK**, and **PyQt**. They all offer a wide range of tools and widgets that you can use to compose a GUI application.

The one I'm going to use for the rest of this chapter is Tkinter. **Tkinter** stands for **Tk interface** and it is the standard Python interface to the Tk GUI toolkit. Both Tk and Tkinter are available on most Unix platforms, macOS X, as well as on Windows systems.

Let's make sure that `tkinter` is installed properly on your system by running this command:

```
$ python -m tkinter
```

It should open a dialog window, demonstrating a simple `Tk` interface. If you can see that, we're good to go. However, if it doesn't work, please search for `tkinter` in the Python official documentation (`https://docs.python.org/3.7/library/tkinter.html`). You will find several links to resources that will help you get up and running with it.

We're going to make a very simple GUI application that basically mimics the behavior of the script we saw in the first part of this chapter. We won't add the ability to save JPGs or PNGs singularly, but after you've gone through this chapter, you should be able to play with the code and put that feature back in by yourself.

So, this is what we're aiming for:

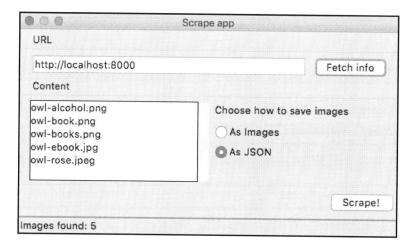

Gorgeous, isn't it? As you can see, it's a very simple interface (this is how it should look on a mac). There is a frame (that is, a container) for the **URL** field and the **Fetch info** button, another frame for the **Listbox** (**Content**) to hold the image names and the radio button to control the way we save them, and finally there is a **Scrape!** button at the bottom. We also have a status bar, which shows us some information.

In order to get this layout, we could just place all the widgets on a root window, but that would make the layout logic quite messy and unnecessarily complicated. So, instead, we will divide the space using frames and place the widgets in those frames. This way we will achieve a much nicer result. So, this is the draft for the layout:

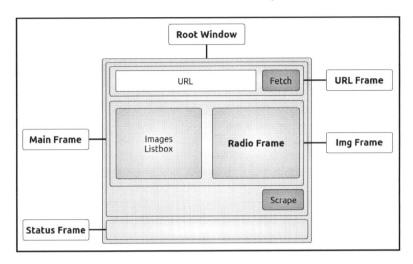

We have a **Root Window**, which is the main window of the application. We divide it into two rows, the first one in which we place the **Main Frame**, and the second one in which we place the **Status Frame** (which will hold the status bar text). The **Main Frame** is subsequently divided into three rows. In the first one, we place the **URL Frame**, which holds the **URL** widgets. In the second one, we place the **Img Frame**, which will hold the **Listbox** and the **Radio Frame**, which will host a label and the radio button widgets. And finally we have the third one, which will just hold the **Scrape** button.

In order to lay out frames and widgets, we will use a layout manager, called **grid**, that simply divides up the space into rows and columns, as in a matrix.

Now, all the code I'm going to write comes from the guiscrape.py module, so I won't repeat its name for each snippet, to save space. The module is logically divided into three sections, not unlike the script version: imports, layout logic, and business logic. We're going to analyze them line by line, in three chunks.

The imports

Imports are like in the script version, except we've lost `argparse`, which is no longer needed, and we have added two lines:

```
# guiscrape.py
from tkinter import *
from tkinter import ttk, filedialog, messagebox
...
```

The first line is quite common practice when dealing with `tkinter`, although in general it is bad practice to import using the `*` syntax. You can incur in name collisions and, if the module is too big, importing everything would be expensive.

After that, we import `ttk`, `filedialog`, and `messagebox` explicitly, following the conventional approach used with this library. `ttk` is the new set of styled widgets. They behave basically like the old ones, but are capable of drawing themselves correctly according to the style your OS is set on, which is nice.

The rest of the imports (omitted) is what we need in order to carry out the task you know well by now. Note that there is nothing we need to install with `pip` in this second part; we already have everything we need.

The layout logic

I'm going to paste it chunk by chunk so that I can explain it easily to you. You'll see how all those pieces we talked about in the layout draft are arranged and glued together. What I'm about to paste, as we did in the script before, is the final part of the `guiscrape.py` module. We'll leave the middle part, the business logic, for last:

```
if __name__ == "__main__":
    _root = Tk()
    _root.title('Scrape app')
```

As you know by now, we only want to execute the logic when the module is run directly, so that first line shouldn't surprise you.

In the last two lines, we set up the main window, which is an instance of the `Tk` class. We instantiate it and give it a title. Note that I use the prepending underscore technique for all the names of the `tkinter` objects, in order to avoid potential collisions with names in the business logic. I just find it cleaner like this, but you're allowed to disagree:

```
_mainframe = ttk.Frame(_root, padding='5 5 5 5')
_mainframe.grid(row=0, column=0, sticky=(E, W, N, S))
```

Here, we set up the **Main Frame**. It's a `ttk.Frame` instance. We set `_root` as its parent, and give it some `padding`. The `padding` is a measure in pixels of how much space should be inserted between the inner content and the borders in order to let our layout breathe a little, otherwise we have a *sardine effect*, where widgets are packed too tightly.

The second line is more interesting. We place this `_mainframe` on the first `row` (0) and first `column` (0) of the parent object (`_root`). We also say that this frame needs to extend itself in each direction by using the `sticky` argument with all four cardinal directions. If you're wondering where they came from, it's the `from tkinter import *` magic that brought them to us:

```
_url_frame = ttk.LabelFrame(
    _mainframe, text='URL', padding='5 5 5 5')
_url_frame.grid(row=0, column=0, sticky=(E, W))
_url_frame.columnconfigure(0, weight=1)
_url_frame.rowconfigure(0, weight=1)
```

Next, we start by placing the **URL Frame** down. This time, the parent object is `_mainframe`, as you will recall from our draft. This is not just a simple `Frame`, it's actually a `LabelFrame`, which means we can set the text argument and expect a rectangle to be drawn around it, with the content of the text argument written in the top-left part of it (check out the previous picture if it helps). We position this frame at (0, 0), and say that it should expand to the left and to the right. We don't need the other two directions.

Finally, we use `rowconfigure` and `columnconfigure` to make sure it behaves correctly, should it need to resize. This is just a formality in our present layout:

```
_url = StringVar()
_url.set('http://localhost:8000')
_url_entry = ttk.Entry(
    _url_frame, width=40, textvariable=_url)
_url_entry.grid(row=0, column=0, sticky=(E, W, S, N), padx=5)
_fetch_btn = ttk.Button(
    _url_frame, text='Fetch info', command=fetch_url)
_fetch_btn.grid(row=0, column=1, sticky=W, padx=5)
```

Here, we have the code to lay out the URL textbox and the `_fetch` button. A textbox in this environment is called `Entry`. We instantiate it as usual, setting `_url_frame` as its parent and giving it a width. Also, and this is the most interesting part, we set the `textvariable` argument to be `_url`. `_url` is a `StringVar`, which is an object that is now connected to `Entry` and will be used to manipulate its content. Therefore, we don't modify the text in the `_url_entry` instance directly, but by accessing `_url`. In this case, we call the `set` method on it to set the initial value to the URL of our local web page.

We position `_url_entry` at (0, 0), setting all four cardinal directions for it to stick to, and we also set a bit of extra padding on the left and right edges using `padx`, which adds padding on the *x*-axis (horizontal). On the other hand, `pady` takes care of the vertical direction.

By now, you should get that every time you call the `.grid` method on an object, we're basically telling the grid layout manager to place that object somewhere, according to rules that we specify as arguments in the `grid()` call.

Similarly, we set up and place the `_fetch` button. The only interesting parameter is `command=fetch_url`. This means that when we click this button, we call the `fetch_url` function. This technique is called **callback**:

```
_img_frame = ttk.LabelFrame(
    _mainframe, text='Content', padding='9 0 0 0')
_img_frame.grid(row=1, column=0, sticky=(N, S, E, W))
```

This is what we called **Img Frame** in the layout draft. It is placed on the second row of its parent `_mainframe`. It will hold the **Listbox** and the **Radio Frame**:

```
_images = StringVar()
_img_listbox = Listbox(
    _img_frame, listvariable=_images, height=6, width=25)
_img_listbox.grid(row=0, column=0, sticky=(E, W), pady=5)
_scrollbar = ttk.Scrollbar(
    _img_frame, orient=VERTICAL, command=_img_listbox.yview)
_scrollbar.grid(row=0, column=1, sticky=(S, N), pady=6)
_img_listbox.configure(yscrollcommand=_scrollbar.set)
```

This is probably the most interesting bit of the whole layout logic. As we did with `_url_entry`, we need to drive the contents of `Listbox` by tying it to an `_images` variable. We set up `Listbox` so that `_img_frame` is its parent, and `_images` is the variable it's tied to. We also pass some dimensions.

The interesting bit comes from the _scrollbar instance. Note that, when we instantiate it, we set its command to _img_listbox.yview. This is the first half of the contract between Listbox and Scrollbar. The other half is provided by the _img_listbox.configure method, which sets yscrollcommand=_scrollbar.set.

By providing this reciprocal bond, when we scroll on Listbox, Scrollbar will move accordingly and vice versa, when we operate Scrollbar, Listbox will scroll accordingly:

```
_radio_frame = ttk.Frame(_img_frame)
_radio_frame.grid(row=0, column=2, sticky=(N, S, W, E))
```

We place the **Radio Frame**, ready to be populated. Note that Listbox is occupying (0, 0) on _img_frame, Scrollbar (0, 1), and therefore _radio_frame will go in (0, 2):

```
_choice_lbl = ttk.Label(
    _radio_frame, text="Choose how to save images")
_choice_lbl.grid(row=0, column=0, padx=5, pady=5)
_save_method = StringVar()
_save_method.set('img')
_img_only_radio = ttk.Radiobutton(
    _radio_frame, text='As Images', variable=_save_method,
    value='img')
_img_only_radio.grid(
    row=1, column=0, padx=5, pady=2, sticky=W)
_img_only_radio.configure(state='normal')
_json_radio = ttk.Radiobutton(
    _radio_frame, text='As JSON', variable=_save_method,
    value='json')
_json_radio.grid(row=2, column=0, padx=5, pady=2, sticky=W)
```

Firstly, we place the label, and we give it some padding. Note that the label and radio buttons are children of _radio_frame.

As for the Entry and Listbox objects, Radiobutton is also driven by a bond to an external variable, which I called _save_method. Each Radiobutton instance sets a value argument, and by checking the value on _save_method, we know which button is selected:

```
_scrape_btn = ttk.Button(
    _mainframe, text='Scrape!', command=save)
_scrape_btn.grid(row=2, column=0, sticky=E, pady=5)
```

On the third row of _mainframe we place the **Scrape** button. Its command is save, which saves the images to be listed in Listbox, after we have successfully parsed a web page:

```
_status_frame = ttk.Frame(
    _root, relief='sunken', padding='2 2 2 2')
_status_frame.grid(row=1, column=0, sticky=(E, W, S))
_status_msg = StringVar()
_status_msg.set('Type a URL to start scraping...')
_status = ttk.Label(
    _status_frame, textvariable=_status_msg, anchor=W)
_status.grid(row=0, column=0, sticky=(E, W))
```

We end the layout section by placing down the status frame, which is a simple ttk.Frame. To give it a little status bar effect, we set its relief property to 'sunken' and give it a uniform padding of two pixels. It needs to stick to the left, right, and bottom parts of the _root window, so we set its sticky attribute to (E, W, S).

We then place a label in it and, this time, we tie it to a StringVar object, because we will have to modify it every time we want to update the status bar text. You should be acquainted with this technique by now.

Finally, on the last line, we run the application by calling the mainloop method on the Tk instance:

```
_root.mainloop()
```

Please remember that all these instructions are placed under the if __name__ == "__main__": clause in the original script.

As you can see, the code to design our GUI application is not hard. Granted, at the beginning, you have to play around a little bit. Not everything will work out perfectly at the first attempt, but I promise you it's very easy and you can find plenty of tutorials on the web. Let's now get to the interesting bit, the business logic.

The business logic

We'll analyze the business logic of the GUI application in three chunks. There is the fetching logic, the saving logic, and the alerting logic.

Fetching the web page

Let's start with the code to fetch the page and images:

```
config = {}

def fetch_url():
    url = _url.get()
    config['images'] = []
    _images.set(())  # initialised as an empty tuple
    try:
        page = requests.get(url)
    except requests.RequestException as err:
        _sb(str(err))
    else:
        soup = BeautifulSoup(page.content, 'html.parser')
        images = fetch_images(soup, url)
        if images:
            _images.set(tuple(img['name'] for img in images))
            _sb('Images found: {}'.format(len(images)))
        else:
            _sb('No images found')
        config['images'] = images

def fetch_images(soup, base_url):
    images = []
    for img in soup.findAll('img'):
        src = img.get('src')
        img_url = f'{base_url}/{src}'
        name = img_url.split('/')[-1]
        images.append(dict(name=name, url=img_url))
    return images
```

First of all, let me explain that `config` dictionary. We need some way of passing data between the GUI application and the business logic. Now, instead of polluting the global namespace with many different variables, my personal preference is to have a single dictionary that holds all the objects we need to pass back and forth, so that the global namespace isn't clogged up with all those names, and we have a single, clean, easy way of knowing where all the objects that are needed by our application are.

In this simple example, we'll just populate the `config` dictionary with the images we fetch from the page, but I wanted to show you the technique so that you have at least one example. This technique comes from my experience with JavaScript. When you code a web page, you often import several different libraries. If each of these cluttered the global namespace with all sorts of variables, there might be issues in making everything work, because of name clashes and variable overriding.

So, it's much better to leave the global namespace as clean as we can. In this case, I find that using one `config` variable is more than acceptable.

The `fetch_url` function is quite similar to what we did in the script. First, we get the `url` value by calling `_url.get()`. Remember that the `_url` object is a `StringVar` instance that is tied to the `_url_entry` object, which is an `Entry`. The text field you see on the GUI is the `Entry`, but the text behind the scenes is the value of the `StringVar` object.

By calling `get()` on `_url`, we get the value of the text, which is displayed in `_url_entry`.

The next step is to prepare `config['images']` to be an empty list, and to empty the `_images` variable, which is tied to `_img_listbox`. This, of course, has the effect of cleaning up all the items in `_img_listbox`.

After this preparation step, we can try to fetch the page, using the same `try/except` logic we adopted in the script at the beginning of the chapter. The one difference is the action we take if things go wrong. We call `_sb(str(err))`. `_sb` is a helper function whose code we'll see shortly. Basically, it sets the text in the status bar for us. Not a good name, right? I had to explain its behavior to you–food for thought.

If we can fetch the page, then we create the `soup` instance, and fetch the images from it. The logic of `fetch_images` is exactly the same as the one explained before, so I won't repeat myself here.

If we have images, using a quick tuple comprehension (which is actually a generator expression fed to a tuple constructor) we feed the `_images` as `StringVar` and this has the effect of populating our `_img_listbox` with all the image names. Finally, we update the status bar.

If there were no images, we still update the status bar, and at the end of the function, regardless of how many images were found, we update `config['images']` to hold the `images` list. In this way, we'll be able to access the images from other functions by inspecting `config['images']` without having to pass that list around.

Saving the images

The logic to save the images is pretty straightforward. Here it is:

```
def save():
    if not config.get('images'):
        _alert('No images to save')
        return

    if _save_method.get() == 'img':
        dirname = filedialog.askdirectory(mustexist=True)
        _save_images(dirname)
    else:
        filename = filedialog.asksaveasfilename(
            initialfile='images.json',
            filetypes=[('JSON', '.json')])
        _save_json(filename)

def _save_images(dirname):
    if dirname and config.get('images'):
        for img in config['images']:
            img_data = requests.get(img['url']).content
            filename = os.path.join(dirname, img['name'])
            with open(filename, 'wb') as f:
                f.write(img_data)
        _alert('Done')

def _save_json(filename):
    if filename and config.get('images'):
        data = {}
        for img in config['images']:
            img_data = requests.get(img['url']).content
            b64_img_data = base64.b64encode(img_data)
            str_img_data = b64_img_data.decode('utf-8')
            data[img['name']] = str_img_data

        with open(filename, 'w') as ijson:
            ijson.write(json.dumps(data))
        _alert('Done')
```

When the user clicks the **Scrape!** button, the save function is called using the callback mechanism.

The first thing that this function does is check whether there are actually any images to be saved. If not, it alerts the user about it, using another helper function, _alert, whose code we'll see shortly. No further action is performed if there are no images.

On the other hand, if the `config['images']` list is not empty, `save` acts as a dispatcher, and it calls `_save_images` or `_save_json`, according to which value is held by `_same_method`. Remember, this variable is tied to the radio buttons, therefore we expect its value to be either `'img'` or `'json'`.

This dispatcher is a bit different from the one in the script. According to which method we have selected, a different action must be taken.

If we want to save the images as images, we need to ask the user to choose a directory. We do this by calling `filedialog.askdirectory` and assigning the result of the call to the `dirname` variable. This opens up a nice dialog window that asks us to choose a directory. The directory we choose must exist, as specified by the way we call the method. This is done so that we don't have to write code to deal with a potentially missing directory when saving the files.

Here's how this dialog should look on a mac:

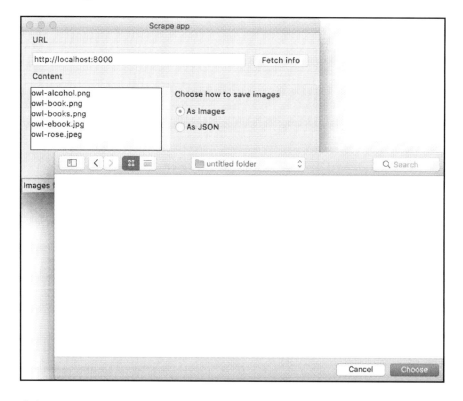

If we cancel the operation, `dirname` will be set to `None`.

Before finishing analyzing the logic in `save`, let's quickly go through `_save_images`.

It's very similar to the version we had in the script so just note that, at the beginning, in order to be sure that we actually have something to do, we check on both `dirname` and the presence of at least one image in `config['images']`.

If that's the case, it means we have at least one image to save and the path for it, so we can proceed. The logic to save the images has already been explained. The one thing we do differently this time is join the directory (which means the complete path) to the image name, by means of `os.path.join`.

At the end of `_save_images`, if we saved at least one image, we alert the user that we're done.

Let's go back now to the other branch in `save`. This branch is executed when the user selects the **As JSON** radio button before pressing the **Scrape** button. In this case, we want to save a file; therefore, we cannot just ask for a directory. We want to give the user the ability to choose a filename as well. Hence, we fire up a different dialog: `filedialog.asksaveasfilename`.

We pass an initial filename, which is proposed to the user–they have the ability to change it if they don't like it. Moreover, because we're saving a JSON file, we're forcing the user to use the correct extension by passing the `filetypes` argument. It is a list, with any number of two-tuples *(description, extension)*, that runs the logic of the dialog.

Here's how this dialog should look on a macOS:

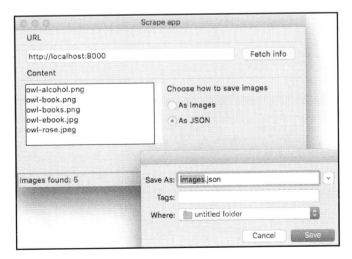

Once we have chosen a place and a filename, we can proceed with the saving logic, which is the same as it was in the previous script. We create a JSON object from a Python dictionary (`data`) that we populate with key/value pairs made by the `images` name and Base64-encoded content.

In `_save_json` as well, we have a little check at the beginning that makes sure that we don't proceed unless we have a filename and at least one image to save. This ensures that if the user presses the **Cancel** button, nothing bad happens.

Alerting the user

Finally, let's see the alerting logic. It's extremely simple:

```
def _sb(msg):
    _status_msg.set(msg)

def _alert(msg):
    messagebox.showinfo(message=msg)
```

That's it! To change the status bar message all we need to do is to access `_status_msg` `StringVar`, as it's tied to the `_status` label.

On the other hand, if we want to show the user a more visible message, we can fire up a message box. Here's how it should look on a mac:

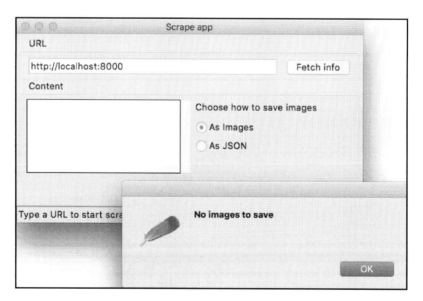

The `messagebox` object can also be used to warn the user (`messagebox.showwarning`) or to signal an error (`messagebox.showerror`). But it can also be used to provide dialogs that ask us whether we're sure we want to proceed or if we really want to delete that file, and so on.

If you inspect `messagebox` by simply printing out what `dir(messagebox)` returns, you'll find methods such as `askokcancel`, `askquestion`, `askretrycancel`, `askyesno`, and `askyesnocancel`, as well as a set of constants to verify the response of the user, such as `CANCEL`, `NO`, `OK`, `OKCANCEL`, `YES`, and `YESNOCANCEL`. You can compare these to the user's choice so that you know the next action to execute when the dialog closes.

How can we improve the application?

Now that you're accustomed to the fundamentals of designing a GUI application, I'd like to give you some suggestions on how to make ours better.

We can start with the code quality. Do you think this code is good enough, or would you improve it? If so, how? I would test it, and make sure it's robust and caters for all the various scenarios that a user might create by clicking around on the application. I would also make sure the behavior is what I would expect when the website we're scraping is down for any reason.

Another thing that we could improve is the naming. I have prudently named all the components with a leading underscore, both to highlight their somewhat *private* nature, and to avoid having name clashes with the underlying objects they are linked to. But in retrospect, many of those components could use a better name, so it's really up to you to refactor until you find the form that suits you best. You could start by giving a better name to the _sb function!

For what concerns the user interface, you could try to resize the main application. See what happens? The whole content stays exactly where it is. Empty space is added if you expand, or the whole widgets set disappears gradually if you shrink. This behavior isn't exactly nice, therefore one quick solution could be to make the root window fixed (that is, unable to resize).

Another thing that you could do to improve the application is to add the same functionality we had in the script, to save only PNGs or JPGs. In order to do this, you could place a combo box somewhere, with three values: All, PNGs, JPGs, or something similar. The user should be able to select one of those options before saving the files.

Even better, you could change the declaration of `Listbox` so that it's possible to select multiple images at the same time, and only the selected ones will be saved. If you manage to do this (it's not as hard as it seems, believe me), then you should consider presenting the `Listbox` a bit better, maybe providing alternating background colors for the rows.

Another nice thing you could add is a button that opens up a dialog to select a file. The file must be one of the JSON files the application can produce. Once selected, you could run some logic to reconstruct the images from their Base64-encoded version. The logic to do this is very simple, so here's an example:

```
with open('images.json', 'r') as f:
    data = json.loads(f.read())

for (name, b64val) in data.items():
    with open(name, 'wb') as f:
        f.write(base64.b64decode(b64val))
```

As you can see, we need to open `images.json` in read mode, and grab the `data` dictionary. Once we have it, we can loop through its items, and save each image with the Base64-decoded content. I'll leave it up to you to tie this logic to a button in the application.

Another cool feature that you could add is the ability to open up a preview pane that shows any image you select from `Listbox`, so that the user can take a peek at the images before deciding to save them.

Finally, one last suggestion for this application is to add a menu. Maybe even a simple menu with **File** and **?** to provide the usual **Help** or **About**. Just for fun. Adding menus is not that complicated; you can add text, keyboard shortcuts, images, and so on.

Where do we go from here?

If you are interested in digging deeper into the world of GUIs, then I'd like to offer you the following suggestions.

The turtle module

The turtle module is an extended reimplementation of the eponymous module from the Python standard distribution up to version Python 2.5. It's a very popular way to introduce children to programming.

It's based on the idea of an imaginary turtle starting at (0, 0) in the Cartesian plane. You can programmatically command the turtle to move forward and backward, rotate, and so on; by combining all the possible moves, all sorts of intricate shapes and images can be drawn.

It's definitely worth checking out, if only to see something different.

wxPython, PyQt, and PyGTK

After you have explored the vastness of the tkinter realm, I'd suggest you explore other GUI libraries: wxPython (https://www.wxpython.org/), PyQt (https://riverbankcomputing.com/software/pyqt/intro), and PyGTK (https://pygobject.readthedocs.io/en/latest/). You may find out one of these works better for you, or it makes it easier for you to code the application you need.

I believe that coders can realize their ideas only when they are conscious of what tools they have available. If your toolset is too narrow, your ideas may seem impossible or extremely hard to realize, and they risk remaining exactly what they are, just ideas.

Of course, the technological spectrum today is humongous, so knowing everything is not possible; therefore, when you are about to learn a new technology or a new subject, my suggestion is to grow your knowledge by exploring breadth first.

Investigate several things, and then go deep with the one or the few that looked most promising. This way you'll be able to be productive with at least one tool, and when the tool no longer fits your needs, you'll know where to dig deeper, thanks to your previous exploration.

The principle of least astonishment

When designing an interface, there are many different things to bear in mind. One of them, which for me is the most important, is the law or **principle of least astonishment**. It basically states that if in your design a necessary feature has a high astonishing factor, it may be necessary to redesign your application. To give you one example, when you're used to working with Windows, where the buttons to minimize, maximize, and close a window are on the top-right corner, it's quite hard to work on Linux, where they are at the top-left corner. You'll find yourself constantly going to the top-right corner only to discover once more that the buttons are on the other side.

If a certain button has become so important in applications that it's now placed in a precise location by designers, please don't innovate. Just follow the convention. Users will only become frustrated when they have to waste time looking for a button that is not where it's supposed to be.

The disregard for this rule is the reason why I cannot work with products such as Jira. It takes me minutes to do simple things that should require seconds.

Threading considerations

This topic is outside the scope of this book, but I do want to mention it.

If you are coding a GUI application that needs to perform a long-running operation when a button is clicked, you will see that your application will probably freeze until the operation has been carried out. In order to avoid this, and maintain the application's responsiveness, you may need to run that time-expensive operation in a different thread (or even a different process) so that the OS will be able to dedicate a little bit of time to the GUI every now and then, to keep it responsive.

Gain a good grasp of the fundamentals first, and then have fun exploring them!

Summary

In this chapter, we worked on a project together. We have written a script that scrapes a very simple web page and accepts optional commands that alter its behavior in doing so. We also coded a GUI application to do the same thing by clicking buttons instead of typing on a console. I hope you enjoyed reading it and following along as much as I enjoyed writing it.

We saw many different concepts, such as working with files and performing HTTP requests, and we talked about guidelines for usability and design.

I have only been able to scratch the surface, but hopefully you have a good starting point from which to expand your exploration.

Throughout the chapter, I have pointed out several different ways you could improve the application, and I have challenged you with a few exercises and questions. I hope you have taken the time to play with those ideas. You can learn a lot just by playing around with fun applications like the one we've coded together.

In the next chapter, we're going to talk about data science, or at least about the tools that a Python programmer has when it comes to facing this subject.

13
Data Science

"If we have data, let's look at data. If all we have are opinions, let's go with mine."

– Jim Barksdale, former Netscape CEO

Data science is a very broad term and can assume several different meanings based on context, understanding, tools, and so on. There are countless books on this subject, which is not suitable for the faint-hearted.

In order to do proper data science, you need to, at the very least, know mathematics and statistics. Then, you may want to dig into other subjects, such as pattern recognition and machine learning and, of course, there is a plethora of languages and tools you can choose from.

I won't be able to talk about everything here. Therefore, in order to render this chapter meaningful, we're going to work on a cool project together instead.

Around the year 2012/2013, I was working for a top-tier social media company in London. I stayed there for two years, and I was privileged to work with several people whose brilliance I can only start to describe. We were the first in the world to have access to the Twitter Ads API, and we were partners with Facebook as well. That means a lot of data.

Our analysts were dealing with a huge number of campaigns and they were struggling with the amount of work they had to do, so the development team I was a part of tried to help by introducing them to Python and to the tools Python gives you to deal with data. It was a very interesting journey that led me to mentor several people in the company and eventually took me to Manila where, for two weeks, I gave intensive training in Python and data science to the analysts over there.

The project we're going to do in this chapter is a lightweight version of the final example I presented to my students in Manila. I have rewritten it to a size that will fit this chapter, and made a few adjustments here and there for teaching purposes, but all the main concepts are there, so it should be fun and instructional for you.

Specifically, we are going to explore the following:

- The Jupyter Notebook
- Pandas and NumPy: main libraries for data science in Python
- A few concepts around Pandas's `DataFrame` class
- Creating and manipulating a dataset

Let's start by talking about Roman gods.

IPython and Jupyter Notebook

In 2001, Fernando Perez was a graduate student in physics at CU Boulder, and was trying to improve the Python shell so that he could have the niceties he was used to when he was working with tools such as Mathematica and Maple. The result of that effort took the name **IPython**.

In a nutshell, that small script began as an enhanced version of the Python shell and, through the effort of other coders and eventually with proper funding from several different companies, it became the wonderful and successful project it is today. Some 10 years after its birth, a Notebook environment was created, powered by technologies such as WebSockets, the Tornado web server, jQuery, CodeMirror, and MathJax. The ZeroMQ library was also used to handle the messages between the Notebook interface and the Python core that lies behind it.

The IPython Notebook has become so popular and widely used that, over time, all sorts of goodies have been added to it. It can handle widgets, parallel computing, all sorts of media formats, and much, much more. Moreover, at some point, it became possible to code in languages other than Python from within the Notebook.

This has led to a huge project that at some stage has been split into two: IPython has been stripped down to focus more on the kernel part and the shell, while the Notebook has become a brand new project called **Jupyter**. Jupyter allows interactive scientific computations to be made in more than 40 languages.

This chapter's project will all be coded and run in a Jupyter Notebook, so let me explain in a few words what a Notebook is.

A Notebook environment is a web page that exposes a simple menu and the cells in which you can run Python code. Even though the cells are separate entities that you can run individually, they all share the same Python kernel. This means that all the names that you define in a cell (the variables, functions, and so on) will be available in any other cell.

 Simply put, a Python kernel is a process in which Python is running. The Notebook web page is, therefore, an interface exposed to the user for driving this kernel. The web page communicates to it using a very fast messaging system.

Apart from all the graphical advantages, the beauty of having such an environment lies in the ability to run a Python script in chunks, and this can be a tremendous advantage. Take a script that is connecting to a database to fetch data and then manipulate that data. If you do it in the conventional way, with a Python script, you have to fetch the data every time you want to experiment with it. Within a Notebook environment, you can fetch the data in a cell and then manipulate and experiment with it in other cells, so fetching it every time is not necessary.

The Notebook environment is also extremely helpful for data science because it allows for step-by-step introspection. You do one chunk of work and then verify it. You then do another chunk and verify again, and so on.

It's also invaluable for prototyping because the results are there, right in front of your eyes, immediately available.

If you want to know more about these tools, please check out `ipython.org` and `jupyter.org`.

I have created a very simple example Notebook with a `fibonacci` function that gives you the list of all the Fibonacci numbers smaller than a given `N`. In my browser, it looks like this:

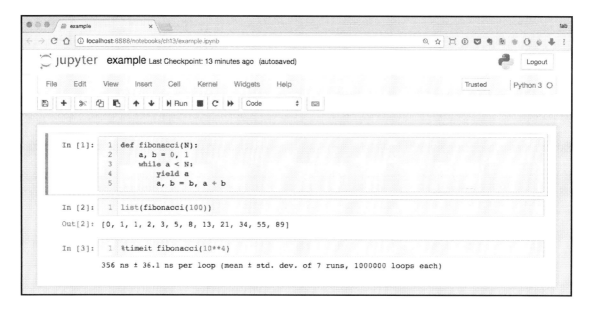

Every cell has an **In []** label. If there's nothing between the brackets, it means that a cell has never been executed. If there is a number, it means that the cell has been executed, and the number represents the order in which the cell was executed. Finally, **a *** means that the cell is currently being executed.

You can see in the picture that in the first cell I have defined the `fibonacci` function, and I have executed it. This has the effect of placing the `fibonacci` name in the global frame associated with the Notebook, therefore the `fibonacci` function is now available to the other cells as well. In fact, in the second cell, I can run `fibonacci(100)` and see the results in **Out [2]**. In the third cell, I have shown you one of the several magic functions you can find in a Notebook in the second cell. **%timeit** runs the code several times and provides you with a nice benchmark for it. All the measurements for the list comprehensions and generators I did in `Chapter 5`, *Saving Time and Memory*, were carried out with this nice feature.

You can execute a cell as many times as you want, and change the order in which you run them. Cells are very malleable, you can also put in markdown text or render them as headers.

Markdown is a lightweight markup language with plain text formatting syntax designed so that it can be converted to HTML and many other formats.

Also, whatever you place in the last row of a cell will be automatically printed for you. This is very handy because you're not forced to write `print(...)` explicitly.

Feel free to explore the Notebook environment; once you're friends with it, it's a long-lasting relationship, I promise.

Installing the required libraries

In order to run the Notebook, you have to install a handful of libraries, each of which collaborates with the others to make the whole thing work. Alternatively, you can just install Jupyter and it will take care of everything for you. For this chapter, there are a few other dependencies that we need to install. You can find them listed in `requirements/requirements.data.science.in`. To install them, please take a look at `README.rst` in the root folder of the project, and you will find instructions specifically for this chapter.

Using Anaconda

Sometimes installing data science libraries can be extremely painful. If you are struggling to install the libraries for this chapter in your virtual environment, an alternative choice you have is to install Anaconda. Anaconda is a free and open source distribution of the Python and R programming languages for data science and machine-learning-related applications that aims to simplify package management and deployment. You can download it from the `anaconda.org` website. Once you have installed it in your system, take a peek at the various requirements for this chapter and install them through Anaconda.

Starting a Notebook

Once you have all the required libraries installed, you can either start a Notebook with the following command or by using the Anaconda interface:

```
$ jupyter notebook
```

You will have an open page in your browser at this address (the port might be different): `http://localhost:8888/`. Go to that page and create a new Notebook using the menu. When you feel comfortable with it, you're ready to go. I strongly encourage you to try and get a Jupyter environment running, before you proceed reading on. It is an excellent exercise sometimes to have to deal with difficult dependencies.

Our project will take place in a Notebook, therefore I will tag each code snippet with the cell number it belongs to, so that you can easily reproduce the code and follow along.

If you familiarize yourself with the keyboard shortcuts (look in the Notebook's **Help** section), you will be able to move between cells and handle their content without having to reach for the mouse. This will make you more proficient and way faster when you work in a Notebook.

Let's now move on and talk about the most interesting part of this chapter: data.

Dealing with data

Typically, when you deal with data, this is the path you go through: you fetch it, you clean and manipulate it, and then you inspect it, and present results as values, spreadsheets, graphs, and so on. I want you to be in charge of all three steps of the process without having any external dependency on a data provider, so we're going to do the following:

1. We're going to create the data, simulating the fact that it comes in a format that is not perfect or ready to be worked on
2. We're going to clean it and feed it to the main tool we'll use in the project such as `DataFrame` from the `pandas` library
3. We're going to manipulate the data in `DataFrame`
4. We're going to save `DataFrame` to a file in different formats
5. We're going to inspect the data and get some results out of it

Setting up the Notebook

First things first, let's produce the data. We start from the `ch13-dataprep` Notebook:

```
#1
import json
import random
from datetime import date, timedelta
import faker
```

Cell #1 takes care of the imports. We have already encountered them, apart from `faker`. You can use this module to prepare fake data. It's very useful in tests, when you prepare your fixtures, to get all sorts of things such as names, email addresses, phone numbers, and credit card details. It is all fake, of course.

Preparing the data

We want to achieve the following data structure: we're going to have a list of user objects. Each user object will be linked to a number of campaign objects. In Python, everything is an object, so I'm using this term in a generic way. The user object may be a string, a dictionary, or something else.

A **campaign** in the social media world is a promotional campaign that a media agency runs on social media networks on behalf of a client. Remember that we're going to prepare this data so that it's not in perfect shape (but it won't be that bad either...):

```
#2
fake = faker.Faker()
```

Firstly, we instantiate the `Faker` that we'll use to create the data:

```
#3
usernames = set()
usernames_no = 1000

# populate the set with 1000 unique usernames
while len(usernames) < usernames_no:
    usernames.add(fake.user_name())
```

Then we need usernames. I want 1,000 unique usernames, so I loop over the length of the `usernames` set until it has 1,000 elements. A `set` method doesn't allow duplicated elements, therefore uniqueness is guaranteed:

```
#4
def get_random_name_and_gender():
    skew = .6  # 60% of users will be female
    male = random.random() > skew
    if male:
        return fake.name_male(), 'M'
    else:
        return fake.name_female(), 'F'

def get_users(usernames):
    users = []
    for username in usernames:
```

```
        name, gender = get_random_name_and_gender()
        user = {
            'username': username,
            'name': name,
            'gender': gender,
            'email': fake.email(),
            'age': fake.random_int(min=18, max=90),
            'address': fake.address(),
        }
        users.append(json.dumps(user))
    return users

users = get_users(usernames)
users[:3]
```

Here, we create a list of `users`. Each `username` has now been augmented to a full-blown `user` dictionary, with other details such as `name`, `gender`, and `email`. Each `user` dictionary is then dumped to JSON and added to the list. This data structure is not optimal, of course, but we're simulating a scenario where users come to us like that.

Note the skewed use of `random.random()` to make 60% of users female. The rest of the logic should be very easy for you to understand.

Note also the last line. Each cell automatically prints what's on the last line; therefore, the output of `#4` is a list with the first three `users`:

```
['{"username": "samuel62", "name": "Tonya Lucas", "gender": "F", "email":
"anthonyrobinson@robbins.biz", "age": 27, "address": "PSC 8934, Box
4049\\nAPO AA 43073"}',
 '{"username": "eallen", "name": "Charles Harmon", "gender": "M", "email":
"courtneycollins@hotmail.com", "age": 28, "address": "38661 Clark Mews Apt.
528\\nAnthonychester, ID 25919"}',
 '{"username": "amartinez", "name": "Laura Dunn", "gender": "F", "email":
"jeffrey35@yahoo.com", "age": 88, "address": "0536 Daniel Court Apt.
541\\nPort Christopher, HI 49399-3415"}']
```

I hope you're following along with your own Notebook. If you are, please note that all data is generated using random functions and values; therefore, you will see different results. They will change every time you execute the Notebook.

In the following code #5 is the logic to generate a campaign name:

```
#5
# campaign name format:
# InternalType_StartDate_EndDate_TargetAge_TargetGender_Currency
def get_type():
    # just some gibberish internal codes
    types = ['AKX', 'BYU', 'GRZ', 'KTR']
    return random.choice(types)

def get_start_end_dates():
    duration = random.randint(1, 2 * 365)
    offset = random.randint(-365, 365)
    start = date.today() - timedelta(days=offset)
    end = start + timedelta(days=duration)
    def _format_date(date_):
        return date_.strftime("%Y%m%d")
    return _format_date(start), _format_date(end)

def get_age():
    age = random.randint(20, 45)
    age -= age % 5
    diff = random.randint(5, 25)
    diff -= diff % 5
    return '{}-{}'.format(age, age + diff)

def get_gender():
    return random.choice(('M', 'F', 'B'))

def get_currency():
    return random.choice(('GBP', 'EUR', 'USD'))

def get_campaign_name():
    separator = '_'
    type_ = get_type()
    start, end = get_start_end_dates()
    age = get_age()
    gender = get_gender()
    currency = get_currency()
    return separator.join(
        (type_, start, end, age, gender, currency))
```

Analysts use spreadsheets all the time, and they come up with all sorts of coding techniques to compress as much information as possible into the campaign names. The format I chose is a simple example of that technique—there is a code that tells us the campaign type, then the start and end dates, then the target `age` and `gender`, and finally the currency. All values are separated by an underscore.

In the `get_type` function, I use `random.choice()` to get one value randomly out of a collection. Probably more interesting is `get_start_end_dates`. First, I get the duration for the campaign, which goes from one day to two years (randomly), then I get a random offset in time which I subtract from today's date in order to get the start date. Given that an offset is a random number between -365 and 365, would anything be different if I added it to today's date instead of subtracting it?

When I have both the start and end dates, I return a stringified version of them, joined by an underscore.

Then, we have a bit of modular trickery going on with the age calculation. I hope you remember the modulo operator (%) from `Chapter 2`, *Built-in Data Types*.

What happens here is that I want a date range that has multiples of five as extremes. So, there are many ways to do it, but what I do is to get a random number between 20 and 45 for the left extreme, and remove the remainder of the division by 5. So, if, for example, I get 28, I will remove 28 % 5 = 3 from it, getting 25. I could have just used `random.randrange()`, but it's hard to resist modular division.

The rest of the functions are just some other applications of `random.choice()` and the last one, `get_campaign_name`, is nothing more than a collector for all these puzzle pieces that returns the final campaign name:

```
#6
# campaign data:
# name, budget, spent, clicks, impressions
def get_campaign_data():
    name = get_campaign_name()
    budget = random.randint(10**3, 10**6)
    spent = random.randint(10**2, budget)
    clicks = int(random.triangular(10**2, 10**5, 0.2 * 10**5))
    impressions = int(random.gauss(0.5 * 10**6, 2))
    return {
        'cmp_name': name,
        'cmp_bgt': budget,
        'cmp_spent': spent,
```

```
        'cmp_clicks': clicks,
        'cmp_impr': impressions
    }
```

In #6, we write a function that creates a complete campaign object. I used a few different functions from the `random` module. `random.randint()` gives you an integer between two extremes. The problem with it is that it follows a uniform probability distribution, which means that any number in the interval has the same probability of coming up.

Therefore, when dealing with a lot of data, if you distribute your fixtures using a uniform distribution, the results you get will all look similar. For this reason, I chose to use `triangular` and `gauss`, for `clicks` and `impressions`. They use different probability distributions so that we'll have something more interesting to see in the end.

Just to make sure we're on the same page with the terminology: `clicks` represents the number of clicks on a campaign advertisement, `budget` is the total amount of money allocated for the campaign, `spent` is how much of that money has already been spent, and `impressions` is the number of times the campaign has been fetched, as a resource, from its source, regardless of the number of clicks that were performed on the campaign. Normally, the amount of `impressions` is greater than the number of `clicks`.

Now that we have the data, it's time to put it all together:

```
#7
def get_data(users):
    data = []
    for user in users:
        campaigns = [get_campaign_data()
                     for _ in range(random.randint(2, 8))]
        data.append({'user': user, 'campaigns': campaigns})
    return data
```

As you can see, each item in `data` is a dictionary with a `user` and a list of campaigns that are associated with that `user`.

Cleaning the data

Let's start cleaning the data:

```
#8
rough_data = get_data(users)
rough_data[:2]  # let's take a peek
```

We simulate fetching the data from a source and then inspect it. The Notebook is the perfect tool for inspecting your steps. You can vary the granularity to your needs. The first item in `rough_data` looks like this:

```
{'user': '{"username": "samuel62", "name": "Tonya Lucas", "gender": "F",
"email": "anthonyrobinson@robbins.biz", "age": 27, "address": "PSC 8934,
Box 4049\\nAPO AA 43073"}',
    'campaigns': [{'cmp_name': 'GRZ_20171018_20171116_35-55_B_EUR',
      'cmp_bgt': 999613,
      'cmp_spent': 43168,
      'cmp_clicks': 35603,
      'cmp_impr': 500001},
    ...
    {'cmp_name': 'BYU_20171122_20181016_30-45_B_USD',
      'cmp_bgt': 561058,
      'cmp_spent': 472283,
      'cmp_clicks': 44823,
      'cmp_impr': 499999}]}
```

So, we now start working on it:

```
#9
data = []
for datum in rough_data:
    for campaign in datum['campaigns']:
        campaign.update({'user': datum['user']})
        data.append(campaign)
data[:2]  # let's take another peek
```

The first thing we need to do in order to be able to feed `DataFrame` with this `data` is to denormalize it. This means transforming `data` into a list whose items are campaign dictionaries, augmented with their relative `user` dictionary. Users will be duplicated in each campaign they belong to. The first item in `data` looks like this:

```
{'cmp_name': 'GRZ_20171018_20171116_35-55_B_EUR',
  'cmp_bgt': 999613,
  'cmp_spent': 43168,
  'cmp_clicks': 35603,
  'cmp_impr': 500001,
  'user': '{"username": "samuel62", "name": "Tonya Lucas", "gender": "F",
"email": "anthonyrobinson@robbins.biz", "age": 27, "address": "PSC 8934,
Box 4049\\nAPO AA 43073"}'}
```

You can see that the `user` object has been brought into the campaign dictionary, which was repeated for each campaign.

Now, I would like to help you and offer a deterministic second part of the chapter, so I'm going to save the data I generated here so that I (and you, too) will be able to load it from the next Notebook, and we should then have the same results:

```
#10
with open('data.json', 'w') as stream:
    stream.write(json.dumps(data))
```

You should find the `data.json` file in the source code for the book. Now we are done with `ch13-dataprep`, so we can close it, and open up `ch13`.

Creating the DataFrame

First, we have another round of imports:

```
#1
import json
import calendar
import numpy as np
from pandas import DataFrame
import arrow
import pandas as pd
```

The `json` and `calendar` libraries come from the standard library. `numpy` is the NumPy library, the fundamental package for scientific computing with Python. NumPy stands for Numeric Python, and it is one of the most widely-used libraries in the data science environment. I'll say a few words about it later on in this chapter. `pandas` is the very core upon which the whole project is based. **Pandas** stands for **Python Data Analysis Library**. Among many other things, it provides `DataFrame`, a matrix-like data structure with advanced processing capabilities. It's customary to import `DataFrame` separately and then to `import pandas as pd`.

`arrow` is a nice third-party library that speeds up dealing with dates dramatically. Technically, we could do it with the standard library, but I see no reason not to expand the range of the example and show you something different.

After the imports, we load the `data` as follows:

```
#2
with open('data.json') as stream:
    data = json.loads(stream.read())
```

And finally, it's time to create `DataFrame`:

```
#3
df = DataFrame(data)
df.head()
```

We can inspect the first five rows using the `head` method of `DataFrame`. You should see something like this:

	cmp_bgt	cmp_clicks	cmp_impr	cmp_name	cmp_spent	user
0	847110	62554	499997	KTR_20190324_20201106_20-35_F_EUR	39383	{"username": "trevorwood", "name": "Monica Bro...
1	510835	36176	500001	GRZ_20170521_20180724_30-45_B_GBP	210452	{"username": "trevorwood", "name": "Monica Bro...
2	720897	62299	500001	KTR_20171218_20180208_30-40_F_GBP	342507	{"username": "trevorwood", "name": "Monica Bro...
3	610337	46084	500000	AKX_20190124_20200804_40-45_B_USD	224361	{"username": "trevorwood", "name": "Monica Bro...
4	587428	15676	500000	BYU_20170823_20170903_35-55_F_EUR	449387	{"username": "trevorwood", "name": "Monica Bro...

Jupyter renders the output of the `df.head()` call as HTML automatically. In order to have a text-based output, simply wrap `df.head()` in a `print` call.

The `DataFrame` structure is very powerful. It allows us to manipulate a lot of its contents. You can filter by rows, columns, aggregate on data, and many other operations. You can operate with rows or columns without suffering the time penalty you would have to pay if you were working on data with pure Python. This happens because, under the covers, `pandas` is harnessing the power of the NumPy library, which itself draws its incredible speed from the low-level implementation of its core.

Using `DataFrame` allows us to couple the power of NumPy with spreadsheet-like capabilities so that we'll be able to work on our data in a fashion that is similar to what an analyst could do. Only, we do it with code.

But let's go back to our project. Let's see two ways to quickly get a bird's eye view of the data:

```
#4
df.count()
```

`count` yields a count of all the non-empty cells in each column. This is good to help you understand how sparse your data can be. In our case, we have no missing values, so the output is:

```
cmp_bgt        5037
cmp_clicks     5037
cmp_impr       5037
cmp_name       5037
cmp_spent      5037
user           5037
dtype: int64
```

Nice! We have 5,037 rows, and the data type is integers (`dtype: int64` means long integers because they take 64 bits each). Given that we have 1,000 users and the amount of campaigns per user is a random number between 2 and 8, we're exactly in line with what I was expecting:

```
#5
df.describe()
```

The `describe` method is a nice, quick way to introspect a bit further:

```
            cmp_bgt         cmp_clicks          cmp_impr        cmp_spent
count   5037.000000       5037.000000       5037.000000      5037.000000
mean  496930.317054      40920.962676     499999.498312    246963.542783
std   287126.683484      21758.505210          2.033342    217822.037701
min     1057.000000        341.000000     499993.000000       114.000000
25%   247663.000000      23340.000000     499998.000000     64853.000000
50%   491650.000000      37919.000000     500000.000000    183716.000000
75%   745093.000000      56253.000000     500001.000000    379478.000000
max   999577.000000      99654.000000     500008.000000    975799.000000
```

As you can see, it gives us several measures, such as `count`, `mean`, `std` (standard deviation), `min`, and `max`, and shows how data is distributed in the various quadrants. Thanks to this method, we already have a rough idea of how our data is structured.

Let's see which are the three campaigns with the highest and lowest budgets:

```
#6
df.sort_index(by=['cmp_bgt'], ascending=False).head(3)
```

This gives the following output:

	cmp_bgt	cmp_clicks	cmp_impr	cmp_name
3321	999577	8232	499997	GRZ_20180810_20190107_40-55_M_EUR
2361	999534	53223	499999	GRZ_20180516_20191030_25-30_B_EUR
2220	999096	13347	499999	KTR_20180620_20190809_40-50_F_USD

And a call to tail shows us the ones with the lowest budgets:

```
#7
df.sort_values(by=['cmp_bgt'], ascending=False).tail(3)
```

Unpacking the campaign name

Now it's time to increase the complexity. First of all, we want to get rid of that horrible campaign name (cmp_name). We need to explode it into parts and put each part in one dedicated column. In order to do this, we'll use the apply method of the Series object.

The pandas.core.series.Series class is basically a powerful wrapper around an array (think of it as a list with augmented capabilities). We can extrapolate a Series object from DataFrame by accessing it in the same way we do with a key in a dictionary, and we can call apply on that Series object, which will run a function feeding each item in the Series to it. We compose the result into a new DataFrame, and then join that DataFrame with df:

```
#8
def unpack_campaign_name(name):
    # very optimistic method, assumes data in campaign name
    # is always in good state
    type_, start, end, age, gender, currency = name.split('_')
    start = arrow.get(start, 'YYYYMMDD').date()
    end = arrow.get(end, 'YYYYMMDD').date()
    return type_, start, end, age, gender, currency

campaign_data = df['cmp_name'].apply(unpack_campaign_name)
campaign_cols = [
    'Type', 'Start', 'End', 'Age', 'Gender', 'Currency']
campaign_df = DataFrame(
    campaign_data.tolist(), columns=campaign_cols, index=df.index)
campaign_df.head(3)
```

Within `unpack_campaign_name`, we split the campaign `name` in parts. We use `arrow.get()` to get a proper `date` object out of those strings (`arrow` makes it really easy to do it, doesn't it?), and then we return the objects. A quick peek at the last line reveals:

```
    Type      Start         End     Age  Gender  Currency
0   KTR   2019-03-24   2020-11-06   20-35     F        EUR
1   GRZ   2017-05-21   2018-07-24   30-45     B        GBP
2   KTR   2017-12-18   2018-02-08   30-40     F        GBP
```

Nice! One important thing: even if the dates appear as strings, they are just the representation of the real `date` objects that are hosted in `DataFrame`.

Another very important thing: when joining two `DataFrame` instances, it's imperative that they have the same `index`, otherwise `pandas` won't be able to know which rows go with which. Therefore, when we create `campaign_df`, we set its `index` to the one from `df`. This enables us to join them. When creating this `DataFrame`, we also pass the column's names:

```
#9
df = df.join(campaign_df)
```

And after `join`, we take a peek, hoping to see matching data:

```
#10
df[['cmp_name'] + campaign_cols].head(3)
```

The truncated output of the preceding code snippet is as follows:

```
                           cmp_name  Type      Start         End
0   KTR_20190324_20201106_20-35_F_EUR  KTR  2019-03-24   2020-11-06
1   GRZ_20170521_20180724_30-45_B_GBP  GRZ  2017-05-21   2018-07-24
2   KTR_20171218_20180208_30-40_F_GBP  KTR  2017-12-18   2018-02-08
```

As you can see, `join` was successful; the campaign name and the separate columns expose the same data. Did you see what we did there? We're accessing `DataFrame` using the square brackets syntax, and we pass a list of column names. This will produce a brand new `DataFrame`, with those columns (in the same order), on which we then call the `head()` method.

Unpacking the user data

We now do the exact same thing for each piece of `user` JSON data. We call `apply` on the `user` series, running the `unpack_user_json` function, which takes a JSON `user` object and transforms it into a list of its fields, which we can then inject into a brand new `DataFrame`, `user_df`. After that, we'll join `user_df` back with `df`, like we did with `campaign_df`:

```
#11
def unpack_user_json(user):
    # very optimistic as well, expects user objects
    # to have all attributes
    user = json.loads(user.strip())
    return [
        user['username'],
        user['email'],
        user['name'],
        user['gender'],
        user['age'],
        user['address'],
    ]

user_data = df['user'].apply(unpack_user_json)
user_cols = [
    'username', 'email', 'name', 'gender', 'age', 'address']
user_df = DataFrame(
    user_data.tolist(), columns=user_cols, index=df.index)
```

Very similar to the previous operation, isn't it? We should also note here that, when creating `user_df`, we need to instruct `DataFrame` about the column names and the `index`. Let's join and take a quick peek:

```
#12
df = df.join(user_df)

#13
df[['user'] + user_cols].head(2)
```

The output shows us that everything went well. We're good, but we're not done yet. If you call df.columns in a cell, you'll see that we still have ugly names for our columns. Let's change that:

```
#14
better_columns = [
    'Budget', 'Clicks', 'Impressions',
    'cmp_name', 'Spent', 'user',
    'Type', 'Start', 'End',
    'Target Age', 'Target Gender', 'Currency',
    'Username', 'Email', 'Name',
    'Gender', 'Age', 'Address',
]
df.columns = better_columns
```

Good! Now, with the exception of 'cmp_name' and 'user', we only have nice names.

Completing the datasetNext step will be to add some extra columns. For each campaign, we have the numbers of clicks and impressions, and we have the amounts spent. This allows us to introduce three measurement ratios: **CTR**, **CPC**, and **CPI**. They stand for **Click Through Rate**, **Cost Per Click**, and **Cost Per Impression**, respectively.

The last two are straightforward, but CTR is not. Suffice it to say that it is the ratio between clicks and impressions. It gives you a measure of how many clicks were performed on a campaign advertisement per impression—the higher this number, the more successful the advertisement is in attracting users to click on it:

```
#15
def calculate_extra_columns(df):
    # Click Through Rate
    df['CTR'] = df['Clicks'] / df['Impressions']
    # Cost Per Click
    df['CPC'] = df['Spent'] / df['Clicks']
    # Cost Per Impression
    df['CPI'] = df['Spent'] / df['Impressions']
calculate_extra_columns(df)
```

I wrote this as a function, but I could have just written the code in the cell. It's not important. What I want you to notice here is that we're adding those three columns with one line of code each, but DataFrame applies the operation automatically (the division, in this case) to each pair of cells from the appropriate columns. So, even if they are masked as three divisions, these are actually *5037 * 3* divisions, because they are performed for each row. Pandas does a lot of work for us, and also does a very good job of hiding the complexity of it.

The function, `calculate_extra_columns`, takes `DataFrame`, and works directly on it. This mode of operation is called **in-place**. Do you remember how `list.sort()` was sorting the list? It is the same deal. You could also say that this function is not pure, which means it has side effects, as it modifies the mutable object it is passed as an argument.

We can take a look at the results by filtering on the relevant columns and calling `head`:

```
#16
df[['Spent', 'Clicks', 'Impressions',
    'CTR', 'CPC', 'CPI']].head(3)
```

This shows us that the calculations were performed correctly on each row:

```
    Spent  Clicks  Impressions      CTR       CPC       CPI
0   39383   62554       499997  0.125109  0.629584  0.078766
1  210452   36176       500001  0.072352  5.817448  0.420903
2  342507   62299       500001  0.124598  5.497793  0.685013
```

Now, I want to verify the accuracy of the results manually for the first row:

```
#17
clicks = df['Clicks'][0]
impressions = df['Impressions'][0]
spent = df['Spent'][0]
CTR = df['CTR'][0]
CPC = df['CPC'][0]
CPI = df['CPI'][0]
print('CTR:', CTR, clicks / impressions)
print('CPC:', CPC, spent / clicks)
print('CPI:', CPI, spent / impressions)
```

This yields the following output:

```
CTR: 0.1251087506525039 0.1251087506525039
CPC: 0.6295840393899671 0.6295840393899671
CPI: 0.0787664725988356 0.0787664725988356
```

This is exactly what we saw in the previous output. Of course, I wouldn't normally need to do this, but I wanted to show you how can you perform calculations this way. You can access `Series` (a column) by passing its name to `DataFrame`, in square brackets, and then you access each row by its position, exactly as you would with a regular list or tuple.

We're almost done with our `DataFrame`. All we are missing now is a column that tells us the duration of the campaign and a column that tells us which `day` of the week corresponds to the start date of each campaign. This allows me to expand on how to play with `date` objects:

```
#18
def get_day_of_the_week(day):
    number_to_day = dict(enumerate(calendar.day_name, 1))
    return number_to_day[day.isoweekday()]

def get_duration(row):
    return (row['End'] - row['Start']).days

df['Day of Week'] = df['Start'].apply(get_day_of_the_week)
df['Duration'] = df.apply(get_duration, axis=1)
```

We used two different techniques here but first, the code.

`get_day_of_the_week` takes a `date` object. If you cannot understand what it does, please take a few moments to try to understand for yourself before reading the explanation. Use the inside-out technique like we've done a few times before.

So, as I'm sure you know by now, if you put `calendar.day_name` in a `list` call, you get `['Monday', 'Tuesday', 'Wednesday', 'Thursday', 'Friday', 'Saturday', 'Sunday']`. This means that, if we enumerate `calendar.day_name` starting from 1, we get pairs such as `(1, 'Monday')`, `(2, 'Tuesday')`, and so on. If we feed these pairs to a dictionary, we get a mapping between the days of the week as numbers (1, 2, 3, ...) and their names. When the mapping is created, in order to get the name of a day, we just need to know its number. To get it, we call `date.isoweekday()`, which tells us which day of the week that date is (as a number). You feed that into the mapping and, boom! You have the name of the day.

`get_duration` is interesting as well. First, notice it takes an entire row, not just a single value. What happens in its body is that we perform a subtraction between a campaign's end and start dates. When you subtract `date` objects, the result is a `timedelta` object, which represents a given amount of time. We take the value of its `.days` property. It is as simple as that.

Now, we can introduce the fun part, the application of those two functions.

The first application is performed on a `Series` object, like we did before for `'user'` and `'cmp_name'`; there is nothing new here.

The second one is applied to the whole `DataFrame` and, in order to instruct `pandas` to perform that operation on the rows, we pass `axis=1`.

We can verify the results very easily, as shown here:

```
#19
df[['Start', 'End', 'Duration', 'Day of Week']].head(3)
```

The preceding code yields the following output:

```
       Start          End  Duration Day of Week
0  2019-03-24   2020-11-06       593      Sunday
1  2017-05-21   2018-07-24       429      Sunday
2  2017-12-18   2018-02-08        52      Monday
```

So, we now know that between the 24th of March, 2019 and the 6th of November, 2020 there are 593 days, and that the 24th of March, 2019 is a Sunday.

If you're wondering what the purpose of this is, I'll provide an example. Imagine that you have a campaign that is tied to a sports event that usually takes place on a Sunday. You may want to inspect your data according to the days so that you can correlate them to the various measurements you have. We're not going to do it in this project, but it was useful to see, if only for the different way of calling `apply()` on `DataFrame`.

Cleaning everything up

Now that we have everything we want, it's time to do the final cleaning; remember we still have the `'cmp_name'` and `'user'` columns. Those are useless now, so they have to go. Also, I want to reorder the columns in `DataFrame` so that it is more relevant to the data it now contains. In order to do this, we just need to filter `df` on the column list we want. We'll get back a brand new `DataFrame` that we can reassign to `df` itself:

```
#20
final_columns = [
    'Type', 'Start', 'End', 'Duration', 'Day of Week', 'Budget',
    'Currency', 'Clicks', 'Impressions', 'Spent', 'CTR', 'CPC',
    'CPI', 'Target Age', 'Target Gender', 'Username', 'Email',
    'Name', 'Gender', 'Age'
]
df = df[final_columns]
```

I have grouped the campaign information at the beginning, then the measurements, and finally the user data at the end. Now our `DataFrame` is clean and ready for us to inspect.

Before we start going crazy with graphs, what about taking a snapshot of `DataFrame` so that we can easily reconstruct it from a file, rather than having to redo all the steps we did to get here. Some analysts may want to have it in spreadsheet form, to do a different kind of analysis than the one we want to do, so let's see how to save `DataFrame` to a file. It's easier done than said.

Saving the DataFrame to a file

We can save `DataFrame` in many different ways. You can type `df.to_` and then press *Tab* to make autocompletion pop up, to see all the possible options.

We're going to save `DataFrame` in three different formats, just for fun. First, CSV:

```
#21
df.to_csv('df.csv')
```

Then JSON:

```
#22
df.to_json('df.json')
```

And finally, in an Excel spreadsheet:

```
#23
df.to_excel('df.xls')
```

The CSV file looks like this (output truncated):

```
,Type,Start,End,Duration,Day of Week,Budget,Currency,Clicks,Im
0,KTR,2019-03-24,2020-11-06,593,Sunday,847110,EUR,62554,499997
1,GRZ,2017-05-21,2018-07-24,429,Sunday,510835,GBP,36176,500001
2,KTR,2017-12-18,2018-02-08,52,Monday,720897,GBP,62299,500001,
```

And the JSON one looks like this (again, output truncated):

```
{
  "Age": {
    "0": 29,
    "1": 29,
    "10": 80,
```

So, it's extremely easy to save `DataFrame` in many different formats, and the good news is that the reverse is also true: it's very easy to load a spreadsheet into `DataFrame`. The programmers behind `pandas` went a long way to ease our tasks, something to be grateful for.

Visualizing the results

Finally, the juicy bits. In this section, we're going to visualize some results. From a data science perspective, I'm not very interested in going deep into analysis, especially because the data is completely random, but still, this code will get you started with graphs and other features.

Something I learned in my life, and this may come as a surprise to you, is that—*looks also count*, so it's very important that when you present your results, you do your best to *make them pretty*.

First, we tell `pandas` to render graphs in the cell output frame, which is convenient. We do it with the following:

```
#24
%matplotlib inline
```

Then, we proceed with some styling:

```
#25
import matplotlib.pyplot as plt
plt.style.use(['classic', 'ggplot'])
import pylab
pylab.rcParams.update({'font.family' : 'serif'})
```

Its purpose is to make the graphs we will look at in this section a little bit prettier. You can also instruct the Notebook to do this when you start it from the console by passing a parameter, but I wanted to show you this way too since it can be annoying to have to restart the Notebook just because you want to plot something. In this way, you can do it on the fly and then keep working.

We also use `pylab` to set the `font.family` to `serif`. This might not be necessary on your system. Try to comment it out and execute the Notebook, and see whether anything changes.

Now that `DataFrame` is complete, let's run `df.describe()` (#26) again. The results should look something like this:

	Duration	Budget	Clicks	Impressions	Spent	CTR	CPC	CPI	Age
count	5037.000000	5037.000000	5037.000000	5037.000000	5037.000000	5037.000000	5037.000000	5037.000000	5037.000000
mean	358.565019	496930.317054	40920.962676	499999.498312	246963.542783	0.081842	9.179302	0.493928	53.815565
std	212.487827	287126.683484	21758.505210	2.033342	217822.037701	0.043517	16.070602	0.435644	21.286780
min	1.000000	1057.000000	341.000000	499993.000000	114.000000	0.000682	0.001638	0.000228	18.000000
25%	174.000000	247663.000000	23340.000000	499998.000000	64853.000000	0.046680	1.796924	0.129706	35.000000
50%	354.000000	491650.000000	37919.000000	500000.000000	183716.000000	0.075838	4.984735	0.367432	54.000000
75%	545.000000	745093.000000	56253.000000	500001.000000	379478.000000	0.112506	11.166230	0.758953	72.000000
max	730.000000	999577.000000	99654.000000	500008.000000	975799.000000	0.199309	444.365399	1.951598	90.000000

This kind of quick result is perfect for satisfying those managers who have 20 seconds to dedicate to you and just want rough numbers.

Once again, please keep in mind that our campaigns have different currencies, so these numbers are actually meaningless. The point here is to demonstrate the `DataFrame` capabilities, not to get to a correct or detailed analysis of real data.

Alternatively, a graph is usually much better than a table with numbers because it's much easier to read it and it gives you immediate feedback. So, let's graph out the four pieces of information we have on each campaign—`'Budget'`, `'Spent'`, `'Clicks'`, and `'Impressions'`:

```
#27
df[['Budget', 'Spent', 'Clicks', 'Impressions']].hist(
    bins=16, figsize=(16, 6));
```

We extrapolate those four columns (this will give us another `DataFrame` made with only those columns) and call the histogram `hist()` method on it. We give some measurements on the bins and figure sizes, but basically, everything is done automatically.

One important thing: since this instruction is the only one in this cell (which also means, it's the last one), the Notebook will print its result before drawing the graph. To suppress this behavior and have only the graph drawn with no printing, just add a semicolon at the end (you thought I was reminiscing about Java, didn't you?). Here are the graphs:

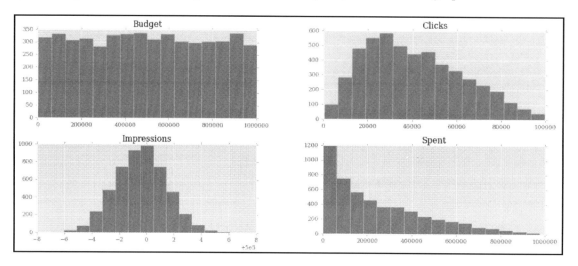

They are beautiful, aren't they? Did you notice the serif font? How about the meaning of those figures? If you go back and take a look at the way we generate the data, you will see that all these graphs make perfect sense:

- **Budget** is simply a random integer in an interval, therefore we were expecting a uniform distribution, and there we have it; it's practically a constant line.
- **Spent** is a uniform distribution as well, but the high end of its interval is the budget, which is moving. This means we should expect something such as a quadratic hyperbole that decreases to the right. And there it is as well.
- **Clicks** was generated with a triangular distribution with a mean roughly 20% of the interval size, and you can see that the peak is right there, at about 20% to the left.
- **Impressions** was a Gaussian distribution, which is the one that assumes the famous bell shape. The mean was exactly in the middle and we had a standard deviation of 2. You can see that the graph matches those parameters.

Good! Let's plot out the measures we calculated:

```
#28
df[['CTR', 'CPC', 'CPI']].hist(
    bins=20, figsize=(16, 6))
```

Here is the plot representation:

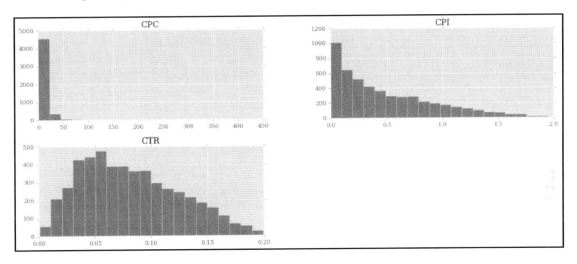

We can see that the **CPC** is highly skewed to the left, meaning that most of the **CPC** values are very low. The **CPI** has a similar shape, but is less extreme.

Now, all this is nice, but if you wanted to analyze only a particular segment of the data, how would you do it? We can apply a mask to DataFrame so that we get another one with only the rows that satisfy the mask condition. It's like applying a global, row-wise if clause:

```
#29
mask = (df.Spent > 0.75 * df.Budget)
df[mask][['Budget', 'Spent', 'Clicks', 'Impressions']].hist(
    bins=15, figsize=(16, 6), color='g');
```

In this case, I prepared `mask` to filter out all the rows for which the amount spent is less than or equal to 75% of the budget. In other words, we'll include only those campaigns for which we have spent at least three-quarters of the budget. Notice that in `mask`, I am showing you an alternative way of asking for a `DataFrame` column, by using direct property access (`object.property_name`), instead of dictionary-like access (`object['property_name']`). If `property_name` is a valid Python name, you can use both ways interchangeably (JavaScript works like this as well).

`mask` is applied in the same way that we access a dictionary with a key. When you apply `mask` to `DataFrame`, you get back another one and we select only the relevant columns on this and call `hist()` again. This time, just for fun, we want the results to be green:

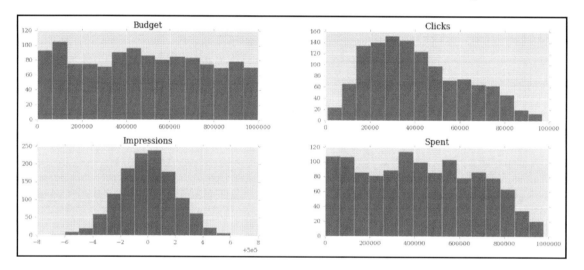

Note that the shapes of the graphs haven't changed much, apart from the **Spent** graph, which is quite different. The reason for this is that we've asked only for the rows where the amount spent is at least 75% of the budget. This means that we're including only the rows where the amount spent is close to the budget. The budget numbers come from a uniform distribution. Therefore, it is quite obvious that the **Spent** graph is now assuming that kind of shape. If you make the boundary even tighter and ask for 85% or more, you'll see the **Spent** graph become more and more like the **Budget** one.

Let's now ask for something different. How about the measure of `'Spent'`, `'Clicks'`, and `'Impressions'` grouped by day of the week:

```
#30
df_weekday = df.groupby(['Day of Week']).sum()
df_weekday[['Impressions', 'Spent', 'Clicks']].plot(
    figsize=(16, 6), subplots=True);
```

The first line creates a new `DataFrame`, `df_weekday`, by asking for a grouping by `'Day of Week'` on `df`. The function used to aggregate the data is an addition.

The second line gets a slice of `df_weekday` using a list of column names, something we're accustomed to by now. On the result, we call `plot()`, which is a bit different to `hist()`. The `subplots=True` option makes `plot` draw three independent graphs:

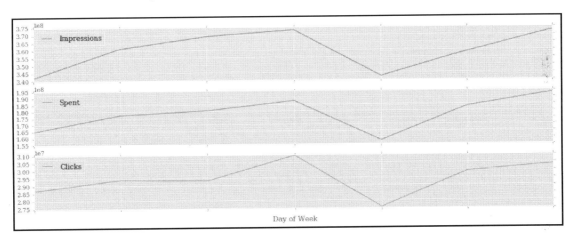

Interestingly enough, we can see that most of the action happens on Sundays and Wednesdays. If this were meaningful data, this would potentially be important information to give to our clients, which is why I'm showing you this example.

Note that the days are sorted alphabetically, which scrambles them up a bit. Can you think of a quick solution that would fix the issue? I'll leave it to you as an exercise to come up with something.

Let's finish this presentation section with a couple more things. First, a simple aggregation. We want to aggregate on `'Target Gender'` and `'Target Age'`, and show `'Impressions'` and `'Spent'`. For both, we want to see `'mean'` and the standard deviation (`'std'`):

```
#31
agg_config = {
    'Impressions': ['mean', 'std'],
    'Spent': ['mean', 'std'],
}
df.groupby(['Target Gender', 'Target Age']).agg(agg_config)
```

It's very easy to do. We will prepare a dictionary that we'll use as a configuration. Then, we perform a grouping on the `'Target Gender'` and `'Target Age'` columns, and we pass our configuration dictionary to the `agg()` method. The result is truncated and rearranged a little bit to make it fit, and shown here:

Target Gender	Target Age	Impressions mean	std	Spent mean
B	20-25	499999.741573	1.904111	218917.000000
	20-30	499999.618421	2.039393	237180.644737
	20-35	499999.358025	2.039048	256378.641975
...		...	...	...
M	20-25	499999.355263	2.108421	277232.276316
	20-30	499999.635294	2.075062	252140.117647
	20-35	499999.835821	1.871614	308598.149254

This is the textual representation, of course, but you can also have the HTML one.

Let's do one more thing before we wrap this chapter up. I want to show you something called a **pivot table**. It's kind of a buzzword in the data environment, so an example such as this one, albeit very simple, is a must:

```
#32
pivot = df.pivot_table(
    values=['Impressions', 'Clicks', 'Spent'],
    index=['Target Age'],
    columns=['Target Gender'],
    aggfunc=np.sum
)
pivot
```

We create a pivot table that shows us the correlation between `'Target Age'` and `'Impressions'`, `'Clicks'`, and `'Spent'`. These last three will be subdivided according to `'Target Gender'`. The aggregation function (`aggfunc`) used to calculate the results is the `numpy.sum` function (`numpy.mean` would be the default, had I not specified anything).

After creating the pivot table, we simply print it with the last line in the cell, and here's a crop of the result:

	Clicks			Impressions			Spent		
Target Gender	**B**	**F**	**M**	**B**	**F**	**M**	**B**	**F**	**M**
Target Age									
20-25	3827736	3703658	3085169	44499977	45999950	37999951	19483613	19852100	21069653
20-30	3079195	2927522	3494013	37999971	36499933	42499969	18025729	19332305	21431910
20-35	3334942	2770677	3045022	40499948	36499954	33499989	20766670	16142070	20676076
20-40	3092064	2662837	3431962	37999984	30999974	40499977	15605660	16776094	20868805

It's pretty clear and provides very useful information when the data is meaningful.

That's it! I'll leave you to discover more about the wonderful world of IPython, Jupyter, and data science. I strongly encourage you to get comfortable with the Notebook environment. It's much better than a console, it's extremely practical and fun to use, and you can even create slides and documents with it.

Where do we go from here?

Data science is indeed a fascinating subject. As I said in the introduction, those who want to delve into its meanders need to be well-trained in mathematics and statistics. Working with data that has been interpolated incorrectly renders any result about it useless. The same goes for data that has been extrapolated incorrectly or sampled with the wrong frequency. To give you an example, imagine a population of individuals that are aligned in a queue. If for some reason, the gender of that population alternated between male and female, the queue would be something like this: F-M-F-M-F-M-F-M-F...

If you sampled it taking only the even elements, you would draw the conclusion that the population was made up only of males, while sampling the odd ones would tell you exactly the opposite.

Of course, this was just a silly example, I know, but it's very easy to make mistakes in this field, especially when dealing with big data where sampling is mandatory and therefore, the quality of the introspection you make depends, first and foremost, on the quality of the sampling itself.

When it comes to data science and Python, these are the main tools you want to look at:

- **NumPy** (http://www.numpy.org/): This is the main package for scientific computing with Python. It contains a powerful N-dimensional array object, sophisticated (broadcasting) functions, tools for integrating C/C++ and Fortran code, useful linear algebra, the Fourier transform, random number capabilities, and much more.
- **Scikit-Learn** (http://scikit-learn.org/): This is probably the most popular machine learning library in Python. It has simple and efficient tools for data mining and data analysis, accessible to everybody, and reusable in various contexts. It's built on NumPy, SciPy, and Matplotlib.
- **Pandas** (http://pandas.pydata.org/): This is an open source, BSD-licensed library providing high-performance, easy-to-use data structures, and data analysis tools. We've used it throughout this chapter.
- **IPython** (http://ipython.org/)/**Jupyter** (http://jupyter.org/): These provide a rich architecture for interactive computing.
- **Matplotlib** (http://matplotlib.org/): This is a Python 2-D plotting library that produces publication-quality figures in a variety of hard-copy formats and interactive environments across platforms. Matplotlib can be used in Python scripts, the Python and IPython shell, Jupyter Notebook, web application servers, and four graphical user interface toolkits.
- **Numba** (http://numba.pydata.org/): This gives you the power to speed up your applications with high-performance functions written directly in Python. With a few annotations, array-oriented and math-heavy Python code can be just-in-time compiled to native machine instructions, similar in performance to C, C++, and Fortran, without having to switch languages or Python interpreters.
- **Bokeh** (http://bokeh.pydata.org/): This is a Python-interactive visualization library that targets modern web browsers for presentation. Its goal is to provide elegant, concise construction of novel graphics in the style of D3.js, but also deliver this capability with high-performance interactivity over very large or streaming datasets.

Other than these single libraries, you can also find ecosystems, such as **SciPy** (`http://scipy.org/`) and the aforementioned **Anaconda** (`https://anaconda.org/`), that bundle several different packages in order to give you something that just works in an "out-of-the-box" fashion.

Installing all these tools and their several dependencies is hard on some systems, so I suggest that you try out ecosystems as well to see whether you are comfortable with them. It may be worth it.

Summary

In this chapter, we talked about data science. Rather than attempting to explain anything about this extremely wide subject, we delved into a project. We familiarized ourselves with the Jupyter Notebook, and with different libraries, such as Pandas, Matplotlib, and NumPy.

Of course, having to compress all this information into one single chapter means I could only touch briefly on the subjects I presented. I hope the project we've gone through together has been comprehensive enough to give you an idea of what could potentially be the workflow you might follow when working in this field.

The next chapter is dedicated to web development. So, make sure you have a browser ready and let's go!

14
Web Development

"Don't believe everything you read on the web."

– Confucius

In this chapter, we're going to work on a website together. By working on a small project, my aim is to open a window for you to take a peek into what web development is, along with the main concepts and tools you should know if you want to be successful with it.

In particular, we are going to explore the following:

- The basic concepts around web programming
- The Django web framework
- Regular expressions
- A brief overview of the Flask and Falcon web frameworks

Let's start with the fundamentals.

What is the web?

The **World Wide Web** (**WWW**), or simply the **web**, is a way of accessing information through the use of a medium called the **internet**. The internet is a huge network of networks, a networking infrastructure. Its purpose is to connect billions of devices together, all around the globe, so that they can communicate with one another. Information travels through the internet in a rich variety of languages, called **protocols**, that allow different devices to speak the same tongue in order to share content.

The web is an information-sharing model, built on top of the internet, which employs the **Hypertext Transfer Protocol** (**HTTP**) as a basis for data communication. The web, therefore, is just one of several different ways information can be exchanged over the internet; email, instant messaging, news groups, and so on, all rely on different protocols.

How does the web work?

In a nutshell, HTTP is an asymmetric **request-response client-server** protocol. An HTTP client sends a request message to an HTTP server. The server, in turn, returns a response message. In other words, HTTP is a **pull protocol** in which the client pulls information from the server (as opposed to a **push protocol**, in which the server pushes information down to the client). Take a look at the following diagram:

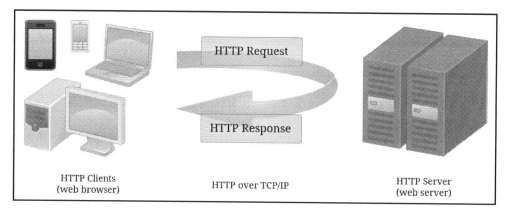

HTTP is based on **TCP/IP** (or the **Transmission Control Protocol/Internet Protocol**), which provides the tools for a reliable communication exchange.

An important feature of the HTTP protocol is that it's *stateless*. This means that the current request has no knowledge about what happened in previous requests. This is a limitation, but you can browse a website with the illusion of being logged in. Under the covers though, what happens is that, on login, a token of user information is saved (most often on the client side, in special files called **cookies**) so that each request the user makes carries the means for the server to recognize the user and provide a custom interface by showing their name, keeping their basket populated, and so on.

Even though it's very interesting, we're not going to delve into the rich details of HTTP and how it works. However, we're going to write a small website, which means we'll have to write the code to handle HTTP requests and return HTTP responses. I won't keep prepending HTTP to the terms request and response from now on, as I trust there won't be any confusion.

The Django web framework

For our project, we're going to use one of the most popular web frameworks you can find in the Python ecosystem: Django.

A **web framework** is a set of tools (libraries, functions, classes, and so on) that we can use to code a website. We need to decide what kind of requests we want to allow to be issued against our web server and how we respond to them. A web framework is the perfect tool for doing that because it takes care of many things for us so that we can concentrate only on the important bits without having to reinvent the wheel.

 There are different types of frameworks. Not all of them are designed for writing code for the web. In general, a **framework** is a tool that provides functionalities to facilitate the development of software applications, products, and solutions.

Django design philosophy

Django is designed according to the following principles:

- **Don't repeat yourself** (DRY): Don't repeat code, and code in a way that makes the framework deduce as much as possible from as little as possible.
- **Loose coupling**: The various layers of the framework shouldn't know about each other (unless absolutely necessary for whatever reason). Loose coupling works best when paralleled with high cohesion. Putting together things which change for the same reason, and spreading apart those which change for different reasons.
- **Less code**: Applications should use the least possible amount of code, and be written in a way that favors reuse as much as possible.
- **Consistency**: When using the Django framework, regardless of which layer you're coding against, your experience will be very consistent with the design patterns and paradigms that were chosen to lay out the project.

The framework itself is designed around the **model-template-view** (**MTV**) pattern, which is a variant of **model-view-controller** (**MVC**), which is widely employed by other frameworks. The purpose of such patterns is to separate concerns and promote code reuse and quality.

The model layer

Of the three layers, this is the one that defines the structure of the data that is handled by the application, and deals with data sources. A **model** is a class that represents a data structure. Through some Django magic, models are mapped to database tables so that you can store your data in a relational database.

A **relational database** stores data in tables in which each column is a property of the data and each row represents a single item or entry in the collection represented by that table. Through the **primary key** of each table, which is that part of the data that allows it to uniquely identify each item, it is possible to establish relationships between items belonging to different tables, that is, to put them into *relation*.

The beauty of this system is that you don't have to write database-specific code in order to handle your data. You just have to configure your models correctly and use them. The work on the database is done for you by the Django **object-relational mapping** (**ORM**), which takes care of translating operations done on Python objects into a language that a relational database can understand: **SQL** (or **Structured Query Language**). We saw an example of ORM in `Chapter 7`, *Files and Data Persistence*, where we explored SQLAlchemy.

One benefit of this approach is that you will be able to change databases without rewriting your code, since all the database-specific code is produced by Django on the fly, according to which database it's connected to. Relational databases speak SQL, but each of them has its own unique flavor of it; therefore, not having to hardcode any SQL in our application is a tremendous advantage.

Django allows you to modify your models at any time. When you do, you can run a command that creates a migration, which is the set of instructions needed to port the database in a state that represents the current definition of your models.

To summarize, this layer deals with defining the data structures you need to handle in your website and gives you the means to save and load them from and to the database by simply accessing the models, which are Python objects.

The view layer

The function of a view is handling a request, performing whatever action needs to be carried out, and eventually returning a response. For example, if you open your browser and request a page corresponding to a category of products in an e-commerce shop, the view will likely talk to the database, asking for all the categories that are children of the selected category (for example, to display them in a navigation sidebar) and for all the products that belong to the selected category, in order to display them on the page.

Therefore, the view is the mechanism through which we can fulfill a request. Its result, the response object, can assume several different forms: a JSON payload, text, an HTML page, and so on. When you code a website, your responses usually consist of HTML or JSON.

The **Hypertext Markup Language**, or **HTML**, is the standard markup language used to create web pages. Web browsers run engines that are capable of interpreting HTML code and render it into what we see when we open a page of a website.

The template layer

This is the layer that provides the bridge between backend and frontend development. When a view has to return HTML, it usually does it by preparing a **context object** (a dictionary) with some data, and then it feeds this context to a template, which is rendered (that is to say, transformed into HTML), and returned to the caller in the form of a response (more precisely, the body of the response). This mechanism allows for maximum code reuse. If you go back to the category example, it's easy to see that, if you browse a website that sells products, it doesn't really matter which category you click on or what type of search you perform, the layout of the products page doesn't change. What does change is the data with which that page is populated.

Therefore, the layout of the page is defined by a template, which is written in a mixture of HTML and Django template languages. The view that serves that page collects all the products to be displayed in the context dictionary, and feeds it to the template, which will be rendered into an HTML page by the Django template engine.

The Django URL dispatcher

The way Django associates a **Uniform Resource Locator** (URL) with a view is by matching the requested URL with the patterns that are registered in a special file. A URL represents a page in a website so `http://mysite.com/categories?id=123` would probably point to the page for the category with ID `123` on my website, while `https://mysite.com/login` would probably be the user login page.

 The difference between HTTP and HTTPS is that the latter adds encryption to the protocol so that the data that you exchange with the website is secured. When you put your credit card details on a website, or log in anywhere, or do anything around sensitive data, you want to make sure that you're using HTTPS.

Regular expressions

The way Django matches URLs to patterns is through a regular expression. A **regular expression** is a sequence of characters that defines a search pattern with which we can carry out operations, such as pattern and string matching, and find/replace.

Regular expressions have a special syntax to indicate things such as digits, letters, and spaces, as well as how many times we expect a character to appear, and much more. A complete explanation of this topic is outside the scope of this book. However, it is a very important subject, so the project we're going to work on together will revolve around it, in the hope that you will be stimulated to find the time to explore it a bit more on your own.

To give you a quick example, imagine that you wanted to specify a pattern to match a date, such as `"26-12-1947"`. This string consists of two digits, one dash, two digits, one dash, and finally four digits. Therefore, we could write it like this: `r'[0-9]{2}-[0-9]{2}-[0-9]{4}'`. We created a class by using square brackets, and we defined a range of digits inside, from `0` to `9`, hence all the possible digits. Then, between curly brackets, we say that we expect two of them. Then a dash, then we repeat this pattern once as it is, and once more, by changing how many digits we expect, and without the final dash. Having a class such as `[0-9]` is such a common pattern that a special notation has been created as a shortcut: `'\d'`. Therefore, we can rewrite the pattern like this: `r'\d{2}-\d{2}-\d{4}'` and it will work exactly the same. That **r** in front of the string stands for **raw**, and its purpose is to prevents python from trying to interpret backslash escape sequences, so that they can be passed as-is to the regular expression engine.

A regex website

So, here we are. We'll code a website that stores regular expressions so that we'll be able to play with them a little bit.

 Before we proceed with creating the project, I'd like to talk about **Cascading Style Sheets (CSS)**. CSS are files in which we specify how the various elements on an HTML page look. You can set all sorts of properties, such as shape, size, color, margins, borders, and fonts. In this project, I have tried my best to achieve a decent result on the pages, but I'm neither a frontend developer nor a designer, so please don't pay too much attention to how things look. Try to focus on how they work.

Setting up Django

On the Django website (`https://www.djangoproject.com/`), you can follow the tutorial, which gives you a pretty good idea of Django's capabilities. If you want, you can follow that tutorial first and then come back to this example. So, first things first; let's install Django in your virtual environment (you will find it is already installed, as it is part of the requirements file):

```
$ pip install django
```

When this command is done, you can test it within a console (try doing it with `bpython`, it gives you a shell similar to IPython but with nice introspection capabilities):

```
>>> import django
>>> django.VERSION
(2, 0, 5, 'final', 0)
```

Now that Django is installed, we're good to go. We'll have to do some scaffolding, so I'll quickly guide you through that.

Starting the project

Choose a folder in the book's environment and change into that. I'll use `ch14`. From there, we can start a Django project with the following command:

```
$ django-admin startproject regex
```

This will prepare the skeleton for a Django project called `regex`. Change into the `regex` folder and run the following:

```
$ python manage.py runserver
```

You should be able to go to `http://127.0.0.1:8000/` with your browser and see the **It worked!** default Django page. This means that the project is correctly set up. When you've seen the page, kill the server with *Ctrl + C* (or whatever it says in the console). I'll paste the final structure for the project now so that you can use it as a reference:

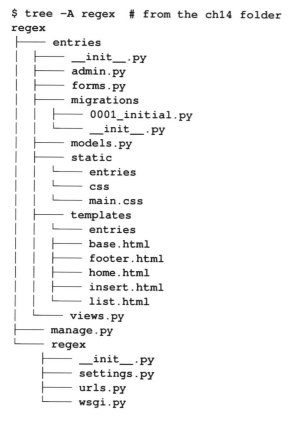

```
$ tree -A regex  # from the ch14 folder
regex
├── entries
│   ├── __init__.py
│   ├── admin.py
│   ├── forms.py
│   ├── migrations
│   │   ├── 0001_initial.py
│   │   └── __init__.py
│   ├── models.py
│   ├── static
│   │   └── entries
│   │   └── css
│   │   └── main.css
│   ├── templates
│   │   └── entries
│   │   ├── base.html
│   │   ├── footer.html
│   │   ├── home.html
│   │   ├── insert.html
│   │   └── list.html
│   └── views.py
├── manage.py
└── regex
    ├── __init__.py
    ├── settings.py
    ├── urls.py
    └── wsgi.py
```

Don't worry if you're missing files, we'll get there. A Django project is typically a collection of several different applications. Each application is meant to provide a functionality in a self-contained, reusable fashion. We'll create just one, called `entries`:

```
$ python manage.py startapp entries
```

Within the `entries` folder that has been created, you can get rid of the `tests.py` module.

Now, let's fix the `regex/settings.py` file in the `regex` folder. We need to add our application to the `INSTALLED_APPS` list so that we can use it (add it at the bottom of the list):

```
INSTALLED_APPS = [
    'django.contrib.admin',
    ...
    'entries',
]
```

Then, you may want to fix the language and time zone according to your personal preference. I live in London, so I set them like this:

```
LANGUAGE_CODE = 'en-gb'
TIME_ZONE = 'Europe/London'
```

There is nothing else to do in this file, so you can save and close it.

Now it's time to apply the **migrations** to the database. Django needs database support to handle users, sessions, and things like that, so we need to create a database and populate it with the necessary data. Luckily, this is very easily done with the following command:

```
$ python manage.py migrate
```

 For this project, we use an SQLite database, which is basically just a file. On a real project, you would use a different database engine, such as MySQL or PostgreSQL.

Creating users

Now that we have a database, we can create a superuser using the console:

```
$ python manage.py createsuperuser
```

After entering the username and other details, we have a user with admin privileges. This is enough to access the Django admin section, so try to start the server:

```
$ python manage.py runserver
```

This will start the Django development server, which is a very useful built-in web server that you can use while working with Django. Now that the server is running, we can access the admin page at `http://localhost:8000/admin/`. I will show you a screenshot of this section later. If you log in with the credentials of the user you just created and head to the **Authentication and Authorization** section, you'll find **Users**. Open that and you will be able to see the list of users. You can edit the details of any user you want as an admin. In our case, make sure you create a different one so that there are at least two users in the system (we'll need them later). I'll call the first user Fabrizio (username: `fab`) and the second one Adriano (username: `adri`), in honor of my father.

By the way, you should see that the Django admin panel comes for free automatically. You define your models, hook them up, and that's it. This is an incredible tool that shows how advanced Django's introspection capabilities are. Moreover, it is completely customizable and extendable. It's truly an excellent piece of work.

Adding the Entry model

Now that the boilerplate is out of the way, and we have a couple of users, we're ready to code. We start by adding the `Entry` model to our application so that we can store objects in the database. Here's the code you'll need to add (remember to use the project tree for reference):

```
# entries/models.py
from django.db import models
from django.contrib.auth.models import User
from django.utils import timezone

class Entry(models.Model):
    user = models.ForeignKey(User, on_delete=models.CASCADE)
    pattern = models.CharField(max_length=255)
    test_string = models.CharField(max_length=255)
    date_added = models.DateTimeField(default=timezone.now)

    class Meta:
        verbose_name_plural = 'entries'
```

This is the model we'll use to store regular expressions in our system. We'll store a pattern, a test string, a reference to the user who created the entry, and the moment of creation. You can see that creating a model is actually quite easy, but nonetheless, let's go through it line by line.

First we need to import the `models` module from `django.db`. This will give us the base class for our `Entry` model. Django models are special classes and much is done for us behind the scenes when we inherit from `models.Model`.

We want a reference to the user who created the entry, so we need to import the `User` model from Django's authorization application and we also need to import the `timezone` model to get access to the `timezone.now()` function, which provides us with a `timezone`-aware version of `datetime.now()`. The beauty of this is that it's hooked up with the `TIME_ZONE` settings I showed you before.

As for the primary key for this class, if we don't set one explicitly, Django will add one for us. A **primary key** is a key that allows us to uniquely identify an `Entry` object in the database (in this case, Django will add an auto-incrementing integer ID).

So, we define our class, and we set up four class attributes. We have a `ForeignKey` attribute that is our reference to the `User` model. We also have two `CharField` attributes that hold the pattern and test strings for our regular expressions. We also have `DateTimeField`, whose default value is set to `timezone.now`. Note that we don't call `timezone.now` right there, it's `now`, not `now()`. So, we're not passing a `DateTime` instance (set at the moment in time when that line is parsed) rather, we're passing a callable, a function that is called when we save an entry in the database. This is similar to the callback mechanism we used in `Chapter 12`, *GUIs and Scripts*, when we were assigning commands to button clicks.

The last two lines are very interesting. We define a `Meta` class within the `Entry` class itself. The `Meta` class is used by Django to provide all sorts of extra information for a model. Django has a great deal of logic under the hood to adapt its behavior according to the information we put into the `Meta` class. In this case, in the admin panel, the pluralized version of `Entry` would be *Entrys*, which is wrong, therefore we need to set it manually. We specify the plural in all lowercase, as Django takes care of capitalizing it for us when needed.

Now that we have a new model, we need to update the database to reflect the new state of the code. In order to do this, we need to instruct Django that it needs to create the code to update the database. This code is called **migration**. Let's create it and execute it:

```
$ python manage.py makemigrations entries
$ python manage.py migrate
```

After these two instructions, the database will be ready to store `Entry` objects.

There are two different kinds of migrations: data and schema migrations. **Data migrations** port data from one state to another without altering its structure. For example, a data migration could set all products for a category as out of stock by switching a flag to `False` or `0`. A **schema migration** is a set of instructions that alter the structure of the database schema. For example, that could be adding an `age` column to a `Person` table, or increasing the maximum length of a field to account for very long addresses. When developing with Django, it's quite common to have to perform both kinds of migrations over the course of development. Data evolves continuously, especially if you code in an agile environment.

Customizing the admin panel

The next step is to hook the `Entry` model up with the admin panel. You can do it with one line of code, but in this case, I want to add some options to customize the way the admin panel shows the entries, both in the list view of all entry items in the database and in the form view that allows us to create and modify them.

All we need to do is to add the following code:

```
# entries/admin.py
from django.contrib import admin
from .models import Entry

@admin.register(Entry)
class EntryAdmin(admin.ModelAdmin):
    fieldsets = [
        ('Regular Expression',
         {'fields': ['pattern', 'test_string']}),
        ('Other Information',
         {'fields': ['user', 'date_added']}),
    ]
    list_display = ('pattern', 'test_string', 'user')
    list_filter = ['user']
    search_fields = ['test_string']
```

This is simply beautiful. My guess is that you probably already understand most of it, even if you're new to Django.

So, we start by importing the `admin` module and the `Entry` model. Because we want to foster code reuse, we import the `Entry` model using a relative import (there's a dot before `models`). This will allow us to move or rename the application without too much trouble. Then, we define the `EntryAdmin` class, which inherits from `admin.ModelAdmin`. The decoration on the class tells Django to display the `Entry` model in the admin panel, and what we put in the `EntryAdmin` class tells Django how to customize the way it handles this model.

First, we specify the `fieldsets` for the create/edit page. This will divide the page into two sections so that we get a better visualization of the content (pattern and test string) and the other details (user and timestamp) separately.

Then, we customize the way the list page displays the results. We want to see all the fields, but not the date. We also want to be able to filter on the user so that we can have a list of all the entries by just one user, and we want to be able to search on `test_string`.

I will go ahead and add three entries, one for myself and two on behalf of my father. The result is shown in the next two screenshots. After inserting them, the list page looks like this:

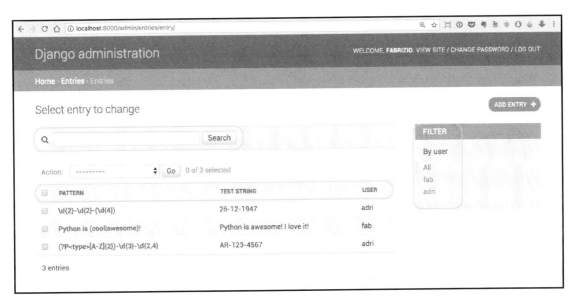

I have highlighted the three parts of this view that we customized in the `EntryAdmin` class. We can filter by user, we can search, and we have all the fields displayed. If you click on a pattern, the edit view opens up.

After our customization, it looks like this:

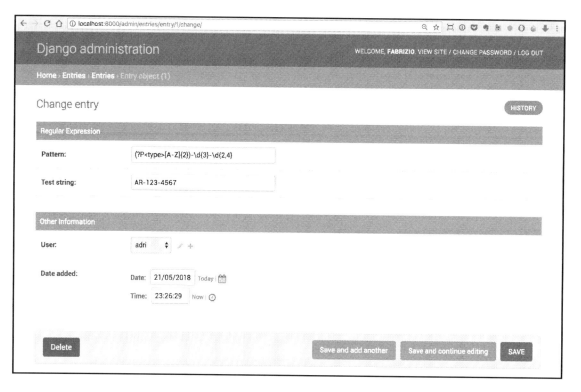

Notice how we have two sections: **Regular Expression** and **Other Information**, thanks to our custom `EntryAdmin` class. Have a go with it, add some entries to a couple of different users, get familiar with the interface. Isn't it nice to have all this for free?

Creating the form

Every time you fill in your details on a web page, you're inserting data in form fields. A **form** is a part of the HTML **Document Object Model (DOM)** tree. In HTML, you create a form by using the `form` tag. When you click on the submit button, your browser normally packs the `form` data together and puts it in the body of a `POST` request. As opposed to `GET` requests, which are used to ask the web server for a resource, a `POST` request normally sends data to the web server with the aim of creating or updating a resource. For this reason, handling `POST` requests usually requires more care than `GET` requests.

When the server receives data from a POST request, that data needs to be validated. Moreover, the server needs to employ security mechanisms to protect against various types of attacks. One attack that is very dangerous is the **cross-site request forgery (CSRF)** attack, which happens when data is sent from a domain that is not the one the user is authenticated on. Django allows you to handle this issue in a very elegant way.

So, instead of being lazy and using the Django admin to create the entries, I'm going to show you how to do it using a Django form. By using the tools the framework gives you, you get a very good degree of validation work already done (in fact, we won't need to add any custom validation ourselves).

There are two kinds of form classes in Django: Form and ModelForm. You use the former to create a form whose shape and behavior depends on how you code the class, what fields you add, and so on. On the other hand, the latter is a type of form that, albeit still customizable, infers fields and behavior from a model. Since we need a form for the Entry model, we'll use that one:

```
# entries/forms.py
from django.forms import ModelForm
from .models import Entry

class EntryForm(ModelForm):
    class Meta:
        model = Entry
        fields = ['pattern', 'test_string']
```

Amazingly enough, this is all we have to do to have a form that we can put on a page. The only notable thing here is that we restrict the fields to only pattern and test_string. Only logged-in users will be allowed access to the insert page, and therefore we don't need to ask who the user is, we already know that. As for the date, when we save an Entry, the date_added field will be set according to its default, therefore we don't need to specify that as well. We'll see in the view how to feed the user information to the form before saving. So, now that the background work is done, all we need is the views and the templates. Let's start with the views.

Writing the views

We need to write three views. We need one for the home page, one to display the list of all entries for a user, and one to create a new entry. We also need views to log in and log out. But thanks to Django, we don't need to write them. I'll paste the code in steps:

```
# entries/views.py
import re
from django.contrib.auth.decorators import login_required
from django.contrib.messages.views import SuccessMessageMixin
from django.urls import reverse_lazy
from django.utils.decorators import method_decorator
from django.views.generic import FormView, TemplateView
from .forms import EntryForm
from .models import Entry
```

Let's start with the imports. We need the `re` module to handle regular expressions, then we need a few classes and functions from Django, and finally, we need the `Entry` model and the `EntryForm` form.

The home view

The first view is `HomeView`:

```
# entries/views.py
class HomeView(TemplateView):
    template_name = 'entries/home.html'

    @method_decorator(
        login_required(login_url=reverse_lazy('login')))
    def get(self, request, *args, **kwargs):
        return super(HomeView, self).get(request, *args, **kwargs)
```

It inherits from `TemplateView`, which means that the response will be created by rendering a template with the context we'll create in the view. All we have to do is specify the `template_name` class attribute to point to the correct template. Django promotes code reuse to a point that if we didn't need to make this view accessible only to logged-in users, the first two lines would have been all we needed.

However, we want this view to be accessible only to logged-in users; therefore, we need to decorate it with `login_required`. Now, historically views in Django were functions; therefore, this decorator was designed to accept a function, and not a method like we have in this class. We're using Django class-based views in this project so, in order to make things work, we need to transform `login_required` so that it accepts a method (the difference being in the first argument: `self`). We do this by passing `login_required` to `method_decorator`.

We also need to feed the `login_required` decorator with `login_url` information, and here comes another wonderful feature of Django. As you'll see after we're done with the views, in Django, you tie a view to a URL through a pattern, consisting of a string which may or may not be a regular expression, and possibly other information. You can give a name to each entry in the `urls.py` file so that when you want to refer to a URL, you don't have to hardcode its value into your code. All you have to do is get Django to reverse-engineer that URL from the name we gave to the entry in `urls.py`, defining the URL and the view that is tied to it. This mechanism will become clearer later. For now, just think of `reverse('...')` as a way of getting a URL from an identifier. In this way, you only write the actual URL once, in the `urls.py` file, which is brilliant. In the `views.py` code, we need to use `reverse_lazy`, which works exactly like `reverse` with one major difference: it only finds the URL when we actually need it (in a lazy fashion). The reason why `reverse_lazy` can be so useful is that sometimes it might happen that we need to reverse an URL from an identifier, but at the moment we call `reverse`, the `urls.py` module hasn't been loaded yet, which causes a failure. The lazy behavior of `reverse_lazy` solves the issue because even if the call is made before the `urls.py` module has been loaded, the actual reversing of the identifier, to get to the related URL, happens in a lazy fashion, later on, when `urls.py` has surely been loaded.

The `get` method, which we just decorated, simply calls the `get` method of the parent class. Of course, the `get` method is the method that Django calls when a `GET` request is performed against the URL tied to this view.

The entry list view

This view is much more interesting than the previous one:

```
# entries/views.py
class EntryListView(TemplateView):
    template_name = 'entries/list.html'

    @method_decorator(
        login_required(login_url=reverse_lazy('login')))
```

```
def get(self, request, *args, **kwargs):
    context = self.get_context_data(**kwargs)
    entries = Entry.objects.filter(
        user=request.user).order_by('-date_added')
    matches = (self._parse_entry(entry) for entry in entries)
    context['entries'] = list(zip(entries, matches))
    return self.render_to_response(context)

def _parse_entry(self, entry):
    match = re.search(entry.pattern, entry.test_string)
    if match is not None:
        return (
            match.group(),
            match.groups() or None,
            match.groupdict() or None
        )
    return None
```

First of all, we decorate the `get` method as we did before. Inside of it, we need to prepare a list of `Entry` objects and feed it to the template, which shows it to the user. In order to do so, we start by getting the `context` dictionary like we're supposed to do, by calling the `get_context_data` method of the `TemplateView` class. Then, we use the ORM to get a list of the entries. We do this by accessing the objects manager, and calling a filter on it. We filter the entries according to which user is logged in, and we ask for them to be sorted in descending order (that `'-'` in front of the name specifies the descending order). The `objects` manager is the default **manager** every Django model is augmented with on creation: it allows us to interact with the database through its methods.

We parse each entry to get a list of matches (actually, I coded it so that `matches` is a generator expression). Finally, we add to the context an `'entries'` key whose value is the coupling of `entries` and `matches`, so that each `Entry` instance is paired with the resulting match of its pattern and test string.

On the last line, we simply ask Django to render the template using the context we created.

Take a look at the `_parse_entry` method. All it does is perform a search on the `entry.test_string` with the `entry.pattern`. If the resulting `match` object is not `None`, it means that we found something. If so, we return a tuple with three elements: the overall group, the subgroups, and the group dictionary.

Notice that `match.groups()` and `match.groupdict()` might return respectively an empty tuple and an empty dict. In order to normalize empty results to a simpler `None`, I use a common pattern in Python by exploiting the `or` operator. `A or B`, in fact, will return `A` if `A` evaluates to a truthy value, or `B` otherwise. Can you think how this might differ from the behavior of the `and` operator?

If you're not familiar with those terms, don't worry, you'll see a screenshot soon with an example. We return `None` if there is no match (which technically is not needed, as Python would do that anyway, but I have included it here for the sake of being explicit).

The form view

Finally, let's examine `EntryFormView`:

```python
# entries/views.py
class EntryFormView(SuccessMessageMixin, FormView):
    template_name = 'entries/insert.html'
    form_class = EntryForm
    success_url = reverse_lazy('insert')
    success_message = "Entry was created successfully"

    @method_decorator(
        login_required(login_url=reverse_lazy('login')))
    def get(self, request, *args, **kwargs):
        return super(EntryFormView, self).get(
            request, *args, **kwargs)

    @method_decorator(
        login_required(login_url=reverse_lazy('login')))
    def post(self, request, *args, **kwargs):
        return super(EntryFormView, self).post(
            request, *args, **kwargs)

    def form_valid(self, form):
        self._save_with_user(form)
        return super(EntryFormView, self).form_valid(form)

    def _save_with_user(self, form):
        self.object = form.save(commit=False)
        self.object.user = self.request.user
        self.object.save()
```

This is particularly interesting for a few reasons. First, it shows us a nice example of Python's multiple inheritance. We want to display a message on the page, after having inserted an `Entry`, so we inherit from `SuccessMessageMixin`. But we want to handle a form as well, so we also inherit from `FormView`.

 Note that, when you deal with mixins and inheritance, you may have to consider the order in which you specify the base classes in the class declaration, as it will affect how methods are found when going up the inheritance chain to serve a call.

In order to set up this view correctly, we need to specify a few attributes at the beginning: the template to be rendered, the form class to be used to handle the data from the `POST` request, the URL we need to redirect the user to in the case of success, and the success message.

Another interesting feature is that this view needs to handle both `GET` and `POST` requests. When we land on the form page for the first time, the form is empty, and that is the `GET` request. On the other hand, when we fill in the form and want to submit the `Entry`, we make a `POST` request. You can see that the body of `get` is conceptually identical to `HomeView`. Django does everything for us.

The `post` method is just like `get`. The only reason we need to code these two methods is so that we can decorate them to require login.

Within the Django form-handling process (in the `FormView` class), there are a few methods that we can override in order to customize the overall behavior. We need to do it with the `form_valid` method. This method will be called when the form validation is successful. Its purpose is to save the form so that an `Entry` object is created out of it, and then stored in the database.

The only problem is that our form is missing the user. We need to intercept that moment in the chain of calls and put the user information in ourselves. This is done by calling the `_save_with_user` method, which is very simple.

First, we ask Django to save the form with the `commit` argument set to `False`. This creates an `Entry` instance without attempting to save it to the database. Saving it immediately would fail because the `user` information is not there.

The next line updates the `Entry` instance (`self.object`), adding the `user` information and, on the last line, we can safely save it. The reason I called `object` and set it on the instance like that was to follow what the original `FormView` class does.

We're fiddling with the Django mechanism here, so if we want the whole thing to work, we need to pay attention to when and how we modify its behavior, and make sure we don't alter it incorrectly. For this reason, it's very important to remember to call the `form_valid` method of the base class (we use `super` for that) at the end of our own customized version, to make sure that every other action that method usually performs is carried out correctly.

Note how the request is tied to each view instance (`self.request`) so that we don't need to pass it through when we refactor our logic into methods. Note also that the user information has been added to the request automatically by Django. Finally, the reason why all the process is split into very small methods like these is so that we can only override those that we need to customize. All this removes the need to write a lot of code.

Now that we have the views covered, let's see how we couple them to the URLs.

Tying up URLs and views

In the `urls.py` module, we tie each view to a URL. There are many ways of doing this. I chose the simplest one, which works perfectly for the extent of this exercise, but you may want to explore this subject more deeply if you intend to work with Django. This is the core around which the whole website logic will revolve; therefore, you should try to get it down correctly. Note that the `urls.py` module belongs to the project folder:

```
# regex/urls.py
from django.contrib import admin
from django.urls import path
from django.contrib.auth import views as auth_views
from django.urls import reverse_lazy
from entries.views import HomeView, EntryListView, EntryFormView

urlpatterns = [
    path('admin/', admin.site.urls),
    path('entries/', EntryListView.as_view(), name='entries'),
    path('entries/insert',
        EntryFormView.as_view(),
        name='insert'),

    path('login/',
        auth_views.login,
        kwargs={'template_name': 'admin/login.html'},
        name='login'),
    path('logout/',
        auth_views.logout,
        kwargs={'next_page': reverse_lazy('home')},
        name='logout'),
```

```
        path('', HomeView.as_view(), name='home'),
    ]
```

If you are familiar with version 1 of Django, you will notice some differences here, as this project is coded in version 2. As you can see, the magic comes from the `path` function, which has recently replaced the `url` function. First, we pass it a path string (also known as a *route*), then the view, and finally a name, which is what we will use in the `reverse` and `reverse_lazy` functions to recover the URL.

Note that, when using class-based views, we have to transform them into functions, which is what `path` is expecting. To do that, we call the `as_view()` method on them.

Note also that the first `path` entry, for the admin, is special. Instead of specifying a URL and a view, it specifies a URL prefix and another `urls.py` module (from the `admin.site` package). In this way, Django will complete all the URLs for the admin section by prepending `'admin/'` to all the URLs specified in `admin.site.urls`. We could have done the same for our entries application (and we should have), but I feel it would have been a bit of overkill for this simple project.

The URL paths defined in this module are so simple that they don't require any regular expression to be defined. Should you need to use a regular expression, you can check out the `re_path` function, which is designed for that purpose.

We also include login and logout functionalities, by employing views that come straight out of the `django.contrib.auth` package. We enrich the declaration with the necessary information (such as the next page, for the logout view, for example) and we don't need to write a single line of code to handle authentication. This is brilliant and saves us a lot of time.

Each `path` declaration must be done within the `urlpatterns` list and on this matter, it's important to consider that, when Django is trying to find a view for a URL that has been requested, the patterns are exercised in order, from top to bottom. The first one that matches is the one that will provide the view for it so, in general, you have to put specific patterns before generic ones, otherwise they will never get a chance to be caught. To show you an example that uses regular expressions in the route declaration, `'^shop/categories/$'` needs to come before `'^shop'` (notice that the `'$'` signals the end of the pattern, and it is not specified in the latter), otherwise it would never be called.

So, models, forms, admin, views, and URLs are all done. All that's left is to take care of the templates. I'll have to be very brief on this part because HTML can be very verbose.

Writing the templates

All templates inherit from a base one, which provides the HTML structure for all others, in a very **object-oriented programming (OOP)** fashion. It also specifies a few blocks, which are areas that can be overridden by children so that they can provide custom content for those areas. Let's start with the base template:

```
# entries/templates/entries/base.html
{% load static from staticfiles %}
<!DOCTYPE html>
<html lang="en">
  <head>
    {% block meta %}
      <meta charset="utf-8">
      <meta name="viewport"
       content="width=device-width, initial-scale=1.0">
    {% endblock meta %}

    {% block styles %}
      <link href="{% static "entries/css/main.css" %}"
       rel="stylesheet">
    {% endblock styles %}

    <title> {% block title %}Title{% endblock title %} </title>
  </head>

  <body>
    <div id="page-content">
      {% block page-content %}
      {% endblock page-content %}
    </div>
    <div id="footer">
      {% block footer %}
      {% endblock footer %}
    </div>
  </body>
</html>
```

There is a good reason to repeat the `entries` folder from the `templates` one. When you deploy a Django website, you collect all the template files under one folder. If you don't specify the paths like I did, you may get a `base.html` template in the entries application, and a `base.html` template in another app. The last one to be collected will override any other file with the same name. For this reason, by putting them in a `templates/entries` folder and using this technique for each Django application you write, you avoid the risk of name collisions (the same goes for any other static file).

There is not much to say about this template, really, apart from the fact that it loads the `static` tag so that we can get easy access to the `static` path without hardcoding it in the template using `{% static ... %}`. The code in the special `{% ... %}` sections is code that defines logic. The code in the special `{{ ... }}` represents variables that will be rendered on the page.

We define five blocks: `styles`, `meta`, `title`, `page-content`, and `footer`, whose purpose is to hold the metadata, style information, title, the content of the page, and the footer, respectively. Blocks can be optionally overridden by child templates in order to provide different content within them.

Here's the footer:

```
# entries/templates/entries/footer.html
<div class="footer">
  Go back <a href="{% url "home" %}">home</a>.
</div>
```

It gives us a nice link to the home page, which comes from the following template:

```
# entries/templates/entries/home.html
{% extends "entries/base.html" %}
{% block title%}Welcome to the Entry website.{% endblock title %}

{% block page-content %}
  <h1>Welcome {{ user.first_name }}!</h1>

  <div class="home-option">To see the list of your entries
    please click <a href="{% url "entries" %}">here.</a>
  </div>
  <div class="home-option">To insert a new entry please click
    <a href="{% url "insert" %}">here.</a>
  </div>
  <div class="home-option">To login as another user please click
    <a href="{% url "logout" %}">here.</a>
  </div>
    <div class="home-option">To go to the admin panel
    please click <a href="{% url "admin:index" %}">here.</a>
```

```
        </div>
{% endblock page-content %}
```

It extends the `base.html` template, and overrides `title` and `page-content`. You can see that basically all it does is provide four links to the user. These are the list of entries, the insert page, the logout page, and the admin page. All of this is done without hardcoding a single URL, through the use of the `{% url ... %}` tag, which is the template equivalent of the `reverse` function.

The template for inserting `Entry` is as follows:

```
# entries/templates/entries/insert.html
{% extends "entries/base.html" %}
{% block title%}Insert a new Entry{% endblock title %}

{% block page-content %}
  {% if messages %}
    {% for message in messages %}
      <p class="{{ message.tags }}">{{ message }}</p>
    {% endfor %}
  {% endif %}

  <h1>Insert a new Entry</h1>
  <form action="{% url "insert" %}" method="post">
    {% csrf_token %}{{ form.as_p }}
    <input type="submit" value="Insert">
  </form><br>
{% endblock page-content %}

{% block footer %}
  <div><a href="{% url "entries" %}">See your entries.</a></div>
  {% include "entries/footer.html" %}
{% endblock footer %}
```

There is some conditional logic at the beginning to display messages, if any, and then we define the form. Django gives us the ability to render a form by simply calling `{{ form.as_p }}` (alternatively, `form.as_ul` or `form.as_table`). This creates all the necessary fields and labels for us. The difference between the three commands is in the way the form is laid out: as a paragraph, as an unordered list, or as a table. We only need to wrap it in form tags and add a submit button. This behavior was designed for our convenience: we need the freedom to shape that `<form>` tag as we want, so Django isn't intrusive on that. Also, note that `{% csrf_token %}`.

It will be rendered into a token by Django and will become part of the data sent to the server on submission. This way, Django will be able to verify that the request was from an allowed source, thus avoiding the aforementioned CSRF issue. Did you see how we handled the token when we wrote the view for the `Entry` insertion? Exactly. We didn't write a single line of code for it. Django takes care of it automatically thanks to a **middleware** class (`CsrfViewMiddleware`). Please refer to the official Django documentation (`https://docs.djangoproject.com/en/2.0/`) to explore this subject further.

For this page, we also use the footer block to display a link to the home page. Finally, we have the list template, which is the most interesting one:

```
# entries/templates/entries/list.html
{% extends "entries/base.html" %}
{% block title%} Entries list {% endblock title %}

{% block page-content %}
 {% if entries %}
  <h1>Your entries ({{ entries|length }} found)</h1>
  <div><a href="{% url "insert" %}">Insert new entry.</a></div>

  <table class="entries-table">
   <thead>
     <tr><th>Entry</th><th>Matches</th></tr>
   </thead>
   <tbody>
    {% for entry, match in entries %}
     <tr class="entries-list {% cycle 'light-gray' 'white' %}">
      <td>
        Pattern: <code class="code">
         "{{ entry.pattern }}"</code><br>
        Test String: <code class="code">
         "{{ entry.test_string }}"</code><br>
        Added: {{ entry.date_added }}
      </td>
      <td>
        {% if match %}
         Group: {{ match.0 }}<br>
         Subgroups:
          {{ match.1|default_if_none:"none" }}<br>
         Group Dict: {{ match.2|default_if_none:"none" }}
        {% else %}
         No matches found.
        {% endif %}
      </td>
     </tr>
    {% endfor %}
```

```
      </tbody>
    </table>
  {% else %}
    <h1>You have no entries</h1>
    <div><a href="{% url "insert" %}">Insert new entry.</a></div>
  {% endif %}
{% endblock page-content %}

{% block footer %}
  {% include "entries/footer.html" %}
{% endblock footer %}
```

It may take you a while to get used to the template language, but really, all there is to it is the creation of a table using a `for` loop. We start by checking whether there are any entries and, if so, we create a table. There are two columns, one for `Entry`, and the other for the match.

In the `Entry` column, we display the `Entry` object (apart from the user), and in the `Matches` column, we display that three-tuple we created in the `EntryListView`. Note that to access the attributes of an object, we use the same dot syntax we use in Python, for example `{{ entry.pattern }}` or `{{ entry.test_string }}`, and so on.

When dealing with lists and tuples, we cannot access items using the square brackets syntax, so we use the dot one as well (`{{ match.0 }}` is equivalent to `match[0]`, and so on). We also use a filter, through the pipe (`|`) operator to display a custom value if a match is `None`.

The Django template language (which is not properly Python) is kept simple for a precise reason. If you find yourself limited by the language, it means you're probably trying to do something in the template that should actually be done in the view, where that logic is more pertinent.

Allow me to show you a couple of screenshots of the *list* and *insert* templates. This is what the list of entries looks like for my father:

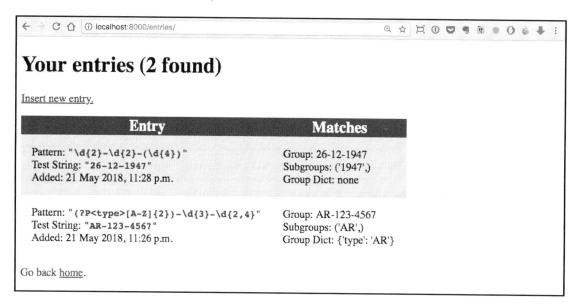

Note how the use of the cycle tag alternates the background color of the rows from white to light gray. Those classes are defined in the `main.css` file.

The `Entry` insertion page is smart enough to provide a few different scenarios. When you land on it at first, it presents you with just an empty form. If you fill it in correctly, it will display a nice message for you (see the following picture). However, if you fail to fill in both fields, it will display an error message before them, alerting you that those fields are required.

Note also the custom footer, which includes both a link to the entries list and a link to the home page:

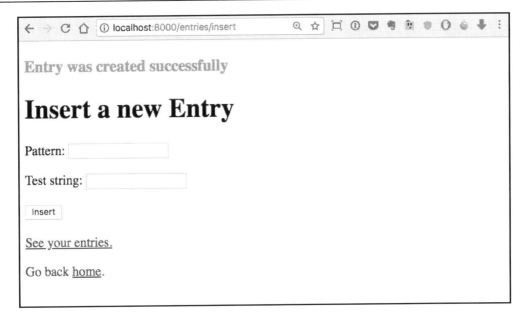

And that's it! You can play around with the CSS styles if you want. Download the code for the book and have fun exploring and extending this project. Add something else to the model, create and apply a migration, play with the templates, there's lots to do!

Django is a very powerful framework, and offers so much more than what I've been able to show you in this chapter, so you should definitely check it out. The beauty of it is that Django is Python, so reading its source code is a very useful exercise.

The future of web development

Computer science is a very young subject, compared to other branches of science that have existed alongside humankind for centuries. One of its main characteristics is that it moves extremely fast. It leaps forward with such speed that, in just a few years, you can see changes that are comparable to real-world changes that took a century to happen. Therefore, as a coder, you must pay attention to what happens in this world, all the time.

Currently, because powerful computers are quite cheap and almost everyone has access to them, the trend is to try to avoid putting too much workload on the backend, and let the frontend handle part of it. Therefore, in the last few years, JavaScript frameworks and libraries, such as jQuery, Backbone and, more recently, React, have become very popular. Web development has shifted from a paradigm where the backend takes care of handling data, preparing it, and serving it to the frontend to display it, to a paradigm where the backend is sometimes just used as an API, a sheer data provider. The frontend fetches the data from the backend with an API call, and then it takes care of the rest. This shift facilitates the existence of paradigms such as **Single-Page Application** (**SPA**), where, ideally, the whole page is loaded once and then evolves, based on the content that usually comes from the backend. E-commerce websites that load the results of a search in a page that doesn't refresh the surrounding structure are made with similar techniques. Browsers can perform asynchronous calls such as **Asynchronous JavaScript and XML** (**AJAX**) that can return data that can be read, manipulated, and injected back into the page with JavaScript code.

So, if you're planning to work on web development, I strongly suggest you to get acquainted with JavaScript (if you're not already), and also with APIs. In the last few pages of this chapter, I'll give you an example of how to make a simple API using two different Python microframeworks: Flask and Falcon.

Writing a Flask view

Flask (`http://flask.pocoo.org/`) is a Python microframework. It provides far fewer features than Django, but if your project is meant to be very small, then it might be a better choice. In my experience though, when developers choose Flask at the beginning of a project, they eventually end up adding plugin after plugin, until they have what I call a Django Frankenstein project. Being agile means having periodically to spend time reducing the technical debt accumulated over time. However, switching from Flask to Django can be a daunting operation, so when starting a new project, make sure you consider its evolution. My cheeky opinion on this matter is very simple: I always go with Django, as I personally prefer it to Flask, but you might disagree with me, so I want to offer you an example.

In your `ch14` folder, create a `flask` folder with the following structure:

```
$ tree -A flask  # from the ch14 folder
flask
├── main.py
└── templates
    └── main.html
```

Basically, we're going to code two simple files: a Flask application and an HTML template. Flask uses Jinja2 as a template engine. It's extremely popular and very fast, to the point that even Django started offering native support for it:

```html
# flask/templates/main.html
<!doctype html>
<title>Hello from Flask</title>
<h1>
  {% if name %}
    Hello {{ name }}!
  {% else %}
    Hello shy person!
  {% endif %}
</h1>
```

The template is almost offensively simple. All it does is change the greeting according to the presence of the `name` variable. A bit more interesting is the Flask application that renders it:

```python
# flask/main.py
from flask import Flask, render_template

app = Flask(__name__)

@app.route('/')
@app.route('/<name>')
def hello(name=None):
    return render_template('main.html', name=name)
```

We create an `app` object, which is a Flask application. We only feed the fully qualified name of the module, which is stored in __name__.

Then, we write a simple `hello` view, which takes an optional `name` argument. In the body of the view, we simply render the `main.html` template, passing to it the `name` argument, regardless of its value.

What's interesting is the routing. Differently from Django's way of tying up views and URLs (the `urls.py` module), in `Flask` you decorate your views with one or more `@app.route` decorators. In this case, we decorate twice: the first line ties the view to the root URL (/), while the second line ties the view to the root URL with a name information (`/<name>`).

Change into the `flask` folder and type (make sure you have either installed Flask with `$ pip install flask` or by installing the requirements in the source code for the book):

```
$ FLASK_APP=main.py flask run
```

You can open a browser and go to `http://127.0.0.1:5000/`. This URL has no name information; therefore, you will see **Hello shy person!** It is written all nice and big. Try to add something to that URL, such as `http://127.0.0.1:5000/Milena`. Hit *Enter* and the page will change to **Hello Milena!** (so you will have said hello to my sister).

Of course, Flask offers you much more than this, but we don't have the room to go through a more complex example. It's definitely worth exploring, though. Several projects use it successfully and it's fun and nice to create websites or APIs with it. Flask's author, Armin Ronacher, is a successful and very prolific coder. He also created or collaborated on several other interesting projects, such as Werkzeug, Jinja2, Click, and Sphinx. He also contributed functionalities to the Python AST module.

Building a JSON quote server in Falcon

Falcon (`http://falconframework.org/`) is another microframework written in Python, which was designed to be light, fast, and flexible. I have seen this relatively young project evolve to become something really popular due to its speed, which is impressive, so I'm happy to show you a tiny example using it. We're going to build an API that returns a random quote from the Buddha.

In your `ch14` folder, create a new one called `falcon`. We'll have two files: `quotes.py` and `main.py`. To run this example, install Falcon and Gunicorn (`$ pip install falcon gunicorn` or the full requirements for the book). Falcon is the framework, and **Gunicorn** (**Green Unicorn**) is a Python WSGI HTTP Server for Unix (which, in layman's terms, means the technology that is used to run the server).

The Web Server Gateway Interface (WSGI) is a simple calling convention for web servers to forward requests to web applications or frameworks written in Python. If you wish to learn more, please checkout `PEP333`, which defines the interface.

When you're all set up, start by creating the `quotes.py` file:

```
# falcon/quotes.py
quotes = [
    "Thousands of candles can be lighted from a single candle, "
    "and the life of the candle will not be shortened. "
    "Happiness never decreases by being shared.",
    ...
    "Peace comes from within. Do not seek it without.",
    ...
]
```

You will find the complete list of quotes in the source code for this book. If you don't have it, you can instead fill in your favorite quotes. Note that not every line has a comma at the end. In Python, it's possible to concatenate strings like that, as long as they are in brackets (or braces). It's called **implicit concatenation**.

The code for the main application is not long, but it is interesting:

```
# falcon/main.py
import json
import random
import falcon
from quotes import quotes

class QuoteResource:
    def on_get(self, req, resp):
        quote = {
            'quote': random.choice(quotes),
            'author': 'The Buddha'
        }
        resp.body = json.dumps(quote)

api = falcon.API()
api.add_route('/quote', QuoteResource())
```

Let's start with the class. In Django we had a `get` method, in Flask we defined a function, and here we write an `on_get` method, a naming style that reminds me of Java/C# event handlers. It takes a request and a response argument, both automatically fed by the framework. In its body, we define a dictionary with a randomly chosen quote, and the author information. Then we dump that dictionary to a JSON string and set the response body to its value. We don't need to return anything, Falcon will take care of it for us.

At the end of the file, we create the Falcon application, and we call `add_route` on it to tie the handler we have just written to the URL we want.

When you're all set up, change to the `falcon` folder and type:

```
$ gunicorn main:api
```

Then, make a request (or simply open the page with your browser) to `http://127.0.0.1:8000/quote`. When I did it, I got this JSON in response:

```
{
  quote: "Peace comes from within. Do not seek it without.",
  author: "The Buddha"
}
```

Within the `falcon` folder, I have left a `stress.py` module for you, which tests how fast our Falcon code is. See if you can make it work by yourself, it should be very easy for you at this point.

Whatever framework you end up using for your web development, try to keep yourself informed about other choices too. Sometimes you may be in situations where a different framework is the right way to go, and having a working knowledge of different tools will give you an advantage.

Summary

In this chapter, we took a look at web development. We talked about important concepts, such as the DRY philosophy and the concept of a framework as a tool that provides us with many things we need in order to write code to serve requests. We also talked about the MTV pattern, and how nicely these three layers play together to realize a request-response path.

Then, we briefly introduced regular expressions, which is a subject of paramount importance, and it's the layer that provides the tools for URL routing.

There are many different frameworks out there, and Django is definitely one of the best and most widely used, so it's worth exploring, especially its source code, which is well written.

There are other very interesting and important frameworks too, such as Flask. They provide fewer features but might be faster, both in execution time and to set up. One that is extremely fast is the Falcon project, whose benchmarks are outstanding.

It's important to get a solid understanding of how the request-response mechanism works, and how the web in general works, so that eventually it won't matter too much which framework you have to use. You will be able to pick it up quickly because it will only be a matter of getting familiar with a way of doing something you already know a lot about.

Explore at least three frameworks and try to come up with different use cases to decide which one of them could be the ideal choice. When you are able to make that choice, you will know you have a good enough understanding of them.

Farewell

I hope that you are still thirsty and that this book will be just the first of many steps you take towards Python. It's a truly wonderful language, well worth learning deeply.

I hope that you enjoyed this journey with me, I did my best to make it interesting for you. It sure was for me, I had such a great time writing these pages.

Python is open source, so please keep sharing it and consider supporting the wonderful community around it.

Until next time, my friend, farewell!

Other Books You May Enjoy

If you enjoyed this book, you may be interested in these other books by Packt:

Secret Recipes of the Python Ninja
Cody Jackson

ISBN: 978-1-78829-487-4

- Know the differences between .py and .pyc files
- Explore the different ways to install and upgrade Python packages
- Understand the working of the PyPI module that enhances built-in decorators
- See how coroutines are different from generators and how they can simulate multithreading
- Grasp how the decimal module improves floating point numbers and their operations
- Standardize sub interpreters to improve concurrency
- Discover Python's built-in docstring analyzer

Python Programming Blueprints
Daniel Furtado, Marcus Pennington

ISBN: 978-1-78646-816-1

- Learn object-oriented and functional programming concepts while developing projects
- The dos and don'ts of storing passwords in a database
- Develop a fully functional website using the popular Django framework
- Use the Beautiful Soup library to perform web scrapping
- Get started with cloud computing by building microservice and serverless applications in AWS
- Develop scalable and cohesive microservices using the Nameko framework
- Create service dependencies for Redis and PostgreSQL

Leave a review - let other readers know what you think

Please share your thoughts on this book with others by leaving a review on the site that you bought it from. If you purchased the book from Amazon, please leave us an honest review on this book's Amazon page. This is vital so that other potential readers can see and use your unbiased opinion to make purchasing decisions, we can understand what our customers think about our products, and our authors can see your feedback on the title that they have worked with Packt to create. It will only take a few minutes of your time, but is valuable to other potential customers, our authors, and Packt. Thank you!

Index

U

Unicode code points 54
Uniform Resource Locator (URL) 444
unit tests
  about 255, 259
  writing 259, 260
Universal Time Coordinated 301
unpacking 124
upcasting 51
usability tests 255
user acceptance testing (UAT) 255
UTF-8 encoding 55

V

variable keyword arguments 124
variable positional arguments 123
views, regex website
  entry list view 455, 456
  form view 458, 459
  home view 454, 455
  writing 454
vim
  using 371

virtual environment (virtualenv)
  about 20
  creating 21, 22, 23
  reference 21

W

web development
  Falcon 470, 472
  Flask 468, 470
  future 467
web framework 441
web
  about 439
  functioning 440
while loop 92, 94
white-box tests 254
World Wide Web (WWW) 439
wxPython 385, 401

Y

yield from expression 163

Z

zip function 145, 148